ANTHOLOGY OF VEDIC HYMNS

ANTHOLOGY OF VEDIC HYMNS:

BEING

A COLLECTION OF HYMNS FROM THE FOUR VEDAS

SVAMI BHUMANANDA SARASVATI

GYAN

Published by

Gyan Publishing House
5, Ansari Road
Daryaganj, New Delhi-110002
Phone: 011-47034999, 9811692060
E-mail: books@gyanbooks.com

Distribution Network
gyanbooks.com
India, USA, Canada, UK, Australia

ISBN: 978-93-7014-213-8 (HB)

First Published, 1935

2nd Impression 2025

Printed at: Gyan Press, Delhi.

ANTHOLOGY OF VEDIC HYMNS
Author: SVAMI BHUMANANDA SARASVATI

Anthology of Vedic Hymns.

Anthology of Vedic Hymns

BEING

A Collection of Hymns from THE FOUR VEDAS

Selected, Translated & Commented upon

BY

SVAMI BHUMANANDA SARASVATI,

VEDIC MISSIONARY.

1935

ॐ

LIST OF CONTENTS.

ॐ

Preface.

"May God bless your righteous endeavour and the noble purpose of the Ramlal Kapur Trust with success."

(Message received from *MAHATMA HANSARAJA JI* on the eve of publishing this volume).

The Revered Mahatma Hansaraja ji has been the guiding spirit in the compilation of the present work which is itself a fruit of the pious wishes of the late Lala Ramlal Kapur, Sole Agent for the Punjab to the Titaghar Paper Mills Co., Bengal. His worthy sons, Ruplal, Hansaraja, Gyanachand and Pyarelal founded, in honour of their revered father, the Ram Lal Kapur Trust donating a decent amount of money towards it for the publication of Vedic works. Intended by the Trust, for circulation in Europe and elsewhere among English-knowing people, the present work was expected to cover not less than 450 pages of matter, but delay having occured on account of unforeseen and inevitable circumstances it has been found desirable to divide the work into two parts terminating this first volume with thirteen verses from the Samavēda

The second part, whenever, wherever and by whomsoever it may be published will contain a detailed critical introduction, some 200 Vedic verses in complete hymns, a full index as in this volume and additional notes. The introduction will contain an elaborate dissertation on Vedic accent also. Thus, the division of the work into two volumes may be considered to be advantageous. But the publication of the second volume must be left to the remote future, though the matter is ready with me, for during these days of materialism and irreligion it is impossible to find publishers for such a work. Hence it is but just that I should heartily tnank the trustees of the Ram Lal Kapur Trust for spending their funds on such a risky venture. If this volume meets with a favourable reception at the hands of the English knowing public, the Ram Lal Kapur Trust themselves may soon help me to issue the second volume also.

This book is not intended for a casual, cursory reading. The holiday or leisure-hour reader of emotional and too often immoral fiction will find nothing in this volume to his taste. It is a religious book intended for the religious and devout seeker after God. It is a very serious work for very careful and serious study. One who seriously and attentively studies this volume will find one's way open into the Temple of Vedic Literature. The many grammatical and exegetical details, if the reader tries to understand and utilise them properly, will enable him to handle the most abstruse and difficult questions in Vedic interpretation with full reliance and mastery. He who studies the notes will not need the help of the translation for he will himself be able to translate the Vedic verse concerned. Those who do not wish to read the notes may skip over them and read the translation itself which can be easily found out from the heading. The translation, it must be borne in mind, is not an ordinary translation. It is a combination of both literal translation and paraphrase. The chief purpose of translation is to convey to the mind of an enquerer in his own idiom or in easier style, the sense of a passage in his own or a different language which he cannot understand. Hence, to substitute mere dictionary equivalents for words unintelligible in themselves, cannot fulfil the purpose of translation. It is just for this reason that the translations of Vedic literature by European scholars and their Indian followers with which Vedic students the world over are provided, have failed to supply the wants of the times. More than a century has passed since Europe got herself introduced into the Temple of Vedic Lore, but even now after such patient and anxious waiting on the part of the world, her sons have the boldness to tell us that Vedic literature is unintelligible and that the Vedas contain nothing but "lies", "mad man's raving" and children's prattle", with a little scattering here and there of some truth and fine poetry ! There never was a more lamentable and unpardonable bungling done on this side of the grave than what they call Vedic research by European Scholars and their Indian followers. Are they really incapable to understand the Vedas, or are the Vedas unfit for human digestion ? Bhartṛhari answered the question for us:—कुरत्नाः स्युः कुपरीक्षका न मणयो येरर्घतः पातिताः. It is not the fault of the jewel if it is undervalued. The jewel is what it is. It is not its business to set down its own price.

The Vedas are not Indian; they belong to the whole world. The establishment of a world literary soviet is necessary for a sincere research into these most ancient records of humanity.

I am conscious that my translation is defective in many places, but all the same, it is a very sincere attempt to clearly convey the idea of the original to the mind of the reader. Having studied the notes and gone through the quotations along with a little patient search into similar passages, anyone will be able to correct my mistakes. The ancillary material is intended to clear and light the way and not to darken it. I have made, in other words, an honest effort to explain things and not to "explain them away". Hence no difficulty, of which I was conscious at the time of writing, have I wilfully evaded, but have squarely faced it and tried to clear it away. Hence it is that I was compelled to quote so many authorities.

There are three types of quotations in this book. The first are from the Vedas themselves and *these alone* are intended *to support or bear out the interpretation.* The second are from Sanskrit philosophical and other literature. These are brought in to expalin a passage merely and not to support or bear it out. It is for this purpose that the august Bhagavadgita is quoted. The beautiful versified translation of this noble work given in the volume is from the one published by Sadhu F. T. Brooks (an English man) from Madras. The third type of quotations are from the Bible, English Poetry, History &c. These are intended simply to illustrate the truths laid down in the Vedic verses. An attempt at comparative study of religion has also compelled me to allude to the Bible.

Wherever there is some sort of criticism, it should be understood, it is not my intention to hurt the feelings of any one but simply to point out what I believe to be right and true.

No one will be more sorry than I myself for the innumerable typographical mistakes. It is silly and unjust to find fault with the press. The Navayuga press has done its very best. I am entirely responsible for and guilty of the horrible blunders. I have now come to know that there can be no "printer's devils"—this is a mere hood-winking phrase—they are all devils of the writer's and proof-reader's making. As a proof-reader I have miserably failed. This is the first time in my life I have ever done any serious proof-reading, and I now know something of that difficult art. I have, however, made a clean breast of the affair in the "Companion" in "Addenda et Corrigenda", which the reader should have near at hand while reading the book. While issuing the second volume, if ever there is a demand for it, I am sure, I shall be able to minimise the mistakes to a surprising extent.

There must be many flaws in the "Errata" as well as the appendices but the reader may find what is given quite enough for his purpose. These parts of the work were written in great hurry almost on the eve of publishing the book. Hence a full list of references to the Nighaṇṭu and Nirukta could not also be prepared.

The lack of an introduction to such a work is inexcusable. The writing of an introduction covering at least some thirty pages of matter dealing with all questions bearing on Vedic interpretation, required at least a month's time since such a task demands reference to a large number of books. The secretary of the trust gave me very short notice terminating the printing. The little time that was available was hardly enough to finish the work that had still to be done to give the book a form fit to be called the first volume, especially as the press had done no printing almost during the first twenty days of March. In addition to this, I must mention that the state of my health also, now a days, has been very unsatisfactory. A gentleman had promised to write a part of the introduction but probably he forgot his word for I have heard nothing from him as yet. If ever there is a chance of issuing a second volume of which I have little hope, that volume will have a detailed critical introduction written by myself for I have learnt by experience not to depend upon others in such matters.

In conclusion I thank Mahāśaya Māmrāja of the D. A. V. College Research Library, Lahore; Pt. Bhagavaddatta, B. A., Research Scholar, Lahore; Pt. Viśvabandhu, Śastri, M. A., M. O. L., and Pt. Bhīmadēva Śarmā Sastri, M. A., M. O. L., both of the Viśvēśvarānanda Research Institute, Lahore; Pt. C. V. Venkatavarada Aiyengar, Bangalore; Pt. Jñyānacandra Śarmā B. A. (national), Homoeopath, Khānēwāl, Dist Mūltān, Punjab; Pt. Gaṇapati, Vedic Missionary, Delhi; the Rev. Svāmi Nityānanda ji Tīrtha, Lahore; Pt. Viśvapriya Śarmā, Śaśtri, Professor, Brāhmamahāvidyālaya, Lahore; the Rev. Svāmi Vedānanda ji Tirtha. Dingā, Gujrat (Punjab); and L. Ramsahae, B. A., B T, Headmaster, L. R. D. A. V. High School, Karachi; for the help they have, in various ways rendered me in the compilation of the work. Some of these gentlemen have helped with books, some with money and some in a purely literary manner helping me in readily checking my grammatical notes whenever I approached them in that connection. I have also to thank Pt. Bhīmasēna, Vidyālaṇkāra, Proprietor of the Navayuga Press and his staff, especially Mōtīrāma Compositor and Rāmaprasāda, Machineman, for the pains they have taken in the work.

The whole manuscript (except the Puruṣa Sūkta) was read out to Pt. Brahmadatta Jijñāsu, Lahore, while he was at Kāśi in September last. He was kind enough to devote some of his precious time for this purpose. He made a number of excellent suggestions all of which have been carried out. The Puruṣa Sūkta with the scholion of the Rev. Maharsi Dayānanda Sarasvati has been included in the book at his suggestion.

I am gateful to Pt. Srīpāda Dāmōdara Satavalekara of Aundh, Satara; Pt. Kṣemakaraṇadāsa Trivēdi, of Jaipur; the Publishers of Pt. Tulsirāma Svāmi's Works, Meerut; L. Haṃsarāja Librarian, D. A. V. College Research Library Lahore; Pt. Ayodhyaprasāda of Calcutta now in America; Messrs. Choudhary and Sons, Benares; and all others whose books I have profitably used in the compilation of this volume.

I am very much obliged also to the Secretary of the Trust, Lala Rūpalal Kapur and his brother Haṃsarāja for their kindly purchasing books for me, and affording necessary conveniences such as board and lodging during the time of writing.

The Sanmārgadarśana a book written in Hindi by my Guru the very revered Svami Sarvadānandaji Mahārāja has been very useful to me in writing on the Sacred Syllable 'Aum' in Chapter III on "The Nature of the Supreme Being." For this I thank his reverence as well as his publisher Mahāśaya Santarāma who also helped me in many ways all the time the work was being done.

The Revered Mahatma Haṃsarajaji guided me throughout in the compilation of the work. He was kind enough to allow me to read out the whole work to him (even the sheets I have now in abeyance) for almost four months for which purpose he set apart a portion of his precious time almost daily. Had it not been for him it is hardly possible I should have undertaken this work, nay, it is doubtful whether such a book should ever have been written. The responsibility, however, about the views expressed in the work devolves on me, for the kind Mahatma, never interfered with my way of dealing with the subject. It is with his blessing, the good wishes of my Guru the Very Rev. Svami Sarvadānandaji and those of another noble son of the Punjab, my kind elderly friend and well-wisher, the revered Master Lakṣmaṇadasa Ārya, B. A., L. T., of Lyallpur, that the book now carries the Vedic message to the English speaking world.

Any suggestions and corrections may kindly be communicated to me c/o the publishers.

स्तुता मया॑ वरदा वेदमाता ।
प्रचोदयन्तां पावमानी द्विजानाम् ॥

A. V. XIX, 71, 1. ab

विद्वानेव विजानाति विद्वज्जनपरिश्रमम् ।
नहि वन्ध्या विजानाति गुर्वीं प्रसववेदनाम् ॥

निन्दन्तु नीतिनिपुणा यदि वा स्तुवन्तु
लक्ष्मीः समाविशतु गच्छतु वा यथेष्टम् ।
अद्यैव वा मरणमस्तु युगान्तरे वा
न्याय्यात्पथः प्रविचलन्ति पदं न धीराः ॥ भर्तृहरेः ॥

यस्मात्कोशादुदभराम वेदम्
तस्मिन्नन्तरव दध्म एनम् ।
कृतमिष्टं ब्रह्मणो वीर्येण
तेन मा देवास्तपसावतेह ॥

A. V. XIX, 72, 2.

॥ ॐ तत्सत् ॐ ॥

Lahore, 31-3-35. **Bhumananda Sarasvati.**

ॐ

The following are a few of the infinite number of the meanings of the sacred syllable 'Aum'.

सच्चिदानन्दः ।
नित्यशुद्धबुद्धमुक्तस्वभावः ।
अनुपमः ।
अजः ।
सर्वशक्तिमान् ।
सर्वजगदुत्पादकः ।
सनातनः ।
सर्वस्वामी ।
अस्मत्पिता ।
सर्वानन्दप्रदः ।
अविद्यान्धकारनिर्मूलकः ।
परमैश्वर्यदायकः ।
अधमोद्धारकः ।
मान्यप्रदः ।
विनयविधिप्रदः ।
निरञ्जनः ।
शर्मदः ।
निर्विकारः ।
सदुपदेशकः ।
सत्यगुणाकरः ।
निरामयः ।
दीनदयाकरः ।
दारिद्र्यविनाशकः ।
सुनीतिवर्धकः ।
राज्यविधायकः ।

अनन्तस्वरूपः ।
अद्वितीयः ।
जगदादिकारणम् ।
निराकारः ।
न्यायकारी ।
सर्वजगदाधारः ।
सर्वमङ्गलमयः ।
करुणाकरः ।
परमसहायकः ।
सकलदुःखविनाशकः ।
विद्यार्कप्रकाशकः ।
साम्राज्यप्रसारकः ।
पतितपावनः ।
विश्वविनोदकः ।
विश्वासविलासकः ।
नायकः ।
नरेशः ।
सर्वान्तर्यामिन् ।
मोक्षप्रदः ।
निर्मलः ।
निरुपद्रवः ।
परमसुखदायकः ।
निर्वैरविधायकः ।
प्रीतिसाधकः ।
शत्रुविनाशकः ।

सर्वबलदायकः । निर्बलपालकः ।
सुधर्मसुप्रापकः । अर्थसुसाधकः ।
सुकामवर्धकः । ज्ञानप्रदः ।
सन्तति-पालकः । धर्मसुशिक्षकः ।
रोगविनाशकः । पुरुषार्थप्रापकः ।
दुर्गुणनाशकः । सिद्धिप्रदः ।
सज्जनसुखदः । दुष्टसुताड़नः ।
गर्वविदारकः । कुक्रोधविदारकः ।
कुलोभविदारकः । परमेशः ।
परेशः । परमात्मा ।
परब्रह्मन् । जगदानन्दकः ।
परमेश्वरः । व्यापकः ।
सूक्ष्मः । अच्छेद्यः ।
अजरः । अमृतः ।
अभयः । निर्बन्धनः ।
अप्रतिमप्रभावः । निर्गुणः ।
अतुलः । विश्वाद्यः ।
विश्ववन्द्यः । विद्वद्विलासकः ।
इत्याद्यनन्तविशेषणवाच्यः ॥

The above explanation is adapted from Maharṣi Dayananda's Āryābhivinaya pp. 13-15 of the edition issued by the Ramlal Kapur Trust.

Anthology of Vedic Hymns.

Prayers and Exhortations.

ओ३म् ॥ विश्वा॑नि देव सवितर्दुरि॒ता॑नि॒ परा॑सुव । य॒द्भ॒द्रं तन्न॒ऽआसु॑व ॥ य० ३० । ३ ॥

Oh Lord God, Creator of the universe (and Source of all great powers), of Holiest nature (and Dispenser of true happiness), be gracious, we beseech Thee, to dispel all our miseries (vices and evil propensities), and to bestow upon us what is good (such as virtuous tendencies, inclination to do benevolent deeds and a righteous disposition).

हि॒र॒ण्य॒ग॒र्भः सम॑वर्त॒ताग्रे॑ भू॒तस्य॑ जा॒तः पति॒रेक॑ऽ आसीत् । स दा॑धार पृ॒थि॒वीं द्यामु॒तेमां कस्मै॑ दे॒वाय॑ ह॒विषा॑ विधेम ॥ य० १३ । ४ ॥

Subduing our minds and living upright lives, we should, with fervent devotion, serve Him Who is Blissful and Holy, the Self-effulgent Creator, (Supporter and Illuminator) of all luminous bodies like the sun, the One Master of the universe Who existed before creation. It is He that sustains this earth, (the intermediate regions) and the vast heavens.

यऽआ॑त्म॒दा ब॑ल॒दा यस्य॒ विश्व॑ऽउ॒पास॑ते प्र॒शिषं॒ यस्य॑ दे॒वाः । यस्य॑ छा॒यामृतं॒ यस्य॑ मृ॒त्युः कस्मै॑ दे॒वाय॑ ह॒विषा॑ विधेम ॥ य० २५ । १३ ॥

Let us apply with heart and soul to observe in our daily life the commaudments of that Bliss-imparting God Who giveth to the devout true knowledge of (Himself as well as) the soul, Who blesses individuals and societies (that remember Him), with strength physical and spiritual, Whom all the enlightened adore, and Whose visible and truthful rule in the universe the righteous acknowledge, Whose shelter leads to emancipation, and disregard of Whom is (misery and) death.

यः प्राणतो निमिषतो महित्वैकऽइद्राजा जगतो बभूव। यऽईशेऽअस्य द्विपदश्चतुष्पदः कस्मै देवाय हविषा विधेम॥ य० २३।३॥

Let us offer all the best that we have, and devoutly resort to that Blissful God, the Giver of all wealth, Who, in His infinite glory, is the One and Sole Ruler of all creation animate and inanimate, bestowing (with His unfathomable wisdom) corporeal existence on all creatures—bipeds (like men), and quadrupeds (like the cow and all other beings).

येन द्यौरुग्रा पृथिवी च दृढा येन स्वः स्तभितं येन नाकः। योऽअन्तरिक्षे रजसो विमानः कस्मै देवाय हविषा विधेम॥ य० ३२।६॥

Let us adore with all the strength of our body, mind and soul, that Blissful Supreme Being, the Lord of all our désires by whom the formidable sun, the earth and other planets are fixed (in their orbits), by whom the quota of happiness and the enjoyment of final beatitude (according to the deserts of each finite being endowed with life) are established on a firm basis, and who (after the period of the dissolution of the cosmos is over), creates the different planets (or worlds) and sets them moving in space (—lets them fly like birds, so to say, in different directions in the sky).

प्रजापते न त्वदेतान्यन्यो विश्वा जातानि परि ता बभूव । यत्कामास्ते जुहुमस्तन्नोऽअस्तु वयं स्याम पतयो रयीणाम् ॥ ऋ० १० । १२१ । १० ॥

O Lord of all creatures, no other than Thou can control and govern all these created things. May the things desiring which we pray to Thee, be ours! May we be lord of all good things of the world.

स नो बन्धुर्जनिता स विधाता धामानि वेद भुवनानि विश्वा । यत्र देवा अमृतमानशानास्तृतीये धामन्नध्यैरयन्त ॥ य० ३२ । १० ॥

He is kind and loving like a brother to His devotees. He is the Producer of the entire universe (seen and unseen). He it is that lends us strength to accomplish our tasks in life. He knows (by direct contact) all the worlds, and the name, place and source of everything (visible and invisible). The Source of final beatitude (infinitely above the vanishing joys of the world and untouched by its shortcomings and miseries), in Him do the enlightened attain to emancipation (and move about having free access to all the worlds, all places and everything according to their wish).

अग्ने नय सुपथा रायेऽअस्मान्विश्वानि देव वयुनानि विद्वान् । युयोध्यस्मज्जुहुराणमेनो भूयिष्ठान्ते नमऽउक्तिं विधेम ॥ य० ४० । १६ ॥

Oh Self-effulgent, Omniscient Lord! we bow unto Thee with profound humility. Cast out from us all debasing and sinful desires and habits and lead us, by the path of righteousness, to the acquisition of all true knowledge that we may enjoy true happiness.

Chapter I.

Worship of the One God.

Rgvēda Mandala I, Sūkta 1

Seer :—Madhucchandas.
Subject :—Adoration of God the Self-effulgent
Metre :—Gāyatrī.
Tone :—Ṣaḍja.

(१) ओ३म् ॥ अग्निमीळे पुरोहितं यज्ञस्य देवमृत्विजम् । होतारं रत्नधातमम् ॥ १ ॥

पदपाठः—अग्निम् । ईळे । पुरःऽहितम् । यज्ञस्य । देवम् । ऋत्विजम् । होतारम् । रत्नऽधातमम् ॥

अन्वयः—अहं यज्ञस्य पुरोहितमृत्विजम् होतारं रत्नधातमं देवमग्निमीळे ॥

Word-meaning &c. :—अग्निम् (√अञ्चु गतिपूजनयोः or √अगि गतौ+नि U. IV, 50)=God the adorable, He who is fit to be approached, known, accepted, adored by all or He, who, being omnipresent, knows or pervades all. ईळे=ईडे (The change of of ड to ळ in Vedic Sanskrit is set forth in the couplet:—अजमध्यस्थडकारस्य ळकारम् बह्वृचा जगुः । अजमध्यस्थ ढकारस्य ळ्हकारम् वै यथाक्रमात् ॥)=I entreat, praise, request. पुरोहितम् (पुरः+√डुधाञ् धारणपोषणयोः+क्त P. I, I, 26 ; III, 2, 102 and VII, 4, 42)=He who supports from all eternity. (पुरस्ताद् दधाति). यज्ञस्य (√यज देवपूजासंगतिकरणदानेषु+नङ् P. III, 3, 90)=all activities from the agnihotra to the aśvamedha sacrifice; all righteous and philanthropic deeds. देवम् (√दिवु क्रीडाविजिगीषाव्यवहारद्युतिस्तुतिमोदमदस्वप्नकांतिगतिषु+अच् P. III, 1, 134)=

donor, imparter of joy or happiness, conqueror, illuminator. **ऋत्विजम्** (**य ऋतौ ऋतौ प्रत्युत्पत्तिकाले संसारं संगतं करोति, सर्वेषु ऋतुषु यजनीयः—ऋतु+ √यज्** P. III, 2, 59 and III, 3, 113)=He who brings together the cosmos at every creation; the only object of adoration in all seasons. **होतारम्** (**√हु दानादनयोः**, some say **आदाने** also.+ **तृन्** P. III, 1, 135 or U. II, 94 and 95)=donor, bestower; He who bestows all gifts upto emancipation; He who receives the adoration offered by devotees, souls who attain liberation and the cosmos at the time of dissolution. **रत्नधातमम्** (**रत्नानि सर्वजनै रमणीयानि प्रकृत्यादि पृथिव्यन्तानि ज्ञानहीरकसुवर्णादीनि जीवेभ्यो दानार्थं दधातीति रत्नधाः। अतिशयेन रत्नधाः स रत्न धातमः—रत्न+ √धा+तमप्** P. II, 2, 19 and V, 3, 55)=the most bounteous bestower of splendid wealth. For details see comments at the end.

Translation :—I glorify God the Self-effulgent, the Supporter of the universe from all eternity, the Illuminator of all activity, the Only Object of adoration in all seasons and the Most Bounteous and the Greatest Donor of splendid wealth.

Purport :—The Vedas unfold the eternal laws according to which the universe, human society and all things are sustained. They are revealed by God, their Author, for the benefit of souls. Every Vedic verse therefore is a statement made by God, and propagated by Him in the whole universe through one of the four original Ṛṣis.

Comment :—This is the first sentence in the original Vedic literature. It is significant that it begins with the name of God Himself and describes His attributes.

Agni is one of the names of God, for in Ṛgvēda I, 164, 46[1] we are told that :—"the wise call the Ador-

1. इन्द्रं मित्रं वरुणमग्निमाहुरथो दिव्यः स सुपर्णो गरुत्मान्।
एकं सद्विप्रा बहुधा वदन्त्यग्निं यमं मातरिश्वानमाहुः॥

able God (Agni), 'Indra'—the Omnipotent, 'Mitra'—the friend of all, 'Varuṇa'—the Holiest, and He also is, (according to them) 'Divya'—the Shining One, 'Suparṇa'—the Protector and Preserver of the universe, 'Garutmān'—the Mighty Spirit. Though He is One Unitary Being they speak of Him in various ways, sometimes calling Him 'Agni'—the Self-effulgent, sometimes, 'Yama'—the Controller of the world and sometimes 'Mātariśvan'—the Life Energy of the universe."

The first verse of the thirty-second chapter of the Yajurvēda[2] voices the same idea :—"Verily He is Agni—the All-knowing, He is Āditya—the Imperishable, He is Vāyu—the mover of all the universe, and verily He is Candramas—the All-blissful Being. Verily He is Sukra—the Holy One, He is Brahman—the Supreme Being. He is Āpah—All pervading and He is Prajāpati—the Lord of all creatures."

The following question put in the Ṛgvēda[3] and the answer to it leave no doubt as to the use of the word Agni to denote the Supreme Being :—"Who is that amongst all the immortal beings possessed of divine attributes whose charming name we shall contemplate ? What is that Being who will give us birth again on earth so that we may see father and mother ?" This is the question; now the answer is :—"We shall contemplate the charming name of Agni—the Self-effulgent God, who is the foremost of all the immortal beings possessed of divine attributes ; He will give us birth again on earth so that we may see father and mother."

---

2. तदेवाग्निस्तदादित्यस्तद्वायुस्तदु चन्द्रमाः । तदेव शुक्रं तद्ब्रह्म ता आपः स प्रजापतिः ॥ 3. कस्य नूनं कतमस्यामृतानां मनामहे चारु देवस्य नाम । को नो मह्या अदितये पुनर्दात्पितरं च दृशेयं मातरं च ॥ अग्नेर्वयं प्रथमस्यामृतानां मनामहे चारु देवस्य नाम । स नो मह्या अदितये पुनर्दात्पितरं च दृशेयं मातरं च ॥ ऋग्वेद १, २४, १ ; २ ॥

Surely the ordinary kitchen-fire, not that blazing in the biggest blasting furnace on earth, nay, not even the sun, can be said to possess the qualifications mentioned in the above verse. Nor can any wise devotee be expected to give vent to the grand emotion embodied in the following verse of the Ṛgveda[4] in addressing the physical fire:—"Oh Lord Omniscient! that I should ever experience myself subsisting in Thee, and that Thou mayest always be immanent in me, in this, indeed, is the fulfilment of all Thy blessings."

In the Brāhmaṇa literature also the word Agni is oftentimes used as a name of God. In the Śatapatha Brāhmaṇa we are told that Brahmā[5] (the Supreme Being), the soul,[6] the creatures[7] and their Protector,[8] the Puruṣa[9] and He whose face is Brahma[10] (the qualification of the highest class in human society) are all called Agni. The last is surely an echo of the Puruṣa, Sūkta, Yajurvēda chapter thirty-one verse eleven,[11] which says:—"In creation, that is, of the Virāṭ-puruṣa the body of all the bodies (see Puruṣ-sūkta verse five), the Brāhmaṇa (the man knowing God and given to teaching and preaching) occupies the position of the face, that is, being created with the best and the highest qualities of head and heart, he is highest in the social scale (according to God's dispensation). The next in order is the Kṣatriya (or the governing and warrior class) who can be said to be the arms of this Puruṣa, created as he is, with such qualities as strength, valour &c. The agricultural and commercial class endowed with qualities neces-

4. यदग्ने स्यामहं त्वं त्वं वा घा स्या अहम् । स्युष्टे सत्या इहाशिषः ॥ ऋ ८, ४४, २३ ॥
5. ब्रह्माग्निः । २ । ४ । २ । ११ ॥ 6. आत्मा वा अग्निः । १ । २ । २ । १ ॥ 7. and 8. अयं वा अग्निः प्रजाश्च प्रजापतिश्च । ६ । १ । २ । ४२ ॥ 9. पुरुषोऽग्निः । १० । ४ । १ । १० ॥ 10. मुखं ह्येतदग्नेर्यद्ब्रह्म । ९ । १ । १ । १० ॥ 11. ब्राह्मणोऽस्य मुखमासीद्बाहू राजन्यः कृतः । ऊरू तदस्य यद्वैश्यः पद्भ्यां शूद्रो अजायत ॥

sary for farming, business &c., occupying the middlemost position in the scale of human society, can be compared to the thighs of this Virāṭ-puruṣa. Finally the Śūdra occupies the position of His feet, being lowest in the social scale on account of such qualities as lack of intelligence and such other faculties."

The Maitryupaniṣad has an inimitable text about the attributes of God, in which the word Agni is used as one of His names:—"This Spirit indeed is Iśāna—the Controller, Śambhu—the Imparter of bliss, Bhava—the Origin of all beings, Rudra—the Dispeller of evil, Prajāpati—the Protector of all creatures, Viśvasṛk—the Creator of the universe, Hiraṇyagarbha—the Producer of all luminous bodies like the sun and moon, Satyam—the Ever-true (being immutable), Prāṇa—the Imparter of vitality to all creatures, Haṃsa—He who gives their gross form to all created objects, Sāsta—the Governor of all, Viṣṇu—the Omnipresent, Nārāyaṇa—the Refuge of all human beings, Arka—He who is fit to be adored by all, Savitā—the Generator of all, Dhātā—maker, Vidhātā—Fashioner, Samrāṭ—the King of all kings, Indra—the Omnipotent, Indu—the Imparter of joy, He who like the fire imparts energy to all diffusing luster through the globe of luster endowed with thousands of eyes, so to say, being infinitely more beneficial than the fire, He should be searched after by one desirous to know Him discarding all inclinations to harm any creature."[12]

In Yāska's Nirukta[13] the word agni is explained as follows:—"Agni is so called because it takes a leading

12. एष हि खल्वात्मेशानः शंभुर्भवो रुद्रः । प्रजापतिर्विश्वसृग्घिरण्यगर्भः सत्यं प्राणो हंसः शास्ता विष्णुर्नारायणोऽर्कः सविता धाता विधाता सम्राडिन्द्र इन्दुरिति य एष तपत्यग्निरिवाग्निनापिहितः सहस्राक्षेण हिरण्मयेनाण्डेन एष वा जिज्ञासितव्योऽन्वेष्टव्यः सर्वभूतेभ्योऽभयं दत्त्वा । ६ । ८ ॥

13. अग्निः कस्मात् । अग्रणीर्भवति । अग्रं यज्ञेषु प्रणीयते । अङ्गं नयति सन्नममानः ।

part in all human affairs, (becomes, so to say, leader-agraṇī). It is also carried in front in all sacrificial ceremonies. Or it is so called because when set to anything it occupies the whole object and makes it, as it were, a part of itself, 'angam nayati'. The exigete Sthāulāṣṭhīvi considers the word agni to denote the parching or scoarching effect which is destructive of viscidity, 'na knōpayati'. According to Śakapūṇi it is made up of three verbs, viz., √i to go, √anjū to go or √dah to burn and √nī to lead. He takes 'a' from the √i, 'ga' from √anjū or √dah and lastly 'ni' from √nī." Hence the word is formed according to this explanation as follows :—

(1) अग्रं नयति=अग्र+√नी=अग्+नि=अग्नि।
(2 अग्रे नीयते=अग्र+√नी= ,, . ,,
(3) न क्नोपयति=अ+√क्नूयी+क्विन्=अ+क्न्+इ=अग्नि।
(4) √इ+√अञ्जू+√नी=अ+ज्+नी=अग्नि।
(5) √इ+√दह्+√नी=अ+ह्+नी=अग्नि।

Yāska's explanation (Nir. VII, 15) [14] of the present verse also is noteworthy. He explains the form ईळे to mean याचामि—I beg or entreat. According to him the root √īḍ here signifies the act of entreaty or reverence. In the 12th section of the 2nd chapter of his work he derives the word पुरोहित from the adverb पुरस्+the root धा i.e., पुर एनं दधति=पुरस्+धा+क्त=पुरः+हित, P. VII, 4, 42. The word देव he derives in two ways viz., from the √दा to give, or √दीप् or √द्युत both meaning to shine, or illumine; and from the noun दिव् meaning the heavens :—दिवि तिष्ठति=दिव्+घञ्=देव. The words देव and देवता he says are synonymous. Aurṇavābha,

अक्नोपनो भवतीति स्थौलाष्ठीविः। न क्नोपयति न स्नेहयति। त्रिभ्य आख्यातेभ्यो जायत इति शाकपूणिरितादक्ताद्दग्धाद्वा नीतात्। स खल्वेतेरकारमादत्ते गकारमनक्तेर्वा दहतेर्वा नीः परः॥ निरुक्त ७। १४॥

[14] अग्निमीळेऽग्निं याचामि। ईळिरध्येषणाकर्मा पूजाकर्मा वा। पुर एनं दधतीति पुरोहितः। देवो दानाद्वा दीपनाद्वा द्योतनाद्वा द्युस्थानो भवतीति वा। यो देवः सा देवता। होतारं ह्वातारम्। जुहोतेर्होतेत्यौर्णवाभः। रत्नधातमं रमणीयानां धनानां दातृतमम्॥

says Yaska, derives the word होतृ from the root √हु in the sense of दान and अदन or आदान, whereas he himself takes it to be formed from the root √ह्वे to invoke upon. He derives यज्ञ from the root याच् also. याच्ञो भवन्ति इति याच्ञ=यज्ञ=यज्ञ. Three other derivations of this word he gives as follows :—(1) In a sacrifice oblations are offered with the recitation of verses from the Yajurveda and hence it is moistened, so to say, with them. यजुस्+√उन्दि्+क्त=यजुस्+उन्न=यज्+न=यज्ञ. (2) During sacrifices antelope-hides or spread for the sacrificers to sit on, hence :—अजिन (hide), अज् इ न—य्+अज्+न=यज्ञ. This is according to Aupamanyava. (3) A sacrifice is carried on, accomplished, by verses of the Yajurveda, therefore यजुस्+√नी=यज्+न=यज्ञ[15].

Yaska makes a very significant remark also on the multiplicity of the names of God. He says[16]:—"On account of the Omnipotence of the Deity, the One Supreme Being is variously extolled, as a result of which it appears that the different aspects (attributes &c.,) of the One, appear to be different deities.

(२) अ॒ग्निः पूर्वे॑भि॒र्ऋषि॑भि॒रीड्यो॒ नूत॑नैरु॒त। स दे॒वाँ एह व॑क्षति ॥ २ ॥

पदपाठ :—अ॒ग्निः। पूर्वे॑भिः। ऋषि॑भिः। ईड्यः। नूत॑नैः। उ॒त। सः। दे॒वान्। आ। इ॒ह। व॒क्ष॒ति॒॥

अन्वय :—योऽयमग्निः पूर्वेभिरुत नूतनैर्ऋषिभिरीड्योऽस्ति स इह देवानावक्षति ॥

Word-meaning &c. :—पूर्वेभिः (√पूर्व निमन्त्रणे निवासे वा+अच्)=by the ancient, the preceding according to

---

15. यज्ञः कस्मात्। प्रस्य.तं यजतिकर्मेति नैरुक्ताः। याच्ञो भवतीति वा। यजुरुन्नो भवतीति वा। बहुकृष्णाजिन इत्यौपमन्यवः। यजूंष्येनं नयन्तीति वा॥ निरुक्त ३। १९॥

16. माहाभाग्याद्देवताया एक आत्मा बहुधा स्तूयते। एकस्यात्मनोऽन्ये देवाः प्रत्यङ्गानि भवन्ति॥ निरुक्त ७। ४॥

human computation. ऋषिभिः (√ऋषी गतौ+इन् U. IV, 120)=a sage, a seer; the vital air; ratiocination. ईड्यः (√ईड् स्तुतौ+क्यप् P. III, 1, 109)=fit to be praised, adored or sought after. नूतनैः (नव+तनप् by Varitka नवस्य नू त्नमनप्त्नखाश्च)=by the modern or present according to human computation. पूर्वेभिर्ऋषिभिः=by men (living in the past or present age) well versed in the Vedic lores guiding the masses by teaching and preaching; with the vital air that subsists in the primordial matter the cause of the cosmos; by means of ratioci. nation on the part of the enlightened who taught the Vedic lores in the past. नूतनैर्ऋषिभिः=by brahmacaris or studencs of the Vedic lore; by the vital air that enlivens bodies and the cosmos which are the effects of primordial matter; through ratiocination by modern scholars well versed in the Vedic lores. (The words ancient and modorn are used with reference to human computation and have nothing to do with God to Whom everything is present). उत=also. देवान् √दिवु +अच्)=perfect limbs and senses, perfect attainments such as advanced learning, seasons of great joy and perfect happiness; all great powers and good gifts. इह=here in this world; during this life, in the soul. आ—वक्षति (आ वहतु)=may He bestow on us.

Translation :—May God the Self-effulgent, (Omnipotent, the Internal Regulator and Illuminator of all beings), worthy of being glorified and sought after by both the preceptors (ancient and modern according to human computation) and the students of the Vedic lores (or Who deserves to be praised and sought after by a regulation of the vital air in the bodies and the cosmos that are effects, in harmony with the subtle vital air which subsists eternally in the primordial matter the cause, or by means of ratiocination of enlightened men well versed in the Vedic lores who lived in the past and are still living in the present according to hman consideration), bestow on us all great powers and good gifts (like perfect limbs and senses, advanced learning and seasons of great joy and happiness).

Purport:—The end of all learning and teaching, of regulations of breath and other Yogic exercises, as well as of ratiocination should be the glorification of God and conformity to His will.

Comment:—By 'ancient'-pūrve are meant such as are learned in the Vedic lores irrespective of the age to which they belong for the idea of past and present depends upon human computation whereas to God, the Author of the Vedas, everything is present in as much as all things do always exist in some form or other, gross or subtle, manifested or unmanifested. By modern—'navīna' students of the Vedic lores are intended and not scholars and sages of the present age who also are designated 'pūrve' by the verse. The word 'ṛṣi' denotes men who understand the Vedic law, and are engaged in the propagation of righteousness and learning. Preaching and practising the truth they are the benefactors of mankind. Guileless and ever industrious, they take recourse to God for the attainment of uprightness in life and emancipation after and investigate into heat and such other natural phenomena for the service of humanity. The word 'ṛṣi' according to Yāska[1] means a seer—one endowed with keenness of vision. But Aupamanyava says that a 'ṛṣi' is he who has understood the Vedic law, in support of which interpretation he cites a Brāhmaṇa passage meaning that the eternal Vedic law was revealed in the vision of these seers undergoing austerities and this is why they are called 'seers'. Yāska clearly

1. ऋषिर्दर्शनात् । स्तोमान्ददर्शेत्यौपमन्यवः । तद्यदेनांस्तपस्यमानान्ब्रह्म स्वयम्भ्वभ्यानर्षत्त ऋषयोऽभवंस्तदृषीणामृषित्वमिति विज्ञायते ॥ निरुक्त २ । ११ ॥

states[2] that a 'ṛṣi' is so called because he or she visualises (understands fully) vedic verses having many and different significations. Elsewhere he narrates what work these ṛṣis have done in these words[3] :— "There were once enlightened persons who had visualised (fully understood and lived up to) the law of righteousness ; they, through their teaching, laid bare the meaning of Vedic texts for such as were unable to understand the Vedas. Later on there came a time when people were unable to understand the Vedas even through these teachings of the ancient seers. For such people, later scholars compiled this Vedic dictionary (the Nighaṇṭu and Nirukta) so that they may, with some effort, be able to grasp the meaning of Vedic texts."

By 'ṛṣi' is also meant a process of reasoning adopted in making difficult or abstruse matters clear. In his beautiful commentary on Ṛgvēda I, 164, 39 Yāska[4] says that Vedic statements are to be interpreted on the basis of such other Vedic texts as are relevent to the purpose and also through a right process of reasoning, but never severed from their context as this latter always has its influence on the sense of a text. A person not endowed with vision or void of purity and austerity of life cannot understand the Vedas. In chapter I section 14 it has already been pointed out that men well-versed in all the ancillary

---

2. एवमुच्चावचैरभिप्रायैर्ऋषीणां मन्त्रदृष्टयो भवन्ति ॥ निरुक्त ७ । ३ ॥

3. साक्षात्कृतधर्माण ऋषयो बभूवुस्तेऽवरेभ्योऽसाक्षात्कृतधर्मभ्य उपदेशेन मन्त्रान्सम्प्रादुरुपदेशाय ग्लायन्तोऽवरे बिल्मग्रहणायेमं ग्रन्थं समाम्नासिषुर्वेदं च वेदाङ्गानि च । निरुक्त १ । २० ॥

4. न तु पृथक्त्वेन मन्त्रा निर्वक्तव्याः प्रकरणश एव तु निर्वक्तव्या न ह्येषु प्रत्यक्षमस्त्यनृषेरतपसो वा पारोवर्यवित्सु तु खलु वेदितृषु भूयोविद्यः प्रशस्योभवतीत्युक्तं । पुरस्तान्मनुष्या वा ऋषिषूत्क्रामत्सु देवानब्रुवन्को न ऋषिर्भविष्यतीति । तेभ्य एतं तर्कमृषिं प्रायच्छन्मन्त्रार्थचिन्ताभ्यूहमभ्यूढं तस्माद्यदेव किंचानूचानोऽभ्यूहत्यार्षं तद्भवति । निरुक्त १३ । १२ ॥

lores alone can grasp the meaning of Vedic texts But such 'ṛṣis' are not always available. Hence Yāska cites a legend to point out the necessity and sufficiency of the right sort of reasoning to interpret the Vedas. "When the 'ṛṣis' were nowhere to be found the people asked the enlightened (leaders) as to who would guide them in matters of Vedic interpretation as a seer now. They, in reply, mentioned reasoning as a factor to take the place of ṛṣis in deciding the sense of Vedic texts. Hence, whatever import a scholar traces in a Vedic text by a right process of reasoning becomes equal to the result of a seer's vision." This process of reasoning is described by Gotama[5] as 'an enquiry into the causes or reasons of a thing with a view to arrive at the truth.

The word 'ṛṣi' also means the vital air which interpretation is given in the Śatapatha Brāhmaṇa VII, 2, 1, 5[6].

The word 'ṛtu' according to Śatapatha Br. VII, 2, 2, 26[7] has all the meanings of the word 'dēva'.

Yāska in Nirukta VII, 16[8] says that the word 'agni' in this verse does not mean the kitchen fire, but it denotes the two luminous bodies of the upper regions 'uttarē jyōtiṣī', that is electricity (lightening) subsisting in the mid region and the sun in the celestial. The words 'uttarē jyōtiṣī' also mean the two highest luminous beings, namely, the Supreme Being, and the soul. Yāska does, really seem to mean here the Supreme Being also.

(३) अग्निना रयिमश्नवत्पोषमेव दिवेदिवे ।
यशसं वीरवत्तमम् ॥ ३ ॥

---

5. अविज्ञाततत्त्वेऽर्थे कारणोपपत्तितस्तत्त्वज्ञानार्थमूहस्तर्कः । न्याय १ । १ । ४० ॥

6. प्राणा ऋषयः । 7. ऋतवो वै देवाः ।

8. स न मन्येतायमेवाग्निरित्यप्येते उत्तरे ज्योतिषी अग्नी उच्येते । ततो नु मध्यमः ।

पदपाठः—अग्निना । रयिम् । अश्नवत् । पोषम् । एव । दिवेऽदिवे । यशसम् । वीरवत्ऽतमम् ॥

अन्वयः—मनुष्योऽग्निनैव दिवेदिवे पोषं यशसं वीरवत्तमं रयिमश्नवत् ॥

Word-meaning &c. :—**अग्निना**=by fervently adoring God the Self-effulgent. **रयिम**=such excellent wealth (possessions) as learning, riches &c. (Nig. II, 9). **अश्नवत्** (Vedic subjunctive parasmaipadi form used instead of the atmanepadi)=obtains. **पोषम्** (√**पुष पुष्टौ+घञ्** P. III, 3, 18)=imparting happiness by strengthening body, mind and soul. **एव**=only, alone. **दिवेदिवे**=day by day, everyday (Nig. II, 9). **यशसम** (**युद्+√अश् देवन+असुन्** P. I, 1, 46; U. IV, 191 and 189)=that brings great fame. **वीरवत्तमम्** (**वीर+मतुप्+तमप्** P. V, 2, 94; VIII, 2, 9 and V, 3, 55) consisting of the strongest, bravest and the most accomplished of off-spring and relations.

Translation :—By fervent adoration of God the Self-effulgent alone, does the devotee day by day obtain from Him such excellent possessions as impart happiness through the strengthening of body, mind and soul—possessions which bring great fame and include the strongest, (bravest and the most accomplished) of offspring (and relations).

Purport :—In this verse the word agni is used with a double meaning, namely, God and heat. A man who lives in conformity with the will of God, scientifically investigates into the properties and uses of heat in its various forms and utilises it in arts and crafts, will amass immense wealth, win great fame and have noble off-spring and relations.

The term heat (agni) here stands for light, fire, steam, electricity &c., and by implication signifies all natural phenomena that are necessary for the formation and sustenance of the cosmos. A scientist should see at the back of all these the August Author of Nature herself, for all these agencies work only in obedience to His Omnipotent Sanction. As the Upaniṣad says:—"Fire burns in accordance with His Law, the Sun diffuses light and heat in submission to His Will, and electricity and air in humble obedience to His Dictates render service according to their capabilities. Nay, the fifth, and the most formidable of all these, death, also depends upon His Almighty Will."*

(४) अग्ने यं यज्ञमध्वरं विश्वतः परिभूरसि । स इद्देवेषु गच्छति ॥ ४ ॥

पदपाठः—अग्ने । यम् । यज्ञम् । अध्वरम् । विश्वतः । परिऽभूः । असि । सः । इत् । देवेषु । गच्छति ॥

अन्वयः—हे अग्ने त्वं यमध्वरं यज्ञं विश्वतः परिभूरसि तथायमग्निरपि संपादयितास्ति स इद्देवेषु गच्छति ॥

Word-meaning &c. :—**अग्ने**=Oh Self-effulgent God! **यम्**=which. **यज्ञम्**—the propagation of true learning and the imparting of benefits to others; good or righteous works, such as propitiation of the enlightened, associating with the righteous and giving of charity of various types to the deserving and needy; creation, sustenance and dissolution of the universe on the part of God; praise, prayer and worship offered to God. **अध्वरम्**=(न+√ध्वृ हिंसायाम्+अच् Nig. II, 19; P. III, 1, 134; and Nir. I, 8)=free from any sort of injury to any being. **विश्वतः** (विश्व+तसि P. V, 4, 48)=pervading all, being omnipresent and hence from the side of everything. **परिभूः** (परि सर्वतो भावे Nir. I, 3+√भू+क्विप् P. III, 2, 76)=Supporting or protecting in every way.

* भयादस्याग्निस्तपति भयात्तपति सूर्यः । भयादिन्द्रश्च वायुश्च मृत्युर्धावति पञ्चमः ॥ क० ६ । ३ ॥

असि=thou art. सः=that (yajña). इत्=verily. देवेषु=to the enlightened, wise or all beneficent beings and objects. गच्छति=goes to, reaches, resorts to, for the good of all.

Translation :—Oh Self-effulgent God! being immanent in everything, Thou dost (by means of heat and other natural phenomena of Thy making, through Thy Providence and along with the sustenance of the cosmos) thoroughly protect from all sides, all good works (such as the adoration and contemplation of Thy Divine Majesty, the propagation of righteousness and true learning, giving charity to the deserving and needy, honouring the wise and associating with the virtuous) which are entirely harmless (in themselves but beneficial to all beings) and, it is ordained by Thee that these righteous works should be in the hands of the enlightened for the good of all.

Purport :—As God the Omnipresent always protects the abovementioned righteous deeds from all sides they become endowed with the capacity to impart beneficent properties. Hence it is that heat created by God as possessing such attributes is instrumental in the propagation of beneficial arts and crafts. A learned but righteous and industrious man alone deserves to have these advantages.

(५) अग्निर्होता कविक्रतुः सत्यश्चित्रश्रवस्तमः

देवो देवेभिरागमत् ॥ ५ ॥

पदपाठः—अग्निः । होता । कविऽक्रतुः । सत्यः । चित्रश्रवःऽतमः ।

देवः । देवेभिः । आ । गमत् ॥

अन्वयः—यः सत्यश्चित्रश्रवस्तमः कविक्रतुर्होता देवोऽग्निः परमेश्वरः स देवेभिः सहागमत् ॥

Word-meaning &c. :—अग्निः=God the Self-effulgent होता=bestower of the best gifts; receiver, holder and supporter of the earth and other planets. कविक्रतुः (√कु शब्दे + इ U. IV, 139 or √क्रमु पादविक्षेपे + इण् or √कव गत्यर्थे + इण् = कवि[1] + √डुकृञ् करणे + क्रतु U. I. 76 = क्रतुः। कविश्चासौ क्रतुश्च P. II, 1, 57) = Omniscient Creator of the atomic matter &c., endowed with various properties; the Author and Revealer of the Vedic lores embodying principles forming the basis of all sciences and arts. सत्यः (√अस भुवि + शतृ + यत् P. III, 2, 124 and IV, 4, 98) = beneficial to the righteous[2]; immutable. चित्रश्रवः (√चि चयने + क्त्र U. IV, 174 = चित्र + √श्रु श्रवणे + असुन् U. IV, 189 = श्रवः चित्रमद्भुतं श्रवणं यस्य सः P. II, 2, 24 = चित्रश्रवः + तमप् P. V, 3, 55) = He Whose glory is most wonderful to here about; of Whose glory people hear but hardly understand. देवः = the Self-refulgent Illuminator of all; He Whose light illuminates all; Who guides or impels all beings. देवेभिः (Vedic for देवैः) = with the enlightened; with beneficent attributes. आ-गमत् (Aorist लुङ् form without the augment अट् P. III, 3, 6) = may He come to us; may we attain to Him; may He be accessible to us.

Translation:—May God the Self-effulgent, the Giver of the best blessings, the Omniscient Creator of (atomic matter with its various properties and its expanse) the whole cosmos, the Benefactor of the righteous (and industrious), Whose glory is most wonderful to hear (and know about),—the Light that illuminates all—be accessible to us (His devotees).

Purport:—The word 'agni' here means both God and the natural phenomenon of heat, since God being

---

1. मेधावी कविः। क्रान्तदर्शनो भवति कवतेर्वा ॥ निरुक्त १२ । १३ ॥ कविः क्रान्तदर्शनः। अथवा कवतेर्धातोर्गत्यर्थस्य कविः। गच्छत्यसौ नित्यम्। किंच कविशब्दादेव प्रासादीत्यनुवर्तमानादि ॥ द. इ ॥ कविः कस्मात्। क्रान्तदर्शन इत्यादि क्रमतेः। कवतेर्वा गतिकर्मणः एतं रूपम्। क्रान्तं दूरं गतं दर्शनं प्रकाशरूपं विज्ञानमस्य। यद्वा कवतेस्तदा कविर्गन्ता गच्छत्यसौ नित्यम्। अवगन्ता वा सर्वस्य ज्ञाता। केचित्तु कवतेः शब्दकर्मणः। अस्मिन्नेव नामकरणे शब्दकारी कविरुच्यते ॥ स्क. भा ॥

2. सत्यं कस्मात्। सत्सु तायते सत्प्रभवं भवतीति वा ॥ निरुक्त ३ । १३ ॥

Omniscient, Imperishable, Omnipotent—the Maker and Refuge of all—in Whom all creatures live and move and have their being, is the Illuminator of all; and the physical heat by its power of attraction or gravitation (as in the sun) is the means to keep material objects intact.

Comment:—In this verse the incomprehensible Majesty of God is hinted at. His glory is so wonderful that few of those who hear of it understand all that is said about Him and still fewer realise Him and live up to their experience. It is said in the Kathopaniṣad[3] :—"Many do not have the good fortune to hear about Him, and of those that hear of Him many fail to realise Him. A person capable of teaching about the real nature of God is a rarity and even if such a one be available, the person wishing to learn about Him should have care and presence of mind in doing so. It is only then that he will be one of the few that know about Him and if he is really a man of fortitude, he will then act up to what he has learnt."

The same sentiment is voiced by the Bhagvadgita[4] in its beautiful style as follows :—

"As 'Wonderful', seeing Him, someone beholds ;
As 'Wonderful', speaking another describes Him ;
As 'Wonderful', hearing of Him, a third hears :
Yet e'en after hearing, not one of them *knows*."

God, in this stanza is called 'kavi'—poet. A poet's work, it is generally admitted, is creative, for which genius of a high order is necessary. The intellectual calibre of a human poet is thus compared to the Omniscience of God. Just as God knows His

---

[3] श्रवणायापि बहुभिर्यो न लभ्यः शृण्वन्तोऽपि बहवो यं न विद्युः । आश्चर्योऽस्य वक्ता कुशलोऽस्य लब्धाश्चर्यो ज्ञाता कुशलानुशिष्टः ॥ क. १ । १६ ॥

[4] आश्चर्यवत्पश्यति कश्चिदेनमाश्चर्यवद्वदति तथैव चान्यः । आश्चर्यवच्चैनमन्यः शृणोति श्रुत्वाप्येनं वेद न चैव कश्चित् ॥ २ । २९ ॥

subject thoroughly a human poet also must understand his own topic well to be able to express his thoughts about it in a vivid and attractive manner, but entirely in conformity with truth and Nature. He is, thus, able to tell something new, impart some valuable instrnction on morality or explain some difficult matter in a few choice words full of suggestion. It is only in this sense that a human poet is said to 'create'.

In the Atharvaveda[5] this idea is expressed in a few but impressive words, thus:—"Man neither sees nor can abandon (overlook) Him (the Lord God Omnipresent) Who is (always) close to him. Of the making of such God the Effulgent is this Poem which neither perishes nor decays."

This Poem of the Almighty Poet is two-fold. The first is visible in the universe around us of which the Ṛgvēda[6] sings in the following strains:—"(Oh men!) He has spread the waters in the rays of the Sun, has given vigorous speed to horses and put milk in the udder of the cow. Varuṇa (God the Great) has placed intelligence in our hearts, has diffused heat through space, set the Sun in the high heavens and made the essence of all organic bodies (beings) subsist in the cloud."

"Varuṇa (the Great God) has very ably made the cloud that pours waters downwards, atmosphere and the earth. Therewith the Supreme Being, the

[5] अन्ति सन्तं न जहात्यन्ति सन्तं न पश्यति । देवस्य पश्य काव्यं न ममार न जीर्यति ॥ १० । ८ । ३२ ॥

[6] वनेषु व्यन्तरिक्षं ततान वाजमर्वत्सु पय उस्रियासु । हृत्सु क्रतुं वरुणो अप्स्वग्निं दिवि सूर्यमदधात्सोममद्रौ ॥ ५ । ८५ । २ ॥ नीचीनबारं वरुणः कबन्धं प्र ससर्ज रोदसी अन्तरिक्षम् । तेन विश्वस्य भुवनस्य राजा यवं न वृष्टिर्व्युनत्ति । ३ ॥ यस्येमे हिमवन्तो महित्वा यस्य समुद्रं रसया सहाहुः । यस्येमाः प्रदिशो पश्य बाहू कस्मै देवाय हविषा विधेम । ऋ० । १० । १२१ । ४ ॥ येन द्यौरुग्रा पृथिवी च दृढा येन स्वः स्तभितं येन नाकः । योऽन्तरिक्षे रजसो विमानः कस्मै देवाय हविषा विधेम । ५ ॥ यं क्रन्दसी अवसा तस्तभाने अभ्यैक्षेतां मनसा रेजमाने । यत्राधि सूर उदितो विभाति कस्मै देवाय हविषा विधेम । ६ ॥

Illuminator of the entire universe moistens the earth just as the shower of rain bedews barley (and other cereals that they may grow) to make us happy".

"Whose greatness these snowy mountains and the ocean with its waters proclaim ; Whose arms are these vast regions ; He, it is to Whom we shall offer our prayers."

"By Whom the heavenly bodies are uplifted and the earth is made stable ; by Whom the atmosphere and the heavens are established, Who pervades the entire space by His Spiritual Essence ; He, it is to Whom we shall offer our prayers."

"To Whom the earth and heavens look up, being upheld by His protection, and moved by His will ; in Whom the Sun rises and shines forth ; He it is to Whom we shall offer our prayers".

The Nasadiya and Puruṣa hymns given elsewhere in this book should also be seen in this connection.

The other Poem of this Almighty Poet is the Eternal Law revealed in the shape of the four Vedas. In the Yajurveda[7] we shall find a verse which states the purpose of the Vedas and for whom they are intended in the following words :—"Oh men ! as I have given this Word (i. e. the four Vedas) which is the word of salvation for all mankind, namely, for the Brahmaṇas (those who are engaged in the propagation of sacred knowledge), for the Kṣatriyas (those who look after state affairs or the government of the country), for the Śūdras (those engaged in manual work or service), for the Vaiśyas (those who are devoted to agriculture and commerce), for those who are my dependents (women and servants) and even for them who are of low dignity (in society but of good inclinations), so should you also do &c."

[7] यथेमां वाचं कल्याणीमावदानि जनेभ्यः । ब्रह्मराजन्याभ्यां शूद्राय चार्याय च स्वाय चारणाय । २६ । २ ॥

The Atharvavēda[8] X, 7, 20 describes in figurative language this Divine Poem the gist of which can be given in the following words:—"Who is that Great Being who revealed the Ṛgvēda, the Yajurvēda, the Sāmavēda and the Atharvavēda? He is the Supreme Spirit Who has created the universe and sustains it."

The eighth[9] stanza of the 40th chapter of the Yajurvēda relates:—"That Supreme Being overspreads all. He is entirely Spirit, All-energy, All-powerful, Pure, Perfect, Omniscient, Inward Controller of all, Ruler of all, Eternal and Self-existent. He has from all eternity been teaching uncreated immortal human souls, the true knowledge of things through the revelation of the Veda—His eternal knowledge."

The first verse[10] of the 49th hymn of the 10th book of the Ṛgvēda, Atharvavēda XI 7, 5[11], XIX, 68, 1[12], a translation of all three of which is subjoined and the Samjñāna Sūkta R. V. X, 71; given elsewhere, may be read in this connection:—"I give my devotee the best wealth (which he has won by the deeds of his past life); I reveal knowledge in the form of the Vedas, hence all truly wise people offer me thanks. I encourage the righteous and industrious, and I surely see him that is not such, for, the maintenance and

---

8 यस्मादृचो अपातक्षन्यजुर्यस्मादपाकषन् । सामानि यस्य लोमान्यथर्वाङ्गिरसो मुखम् । १० । ७ । २० ॥

9 स पर्यगाच्छुक्रमकायमव्रणमस्नाविरंशुद्धमपापविद्धम् । कविर्मनीषी परिभूः स्वयम्भूर्याथातथ्यतोऽर्थान्व्यदधाच्छाश्वतीभ्यः समाभ्यः ॥

10 अहं दां गृणते पूर्व्यं वस्वहं ब्रह्म कृणवं मह्यम् वर्धनम् । अहम् भुवं यजमानस्य चोदितायज्वनः साक्षि विश्वस्मिन् भरे ॥

11 ऋक्साम यजुरुच्छिष्टे उद्गीथः प्रस्तुतं स्तुतम् । हिङ्कार उच्छिष्टे स्वरः साम्नो मेडिश्च तन्मयि ॥

12 अव्यसश्च व्यचसश्च बिलं विष्यामि मायया । ताभ्यामुद्धृत्य वेदमथ कर्माणि कृण्महे ॥

support of all depend upon me." "The Ṛgveda, the Sāmaveda, the Yajurveda, the Udgītha (the sacred syllable 'Aum'), hymns of praise, the sound 'hiṃ' (made in the Sāman chant), accent and pitch, and the seven notes of music are all in the Surpassing Lord Brahma (i. e., they are originally taught by Him). May I attain to all these". "I find out the secret of the (relation between) the non-pervasive (the individual soul) and the All-pervasive (the Supreme Being) by means of my intelligence. In this connection we should regard the Vedas to be the Supreme source of right knowledge to follow in our walk of life (up to emancipation)."

(६) यदङ्ग दाशुषे त्वमग्ने भद्रं करिष्यसि । तवेत्तत्सत्यमङ्गिरः ॥ ६ ॥

पदपाठः—यत् । अङ्ग । दाशुषे । त्वम् । अग्ने । भद्रम् । करिष्यसि । तव । इत् । तत् । सत्यम् । अङ्गिरः ॥

अन्वयः—हे अङ्गिरोऽङ्गाग्ने त्वं यद्दाशुषे भद्रं करिष्यसि तत्तवेत्सत्यं व्रतमस्ति ॥

Word-meaning &c. :—यत्=यस्मात्=wherefore ; that. अङ्ग=Oh Friend (of all ! दाशुषे √दाशृ दाने+क्वसु P. III, 2, 107)=to the charitably inclined, to him who offers his, life, property, soul—all—to God ; to him who is industrious in righteous works[1]. भद्रम् (√भदि कल्याणे सुखे च +रन् U. II, 28, or according to the Nirukta[2] √भज सेवायाम्+रन् or अभि+√द्रु गतौ+ड ; or √भू सत्तायाम्+शतृ P. III, 2, 124+√रमु क्रीडायाम्+ड or भाजन+र in the sense of मतुप्)=beneficient ; that which all the wise take

---

[1] यजमानो वै दाश्वान् । श० २ । १ । ४ । १८ ॥

[2] भद्रं भगेन व्याख्यातम् । भजनीयम् । भूतानामभिद्रवणीयम् । भवद्रमयतीति वा भाजनवद्वा । निरुक्त ४ । १० ॥

recourse to; what makes all creatures happy during its possession; what yields happiness to the deserving. कारिष्यसि=करोषि=Thou dost. तव=Thine. तत्=तस्मात्=therefore. सत्यम्=true, lasting. अङ्गिरः (√अगि गत्यर्थे+असि U. IV, 235; √अङ्ग पदे लक्षणे च+आरन् U. III, 134=अङ्गारः; अङ्गारेषु भवः अङ्गिरः Nir. III, 17)=immanent in or pervading the human body in all its various parts (अङ्ग); pervading all the divisions of the material universe; Inner Self; the vital air[3].

Translation:—Oh Self-effulgent God, Friend of all! Oh Inner Self of the universe and the human soul! upon that good man who out of charity and without expecting any return generously gives to the needy and deserving (and who offers his property, body and soul, everything, to Thee the Bestower of all benefits), Thou dost confer all good things (including the bliss of final beatitude). To grant such great and lasting) gifts is quite in accordance with Thy Divine Nature (and lies only in Thy power).

Purport:—God is just and the Friend and Well-wisher of all. To obtain happiness in life, therefore, man ought to worship Him alone and none else, since to bestow happiness on creatures is the nature of this Almighty God the Illuminator of all, and no other being has the power to do so.

Comment:—In this verse God is called the Friend of all. It must be remembered here that one of the names of God is 'Mitra' i. e., Friend. The verse इन्द्रं मित्रं वरुणमग्निमाहुः &c., quoted in the beginning of this chapter should be referred to in this connection.

(७) उप त्वाग्ने दिवेदिवे दोषावस्तर्धिया वयम् ।
नमो भरन्त एमसि ॥ ७ ॥

---

[3] प्राणो वा अङ्गिराः ॥ श० ६ । ३ । ७ । ३ ॥ अयास्यः (आस्यः) वा अङ्गानां रसः ॥ श० १४ । १ । १ । ८ ॥ गार्हपत्योपायिव्याकिनाङ्गारेषु वसतीत्यङ्गिराः ॥ स्क० आ० नि० १ । १७ ॥

पदपाठः—उप॑ । त्वा॒ । अ॒ग्ने॒ । दि॒वेऽदि॑वे । दोषा॑ऽवस्तः । धि॒या । व॒यम् । नमः॑ । भर॑न्तः । आ । इ॒मसि॒ ॥

अन्वयः—हे अग्ने वयम् धिया दिवेदिवे दोषावस्तस्त्वा भरन्तो नमः कुर्वन्तश्चोपैमासि ॥

Word-meaning &c. :—उप एमसि (आ+ √इण् गतौ = we approach with humility. दिवेदिवे (√दिवु क्रीडाविजिगीषाव्यवहारद्युतिस्तुतिमदमोदस्वप्नकान्तिगतिषु)=for the attainment of the light of true knowledge (and nothing else); day by day (Nig. I, 9). दोषावस्तः (दोषा=night, Nig. I, 7 वस्तः=day Nig. I, 9)=day and night; morning and evening. धिया (√ध्यै चिन्तायाम्+क्विप् P. III, 2, 178 and Vārtika ध्यायतेः संप्रसारणं च)=by means of our intellect and mind; by understanding and deeds; by thought word and deed. नमः=adoring Thee. भरन्तः (√डुभृञ् धारणपोषणयोः+शतृ P. III, 2 124)=in a spirit of fervent adoration.

Translation :—Oh Lord God ! in a spirit of humility and fervent devotion we approach Thy Divine Majesty morning and evening with our thoughts, (words) and actions befitting to that end that Thou wilt bless us with the light of true spiritual knowledge.

Purport :—God sees all ; He is Omnipresent and deserving of our adoration. Hence it is but just that we should not forget Him while engaged in any of the tasks of our daily life. It is only in this way that we can secure His grace which will save us from falling away any time from the truth. The reason is, being All-knowing and All-seeing, He is in every way acquainted with all our deeds and plans. This knowledge will help us a good deal in time of temptation.

(८) राज॑न्तमध्व॒राणां॑ गो॒पामृ॒तस्य॒ दीदि॑विम् । वर्ध॑मान॒ं स्वे दमे॑ ॥ ८ ॥

पदपाठः—राजन्तम्। अध्वराणाम्। गोपाम्। ऋतस्य। दीदिविम्। वर्धमानम्। स्वे। दमे॥

अन्वयः—वयं स्वे दमे वर्धमानम्राजन्तमध्वराणां गोपामृतस्य दीदिविं (परमेश्वरं नित्यमुपैमासि)॥

Word-meaning &c. :—राजन्तम् (√राजृ दीप्तौ+शतृ P. III, 2, 124)=glorious; shining. अध्वराणाम्=of righteous deeds or men. गोपाम् (√गम्लृ गतौ+डो U. II, 67 +√पा रक्षणे+क्विप् P. III, 2, 76)=Protector of the earth and other planets. ऋतस्य (√ऋ गतिप्रापणयोः+क्त P. III, 2, 102)=of the Divine Law; of the four Vedas unfolding all the true lores; of the eternal cause of the universe; of truth. (Nig. III, 10 and V, 4), दीदिविम् (√दिवु क्रीडा &c.+क्विन् U. IV. 55)=showing everything clearly. वर्धमानम् (√वृधु वृद्धौ+शानच् P. III, 1, 124 and VIII, 2, 82)=ever increasing; never decreasing. स्वे=in His own. दमे (√दमु उपशमे+घञ् P. III, 3, 121)=in His most blissful state; in His glory in the state af emancipation in which there is no suffering and no lack.

Translation :—We should always approach the August and All-pervading Divine Presence of God the Self-effulgent, in a spirit of sincere humility. He is the Divine Light that illuminates the inner self of all human beings and shows them everything clearly. He is the Mighty Force that impels all righteous men to deeds of self-sacrifice and the good of all creatures. He is the Sustainer of this earth and other planets, and He is the Author and Guardian of the Eternal Vedic Law. He is in His never decreasing state of Bliss

Purport :—The Supreme Being untainted by the shortcomings of decay and lack of knowledge, directing all souls (embodied and disembodied) in the path of truth, protecting the truthful and sustaining the cosmos, ever remains in His state of pure existence and bliss. Worshipping Him, we too shall always rejoice in prosperity and the possession of right knowledge, attaining thereby our destined goal of a progressive life here and emancipation hereafter.

(९) स नः पितेव सूनवेऽग्ने सूपायनो भव ।
सचस्वा नः स्वस्तये ॥ ९ ॥

पदपाठः—सः । नः । पिताऽइव । सूनवे । अग्ने । सुऽउपायनः । भव । सचस्व । नः । स्वस्तये ॥

अन्वयः—हे अग्ने स त्वं सूनवे पितेव नः सूपायनो भव । एवं नः स्वस्तये सचस्व ॥

Word-meaning &c. :—सः=that; He who is described in the above verses. पिता (√पा रक्षणे+तृन् U. II, 94)=Father. इव=like. सूनवे (√षूङ् प्राणिप्रसवे+नु U. III, 32 and 35)=to a son. सूपायनः (सुष्ठूपगतमयनं यस्मात्सः P. II, 2, 24)=He who bestows upon His devotees such beneficient knowledge as will enable them to obtain all excellent objects and means necessary to attain happiness in this life and emancipation hereafter. भव (√भू सत्तायाम्)=be Thou. सचस्व (√षच समवाये)=join; unite; bring together. स्वस्ति (सुष्ठु अस्ति वर्तत इति U. IV, 180)=for welfare and happiness.

Translation:—Oh Self-effulgent God, Who art thus praised by the Vedas and the righteous! just as a (loving and prudent) father provides his son with such useful education as will help him to go peacefully through life, vouchsafe us, we beseech Thee, such beneficient knowledge as will enable us to attain all things necessary to make life happy (on earth and obtain salvation after death). Do Thou also grant us the grace to be united (in Thee) for mutual welfare (whether in prosperity or adversity).

Purport :—This stanza through a beautiful simile compares God and all men and women to an earthly father and his sons and daughters. It teaches that all human beings should trust each other, be united and adore the One God which is the only way to secure happiness. The following prayer should be offered to God by every devout person and a sincere effort made to act up to it :—"Oh Lord God Almighty! protect us and always bestow on us good qualities and enjoin us in good works. A kind father brings up his children with care, provides them with a good education, trains them to have a good character and to be able to do something, so that they may successfully undertake great affairs. We beseech Thee Who art Omniscient and Omnipotent to be such a Father to us and grant us the grace to live worthy lives."

Comment :—This verse lays stress on two important points, namely, the Fatherhood of God and necessity of union among mankind for mutual welfare. The whole world, it says, is a huge family and God is its Head—the Father par excellence ! If all the prevailing religions in this world had attempted to impart such teaching, there should have been no wars, no strifes and no quarrels, and no bolshevism, no socialism and no communalism. The ideas about the Supreme Being, imparted by most of the religions now practised, or preached are radically wrong and unwholesome. The superior Vedic teaching can therefore be only a cry in the wilderness having no force to penerate ears and persuade hearts that have been fully poisoned by one—sided, man-made systems of thought. It is necessary that the salutary and eternal teaching of the Vedas embodied in this beautiful verse be preached all over the world. This is the only cure for the ills of modern human society.

Concluding remarks :—In this very first hymn of the Ṛgvēda, the first of the four Vēdas we are taught about the nature of the One God and the necessity of adoring Him alone. In the first five verses which treat of the importance of both material and spiritual knowledge, the word 'Agni' means God as well as heat. The next four verses describe the nature of God and lay down the method of His adoration.

THE ONENESS OF GOD.

The first-thing taught in this hymn about God is that he is One. European scholars and their Indian followers are not inclined to admit that the Vedic teaching about God is monotheistic. It should be seen what the Vedas say about themselves in this connection.

At the end of this chapter the 2nd section (paryāya) of the 4th hymn of the 13th book of the Atharvavēda is given in which it is clearly stated that He is only One. The hymn itself calls Him 'Rohita' the Most High which can only mean the Supreme Being since in verses 2-5 of the first section He is said to be called by various names. The attributes which the hymn assigns to 'Rohita' do not justify our taking that word to mean the sun. A few, only, of the innumerable other texts can be cited here in support of this view. For example in Ṛgvēda I, 7, 9[1] it is said :—

"The Omnipotent God Who rules over human beings, the eight Vasus (which contain all created things, viz ; the fire, the earth, the air, the intermediate regions between the earth and the sun, the sun, the regions illumined by his rays and called the heavens, the moon and the constellations) and all the

[1] य एकश्चर्षणीनां वसूनामिरज्यति । इन्द्रः पञ्चक्षितीनाम् ॥

five types of different worlds (the lowest, the middling, the good, the better and the best), is *Only One.*"

In I, 84, 7[2] of the same Veda we are told :—"Oh friend! the Omnipotent God, the Supreme Ruler of all, Who possesses incomparable strength and Who variously bestows on the mortal man that is charitably disposed means to live in happiness, is *Only One.*"

Ṛgvēda VI, 36, 4[3] says :—"Oh Omnipotent God! Thou art the *Sole* Master of all mankind and the *Sole* and Supreme Ruler of the whole universe. Being Such and, being praised (by us), let Thou flow upon us streams of such perfectly bliss-imparting wealth (as will enable us to live in peace and happiness)."

In Atharvavēda II, 2, 1[4], the following prayer is offered to God :—"Oh Divine Lord! through right knowledge do I approach Thee Who art of wonderful nature, the Supporter of all the worlds, the *Sole* Master of the universe and worthy to be adored and glorified by mankind. Obeisance to Thee! Bless me with Thy company in Thy Most Sublime State."

The following stanza also is noteworthy :—"May the Lord God bless us with happiness, Whose company is secured (by the worthy soul) in His Most Exalted Blissful State, Who is fit to be worshipped (by mankind), the outer covering (so to say) of whose luster is the resplendent sun, Who is the Dispeller of calamities originating from such phenomenon as fire &c., and Who being the *Sole* Master of the universe deserves to be adored and woll served."

---

[2] य एक इद्विदयते वसु मर्ताय दाशुषे । ईशानो अप्रतिष्कुत इन्द्रो अङ्ग ॥

[3] स रायस्खामुपसृजा गृणानः पुरुश्चन्द्रस्य त्वमिन्द्र वस्वः । पतिर्बभूथासमो जनानामेको विश्वस्य भुवनस्य राजा ॥

[4] दिव्यो गन्धर्वो भुवनस्य यस्पतिरेक एव नमस्यो विक्ष्वीड्यः । तं त्वा यौमि ब्रह्मणा दिव्य देव नमस्ते अस्तु दिवि ते सधस्थम् ॥ दिवि स्पृष्टो यजतः सूर्यत्वगवयाता हरसो दैव्यस्य । मृडाद्गन्धर्वो भुवनस्य यस्पतिरेक एव नमस्यः सुशेवाः ॥

"Come all ye together to the Lord of the heavens praising Him in a fitting manner by truthful speech. He is the *Sole* Omnipresent God worthy of being always adored by men. He is the Most Ancient (being Eternal) but yet He dwells in this new abode of His creation. All (virtuous) ways of life lead to Him alone." This also is from the Atharvaveda.[5]

The following texts from the Upanisads very forcibly state this supreme idea of the Oneness of God :—"Just as heat, which is uniform in its nature all over the world (but different from all other objects and though itself formless,) seems to assume the form of any object endowed with shape and size to which it may be applied, so also, God Who is *One*, (though different from all) being the Inner Self of all beings endows every creature by His immanence with its essential and individual form and is inside it as well as outside."[6]

"Just as the sun, whose light is the medium through which the organ of sight of all creatures functions, does not become tainted because someone's eyesight is defective, so also, the Supreme Being Who is *One* does not become affected with the miseries of the finite beings of the world because He is immanent in them, for, He is beyond all this"[7].

"Only those persons of fortitude merit bliss ever continuing undiminished (through the cycle of ages) who see established in their souls that Supreme Being Who is *One*, the Supreme Controller and Inner Self

---

[5] समेत विश्वे वचसा पतिं दिव एको विभूरतिथिर्जनानाम्। स पूर्व्यो नूतनमाविवासत्तं वर्तनिरनु वावृत एकमित्पुरु । अ० ७ । २१ ॥

[6] अग्निर्यथैको भुवनं प्रविष्टो रूपंरूपं प्रतिरूपो बभूव । एकस्तथा सर्वभूतान्तरात्मा रूपंरूपं प्रतिरूपो बहिश्च । क० ५ । ९ ॥

[7] सूर्यो यथा सर्व लोकस्य चक्षुर्न लिप्यते चाक्षुषैर्बाह्यदोषैः। एकस्तथा सर्वभूतान्तरात्मा न लिप्यते लोकदुःखेन बाह्यः । क० ५ । ११ ॥

of all beings and Who disposes in many ways after creation (in the shape of the cosmos, the effect), the causal matter existing in one (atomic) form before"[8]

"That *One* Refulgent God is hidden in all beings. He pervades all and is the Inner Self of all He disburses to each being fruit according to its actions and is the Refuge of all. He is the Seer and Knower of all. His Being is Simple since in it there is no alloy of the three ingredients of matter sattva (light), rajas (activity) and tamas (dullness)"[9].

GOD THE DISPENSER OF ALL GOODS.

In expressions like 'ratnadhātamam', 'dāśuṣe bhadram kariṣye' &c., the second point is suggested in the hymn, viz., that God is the Dispenser of all 'goods'. As such He is described as the Leader, Director and Ruler of all. This idea is variously and very beautifully developed in Vedic literature. The following texts will be useful in making this point clear :—

"Of the living and moving world including mankind and whatever of wealth there is diffused on earth, God Omnipotent is the Supreme Lord. He dispenses riches to the charitably disposed and if we approach Him with humility and glorify Him, He will condescend to pour wealth on us"[10]

"Oh Most Refulgent God! Thine are all the quarters, Thine are the heavens, Thine the earth, Thine this vast expanse of the intermediate region, and

---

[8] एको वशी सर्वभूतान्तरात्मा एकं रूपं बहुधा यः करोति । तमात्मस्थं येऽनुपश्यन्ति धीरास्तेषां सुखं शाश्वतं नेतरेषाम् । क० ५ । १२ ॥

[9] एको देवः सर्वभूतेषु गूढः सर्वव्यापी सर्वभूतान्तरात्मा । कर्माध्यक्षः सर्वभूताधिवासः साक्षी चेताः केवलो निर्गुणश्च । श्वे० ६ ११ ॥

[10] इन्द्रो राजा जगतश्चर्षणीनामधि क्षमि विषुरूपं यदस्ति । ततो दाशुषे वसूनि चोदद्राध उपस्तुतश्चिदर्वाक् ॥ ऋ० ७ । २७ । ३ ॥

Thine all these creatures on the earth endowed with breath and souls"[11].

"The Lord God Almighty is the Master of the heavens. He is the Lord of the earth, of the waters, the mountains and of all great and powerful beings. He is the Master of all men endowed with wisdom. Hence(oh men !) he is to be approached for the safety of one's possessions and for the attainment of all one's wishes"[12].

In this connection the following passages from the Upaniṣads are noteworthy :—"Among. eternal beings, that Supreme Being is the Eternal Par Excellence. Among those endowed with intelligence, He is of surpassing intelligence. He is One and ever Immutable but yet He grants the wishes of the many, (that is, all the souls embodied and disembodied). To those persons of fortitude who see this Supreme Lord installed on the throne of the soul does the peace of emancipation lasting undiminished (till the end of the cycle of ages) belongs, and to none else"[13].

"He, in time is the Protector of the world, He is the Controller of the universe and He remains concealed in the interior of all beings. All great seers and all enlightened men are in commune with Him. Knowing Him thus does man tear through the toils of recurring (births and) deaths (and attain emancipation)"[14].

---

11 तव चतस्रः प्रदिशस्तव द्यौस्तव पृथिवी तवेदमुग्रोर्वन्तरिक्षम् । तवेदं सर्वमात्मन्वद्यत्प्राणत्पृथिवीमनु ॥ अ० ११ । २ । १० ॥

12 इन्द्रो दिव इन्द्र ईशे पृथिव्या इन्द्रो अपामिन्द्र इत्पर्वतानाम् । इन्द्रो वृधामिन्द्र इन्मेधिराणामिन्द्रः क्षेमे योगे हव्य इन्द्रः ॥ ऋ० १० । ८९ । १० ॥

13 नित्यो नित्यानां चेतनश्चेतनानामेको बहूनां यो विदधाति कामान् । तमात्मस्थं येऽनुपश्यंति धीरास्तेषां शान्तिः शाश्वती नेतरेषाम् ॥ क० ५ । १३ ॥

14 स एव काले भुवनस्य गोप्ता विश्वाधिपः सर्वभूतेषु गूढः । यस्मिन्युक्ता ब्रह्मर्षयो देवताश्च तमेवं ज्ञात्वा मृत्युपाशांश्छिनत्ति ॥ श्वे० ४ । १५ ॥

GOD THE FATHER OF ALL.

Another very beautiful idea hinted at in this hymn is the fatherhood of God. There are a large number of verses in all the four Vedas which expatiate upon this idea. A few are given below :—

"Oh wise man ! know thou that God Almighty is our Protector (from all evil), our Guardian, our Omnipresent Director (towards the goal of our life), our Friend, the most fatherly *Father* of the kindest of fathers, and He is the Maker of the whole world. To him who desires (justly, it should be remembered), He has in His possession all good things to give"[15].

"Oh Protector of the cosmos ! Thou art the Controller of this Divine Speech (in the shape of the Vedas) which the enlightened safeguard in all their dealings and which, we and all noble and good souls, call the Most Excellent. Condescend to teach, (we beseech Thee), to man, Thy *son*, and keep in contentment all beings that are beneficial"[16].

"He Who is our *Father*, the Producer of all things, the Assigner to souls of fruit according to their deeds, Who knows all the worlds (or spheres of existence by personal contact), and the origin (or name) of all things (seen and unseen), Who out of His infinite wisdom gives their designations (according to their attributes or properties) to all enlightened souls (assuming bodies such as sages, seers &c., and the earth and other worlds), is One (without a second, doing all this without the assistance of a servant, helper, deputy or son). He is the only One about Whom we

---

[15] त्राता नो बोधि दद्दशान आपिरभिख्याता मर्डिता सोम्यानाम् । सखा पिता पितृतमः पितृणां कर्तेमु लोकमुशते वयोधाः ॥ ऋ० ४ । १७ । १७ ॥

[16] ब्रह्मणस्पते त्वमस्य यन्ता सूक्तस्य बोधि तनयं च जिन्व । विश्वं तद्भद्रं यदवन्ति देवा बृहद्वदेम विदथे सुवीराः ॥ यजु० ३४ । ५८ ॥

can profitably enquire, and Him do all other beings approach"[17].

In these texts God is called the Father because He creates and protects all beings. The term is thus used logically, in its full significance to denote God Who is the Most Perfect Father, and the Only One deserving that epithet in its fullest sense. The human father is only a very faint specimen—a mere miniature—of the Sublime Fatherhood which is an essential attribute of God.

GOD THE FRIEND.

The hymn calls God a friend as well. In some of the above quotations this aspect of the nature of the Supreme Being is described in clear terms. In the 35th[18] stanza of the 14th chapter of the Yajurvēda God is called 'Mitra' friend, and in the 33rd[19] stanza of the 13th chapter 'Viṣṇu', God Omnipresent is said to be a proper Friend of the human soul'.

God is called a 'proper or worthy Friend' of the individual soul in the 9th[20] and 10th[21] verses of the 11th hymn of the 5th book of the Atharvavēda. That hymn treats of the highest knowledge—brahmavidyā—right knowledge of the Supreme Being, by the acquisition of which man rises so high in his spiritual life that he begins to have, after rigorous discipline which be-

---

17 यो नः पिता जनिता यो विधाता धामानि वेद भुवनानि विश्वा । यो देवानां नामधा एक एव तं सम्प्रश्नम्भुवना यन्त्यन्या ॥ यजु० १६ । २७ ॥

18 नमो मित्रस्य वरुणस्य चक्षसे महो देवाय तदृतं सपर्यत । दूरे दृशे देवजाताय केतवे दिवस्पुत्राय सूर्याय शंसत ॥

19 विष्णोः कर्माणि पश्यत यतो व्रतानि पस्पशे । इन्द्रस्य युज्यः सखा ॥

20 या ते स्तोत्राण्युद्यतानि मर्त्यन्त्वा्स्वासु मानुषीषु विक्षु । देहि नु मे यन्मे अदत्तो असि युज्यो मे सप्तपदः सखासि ॥

21 समा नौ बन्धु वरुण समा जा वेदाहं तद्यन्नावेषा समा जा । ददामि तद्यत्ते अदत्तो अस्मि युज्यस्ते सप्तपदः सखास्मि ॥

comes quite easy for him, intimate communion with God. This idea is very beautifully pictured in the two verses by a simile in which the process of yogic self-discipline undergone by the devotee is compared to the treading of seven steps together (saptapadı) by the bride and the bridegroom during the marriage ceremony. In the case of the devotee this consists in his meditation on the Supreme Being concentrating his attention on the seven places in the body, namely, from the seat up to the crown, the technical names of which are 'bhūh' or mūlādhāra-cakra, 'bhuvah' or svādhiṣṭhāna-cakra, 'svah' or maṇipūrakacakra, 'mahah' or anāhata-cakra, 'janah' or viśuddhacakra, 'tapah' or ājñācakra and, 'satyam' or sahasrāracakra. By gradually proceeding in meditation through these, the devotee, when he reaches the seventh or highest place, becomes aware of the Omnipresent nature of God and begins to feel His existence in his own being. He then begins to feel the lack of one great thing viz, true and Supreme joy—brahmānanda which he then demands of God. This is the matter of the two beautiful texts mentioned above a translation of which is given below :—

"Oh Lord! may hymns of praise approach Thy throne of grace lifted up in all the quarters of the universe inhabited by human beings, (resounding through space). Oh bestow on me that, I beseech Thee, which Thou hast not as yet bestowed upon me (i. e., perfect joy), for, Thou, Oh Lord! art my worthy Friend, Whom I have won by scaling the seven rungs of the ladder of spiritual discipline and,

"Oh Most Excellent Lord we both are brothers and our nature is akin (i. e. we are both entirely spiritual beings). (To this God replies) I know, oh devotee! that our nature is akin. I now give thee that which I did not give thee before, for thou hast properly won my friendship by scaling the seven rungs of the ladder of spiritual discipline."

These passages are quite ample to explain what sort of friendship there is between God and man according to the Vedas.

GOD AS THE POET.

The hymn calls God also a poet. The following extracts are quite enough to show what this means.

In Atharvaveda V, 11, 3[22] we are told that God's might is most incomprehensible when we consider his poem. In the next[23] verse it is said there is none to surpass Him in this connection.

In the Sāmaveda I, 30, 32, 42[24] 'Agni'—God the Self-effulgent is called a poet.

Considering the sense with which it is replete, it can be justly said that the first hymn of the Ṛgvēda, sets in a nutshell the whole teaching of the Vedas and is truly representative of those four Divine Volumes.

Atharvavēda XIII, 4 (2).

Seer—Brahmasvayambhu.

Subject—Rōhita Āditya, i. e., praise of the Most High (God), Immutable.

Metre—(1) Bhurik sāmnī triṣṭubh ; (2) Āsurī pankti ; (3) and (6), Prājāpatya Anuṣṭubh ; (4) and (5) Āsurī gāyatrī.

---

22 सत्यमहं गभीरः काव्येन सत्यं जातेनास्मि जातवेदाः &c. ॥

23 न त्वदन्यः कवितरः &c. ॥

24 परि वाजपतिः कविरग्निः &c. ॥

कविमग्निमुपस्तुहि &c. ॥

त्वमित्सप्रथा अस्यग्ने त्रातर्ऋतः कविरित्थ दि ॥

(१०) कीर्तिश्च यशश्चाम्भश्च नभश्च ब्राह्मण-
वर्चसं चान्नं चान्नाद्यं च ॥१॥

(११) य एतं देवमेकवृतं वेद ॥२॥

पदपाठ :—कीर्तिः । च । यशः । च । अम्भः । च । नभः । च । ब्राह्मणऽवर्चसम् । च । अन्नम् । च । अन्नऽअद्यम् । च ॥१॥

यः । एतम् । देवम् । एकऽवृतम् । वेद ॥२॥

अन्वय :—कीर्तिश्च यशश्चाम्भश्च नभश्च ब्राह्मणवर्चसं चान्नं चान्नाद्यं च तं पुरुषं प्राप्नुवन्ति य एतमेकवृतं देवं वेद ॥

Word-meaning &c. :—कीर्ति (√कृत्+क्तिन् P III, 3, 94)=Glorification of the attributes of God ; fame from learning &c. च=and. यशः=renown earned by bravery &c. अम्भः (√आप्लृ or √अभि शब्दे+असुन् U. IV, 189 & 210 or the first alone).= prowess, valour. नभः (√णह् बन्धने+असुन् U. IV, 189 & 211.)=power of control, authority. ब्राह्मणवर्चसम्=the luster of the knowledge of God. अन्नम्=food. अन्नाद्यम्=other edibles. (here the link should be supplied viz:—fall to the share of that man) यः=who. एतम्=this. एकवृतम् (एक+√वृत्+क्विप्)=the One Self Existent ; Immutable. देवम्=God. वेद=knows.

Translation :—Fame, renown, prowess, authority luster of the knowledge of God, food and other victuals, —all these—fall to the share of that man who knows This Immutable God.

Purport :—He who realises the One Self-existent God in All His Splendour, rises in the world and attains bliss; for this it is, that those who are enlightened by right knowledge care more for the unseen[25] than the seen.

---

25 परोक्षप्रिया इव हि देवा भवन्ति प्रत्यक्षद्विषः ॥ गो० १ । २ । २१ ॥ परोक्षकामा हि देवाः ॥ श० ६ । १ । १ । २ ॥ ७ । ४ । १ । १६ ॥

(१२) न द्वितीयो न तृतीयश्चतुर्थो नाप्युच्यते ॥३॥

(१३) न पञ्चमो न षष्ठः सप्तमो नाप्युच्यते ॥४॥

(१४) नाष्टमो न नवमो दशमो नाप्युच्यते ॥५॥

पदपाठः—न । द्वितीयः । न । तृतीयः । चतुर्थः । न । अपि उच्यते ॥३॥

न । पञ्चमः न । षष्ठः । सप्तमः । न । अपि । उच्यते ॥४॥

न । अष्टमः । न । नवमः । दशमः । न । अपि । उच्यते ॥५॥

अन्वयः—एष एकवृदेवो न द्वितीयो न तृतीयो नापि चतुर्थ उच्यते । न पञ्चमो न षष्ठो नापि सप्तम उच्यते । नाष्टमो न नवमो नापि दशम उच्यते ॥

Word-meaning &c. :—(In the beginning the link is to be supplied from the past verse viz :—This Unitary God). न=not. द्वितीयः=second. तृतीयः=third. चतुर्थः= fourth. अपि=yet. उच्यते=called. पञ्चम=fifth. षष्ठः=sixth. सप्तमः=seventh. अष्टमः=eighth. नवम:=ninth. दशमः=tenth.

Translation :—This One Immutable God is called neither the second, nor the third nor yet the fourth. He is called neither the fifth nor the sixth nor yet the seventh. He is called neither the eighth, nor the ninth nor yet the tenth

Purport :—The Supreme Being is only One; there is no second, third, fourth or any other God. Hence man should worship only Him and none else. The denial of 2nd to 10th is intended to indicate that the number one represents God in His Simplicity and Independent Nature, and hence is a perfect number, the other being mere multiplies of one. The details of this enumeration with reference to God's Nature are given elsewhere in this book which the reader should please look up. The Vedas assert that the Deity is only One without any other or others, the Supreme Reality; He is the Sole Controller of this universe and has no assistant or agent to help Him in His work. His Nature is unitary, Simple and Unique. Hence to call any human being, however exalted, His representative or helper, would be blasphemy.

(१५) स सर्वस्मै वि पश्यति
यच्च प्राणति यच्च न ॥६॥

पदपाठ :—स । सर्वस्मै । वि । पश्यति । यत् । च । प्राणति । यत् । च । न ॥

अन्वय :—स सर्वस्मै वि पश्यति यच्च प्राणति यच्च न (प्राणति) ॥

Word-meaning &c. :—That; He. सर्वस्मै=for (the good of) all (beings). वि पश्यति=sees or over sees (supervises) in various ways, takes care of in various ways. यत्=whatever. च=and. प्राणति=lives and moves, breathes, is endowed with breath or life. न प्राणति=whatever is not endowed with life, inanimate objects.

Translation :—He takes care of all beings whether animate or inanimate in various ways.

Purport:—The One Unitary God, by His Omnipotence and Omniscience and without the help of any assistant or agent oversees the whole universe with special eye to each individual being. Man should adore Him alone and none else.

(१६) तमिदं निगतं सहः स एष
एक एकवृदेक एव ॥७॥

पदपाठ :—तम् । इदम् । निऽगतम् । सहः । सः । एषः । एकः । एकऽवृत् । एकः । एव ॥

अन्वय :—इदं सहस्तं निगतम् । स एष एक एकवृदेक एवास्ति ॥

Word-meaning &c. :—तम्=to Him; in Him. इदम् this. निगतम्=(नि+√गम्) is surely centered in. सहः (√षह मर्षणे+असुन् U. IV, 189) power, might. सः एषः He Himself. एकः=One. एकवृत्=Sole Being; one alone.=एक एव=only One.

Translation :—All this power (of supervising and supporting the universe) is certainly centred in Him. He is the One, One alone and only One.

Purport :—This verse also denies the existence of human or spirit agents and helpers or officers of God to carry on the work of providing for and supervising the universe. All such power is centred in Him and He alone without a second of any sort performs all this work by His Omnipresent nature. Man should remember this fact and adore Him alone.

(१७) सर्वे अस्मिन्देवा एकवृतो भवन्ति ॥८॥

पदपाठ :—सर्वे । अस्मिन् । देवाः । एकऽवृतः । भवन्ति ॥

अन्वय :—अस्मिन्सर्वे देवा एकवृतो भवन्ति ॥

Word-meaning &c. :—सर्वे=all. अस्मिन्=in Him. देवाः=shining or moving bodies like the sun earth &c.; *luminous forces of Nature; beneficient objects and qualities which sustain the creatures. एकवृतः भवन्ति= unite; become one.

Translation :—All the luminous and moving bodies and forces of nature have all their being in Him.

*These are thirty three and are called the 'thirty three devatas'. Details are given elsewhere in this book which the reader may refer to.

Purport :—All this vast universe after dissolution in its causal form and after creation in its phenomenal state, exists in this One Supreme Being Who pervades it through and through by His Omnipresence and Omnipotence. Hence man should adore Him alone as the One and True God.

Comment :—The whole of the 13th book of the Atharvavēda treats of 'Rōhita Āditya'. As to who this Rōhita Āditya is, the 26th verse of the previous hymn declares in the following words :—"That Rōbita surely (स ह रोहितः) Who makes vegitation [and other means for the sustenance of the creatures] grow (रुहः रुरोह) mounts (रोहति) on the sun (द्याम् अधि) which appears (अजायत) after the black night (कृष्णायाः रात्र्याः) as the purifier [of the world] (पुत्रः), the drawer of the sap [of all things] (अर्जुनः) and as the cause of the abode [=sustenance] of all creatures (वत्सः)*". This means that the devotee, a person of a scientific turn of mind, is advised by the Veda to see the Illuminating Power of God in the sun. Any other way of translating the verse will yield most absurd results. There is no reference to Draupadi and Arjuna in this verse at all. A secondary signification of the word Rōhita is the sun, but then all the benefit the devotee is said to gain in No. 10, p. 39 above, cannot be very easily explained. The fact is, however, true that a devoted servant of science investigating into the processes by which the sun's heat does all the work attributed to it, will, like Sir Raman of the Calcutta University, earn great fame wealth and honour. But the Scriptures go much farther than this and help us to see behind all these natural phenomena, their August Author Himself.

---

* कृष्णायाः पुत्रो अर्जुनो रात्र्या वत्सोऽजायत । स ह द्यामधि रोहति रुहो रुरोह रोहितः ॥ अ० १३ । १ । २६ ॥

There are two simple but important words in v. 10, viz., अन्नम् and अन्नाद्यम्. The first is formed from the root अद् भक्षणे by adding the past participial passive termination क्त after the analogy of P. IV, 4, 85 or as Yaska explains, by putting together the prefix आ, root √णम् प्रह्वत्वे शब्दे च, and the termination क्विप् according to Paṇini III, 2, 178*. It is also formed according to Uṇadi III, 6 and 10 by adding the suffix न to the root √अन प्राणने and inserting the augment नित्. The second, अन्नाद्यम्, means अन्नसमानम् अद्यम्. The word अद्यम् is got by adding the suffix ण्यत् irregularly or one of the suffixes यत् or क्यप् all of which are enjoined by P. III, 1, 95 and 3, 113. In none of these forms, to speak the plain truth, does the idea of killing occur. The idea of something already available in a form fit to eat is the necessary implication of these formations. Victuals only in this sense can be said to be provided by God—Rudra—the Dispeller of all evil. The idea of God's coming to the soccour of the suffering, to save them from any sort of harm is clearly expressed in Y. V. XXX, 3, the first verse which begins this book (q. v.). Food is, in some way, identified with God in as much as it sustains creatures just as He does the cosmos.

The 8th, 9th and 10th verses of the beautiful hymn in praise of food, viz., R. V. I, 187 describe in a very simple style the food of human beings. Even Griffith, whose translation we give below, has been forced to give the sense of the text in plain unequivocal (?) terms.

"Whatever morsel we consume from *waters* or from *plants* of earth, O Soma, *wax thou fat* thereby (Sic !).

"What Soma, we enjoy from thee in *milky food* or *barley-brew*, Vatapi, *grow thou fat thereby*.

---

* अन्नं कस्मात्। आनतं भूतेभ्यः। अत्तेर्वा ॥ नि० ३ । ९ ॥

"O *Vegetable, Cake of meal*, be wholesome, firm, and strengthening : Vatapi *grow thou fat* thereby."*

The above translation cannot at all be accepted as authoritative, as it is at best a very poor rendering if not an intentionally garbled one. It fails to explain the epithets Soma and Vatapi (वातः इव सर्वान् पदार्थान् व्याप्नोति=He Who, like the air, fully pervades all things), and has used the questionable expression barley brew for यवाशिरः which simply means a preparation like porridge prepared from barley. If यवाशिरः is—'barley-brew' गवाशिरः must be cow-brew ! Why should the translator vary his terminology so soon ? There is another absurdity in the translation, viz., the statement that Vatapi will fatten by some one else's consuming the food.

The idea of pervasion of food by God is beautifully stated in syllogistic argument in the Bhagavadgita thus :—

"In food, all Creatures have their birth ;
from Rain does Food in turn proceed ;
From sacrifice, the Fall of Rain ;
the Root of sacrifice is Act ;—
All Act learn thou, from Brahma springs,
Brahma from THAT WHICH KNOWS NOT CHANGE.
Hence BRAHMA, th' ALL-PERVADING ONE,
e'er stands revealed in sacrifice."‡

The above quotation from the Bhagavadgita is an explanation of the following tough upanisadic

* यदपामोषधीनां परिंशमारिशामहे । वातापे पीव इद्भव ॥ यत्ते सोम गवाशिरो यवाशिरो भजामहे । वातापे पीव इद्भव । करम्भ ओषधे भव पीवो वृक उदारथिः । वातापे पीव इद्भव ॥ ऋ० १ । १८७ । ८-१० ॥

‡ अन्नाद्भवन्ति भूतानि पर्जन्यादन्नसम्भवः । यज्ञाद्भवति पर्जन्यो यज्ञः कर्मसमुद्भवः ॥ कर्म ब्रह्मोद्भवं विद्धि ब्रह्माक्षरसमुद्भवं । तस्मात्सर्वगतं ब्रह्म नित्यं यज्ञे प्रतिष्ठितम् ॥ भ० गी० ३ । १४ ; १५ ॥

passage*:—"Some say that food (अन्नम्) is the Supreme Being (ब्रह्म), but this is not right, for, *food rots without vital air*. Some others think that vital air itself is the Supreme Being which also is not correct since the vital air gets 'dried up' without food. Both these devatas (beneficent objects) united together attain supremacy. Hearing of this account Pratṛda said to his father:—"To such a learned man as knows this principle what good can I do or what evil?" His father at this, preventing him with his hand, said, "Oh Pratṛda, don't you question the fact of one's attaining supremacy by uniting these two together." He again added:—"For 'vi' indeed is food, since in food it is that all beings are entered (sheltered) and 'ram' is the vital air indeed, in as much as all these beings sport in it. He who knows this truth (and lives up to it) in him will all (finite) beings be sheltered and in him will they all sport."

A long passage, sections 7-10 of the third part of the Taittirīyopniṣad, praises food and says that it must be regarded with respect.

Food which is extolled in such terms can, surely, involve no injury to any creature. There must be something radically wrong with the way of rendering Vedic statements so as to yield the idea of getting food by killing.

---

* अन्नं ब्रह्मेत्येक आहुस्तन्न तथा । पूयति वा अन्नमृते प्राणात् । प्राणो ब्रह्मेत्येक आहुस्तन्न तथा । शुष्यति वै प्राण ऋतेऽन्नात् । एते ह त्वेव देवते एकधाभूयं भूत्वा परमतां गच्छतः । तद्ध स्माऽह प्रातृदः पितरं किं स्विदेवैवंविदुषे साधु कुर्यां किमेवास्मा असाधु कुर्यामिति । स ह स्माऽह पाणिना । मा प्रातृद कस्त्वेनयोरेकधाभूयं भूत्वा परमतां गच्छतीति । तस्मा उ हैतदुवाच वीत्यन्नं वै व्यन्ने हीमानि सर्वाणि भूतानि विष्टानि रमिति प्राणो वै रं प्राणे हीमानि सर्वाणि भूतानि रमन्ते सर्वाणि ह वा अस्मिन्भूतानि विशन्ति सर्वाणि भूतानि रमन्ते य एवं वेद ॥ बृ० १५ । २ । १ ॥

The hymn also mentions that God cannot be counted along with any other being. He is always first alone. To represent Him only the number one (1) can be used. In the formation of द्वितीय we have two elements viz., the number द्वि and the termination तीय added according to P. V, 2, 54. The next तृतीय is formed in a similar manner by P. V, 2, 55, चतुर्थ and षष्ठ by V, 2, 51, and पञ्चम, सप्तम, अष्टम, नवम and दशम by V, 2, 49. All these ordinal numbers are composite formations serviceable only when a serial arrangement of things having some similarity with one another is spoken of. God is a *Unitary* Being of *Simple* nature and *One without* a second. Therefore, these ordinal numbers cannot be used as adjectives of His Holy Name.

Further details on this point will be found in the comments on Chapter XXXII of the Yajurveda given elsewhere.

Chapter II.

Section I.

The Householder's Morning Prayers.

Yajurveda XXXIV, 34-40.

Seer:—The Sage Vasiṣṭha.

Subject:—Verse 34, invocation of God with different epithets; verses 36 and 38 and 35, 37 and 39, praise of the Supreme Being as the Possessor and Bestower of fortune; verse 40, an appreciation of the dawn and prayer for the enlightenment of the women folk.

Metre:—Stanzas 35, 36, 38 and 40 nicṛt-triṣṭubh; 37, pankti; 39, triṣṭubh.

Tone:—34, niṣada; 35, 36, 38-40 dhaivata; 37 pañcama.

(१८) प्रातर॒ग्निं प्रा॒तरिन्द्रं॑ हवामहे प्रा॒तर्मि॒त्राव॑-
रु॑णा प्रा॒तर॒श्विना॑ । प्रा॒तर्भगं॑ पू॒ष॒णं॑ ब्रह्म॑ण॒स्पतिं॑ प्रा॒तः
सोम॑मु॒त रु॒द्रं हु॑वेम ॥१॥

पदपाठ:—प्रा॒तः । अ॒ग्निम् । प्रा॒तः । इन्द्र॑म् । ह॒वा॒म॒हे॒ । प्रा॒तः ।
मि॒त्रावरु॑णा । प्रा॒तः । अ॒श्विना॑ । प्रा॒तः । भग॑म् । पू॒षण॑म् । ब्रह्म॑णः ।
पति॑म् । प्रा॒तरिति॑ । सोम॑म् । उ॒त । रु॒द्रम् । हु॒वे॒म ॥

अन्वयः—हे जगदीश्वर वयं त्वामग्निं प्रातरिन्द्रमिति हवामहे। यथा वयं त्वां प्रातर्मित्रावरुणा प्रातरश्विना प्रातर्भगं पूषणं ब्रह्मणस्पतिं सोममुत प्रातः रुद्रमिति नानानामभिर्हुवेम तथाऽनुगृह्यताम्॥

Word-meaning &c. :—प्रातः (प्र + √अत सातत्यगमने + अरन् U. V, 59). अग्निम्=God the Self-refulgent. इन्द्रम्= God the Omnipotent, Bestower of all bounties. हवामहे (√ह्वेञ् स्पर्धायां शब्दे च P. VI, 1, 34)=we invoke upon; and praise; we meditate upon. मित्रावरुणा (आ for औ vide P. VII, 1, 39)=enlivening the whole universe by His omnipresence just as the two vital airs[1] enliven the body of an animal and therefore all-powerful. अश्विना (P. VII, 1, 39)=the Creator and Illuminator of the sun and moon. (√अशू व्याप्तौ + क्वन् + इनि U. I. 151 and P. V, 2, 115). In the Nirukta XII, 1[2] we have the following:—"The 'two aśvins' are so called from their pervading the whole world one (the moon) by imparting sap to the different beings in it and the other (the sun) by diffusing light over it. The Vedic exigete Āurṇavābha maintains that this word is derived from the noun अश्व meaning 'horse' by affixing to it the termination इनि in the sense of possession. Who are these two aśvins? Some say they are the earth and the sun. Some others think that they are the day and the night while still others maintain that they are the sun and the moon. The historians (those who admit eternal history in the Vedas, however, hold the opinion that अश्विनौ is the name of two benevolent kings (leaders or teachers)[3] of human society." The word is

[1] प्राणापानौ मित्रा वरुणौ॥ तां ६ । १० । ५॥ ६ । ८ । १६॥ तै० ३ । ३ । ६ । ६॥ श० ८ । ४ । २ । ६॥ १२ । ६ । २ । १२॥

[2] अश्विनौ यद्व्यश्नुवाते सर्वं रसेनान्यो ज्योतिषान्यः । अश्वैरश्विनावित्यौर्णवाभः । तत्काबश्विनौ द्यावापृथिव्यावित्येके । अहोरात्रावित्येके । सूर्याचन्द्रमसावित्येके । राजानौ पुण्यकृतावित्यैतिहासिकाः॥ नि० १२ । १॥

[3] आत्मानन्द in his commentary on R.V. I, 164, 27 interprets :—अश्विभ्याम् गुरुशिष्याभ्याम् 'by the two As'vins, i. e., by the tutor and the pupil'.

variously interpreted in the Brahmaṇas[4]. भगम्=(√भज् सेवायाम्+घः P. IV, 3, 118). God the lord of all fortune Who is worth adoration; fortune; things that bring fortune; a man of fortune; virtue, power. In an oft-quoted stanza[5] all the important meanings of this word are given thus:—"All power, righteousness, good-repute, splendour, right knowledge and abstinence from the objects of sense—the name of all these six is 'bhaga'—power, potency, great virtue." The (eight) super human powers mentioned by Patanjali in his treatise[6] on Yoga also come under these. They are "becoming minute like an atom, light like a lump of cotton, acquiring things howsoever far they may be, attaining of one's wishes, becoming huge like a mountain, having power over others but being oneself beyond the power of others, being able to produce and destroy and accomplishing whatever one resolves to do"[7]. पूषणम् (√पुष्+कनिन् U. I. 159)=he who nourishes; the sun[8], the earth[9], the air[10]; cattle[11] &c.; that

---

4 इमे ह वै द्यावापृथिवी प्रत्यक्षमाश्विनाविमे हीदं सर्वमाश्नुवाताम् ॥ श० ४ । १ । ५ । १६ ॥ श्रोत्रे अश्विनौ ॥ श० १२ । ९ । १ । १३ ॥ नासिके अश्विनौ ॥ श० १२ । ९ । १ । १४ ॥ तयो ह वाऽश्विनौ पुरुषाविवाक्ष्योः । एतावेवाश्विनौ ॥ श० १२ । ९ । १ । १२ ॥ आश्विनावध्वर्यू ॥ ऐ० १ । १८ ॥ श० १ । १ । २ । १७ ॥ ३ । ९ । ४ । ३ ॥ तै० ३ । २ । २ । १ ॥ गो० २ । २ । ६ ॥ सयोनी वा अश्विनौ ॥ श० ५ । ३ । १ । ८ ॥

5 ऐश्वर्यस्य समग्रस्य धर्मस्य यशसः श्रियः । ज्ञानवैराग्ययोश्चैव षण्णां भग इतीरणा ॥

6 ततोऽणिमादिप्रादुर्भावः कायसम्पत्तद्धर्मानभिघातश्च ॥ योग० ३ । ४५ ॥

7 अणिमा लघिमा प्राप्तिः प्राकाम्यं महिमा तथा । ईशित्वं च वशित्वं च तथा कामावसायिता ॥

8 अथ यद्रश्मिपोषं पुष्यति तत्पूषा भवति ॥ नि० १२ । १७ । १८ ॥ असौ वै पूषा योऽसौ (सूर्यः) तपति ॥ शां० ५ । २ ॥ गो० २ । १ । २० ॥

9 इयं (पृथिवी) वै पूषा ॥ श० ६ । ३ । २ । ८ ॥ ११ । २ । २ । ६ ॥ ४ । १ । १४ ॥ तै० १ । ७ । २ । ५ ॥

10 अयं वै पूषा योऽयं (वातः) पवतऽएष हीदं सर्वं पुष्यति ॥ श० १४ । २ । १ । ९ ; २ । ३२ ॥

11 पशवो वै पूषा ॥ श० ३ । १ । ४ । ९ ॥ ६ । १ । १ । १० ॥ ५ । २ । ५ । ८ ; ३५ ॥ ऐ० २ । २५ ॥ तै० २ । ८ । ११ । २ ॥ तां० २३ । १६ । ५ ॥ १८ । १ । १६ ॥ अन्नं वै पूषा ॥ शां० १२ । ८ ॥ तै० १ । ७ । ३ । ६ ॥ ३ । ८ । २३ । २ ॥

nourish man by yielding milk and working for him; God[12] the nourisher of all. This word has many other significations also. As the term representing the apotheosis of all these, it would be the name of God. ब्रह्मणस्पतिम् (ब्रह्मणः पतिः)=God[13] the protector of the whole universe, the Vedas, His devotees. सोमम् (√सु+मन् U. I, 140)=the Divine impulse[14] inherent in all creatures that gives them the force of motion. रुद्रम् (√रुदिर् अश्रुविमोचने+रक् U. II, 22)=God who makes the sinners cry by punishing them and who destroys all disease. This word also is extensively commented upon in the Brāhmaṇas[15]. The Nirukta X, 6[16] explains this word as follows:—"The cloud is called 'rudra' because it thunders. (√रु+तुक्+रक्). Or it is so called because it moves along thundering for a long time. (√रु+√द्रु+ड. The vital airs are so called since while leaving the human body they make the

---

[12] (अग्ने) त्वं पूषा विधतः पासि नु त्मना ॥ तै० ३ । ११ । २ । १ ॥

[13] ब्रह्म वै ब्रह्मणस्पतिः ॥ शां० ८ । ५ ॥ ६ । ५ ॥ तां० १६ । ५ । ८ ॥

[14] वर्चः सोमः ॥ श० ५ । २ । ५ । १० ; ११ ॥ क्षत्रं सोमः ॥ ऐ० २ । ३८ ॥ शां० ७ । १० ॥ यशो वै सोमः ॥ श० ४ । २ । ४ । ६ ॥ अन्नं सोमः ॥ शां० ६ । ६ ॥ श० ३ । ३ । ४ । २८ ॥ तां० ६ । ६ । १ ॥ हविर्देवानां सोमः ॥ श० ३ । ५ । ३ । २ ॥ प्राणः सोमः ॥ श० ७ । ३ । १ । २ ॥ रेतः सोमः ॥ शां० १३ । ७ ॥ तै० २ । ७ । ४ । १ ॥ श० ३ । ३ । २ । १ ॥ शुक्रः सोमः (शुक्र=निर्मल, Sāyaṇa) ॥ तां ६ । ६ । ६ ॥ रसः सोमः श० ७ । ३ । १ । ३ ॥ तद्यदमृतं सोमः ॥ श० ६ । ५ । १ । ८ ॥ सर्वं हि सोमः (all things) ॥ श० ५ । ५ । ४ । ११ ॥

[15] यदरोदीत्तस्माद्रुद्रः ॥ श० ६ । १ । ३ । १० ॥ अग्निर्वै रुद्रः ॥ श० ५ । ३ । १ । १० ॥ अथोऽस्मारण्येष्वेव पशुषु रुद्रस्य हेतिं दधाति (a fire-arm, cell &c) श० १२ । ७ । ३ । २० ॥ See also Monier-Williams' Sanskrit-English Dictionary on हेति. रुद्र पशूनां पते ॥ तै० ३ । ११ । ४ । २ ॥ यद्रुद्रश्चन्द्रमास्तेन ॥ शां० ६ । ७ ॥ ज्येष्ठश्च श्रेष्ठश्च देवानाम् ॥ शां० २५ । १३ ॥ घोरो वै रुद्रः ॥ शां० १६ । ७ ॥ उच्छेषणभागो वै रुद्रः ॥ तै० १ । ७ । ८ । ५ ॥ प्राणा वै रुद्राः । प्राणा हीदं सर्वं रोदयन्ति ॥ जै० उ० ४ । २ । ६ ॥ श० ११ । ६ । ३ । ७ ॥ रुद्रा एव महः ॥ गो० १ । ५ । १५ ॥

[16] रुद्रो रौतीति सतः । रोरूयमाणो द्रवतीति वा । रोदयतेर्वा ॥

relations weep and bewail. (√रुद्+रद् U. II, 22). Durgācarya[17] on the last says:—"he worries (harasses, punishes) his foes and makes them weep." Yāska quotes the st. इमा रुद्राय &c. R. V. VII, 46, 1 in commenting on which Maharṣi Svāmi Dayānanda explains[18] the word रुद्राय to mean, a brave warrior who makes his foe weep. In XI, 12 of his Nirukta Yāska quotes R. V. V, 57, 1, on the word रुद्रासः but does not give any synonym of the word. Maharṣi Dayānanda egplains it as: दुष्टानां रोदयितारः—'those who make the wicked weep'. In the purport of the verse given by him, it is clear he takes the word to mean 'learned[19] men.' This chapter of the Nirukta also treats of देवता—learned and enlightened beings or beneficient objects. In Nighaṇṭu III, 16 रुद्र is given among the synonyms of स्तोतृ—he who praises. In the Atharvaveda XI, 5, 12 the first class of brahmacārin, the highest type of Vedic student devoting the best part of his life to study maininining celibracy all the while is compared to a cloud. The cloud is called आदित्य[20] and such a student is also called आदित्य—a synonym of रुद्र. The word रुद्राय in R. V. I, 114, 1, is therefore explained by Maharṣi Dayānanda to mean—he who has studied the Vedas and the ancillary lores living in strict celibacy till the forty-fourth year of his life[21]. Sāyaṇa has failed to give the right interpretation of the term in this verse but he has, however, against the grain, been compelled to give up his pet method of import-

---

17 शत्रूनसौ रोदयति दुःखयति ॥

18 शत्रूणां रोदकाय शूरवीराय ॥

19 यथा तृषातुराय जलं शान्तिकरं भवति तथा विद्वांसो जिज्ञासुभ्यः शान्तिप्रदा भवन्ति ॥

20 पर्जन्य आदित्यः ॥ गो० १ । ४ । १ ॥

21 कृतचतुश्चत्वारिंशद्वर्षब्रह्मचर्याय ॥

ing any fanciful mythology in his commentary here.[22] हुवेम=may we extol ; praise.

Translation:—Oh God, Lord of the universe! give us the grace that we may, early in the morning (rising from the bed), invoke upon Thee the Self-effulgent Illuminator and the Most Bountiful Benefactor of all, Who alone art worthy of adoration being immanent in the whole cosmos like the vital air completely pervading our bodies as inhalation and exhalation. Thou art the Creator of the sun and the moon and Thy Opulence is worthy of devoted adherence. Thou nourishest all and art the Protector of Thy devotees. Thou art the Inner Force that impels all beings and Thou dost punish the sinner and dispel all evil.

Purport:—In this verse the words 'Agni' &c., are all used in a double sense. The one, viz., God in His manifold aspects as conceived by the devotee and called by various epithets accordingly, has already been mentioned. The second sense of 'Agni is fire, i. e., the performance of the 'havana', burning fragrant and nourishing materials in fire in order to diffuse purifying and nourishing particles in the air. 'Indra' means great power or wealth and by this term the devotee is asked to think of means to attain these. 'Mitrāvarṇa' mean inhalation and exhalation also, by which it is hinted that the early morning time is the best for prāṇāyama' or regulations of breathing. By 'Aśvinau' the teacher and the preacher also are meant. It is a well know fact

---

[22] रुद्राय रोदयति सर्वमन्तकाल इति रुद्रः यद्वा रुत्संस राख्यं दुःखं तद्द्रावयत्यपगमयति विनाशयतीति रुद्रः । यद्वा रुतः शब्दरूपा उपनिषदस्ताभिद्रूयते गम्यते प्रतिपाद्यत इति रुद्रः । यद्वा रुच्छब्दात्मिकावाणी तत्प्रतिपाद्यात्मविद्या वा तामुपासकेभ्यो राति ददातीति रुद्रः । यद्वा रुणध्यावृणोतीति रुदन्धकारादि तं द्रृणाति विदारयतीति रुद्रः ॥ After this comes a myth. But how clear and natural is the interpretation given by Maharsi Dayananda !

that the best time for learning something or hearing a sermon or lecture is morning. 'Bhaga' also means one's share and denotes progress in one's position. 'Pūṣan' means nourishing. This indicates strengthening of body and mind. 'Brahmaṇaspati' means a man learned in the Vedas. 'Sōma' means also the essence of medical herbs. Finally 'Rudra' means the soul as well. All these are matters which can be well practised, meditated upon or acquired only at the morning time when the mind is fresh and capable of grasping difficult and higher things.

(१९) प्रातर्जितं भगमुग्रं हुवेम वयं पुत्रमदितेर्यो विधर्ता । आध्रश्चिद्यं मन्यमानस्तुरश्चिद्राजा चिद्यं भगं भक्षीत्याह ॥२॥

पदपाठः—प्रातःऽजितम् । भगम् । उग्रम् । हुवेम । वयम् । पुत्रम् । अदितेः । यः । विऽधर्ता । आध्रः । चित् । यम् । मन्यमानः । तुरः । चित् । राजा । चित् । यम् । भगम् । भक्षि । इति । आह ॥

अन्वयः—हे परमात्मन्वयं प्रातस्त्वां जितमुग्रं भगं हुवेम । त्वमदितेः पुत्रं विधर्ताऽध्रोऽसि । एवंविधं त्वां यो यश्चिद्भगं भक्षीत्याह तच्चिदस्मभ्यं दीयतामिति प्रार्थयामहे ॥

Word-meaning &c. :—जितम् (√जि जये + तुट् + क्विप् P. III, 2, 178 and VI, 1, 71)=victorious, glorious. उग्रम्= full of splendour. अदितेः (√दीङ् क्षये √दो अवखण्डने, or √दाप् लवने + क्तिन् P. III, 3, 113 and VII, 4, 40)=of the intermediate or celestial region. पुत्रम् (√पूञ् पवने + क्त, U. IV, 165 पुरु त्रायते निपरणाद्वा पुंनरकं ततस्त्रायत इति वा पुत् + √त्रैङ् पालने or पुत् + त्रैङ् + ड Nir. II, 11. पुत् + त्रैङ् + ड Ramayana II, 107*, 12=Sons or offspring (singular used for the plural), i. e., the sun, moon and other planets

* पुन्नाम्नो नरकाद्यस्मात्पितरं त्रायते सुतः । तस्मात्पुत्र इति प्रोक्तः पितॄन् यः पाति सर्वतः ॥

and constellations which are situated in the celestial regions. विधर्ता (वि+धृञ् धारणे+तृन् P. III, 2, 135)=who supports in a perfect or special manner. आध्रः (आ+धृञ् धारणे+क P. III, 2, 5 वा० कप्रकरणे मूलविभुजादिभ्य उपसंख्यानम्)=who sustains from all round. चित्=even यं चित्=whatever. तञ्चित्=even that. मन्यमानः (√मन ज्ञाने+शानच् P. III, 3, 124 and VII, 2, 82)=knowing; who knows. तुरः (√तुर त्वरणे+क P. VI, 1, 135)=quick in hearing the prayers of his devotees. राजा=illuminator, ruler of all. भगम्=prosperity, fortune, amenities of life, bliss of God's company. भक्षि=enjoy thou (Vedic form of the imperative, see P. III, 4, 6) इति=thus. आह=Thou hast ordained (third person for the second).

Translation :—Oh Lord God, early in the morning may we invoke upon Thee who art ever victorious and full of glory. Thou art the sustainer of all the planets in the vast celestial (and intermediate) regions. Thou art the ruler of all and Thou art quick in conferring favours on Thy devotees. Knowing these to be Thy attributes, we beseech Thee to bestow whatever happiness (including the bliss of Thy company) which Thou hast even ordained us to enjoy.

Purport :—It is one's duty that one should endeavour according to one's ability, to acquire by fair means all amenitiss of life and wealth too, that he may live in peace and happiness and also help the needy.

(२०) भग प्रणेतर्भग सत्यराधो भगेमां धियमु-
दवाददन्नः । भग प्र णो जनय गोभिरश्वैर्भग प्र नृभिर्नृ-
वन्तः स्याम ॥३॥

पदपाठ :—भग । प्रणेतरिति । प्रऽनेतः । भग । इमाम् । धियम् । उत् । अव । ददत् । नः । भग । प्र । नः । जनय । गोभिः । अश्वैः । भग । प्र । नृऽभिः । नृऽवन्तः । स्याम ॥

अन्वयः—हे भग प्रणेतर्भग सत्यराधो भग त्वं कृपया न इमां धियं ददरस्मानुदव । हे भग नो गोभिरश्वैः प्रजनय । हे भग ! त्वमस्मान्नृभिः प्र जनय यतो वयं नृवन्तः स्याम ॥

Word-meaning &c. :—प्रणेतः (प्र + √णीञ् प्रापणे तृन् P. III, 2, 135)=Creator and leader of all in the right path. सत्यराधः (सत्यं राधः यस्य P. II, 2, 24)=He Who possesses (eternal and) true wealth. भग=He who bestows prosperity on those that live righteously. नः=to us. इमाम्=this. धियम् (√ध्यै चिन्तायाम् + क्विप् P. III. 2, 178)= Understanding or knowledge (of Thy power and splendour). उत् अव=Shield us, protect us. ददत् (√डुदाञ् दाने + शतृ P. III, 2, 124)=giving, granting. गोभिः (√गम्लृ गतौ + डो U. II, 67)=with cows. अश्वैः (√अशू व्याप्तौ + क्वन् U. I, 151)=with horses. गोभिरश्वैः= with earthly possessions consisting of kine and horses. भग=by Thy grace (vocative used in place of the instrumental according to P, VII, 1, 39). प्र स्यात्=may we be well. May we progress in life. नृभिः (√णीञ् प्रापणे + ऋ U. II, 99 and 100)=With men. नृवन्तः (नृ + वतु P. V 2, 94 & VIII. 2, 9)=Possessing brave men. नृभिः नृवन्तः प्रस्याम्=May we advance in life having virtuous and brave men among us to lead us.

Translation :—Oh Adorable God ! Thou art the Maker and Guide of all in the path of truth. Oh Lord of all riches ! Thou art the bestower of true (and eternal) wealth. Please grant us this knowledge (of Thy splendour and power) and shield us from (the) danger (of falling away from Thee). Oh Lord, Dispenser of all power ! bless us with earthly possessions by confering on us kine and horses and may we, by Thy grace, progress in life with virtuous and brave men among us to lead us.

Purport :—Whenever one prays to God or associates with the enlightened, one should not fail to ask for wisdom and seek for high-souled persons.

(२१) उतेदानीं भगवन्तः स्यामोत प्रपित्व उत मध्ये अह्नाम्। उतोदिता मघवन्त्सूर्यस्य वयं देवानां सुमतौ स्याम ॥४॥

पदपाठ :—उत। इदानीम्। भगऽवन्तः। स्याम। उत। प्रऽपित्वे। उत। मध्ये। अह्नाम्। उत। उत्ऽइता। मघऽवन्। सूर्यस्य। वयम्। देवानाम्। सुऽमतौ। स्याम ॥

अन्वयः—हे भगवँस्तव कृपयोत स्वप्रयत्नैर्वयमिदानीं प्रपित्व उताह्नां मध्ये भगवन्तः स्यामोत हे मघवन्त्सूर्यस्योदिता वयं देवानां सुमतौ स्याम ॥

Word-meaning &c. :—इदानीम्=now. भगवन्तः (भग+मतुप् P. V, 2, 94 and VIII, 2, 9)=prosperous. स्याम=may we be. उत=and. प्रपित्वे (प्र+√आप्लृ व्याप्तौ+इत्वन् U. IV, 105)=in great or flourishing state (Nir. III, 19). मध्ये (√मन ज्ञाने+यक् U. IV, 112)=in the midst of. अह्नाम् (न √ओहाक् त्यागे+कनिन् U. I, 156 and 158)=of these days. उदिता (उत्+√इण् गतौ+क्तिन् P. III, 3, 94 and VII, 1, 39)=at sunrize, i. e., from the very beginning of the day when all take to their work. मघवन् (मह पूजायाम् or महि वृद्धौ+कनिन्, U. I. 159)=Most Adorable and Opulent Bestower of riches. सूर्यस्य (√सृ गतौ or √षू प्रेरणे+क्यप—सरत्याकाशमार्गेण सुवति लोकं कर्मणि—P. III, 1, 114)=of the sun. देवानाम्=of the enlightened. सुमतौ (शोभना मतिः—सु+√मन ज्ञाने+क्तिन् P. III, 3, 94 and II, 1, 57)=good counsel. सुमतौ स्याम्=may we have the benefit of the good counsel of.

Translation :—Oh Lord ! (by Thy grace and by our own efforts), may we attain to greatness now, and may we become prosperous and strong in these days. Oh most Adorable and Opulent Bestower of riches, may we, from the rising of the sun—the time for all to work—have the benefit of the good counsel of the enlightened.

Purport :—A devout person should at all times think of disciplining himself or herself spiritually and attaining great powers to be put to use in daily life for the good of all.

(२२) भग॑ एव भग॑वाँ अस्तु देवास्तेन॑ वयं भग॑वन्तः स्याम। तं त्वा॑ भग सर्व इज्जो॑हवीति स नो॑ भग पुरएता भ॑वेह ॥५॥

पदपाठ :—भग॑ः । एव । भग॑ऽवान् । अस्तु । देवाः । तेन॑ । वयम् । भग॑ऽवन्तः । स्याम । तम् । त्वा । भग । सर्वः । इत् । जोहवीति । सः । नः । भग । पुरःऽएता । भव । इह ॥

अन्वयः—हे भग ! यो भवाम्भगो भगवानस्तु तेनैव भगवता सह वयं देवा भगवन्तः स्याम । हे भग तम् सर्वो जनस्त्वा जोहवीति स त्वमिह नः पुरएता भव ॥

Word-meaning &c. :—भग=The Bestower of all riches or prosperity ; deserving of the greatest reverence and adoration ; fit to be served. भगवान्=possessing power and glory ; possessing all riches. जोहवीति (√ह्वेञ् आह्वाने frequentative form P. VI, 1, 32 and 33)=invokes upon ; praises ; glorifies. पुरएता (पुरः+√इण् गतौ तृच् P. III, 1, 133)=leader. इह=here ; in this world ; in the life of the house-holder.

Translation :—Oh Revered God ! mayst Thou be the only Object of our service and may all power and glory be Thine, so that we may attain to felicity through Thee alone. Oh Most adorable God ; all people do therefore invoke upon Thee. As such, we beseech Thee, be Thou our Leader here in this world, and guide us in our life as house-holders.

Purport :—Man should associate himself with God the source of all wealth and power, and His enlightened devotees. Thus advancing in life by the grace of God Almighty kinder far than our human parents, man should impart happiness and strength to those that are in need of it.

(२३) समध्वरायोषसो नमन्त दधिक्रावेव शुचये पदाय । अर्वाचीनं वसुविदं भगं नो रथमिवाश्वा वाजिन आवहन्तु ॥६॥

पदपाठ :—सम् । अध्वराय । उषसः । नमन्त । दधिक्राबाऽइव । शुचये । पदाय । अर्वाचीनम् । वसुऽविदम् । भगम् । नः । रथम्ऽइव । अश्वाः । वाजिनः । आ । वहन्तु ॥

अन्वयः—हे जगदीश्वरोषसो दधिक्रावेव शुचये पदायाध्वराय सन्नमन्त । एता वाजिनोऽश्वा रथमिव नोऽर्वाचीनं वसुविदं भगं तवानुग्रहेण प्रापयन्तु ॥

Word-meaning &c. :—सन्नमन्त=favourably inclined (Vedic Subjunctive). अध्वराय=for the accomplishment of virtuous deeds that involve no injury to any one. उषसः (√उष दाहे+असुन् U. IV, 189 and 134)=of the dawn, early morning. दधिक्रावा इव (√डुधाञ् धारणपोषणयोः+कि P. III, 2, 171—दधि+√क्रमु पादविक्षेपे or क्रदि आह्वाने रोदने च +वनिप् P. III, 2, 75, and VI, 4, 41=दधन्तम् क्रमते)=like a well-trained horse[1] उषसः दधिक्रावा इव=starting the day

[1] दधिक्रा दधत् क्रन्दतीति वा दधदाकारी भवतीति वा ॥ नि॰ २ । २१ ॥ निघ॰ १ । १४ a horse ॥

well by making the most of their early morning time when the mind is well-disposed (as then the element of light—सत्त्व—is prominent) and thus 'carrying on' their time (i. e., progressing well through it) like a well-trained horse quietly allowing its rider to mount and then swiftly but carefully proceeding on. This is one way of rendering the expression in which the simile can be explained by taking the devotee to be compared to a well-trained horse. The other way is by instituting a comparison between the dawn and a well-trained horse. The phrase would then have to be explained as follows:—The early morning time becomes most profitable to the man who makes a good use of it allowing him to progress peacefully on through the rest of the day to success, like a well-trained horse which 'bends down' (i. e., quietly stands) and suffers its rider to mount and sit firmly, after which it proceeds in full speed. शुचये (√ईशुचिर् पूतीभावे+इन् U. IV, 120)=for a pure, virtuous, good. पदाय (√पद् गतौ+अच् P. III, 1, 134)=for any object worth acquiring अर्वाचीनम् (अर्वाच्+ख P. V, 4, 8)=new, fresh, modern. वसुविदम् (√वसु निवासे+उ U. I, 10+√विद् लाभे+क P. III, 1, 135=वसूनि विन्दते इति)=that obtains a fortune. भगम्=prosperous condition; fortune. रथम् (√क्रीडने+कथन् U. II, 2) a chariot. अश्वाः=swift.[2] वाजिनः (√वज मार्गसंस्कारगत्योः+घञ् वाज+इनि P. III, 3, 18 and V, 2, 115,=horses. आ वहन्तु=bring from all round.

Translation:—Oh Lord of the universe! It is ordained by Thee that those who understand the great value of their early morning time and put it to a good use, should, thereby be carried forward (peacefully but swiftly) like a rider on the back of a well-trained horse, to success in the performance of great and vir-

---

[2] अश्वः कस्मात् । अश्नुतेऽध्वानम् ॥ नि० २ । २७ ॥ व्याप्नोति ह्यध्वानमन्येभ्यः शीघ्रम् ॥ स्क० भा० ॥

tuous deeds involving no injury to any being, and to the attainment of desirable objects. Grant, we beseech Thee, Oh Lord! that our mornings may, like swift horses conveying a chariot to its destination, carry us on to such a flourishing state as will be distinguished by the acquisition of ever new wealth.

Purport :—Those men are really blessed whom God gives the wisdom to begin and utilise their day properly and acquire learning and power. Such should be sought after.

(२४) अश्वा॑वती॒र्गोम॑ती॒र्न उ॒षासो॑ वी॒रव॑ती॒: सद॑मुच्छन्तु भ॒द्राः । घृ॒तं दुहा॑ना वि॒श्वत॒: प्रपी॑ता यू॒यं पा॑त स्व॒स्तिभि॒: सदा॑ नः ॥७॥

पदपाठ :—अश्वऽवतीः । गोऽमतीः । नः॒ । उ॒षसः॑ । वी॒रऽव॑तीः । सद॑म् । उ॒च्छ॒न्तु । भ॒द्राः । घृ॒तम् । दुहा॑नाः । वि॒श्वतः॑ । प्रऽपी॑ताः । यू॒यम् । पा॒त॒ । स्व॒स्तिऽभिः॑ । सदा॑ । नः॒ ॥

अन्वयः—हे जगदीश्वर तवानुग्रहेणाश्वावतीर्गोमतीरुषस इवाश्वावतीर्गोमतीर्विदुष्यः सदाचारिण्यो नार्यो वीरवतीर्भद्रा घृतं दुहाना विश्वतः प्रपीता अस्माकं सदमुच्छन्तु च यूयं स्वस्तिभिर्नः सदा पात ॥

Word-meaning &c. :—अश्वावतीः[1] (√अशू व्याप्तौ+कन् U. I, 151+मतुप्+ङीप् P. V, 2, 94 & IV, 1, 6)=diffusing dew-water all over (dawn); having precious objects

---

[1] अप्सुजा उ वा अश्वः ॥ श० ७ । ५ । २ । १८ ॥ अप्सुयोनिर्वा अश्वः ॥ तै० ३ । ८ । ४ । ३ ॥ अन्तो वा अश्वः पशूनाम् ॥ तां० २१ । ४ । ६ ॥ तस्मादश्वः पशूनामोजस्वितमः ॥ श० १३ । १ । २ । ६ ॥ वीर्यं वा अश्वः ॥ श० २ । १ । ४ । २४ ॥ वीर्यं=रेतस् (नि० १ । १२ ।)=जल ॥

(women). गोमतीः[2] (√गम् 1st conj.+डो U. II, 67+मतुप्+ङीप् P. V, 2, 94 & IV, 1, 6)=beautified by the rays of the rising sun (dawn); possessing good speech (women). वीरवतीः (√अज् गतिपूजनयोः+रक् U. II, 13=मतुप्+ङीप् P. V, 1. 94 & IV, 1, 6) possessing heroic men—sons and other relatives; who can rouse men to heroic deeds. सदम्(√षद्लृ विषरणगत्यवसादनेषु+अच् P. III, 1, 134) home; assembly. उच्छन्तु (√उच्छ्)=adorn, perfect, complete. भद्राः (√भदि कल्याणे सुखे च+रक् U. II, 28)=of auspicious conduct. घृतम् (√घृ क्षरणे दीप्तौ च+क्त U. III, 80)=water, food. अन्नस्य घृतमेव रसस्तेजः। M. Br. II, 6, 15; उल्वं घृतम् Ś. Br. VI, 6, 2, 15. Is read in the synonyms of water in Nig. I, 12. अन्नमापः। Śankh. Br. XII, 3, 8; आपोऽन्नम्। A. B. VI, 30. Pure and healthy water and food are meant here. दुहानाः (√दुह प्रपूरणे+शानच्+टाप् P. III, 2, 124, and IV, 1, 4) =supplying, providing. विश्वतः (विश्व+तसिल् P. V, 3, 7)= in every way; from all round. प्रपीताः (प्र+√ओप्यायी वृद्धौ+क्त+टाप् P. III, 9, 102 and IV, 1, 4)=growing or advancing fast. यूयम् (=एताः)=they, i. e., the educated and virtuous matrons (second person used for the third). पात (=पान्तु)=may they protect (second person used for the third). स्वस्तिभिः (सु+अस्+ति U. IV, 179 and 180) by such counsels and actions as would confer on us health and happiness.

Translation :—Oh Lord of the universe! bless us with educated and virtuous matrons, resembling the dawn that diffuses cooling dew-water all over space and is attractive on account of the rays of the rising sun,

[2] इमे वै लोका गौर्यद्धि किं च गच्छतीमांस्तल्लोकान् गच्छति ॥ श० ६ । १ । २ । ३५ ॥ इमे लोका गौः ॥ श० ६ । ५ । २ । १७ ॥ अयम्मध्यमो (लोकः) गौः ॥ तां० ४ । १ । ७ ॥ अन्तरिक्षं गौः ॥ ऐ० ४ । १५ ॥ गावो वा आदित्याः ॥ (Sun's rays) ऐ० ४ । १७ ॥ अन्नमु गौः ॥ (food) श० ७ । ५ । २ । १९ ॥ यज्ञो वै गौः ॥ तै० ३ । ९ । ८ । ३ ॥ प्राणो हि गौः ॥ श० ४ । ३ । ४ । २५ ॥ इन्द्रियं वै वीर्यं गावः ॥ श० ५ । ४ । ३ । १० ॥ इडा हि गौः ॥ श० २ । ३ । ४ । ३४ ॥ सरस्वती हि गौः ॥ (good speech) श० १४ । २ । १ । ७ ॥

by their possession of precious objects, good speech, heroic sons and relations, auspicious conduct, and knowing how to provide clean and healthy food and water, that they may perfect our household life and assemblies and advance our welfare in every way by such counsels and actions as would confer on us health and happiness.

Purport :—Women folk should be respected, well-cared for and given a chance to educate and train themselves. If so they will be ever happy and render family life heavenly.

Comment :—This hymn describes the morning time as the best for all endeavours towards mental, spiritual and material advancement. The reason is clear : After complete rest and discontinuance of worldly activity for a sufficient length of time over night, all the soul's faculties get refreshed and the 'lighter side' (sattva) af the material part of the human being becomes prominent, so that the mind is well-disposed to grasp higher and the most difffcult matters at morning time.

Hence it is that all literary and such other activities as require special application of the mind and faculties of the soul are, all over the world, started in the morning. Nay, physical exercise for the building and maintaining of good bodily health essential for higher activities is best taken early in the morning. Considering the great importance of the early morning hours in human life therefore, the following points raised by our prayer-hymn have to be borne in mind.

WHEN SHOULD WE RISE FROM BED ?

In the code of Manu the following statement occurs regarding the time when a man should wake up from bed :—"One should wake up in the morning at the 'hour sacred to God' (Brāhma muhūrta) and contemplate on the maintenance of a righteous standard of living along with (its opposite) the acquisition of wealth. One should consider also the bodily sufferings at the root of these, not forgetting at the same time to meditate on the Supreme Principle (God), the principal object preached by the Vedas[3]." This Brāhma muhūrta is the last[4] 'hour of the night' roughly and covers about three quarters of an hour somewhere at about four o'clock in the morning.

Manu then adds that "having attended to the necessary calls of nature and having washed one's (mouth and) person, one should with a concentrated mind sit (properly in some quiet place) and recite (mentally) the early twilight prayers and again at their own time in the evening the next twilight prayers[5]." Kullūkabhatta in his commentary on this says:—"Then, having got up at the dawn from the bed, one should attend calls of nature if hard pressed and having finished one's ablutions in the manner to be laid down here-in-after, with concentrated mind, remain, mentally reciting for a suffieient length of time, the first twilight prayers and the Holy Gāyatri[6] till the sun comes into sight &c.[7]"

---

[3] ब्राह्मे मुहूर्ते बुध्येत धर्मार्थौ चानुचिन्तयेत् । कायक्लेशांश्च तन्मूलान्वेदतत्त्वार्थमेव च ॥ म० ४ । ९२ ॥

[4] रात्रेश्च पश्चिमे यामे मुहूर्तो ब्राह्म उच्यते ॥ Quoted in Apte's Sankṛt-English dictionary.

[5] उत्थायावश्यकं कृत्वा कृतशौचः समाहितः । पूर्वां संध्यां जपंस्तिष्ठेत्स्वकाले चापरां चिरम् ॥ म० ४ । ९३ ॥

[6] ओ३म् तत्सवितुर्वरेण्यं भर्गो देवस्य धीमहि । धियो यो नः प्रचोदयात् ॥ यजुर्वेद, ३० । २ ॥ Vide details given elsewhere in the book.

[7] तत उषः काले शय्याया उत्थाय सति वेगे मूत्रपुरीषोत्सर्गं कृत्वात्र कृतवक्ष्यमाणशौचोऽनन्यमनाः पूर्वां सन्ध्यां चिरं गायत्रीजपं कुर्वन्नासीतार्कदर्शनात् ॥

THINK OF GOD AS SOON AS YOU WAKE UP.

But what has one to do before the time for the twilight prayers? What should one do no sooner one wakes up? For, to be sure, some time passes between one's waking up and leaving the bed. The injunction about the most serious twilight prayers should not leave one the chance to think that one should let one's mind roam about—go a wool-gathering as they say—during these few minutes. Who knows what may happen? Ten to one, one may fall dead at the very next moment. Hence, one should, at no time in one's life be a beast. A righteous, God-fearing way of life, is the only trait by which man is distinguished from the lower animal.[8] Just at this sacred time, the whole family rising from the bed like one man, should recite this beautiful hymn. The construction—the very wording of it compels the conclusion that it is intended for this purpose. It is pre-eminently the morning prayer that reminds man or woman by force that he or she is a human, a rational, being. After the recitation of this comes the time to do according to what Manu says in his treatise about attending the necessary calls of nature &c.[9] Kullūkabhatta already quoted above, says that one should do so only if hard pressed, but he considers 'śauca', ablutions necessary.

How are these ablutions performed? or what is the method of purification? Manu says that the body is cleansed with water, the mind by a truthful conduct, the soul by right knowledge and austerities and the intellect by good education[10]." That is, ablutions

---

[8] आहारनिद्राभयमैथुनञ्च सामान्यमेतत्पशुभिर्नराणां। धर्मोहि तेषामधिको विशेषो धर्मेण हीनाः पशुभिः समानाः ॥ चाणक्य (?) ॥

[9] See footnote 5 on page 64.

[10] अद्भिर्गात्राणि शुध्यन्ति मनः सत्येन शुध्यति। विद्यातपोभ्यां भूतात्मा बुद्धिर्ज्ञानेन शुध्यति ॥ म० ५ । १०९ ॥

are bodily, mental and spiritual. The first is easy, the second not impossible, but the third is a difficult and long process which must, at every time in ones' daily life, be kept in view.

The second or mental ablution is very necessary, for without it, devotion is impossible. Hence the very first thing a person should do soon after waking from sleep early in the morning is to repeat the Sacred Name of God 'Aum', try to realise that He is present and has waked him or her up to go about the daily task appointed and thus prevent all 'foreign' thoughts from rushing in upon the mind. This will bring about the necessary purification of the mind after which the recitation of the hymn by all the members of the family together in a loud voice, or by each member severally in mind, should be done attentively but not slowly.

MORNING MEDITATION.

Along with the recitation a short meditation is necessary to keep all distracting objects away from the mind. This is, to speak the truth, the beginning of the twilight spiritual exercise. This done, the first or bodily ablutions should be gone through all the while thinking of cleansing one's mind as well as soul. When this act is over, one should, sitting at ease in a quite corner, recite the twilight prayers a subject with which this book is not concerned.

THE SUBJECT OF THE HYMN.

At the top of this section the subject of this hymn has been given in outline. It is, speaking broadly, meditation on the way life is to be spent during the day. As such it resolves into a number of divisions of which the following are most noteworthy:—

I. Recitation of and meditation on the various names of God which indicate how His Providence functions in the universe, and contemplation on our relations with the various institutions and departments of and principal persons concerned with human society as it is within our own part of the world. Also adoption of certain steps for one's own advancement material, mental and spiritual.

II. Associating with the learned and enlightened, congratulating friends and brethren on their success in life or the sudden acquisition of some fortune and rejoicing* with them thereon.

III. Women also should perform the same spiritual exercises and then see to all the household needs. They should keep water and foodstuffs clean and safe. Their duty in life does not end here, for they have also to attend the assemblies or councils of the community along with men and help them with their active cooperation and advice.

Another way of interpreting the hymn is by taking the word 'prātar' to mean the beginning of the day of creation after the night of dissolution. It will then, to give merely the gist of the whole, mean that the whole universe, and the souls that were all in a state of inactivity or torpor, so to say, during the night of 'pralaya' do now, after creation, teem with life and work in their several stations assigned to them by God's Providence.

A third interpretation can be given thus:— When man's life is darkened by ignorance, false knowledge, blemishes and sins, the soul remains, so

---

* In the Bible also morning is considered to be the time for rejoicing, vide Psalms XXX, 5 "...joy cometh in the morning."

to say, unconscious and impotent unable to avail itself of the grace of God ; but when by the company of the enlightened right knowledge dawns on man and he becomes aware of the unsatisfactory state of his own soul he begins to feel the necessity of improvement. He then avails himself of the means afforded by God's Providence and makes headway in spiritual life.

Section II.

Prayers for Noble Intentions.

(to be recited especially while Retiring to Bed).

Yajurvēda XXXIV, 1-6.

Seer :—Śivasaṃkalpa.

Subject :—The mind.

Metre :—Stanza 1, virāṭ-triṣṭubh ; stanzas 2, 4 and 5, triṣṭubh and 3 and 6 svarāṭ-triṣṭubh.

Tone :—Dhaivata.

(२५) ओ३म् ॥ यज्जाग्रतो दूरमुदैति दैवं तदु सुप्तस्य तथैवैति । दूरङ्गमं ज्योतिषां ज्योतिरेकं तन्मे मनः शिवसङ्कल्पमस्तु ॥१॥

पदपाठः—यत् । जाग्रतः । दूरम् । उदैतीत्युत्ऽऐति । दैवम् । तत् । ऊँ इत्यूँ । सुप्तस्य । तथा । एव । एति । दूरङ्गममिति दूरम्ऽगमम् । ज्योतिषाम् । ज्योतिः । एकम् । तत् । मे । मनः । शिवसङ्कल्पमिति शिवऽसङ्कल्पम् । अस्तु ॥

अन्वयः—हे जगदीश्वर त्वदनुग्रहेण यद्दैवं दूरङ्गमञ्ज्योतिषाञ्ज्योतिरेकञ्जाग्रतो दूरमुदैति तदु सुप्तस्य तथैवान्तरेति तन्मे मनः शिवसङ्कल्पमस्तु ॥

Word-meaning &c. :—**यत्**=which **जाग्रतः** (√जागृ निद्राक्षये+शतृ P. III, 2, 124)=in the waking state. **दूरम्** (दुस्+√इण् गतौ+रक् U. II, 13 and 20)=far. **उदैति**=goes, flies, flees. **दैवम्**=(देव+अण् P. IV, 3, 120)=Subsisting in the soul, an instrument of the soul. **तत्**=

that. च=and. तथा एव=in the same manner. एति=returns to the internal sense. दूरङ्गमम् (दूरात् गच्छति इति P. III, 2, 18,=that which goes far, takes cognizance of many objects. ज्योतिषाम् (√द्युत दीप्तौ+इसिन् U. II, 110)=of the sense organs that illumine the objects of the senses. ज्योतिः=illuminator, impeller, mover. एकम्=one, unitary. मे=mine. मनः=mind. शिवसङ्कल्पम् (शिवः सङ्कल्पो यस्य P. II, 2, 24)=having righteous or pious resolves. अस्तु=may be.

Translation :—Oh Lord God, Ruler of the Universe, vouchsafe, I beseech Thee, that my mind the sole illuminator of the sense organs which illuminate the objects of senses, which in the waking state flees far (to different places and different objects) and during sleep returns to the internal sense, may, by Thy grace, be always actuated by righteous resolves.

Purport :—Man's mind engages itself in multifarious affairs during the waking hours, but in sleep, in a way, it reposes. It is the mind that impels the sense organs to do their duty. That man, therefore, who by an active faith in God and the influence of good company cleanses his mind, can easily control it and apply it always only to good objects.

(२६) येन कर्माण्यपसो मनीषिणो यज्ञे कृण्वन्ति विदथेषु धीराः। यदपूर्वं यक्षमन्तः प्रजानां तन्मे मनः शिवसङ्कल्पमस्तु ॥२॥

पदपाठः—येन। कर्माणि। अपसः। मनीषिणः। यज्ञे। कृण्वन्ति। विदथेषु। धीराः। यत्। अपूर्वम्। यक्षम्। अन्तरित्यन्तः। प्रजानामिति प्रऽजानाम्। तत्। मे। मनः इत्यादि पूर्ववत्॥

अन्वयः—हे परमेश्वर तव कृपया ययापसो मनीषिणो धीरा यज्ञे विदथेषु च कृण्वन्ति यदपूर्वं प्रजानामन्तर्यक्षं वर्तते तन्मे मनः शिवसङ्कल्पमस्तु ॥

Word-meaning &c. :—येन=by means of which. कर्माणि (√डुकृञ् करणे+मनिन् U. IV, 145)=works. अपसः (√आप्लृ व्याप्तौ+असुन्+विन् U. IV, 189 and 208; P. V, 2, 121 and 3, 65; also Nig. II, 1)=ever active, always working. मनीषिणः (मनसः ईषा according to the Vartika शकन्ध्वादिषु पररूपं वाच्यं तच्च टेः and the termination इनि, ordained by P. V, 2, 116 or √मनु अवबोधने+ईषन् U. IV, 26 or √ईष गतौ+अ+टाप्=ईषा ; मनसः ईषा+इनि ; P. III, 3, 103 ; IV 1, 4 ; the Vartika quoted above &c. as in the first) wise men who control the mind. यज्ञे=in sacrifice, righteous act, discipline. कृण्वन्ति=perform. विदथेषु (√विद ज्ञाने &c.,+अथ U. III, 113 and 115)=in physical sciences, in warfare, in branches of learning or knowledge. धीराः (धीर्विद्यते येषाम् Nig. III, 15)=wise men; men given to contemplation. अपूर्वम्=possessed of excellent attributes, action and nature, peerless. यक्षम् (√यज्+सन् U. V, 21; P. III, 3, 1 and U. V, 21)=awful; praiseworthy. अन्तः=inside, in the innermost recesses. प्रजानाम्=of creatures.

Translation :—Oh Lord God Almighty ! through whose agency, by Thy grace, the ever industrious wise men given to much thinking, engage themselves in works of piety or learning and teaching, which is peerless and seated in the innermost recesses of all creatures, grant that, that awful mind of mine be ever actuated by noble resolves.

Purport :—One should sanctify oneself by the worship of God, noble thoughts, useful study, and good company which dissociate the mind from evil-ways of life and direct it towards the good.

(२७) यत्प्रज्ञानमुत चेतो धृतिश्च यज्ज्योतिरन्तरमृतम्प्रजासु। यस्मान्न ऋते किञ्चन कर्म क्रियते तन्मे मनः शिवसङ्कल्पमस्तु ॥३॥

पदपाठः—यत्। प्रज्ञानमिति प्रऽज्ञानम्। उत। चेतः। धृतिः। च। यत्। ज्योतिः। अन्तः। अमृतम्। प्रजास्विति प्रऽजासु। यस्मात्। न। ऋते। किम्। चन। कर्म। क्रियते। ०॥

अन्वयः—हे जगदीश्वर तव प्रसादाद्यत्प्रज्ञानं चेत उत धृतिर्यच्च प्रजास्वन्तरमृतं ज्योतिर्यस्मादृते किञ्चन कर्म न क्रियते तन्मे मनः शिवसङ्कल्पमस्तु ॥

Word-meaning &c. :—प्रज्ञानम् (प्र + √ज्ञा मारणतोषणनिशामनेषु + ल्युट् P. III, 3, 15 = the intellect by which concepts of objects of sense are formed. उत = and. चेतः √चिती संज्ञाने + असुन् U. IV, 189) = recollection; memory. धृतिः (√धृञ् धारणे + क्तिन् P. III, 3, 94) = courage; retention. The particle च means to add such other feelings as shame &c. अन्तः = being associated with the soul in the inmost recess. अमृतम् (नञ् + √मृङ् प्राणत्यागे + क्त P. III, 2, 102 and II, 2, 6) = immortal. यस्मात् ऋते = without which. न किम् चन = nothing at all.

Translation :—Oh Lord God! that which is able, by Thy impulse, to take cognition of, retain in memory and recollect the objects of sense, that which is endowed with the feelings of courage &c., and that which is the immortal light placed within the self of all creatures without whose agency no work can be accomplished: may that mind of mine, I beseech Thee, be possessed of noble resolves.

Purport :—The mind has four aspects, viz., the internal sense, cognition, memory and ego. It is therefore the indestructible means which illumine the inner self of all creatures. Hence every one should endeavour to rescue it from the influence of injustice, unrighteousness and prejudice and apply it to works of justice and truth.

(२८) येनेदं भूतं भुवनं भविष्यत्परिगृहीतममृतेन सर्वम्। येन यज्ञस्तायते सप्तहोता तन्मे मनः शिवसंकल्पमस्तु ॥४॥

पदपाठः—येन। इदम्। भूतम्। भुवनम्। भविष्यत्। परिगृहीतमिति परिऽगृहीतम्। अमृतेन। सर्वम्। येन। यज्ञः। तायते। सप्तहोतेति सप्तऽहोता। तत्। मे। मनः। शिवसंकल्पमिति शिवऽसंकल्पम्। अस्तु॥

अन्वयः—हे भगवन्येनामृतेन त्वया साकं वर्तमानेन भूतं भुवनं भविष्यत्सर्वमिदं परिगृहीतं भवति येन च सप्तहोता यज्ञस्तायते तन्मे मनः शिवसङ्कल्पमस्तु॥

Word-meaning &c. :—इदम्=all these movable and immovable beings, the world. भूतम् (√भू सत्तायाम् + क्त P. III, 2, 102)=of the past. भुवनम् (√भू + क्युन् U. II, 80)=of the present. भविष्यत् (√भू + स्य + शतृ P. III, 1, 33; VII, 2, 35; III, 2, 127 and III, 3, 14)=of the future. परिगृहीतम् (परि + √ग्रह ग्रहणे + क्त P. III, 2, 102 and VII, 2, 35)=is fully comprehended. अमृतेन=of the Immortal God. सर्वम् (√सृ गतौ + वन् U. I, 152 and 153)=all. यज्ञः= the sacrifice in the shape of the acquisition of knowledge. तायते (√तनु विस्तारे + यक् P. VI, 4, 44)=is performed. सप्तहोता (सप्त होतारः यस्मिन् P. II, 2, 24)=having seven priests (the Agniṣṭoma); — the five senses, the intellect and the soul (the sacrifice in the shape of the yogic spiritual discipline).

Translation :—Oh Lord! that mind which under Thy immortal impulse is fully able to comprehend the world as it was, is and will be and, under whose authority the sacrifice in the shape of spiritual discipline (*yoga*) is performed by the seven priests, viz., the five sense organs, the soul and the intellect—may that mind of mine, by Thy grace, be moved by right intentions.

Purport:—Rightly disciplined the mind can be a means to acquire knowledge of the whole universe in all the three divisions of time. It should, therefore, be always utilised by man for beneficent objects.

(२६) यस्मिन्नृचः साम यजूंषि यस्मिन्प्रतिष्ठिता रथनाभाविवाराः। यस्मिंश्चित्तं सर्वमोतं प्रजानां तन्मे मनः शिवसङ्कल्पमस्तु ॥५॥

पदपाठः—यस्मिन् । ऋचः । साम । यजूंषि । यस्मिन् । प्रतिष्ठिता । प्रतिस्थितेति प्रतिऽस्थिता । रथनाभाविवेति रथनाभौऽइव । अराः । यस्मिन् । चित्तम् । सर्वम् । ओतमित्याऽउतम् । प्रजानामिति प्रऽजानाम् । तत् । मे । मनः । शिवसङ्कल्पमिति शिवऽसङ्कल्पम् । अस्तु ॥

अन्वयः—हे सर्वेश्वर रथनाभाविवारा यस्मिन्मनस्यृचः साम यजूंषि प्रतिष्ठिता यस्मिन्नथर्वाणः प्रतिष्ठिता भवन्ति यस्मिन्प्रजानां सर्वं चित्तमोतमस्ति तन्मे मनः शिवसङ्कल्पमस्तु ॥

Word-meaning &c. :—ऋचः (ऋचन्ति स्तुवन्ति यया सा —√ऋच स्तुतौ + क्विप् U. II, 57)=the Ṛgveda. साम=the Samaveda. यजूंषि=the Yajurveda. (Add अथर्वाणः=the Atharvaveda). प्रतिष्ठिता (प्रति + √ष्ठा गतिनिवृत्तौ + क्त P. III, 2, 102 and VII, 2, 35)=are inserted. रथनाभौ (रथस्य नाभिः P. II, 2, 8)=in the nave of a cart-wheel. अराः (इयर्ति गच्छत्यनेन — √ऋ गतौ + क P. III, 1, 135)=spokes. चित्तम् (√चिती संज्ञाने + क्त P. III, 2, 102)=knowledge of all things. ओतम् (आ + √वेञ् तन्तुसन्ताने + क्त P. III, 2, 102)=strung; woven.

Translation :—Oh Lord of all, that mind which like the hub of a wheel into which all the spokes are inserted, is the repository of the Ṛgvēda, the Yajurvēda, the Sāmavēda and also the Atharvavēda, the mind on which all the knowledge which creatures have regarding things depends like the pearls of a necklace on the cord on which they are strung—may that mind of mine, by Thy grace, be moved by right intentions (regarding the study and propagation of Vedic teachings).

Purport :—The mind is the receptacle of all worldly knowledge as well as Vedic learning and without it these are inaccessible. Hence, every person should take care to keep it pure with noble thoughts. Once Vedic learning is secured this right intention should concern itself with the right interpretation of Vedic texts so that all may be edified and none scandalised.

(३०) सुषारथिरश्वानिव यन्मनुष्यान्नेनीयते
ऽभीशुभिर्वाजिन इव । हृत्प्रतिष्ठं यदजिरं जविष्ठं तन्मे
मनः शिवसङ्कल्पमस्तु ॥६॥

पदपाठः—सुषारथिः । सुषारथिरिति सुऽसारथिः । अश्वानिवेत्यश्वान्ऽइव । यत् । मनुष्यान् । नेनीयते । अभीशुभिरित्यभीशुऽभिः । वाजिनऽइवेति वाजिनःऽइव । हृत्प्रतिष्ठम् । हृत्प्रतिस्थमिति हृत्ऽप्रतिस्थम् । यत् । अजिरम् । जविष्ठम् । ० ॥

अन्वयः—हे परमेश्वर ! यत्सुषारथिरश्वानिव मनुष्यान्नेनीयते ऽभीशुभिर्वाजिन इव नियच्छति च बलात्सारथिरश्वानिव प्राणिनो नयति यद्धृत्प्रतिष्ठमजिरं जविष्ठमस्तीत्यादिः पूर्ववत् ॥

Word-meaning &c. :—सुषारथिः (शोभनः सारथिः P. II, 1, 57)=a good charioteer. अश्वान्=horses. नेनीयते=drives, takes in any way. **अभीशुभिः** (**अभि + √अशु व्याप्तौ + उ** U. I, 7 ; Nig. I, 5 ; Nir. III, 9 and IX, 16)=by the reins. **वाजिनः**=well trained horses, fleet-foot (Gr.), **हृत्प्रतिष्ठम्** (**हृदि प्रतिष्ठा यस्य** P. II, 2, 24 and 35)=established, dwells, seated, in the heart. **अजिरम्** (**√अज गतौ + किरन्** U. I, 53 ; Nig. II, 15)=swift, going in different directions or to different objects of the senses ; or (**नञ् + √जॄ वयोहानौ + क** P. III, 1, 135)=not affected by old age or imbecility. **जविष्ठम्**=most rapid.

Translation :—Oh God, Supreme Controller! that mind which controls a man (of regulated life), just as a skilful charioteer manages and drives by means of the reins well-trained horses in any direction he likes; and which seated in the heart, is the most rapid in movement and free from decay,—may this mind of mine, by Thy grace, be ever impelled by righteous motives.

Purport :—A foolish man is carried away by his unregulated mind to any object it is attracted by and forcibly kept attached thereto, just as a charioteer drives the horses of the chariot to any place he likes and restrains them there by means of the reins. A wise man, on the contrary, keeps his mind under control and applies it only to what he believes desirable and good. For, this mind, if purified brings happiness and achievement of good deeds, whereas, impelled by impure motives it brings misery and failures If it is subdued it leads to victory, if not subdued it supplants man. Men and women who wish happiness and success in life can, therefore, never be too careful to keep a watch on their minds.

Comment :—This hymn can very profitably be utilised as a prayer while going to bed at night. The evening twilight prayer is quite different from this and is recited much earlier, that is, commenced when the sun is just about to set, it is continued till the stars begin to appear in the sky*. The 'Saṃdhyā' or twilight prayer begins when the day's routine is over. Man is worried by material pursuits of the day which thickly crowd over him during day time but begin to diminish at sunset. Though the day's business may not end now, yet in most cases, it does slacken, thus allowing some time for recreation and devotion. This is however, true only in the case of such as are spiritually-minded whose number all over the world is usually very small. The materially-inclined will not care for evening prayers.

Thus the process of extricating the mind from the trammels of the day's routine begins with the twilight prayers and ends with this hymn. A thoughtful recitation of this hymn accompanied by an examination of conscience will cleanse the mind and fill it with righteous resolves which will remain in it till waking-time. This will help the exercitant, the next morning, to commense life with a very promising start. This step is quite necessary, since the mind being an ever-active and subtle principle will, otherwise, take to a wrong and futile course, even causing bad and harmful dreams at night. The mind is the one means that is available to all rational beings to follow some course, right if they are prudent, wrong if negligent.†

---

* उपास्य पश्चिमां संध्यां सादित्याञ्च यथाविधि । गायत्रीमभ्यसेत्तावद्यावत्ताराणि पश्यति ॥ S. u.

† मनो हि सर्वभूतानां संतनोति शुभाशुभं । अशुभेभ्यस्तदाक्षिप्य शुभेऽर्थे चावधारय ॥ S. u.

Chapter III.

The Nature of the Supreme Being.

(and means to attain Him).

Yajurvēda Ch. XXXII.

Seers :—Verses 1-12 Svayambhubrahma ; 13-15 Medhakāma and verse 16 Srīkāma.

Subject :—God Omnipresent and the means to realise Him.

Metre :—Stanzas 1, 2 and 16 anuṣṭubh ; Stanza 3, nicṛt-pankti ; Stanzas 4 and 5 bhurik-triṣṭubh ; 6, 8-12 nicṛt-triṣṭubh ; Stanza 7, svarad-jagatī ; 13, bhurig-gayatrī ; 14, nicṛdanuṣṭubh and 15 nicṛd-bṛhatī.

Tone :—1, 2, 4 and 16 gāndhāra ; 3 pañcama ; 4-6 and 8-12 dhaivata ; 7 niṣada ; 13 ṣaḍja and 15 madhyama.

(३१) ओ३म् ॥ तदेवाग्निस्तदादित्यस्तद्वायुस्तदु
चन्द्रमाः। तदेव शुक्रं तद्ब्रह्म ता आपः स प्रजापतिः ॥
यजुर्वेदे ३२ । १ ॥

पदपाठः—तत् । एव । अग्निः । तत् । आदित्यः । तत् । वायुः । तत् । ऊँ इत्यूँ । चन्द्रमाः । तत् । एव । शुक्रम् । तत् । ब्रह्म । ताः । आपः । सः । प्रजापतिरिति प्रजाऽपतिः ॥

अन्वयः—हे मनुष्या तदेवाग्निस्तदादित्यस्तद्वायुस्तच्चन्द्रमास्तदेव शुक्रं तद्ब्रह्म ता आपः स उ प्रजापतिरस्त्येवं यूयं विजानीत ॥

Word-meaning &c. :—आदित्यः (नञ्+√दीङ् क्षये or √दो अवखण्डने+क्तिन्+ण्य P. III, 94 and IV, 1, 85)= Imperishable, Immutable. वायुः (√वा गतिगन्धनयोः+उण् U. I, 1)=He who moves, quickens, supports, and destroys all the movable and immovable beings and is the most powerful of all. तत्=that. उ=also ; and. चन्द्रमाः (√चदि आनन्दे+असि U. IV, 228)=He who is the source of happiness and gives it to all others. शुक्रम् (√ईशुचिर् पूतीभावे+रन् U. II, 27)=He who is the most Holy and by Whose Grace or by knowledge of Whom the soul is purified. ब्रह्म (√बृह or बृहि वृद्धौ+मनिन् U. IV, 146)= He who improves, develops the world or brings it to perfection after creating it. आपः (√आप्लृ व्याप्तौ+क्विप् U. II, 58)=He who pervades all and is Omnipresent in the universe. प्रजापतिः=The Lord of all creatures.

Translation :—(Oh men ! know that) He is the Adorable, the Imperishable, the Impeller of all, and the All-blissful Being. Verily He is the Most Holy One, the Supreme Being, the All-pervading and the Lord of all creatures.

Purport :—Men should recognise under different names such as 'Agni' &c , which are secondary, the One Supreme, Omnipresent Being, the Supporter and Controller of the universe and worship Him in spirit. His adoration is the only way to attain true happiness.

(३२) सर्वे निमेषा जज्ञिरे विद्युतः पुरुषादधि ।
नैनमूर्ध्वं न तिर्यञ्चं न मध्ये परि जग्रभत् ॥ २ ॥

पदपाठः—सर्वे । निमेषाऽइति निऽमेषाः । जज्ञिरे । विद्युतऽइति विऽद्युतः । पुरुषात् । अधि । न । एनम् । ऊर्ध्वम । न । तिर्यञ्चम । न । मध्ये । परि । जग्रभत् ॥

अन्वयः—हे मनुष्या यस्माद्विद्युत पुरुषात्सर्वे निमेषा अधि जज्ञिरे तमेनं कोऽपि नोर्ध्वं न तिर्यञ्चं न मध्ये परिजग्रभत्तं यूयं सेवध्वम् ॥

Word-meaning &c. :—सर्वे=all. निमेषाः नि+√मिष स्पर्धायाम्+घञ् P. III, 3, 18)=winking of the eye; shortest period of time as a moment. जज्ञिरे=are produced, born. विद्युतः (वि+√द्युत दीप्तौ+क्विप् P. III, 2, 178) =shining with great splendour. पुरुषात् (√पुर गमने+कुषन् U. IV, 74)=from the Perfect and Omnipresent God. अधि=mostly (construe with जज्ञिरे). न=not. एनम्=this Supreme Being. ऊर्ध्वम्=above. तिर्यञ्चम् (तिरस्+√अञ्चु गतिपूजनयोः+क्विन् P. VI, 3, 94; and III, 2, 59)=slanting in all directions; below. मध्ये (√मन ज्ञाने +य U. IV, 112)=in the middle. सर्वतः (√सृ गतौ+वन् +तसि P. V, 4, 45)=from all sides. परिजग्रभत् (परि+√ग्रह ग्रहणे)=seizes from all sides or completely.

Translation :—Oh men! do you have recourse to that Supreme All-pervading Being shining in His full splendour, by Whose dispensation all the divisions of time have come into existence, and on Whom none can lay hold either from above, below or the middle.

Purport :—God is Almighty and it is from Him that prevailing systems of calculating time have originated. As He is Omnipresent one cannot say whether He is above, below or in the middle of, any place. All should endeavour to realise Him through spiritual discipline and then resort to Him. Place cannot be predicated of God nor can time be, since He always exists and everything is ever present in His Omniscient Mind. It also indicates that one cannot seize God by His upper, middle or lower part since He has no body. Hence when we speak of realising God we are simply using our human idiom. We mean that our tarnished vision is unable to reflect Him and that a change of attitude is necessary.

---

* पूर्वेषामपि गुरुः कालेनानवच्छेदात् ॥ यो० १ । २६ ॥

(३३) न तस्य॑ प्रति॒मा अ॑स्ति॒ यस्य॒ नाम॑ म॒हद्यशः॑। हि॒र॒ण्य॒ग॒र्भ इत्ये॒ष मा मा॑ हिं॒सी॒दित्ये॒षा य॒स्मान्न जा॒त इत्ये॒षः॥ ३

पदपाठः—न। तस्य॑। प्र॒ति॒मेति॑ प्रति॒ऽमा। अ॒स्ति॒। यस्य॑। नाम॑। म॒हत्। यशः॑। हि॒र॒ण्य॒ग॒र्भ इति॑ हिरण्यऽग॒र्भः। इति॑। ए॒षः। मा। मा॒। हिं॒सी॒त्। इति॑। ए॒षा। य॒स्मा॑त्। न। जा॒तः इति॑। ए॒षः॥

अन्वयः—हे मनुष्या यस्य महद्यशो नामास्ति यो हिरण्यगर्भ इत्येषो यस्य मा मा हिंसीदित्येषा यस्मान्न जात इत्येष उपासनीयोऽस्ति तस्य प्रतिमा नास्ति। यद्वा—हिरण्यगर्भ इत्येष (य० २५। १०-१३) उक्तोऽनुवाको मा मा हिंसीदित्येषोक्ता (य० १२। १०२) ऋग्यस्मान्न जात इत्येष (य० ८। ३६। ३७) उक्तोऽनुवाकश्च यस्य नाम महद्यशोऽस्ति तस्य प्रतिमा नास्ति॥

Word-meaning &c. :—न=not. तस्य=His; of that Well-known God. प्रतिमा (प्रतिमीयते यया सा। प्रति+√माङ् माने+क्विप् P. III, 2, 178)=likeness, image, something to measure with. अस्ति=is. यस्य=Whose. नाम (√म्ना अभ्यासे +मनिन् U. IV, 151)=name; worship of the name. महत्=great. यशः=glory; good deeds which bring a good name. हिरण्यगर्भः=the source of all luminaries. इति=thus, as mentioned in the part of the hymn commencing "Hiraṇyagarbha" (Y. V. XXV, 10-13). एषः= as He is; the part of the hymn (Y. V. VIII, 36 and 37). मा=may not. मा=me. हिंसीत्=destroy, punish. एषा= that verse (Y. V. XII, 102), intention. यस्मात्=wherefore. जातः=born; known.

Translation :—There can be no image or measure of that Great God the worship of Whose Name on the part of man is nothing but doing good deeds such as works of piety redounding to his fame (in imitation of His own Holy attributes, deeds and nature). The Source of all luminous existents (such as the sun &c.), He is clearly seen pervading the universe and as the devotee also, is actuated by the wish that the Lord may not be hidden from his mind's eye. Another reason is that He is unborn.

Purport :—God never assumes any body and has therefore no form or shape that can be measured or divided. To obey His commandments is equal to reciting His name, a mere oral repetition being good-for-nothing. He surely confers benefits on those who adore Him, and His glory, as possessing such attributes is repeatedly sung in the Vedas. He does not die nor undergo any change or decay like finite beings. Man should worship only Him, for, by the adoration of any other being he would incur sin and as a result come to grief sooner or later.

Comment :—This verse condemns the use of images for the purpose of concentrating the mind in meditating on God. As He is All-pervading, formless and subtle, no image however skilfully made, can represent Him. An idol distracts the mind and interferes with meditation rather than help in its progress. So also a mere oral repetition of God's names is a futile exercise. Besides, His names are innumerable and discretion is necessary to select one for any particular purpose, whereas the sacred syllable 'Aum' represents[1] Him in the best possible manner, connoting all His attributes and is therefore useful for all purposes. This verbal repetition of 'Aum' though an excellent action in itself, cannot fetch any good to the person repeating, unless this act is backed by meditation on the meanings of the syllable and good deeds such as charity &c., and unless his or her life is reformed[2]. All prayers and ejaculations must therefore be accompanied by practical action.

---

[1] तस्य वाचकः प्रणवः ॥ योग॰ १ । १ । २७ ॥

[2] तज्जपस्तदर्थभावनम् ॥ योग॰ १ । १ । २८ ॥

It will not be out of place to make certain observations here on the nature of God's names. They can be divided into two classes, viz., first, such as connote all His attributes, deeds and nature and second, those which specify only some of them and are secondary according to the 1st verse. To the first class belongs the sacred particle 'Aum' alone, and all other names fall under the second category.

The word 'Aum' is made up of the three letters[3] 'a', 'u', 'm' each of which signifies a number of God's names. 'A' stands for, 'Virat', 'Agni' and 'Viśwa'; 'u' for 'Hiraṇyagarbha', 'Vāyu', and 'Taijasa' and 'm' represents, 'Iśvara', 'Āditya', and 'Prajña'. Of these 'Agni'[4] and 'Virāt'[5] are explained elsewhere in detail. Hiraṇyagarbha' from 'hiraṇya', light[6] and 'garbha', source, means One who is the source and support of all light and luminous bodies, such as the sun. 'Viśva', derived from the root 'viś' to enter and suffix 'va', means God, since the whole universe and all the objects in the universe enter, i. e., are sheltered in Him and He enters or pervades all of them. 'Vāyu', from the root 'vā' to move or kill, suffix 'uṇ' and augment 'yuk' means One who is the life and support of the universe, the cause of its dissolution, mightier than the mightiest 'Tāijasa' is got by adding the suffix 'aṇ' to 'tējas' meaning light which itself is a composite of the root 'tij' to whet and Uṇādi suffix 'asun'. It means One Who is resplendent and gives light to the sun and other luminous bodies. 'Iśvara' derived from the root 'iś' to be powerful, to rule and

---

[3] See the Maṇḍūkyopaniṣad in this connection.
[4] See notes on No. 1 in this book.
[5] See notes on the word in the Puruṣa hymn in this book.
[6] तेजो हिरण्यम् ॥ तै० ३।१२।५।१२ ॥ ज्योतिर्हिरण्यम् ॥ गो० १।२।२१ ॥ श० ४।३।१।२१ ॥

termination 'varac' connotes One Whose knowledge and power are infinite. 'Āditya' is a secondary formation from 'aditi' compounded with the suffix 'ṇya'. 'Aditi' itself is formed of 'a' negative particle, root 'dō' to cut and suffix 'ktic' ('ktin' in the feminine gender). It means immortal i. e., One who never dies or decays. 'Prājña is got by adding the termination 'aṇ', to the word prajña, itself composed of the prefix 'pra', root 'jña' to know and suffix 'ka'. It means One whose knowledge is perfect or Who is Omniscient.

Thus this sacred syllable 'Aum', combining within itself nine of the most sublime names of the Supreme Being connotes His nature, attributes and deeds in the best possible manner. It is an underived and undeclinable word, representing in its fullest connotation only God. As a word signifying a human being or anything else it does not possess this characteristic.

'Aum' is also taken, from time immemorial to be one single[7] letter and hence the suffix 'kāra'[8] is added to it to signify this idea. As such it is described as 'ēkākṣara'[9]—the one letter, or 'ēkākṣara brahma'—the one-lettered symbol of the Supreme Being.

This sacred word is also formed by adding the suffix 'man' to the root 'av' having the following nineteen significations[10] viz., protection, motion, desire, pleasure, satisfaction, attainment, entrance, hearing, owning, entreaty, action, wish, light, obtaining, embracing, killing, giving, division, and development.

---

7 अथैकस्यैवाक्षरस्य रसं (प्रजापतिः) नाशक्नोदाप्तुम्। ओमित्येतस्यैव। सेयं वागभवत्। ओमेव नामैषा ॥ जै० उ० १।१।६।७॥ तदेतदक्षरं (ओङ्कारं) ब्राह्मणोयं कामभिरध्यादि। गो० १।१।२२॥

8 वर्णात्कारः ॥ वार्तिक on P. III, 3, 108.

9 ओमित्येकाक्षरं ब्रह्म व्याहरन्मामनुस्मरन् ॥ गीता ८।१३॥

10 अव रक्षणगतिकान्तिप्रीतितृप्त्यवगमप्रवेशश्रवणस्वाम्यर्थयाचनक्रियेच्छादीप्त्यवाप्त्यालिङ्गनहिंसादानभागवृद्धिषु ॥ धातुपाठे ॥

Each of these as applied to God would connote the following ideas:—

1. Protection:—He, who directly or through some medium or media is the protector of all.

2. Motion:—There are three types of motion, viz,:—knowledge, movement and attainment. He is the Knower of every thing as it is. Himself being Immovable He is the cause of the motion of the world which ever keeps on moving. Being all-pervading He is omnipresent and therefore always available to all. These are the significations of the three ideas of metaphorical motion. As general motion it will connote God the Propagator of effort preceded by knowledge everywhere to keep the world going according to certain laws.

3. Desire:—Though Himself free from desire, He is the fulfilment of the desires of all souls.

4. Love:—His Essence being Bliss, He is the Object of the love of all.

5. Satisfaction:—Being Himself essentially peaceful, He yet always yields joy to His devotees.

6. Attainment:—Being essentially Auspicious, He is the donor of final beatitude to souls.

7. Entrance:—Being the subtlest, He is the Inner Self of all.

8. Hearing:—Being the framer of the organ of audition, He is the efficient cause of the hearing of gross, subtle and hidden sounds.

9. Owning:—Being the Self-existent Controller of all, He is the Master of all.

10. Entreaty:—Being endowed with all power, He is always the protector of all, to whom all approach with their entreaties.

11. Action :—Being the Framer of the world in formation, He is the imparter of activity with previous knowledge. Gross effort itself is called action. This is a species of the above motion.

12. Wish :—Being Himself free from any wish, He reveals auspicious wishes for souls.

13. Light :—Being essentially Effulgent, He is the expeller of the darkness in the form of wrong knowledge.

14. Obtaining :—Though beyond the senses, extremely subtle and uncognisable, He reveals His true form in the pure heart of His devotee.

15. Embracing :—Being always and everywhere present through the relation of the Pervader and the pervaded, He is related to all.

16. Killing :—He who destroys the ignorance, wrong knowledge, hostile feelings and dissensions among those that live according to Vedic teachings.

17. Giving :—He Who gives to souls at the very beginning of the creation a right understanding of things tending towards their happiness.

18. Division :—He Who is, at the time of dissolution, the cause of division of the world, that is reverting of the visible gross universe to its subtle, invisible form.

19. Development :—He Who, for the formation of the world at the time of creation is the Efficient Cause of the development of the primordial or elementary matter into its gross form so that souls may enjoy the residua of their past actions.

These nineteen connotations, if expanded according to the rules of grammar, would reveal the word 'Aum' to have infinite significations. Hence, the meanings of this word being unlimited and therefore beyond human ken, it is rightly called the greatest name of the Supreme Being[11].

By calling 'Aum' an indeclinable particle it is intended to bring to our mind that it undergoes no change by the addition of any suffix indicating number, gender or case as other words invariably do. No sooner such terminations come into contact with it they merge into it leaving no traces of their individuality behind. E. g 'vṛkṣam' + 'am' accusative singular termination, becomes 'vṛkṣam'; vṛkṣam paśya— 'look at the tree', but 'Aum smara'—remember God and not 'aumam'.

This latter word 'Aum' formed from the root 'av' is a derived one, whereas, the former one consisting of the letters 'a', 'u' and 'ma', signifying the nine names of the Supreme Being, is underived, i. e., it is not made up by putting together a root and a suffix or termination.

Mathematically also the sacred word 'Aum' is suggestive of the Omnipotent Nature of the Supreme Being. The number nineteen to which the meanings of the root 'av' total up, is made up of the two digits nine (9), in the unit's place and one (1), in the ten's place. The number one (1) is a subtle and perfect digit present in all the other numbers of the notation and the essence of the other numbers is represented by it. The other numbers are gross and excepting nine, all are imperfect. One begins the scale and nine completes it, whereas other numbers are merely got by adding two or more of these nine together. The other numbers can be got by addition, subtraction,

[11] Maharṣi Dayānanda Sarasvatī develops the word Aum in eighty-seven ways in his explanation of it in connection with R. V. I, 1, 1 in the beginning of his 'Āryābhivinaya'. Vide frontispiece.

division or multiplication, but not so 1, which is entirely independent and self-existent. It declares itself in the beginning, middle and end of all other numbers. In this manner it is really a good representation of the independent, perfect and subtle nature of the Supreme Being.

The number nine is not an independent number, but perfect certainly it is. Hence it is that the scale of notation terminates with it. By the addition of one a number increases and by a successive subtraction of one it goes on dwindling The nature of nine is different from that of the other numbers for when 1 is added to it, 1. itself remains and nine is changed into a cipher without losing its perfect nature. This is the reason why the cipher occupies such an important place in Arithmetic that if it were to be removed that science would cease to enjoy the reputation of a science.

The difference between nine (9) and cipher is only one of form and not essence. This fixed principle is perceptible when we remove cipher from any number containing it, for then the number is reduced only by nine or a multiple of nine. If 0 is removed from 101 we have 11 that is we have really removed 90 which is ten times 9. Removing 0 from 90 we get 9, i. e., 9 times 9 or 81 have been removed. In 81, the two digits added up yield 9. Hence by adding to or taking a cipher from any number we are adding to or subtracting nine or a multiple of nine from the number concerned.

Now the reader will ponder over this number 19 the total of the connotations of the root 'ava'. The digit 'one' is perfect and independent by nature and 9 is ever a perfect number. The number 1 is the beginning and nine the end. The word 'Aum' derived from the root 'ava' thus connotes the perfect and independent attributes, deeds and nature of God.

In the number 10, the cipher is really the representative of nine which latter, having absorbed other numbers, has assumed that form. The number 1 is the symbol of God Who in the beginning, end and middle of all (or before during and after creation)[12] remains in His own immutable form, and the cipher denotes the primordial matter—Prakṛti. Just as the tiny seed includes the tree in itself and there is no distinction apparent in the existence of the two, so also at the time of dissolution the whole universe is dismantled and assuming a subtle form is absorbed in the primordial matter. It is impossible to realise this state by thought or argument. Only deep sleep can be its true example. Hence it is that in deep sleep one hour and a thousand years are alike. In the state of sleep every creature forgets its own self and in the waking state gets itself ensnared in the meshes of differentiation. The world also, that merges in the primordial matter at the time of dissolution through the design and (if the word be allowed), the effort, of the Supreme Being assumes a subtle and visible form. The liberated souls that have, through right knowledge and purification of the self loosening themselves from the fetters of false knowledge, attained to the cognition of self and the knowledge of God, are like the number 9. The other souls, endowed with the causative body which is also called false knowledge or Prakṛti, devoid of cognition of self and hence fettered, are like the numbers from 2 to 8. The differentiation that is noticeable in these numbers by processes of addition or multiplication is the activity of the fetter-

[12] See comments on the Nāsadiya hmyn given elsewhere in this book.

ed souls that involves them in a cycle of births and deaths. Such of them as achieve perfection through devotion to God attain liberation when the flow of actions is obstructed and the universe is lost sight of in dissolution. But as souls are eternal, ordaining of activity is also eternal in succession though not in essence. Therefore it would mean that the state of liberation is not eternal. Its limits would cover an enormous period of 311,040,000,000,000 years.

Thus, mathematically considered the word 'Aum' is full of suggestions that make it a proper symbol for the Supreme Being.

The underived word 'Aum' made up of the three letters 'a', 'u' and 'm' is also full of suggestions. The vowels 'a' and 'u' are either short, long or prolated and 'm' is either a consonant, or a vocal or nasal sound. Thus each has three states and each connotes three of the names of the Supreme Being already mentioned at the commencement of this Comment. The history of the association of these names with the letters is not known, but all the same the association serves a very great and useful purpose.

The first of these three letters 'a' is the first of the alphabet all the world over. Tiruvalluva Nāyanār the author of the beautiful ancient Tamil work on Morality says at the commencement[13] of his treatise that "as the alphabet (of any language) begins with the letter 'a' so the universe has its source in the Lord God the Beginning of all." The older work Bhagavadgita[14] has, "of letters, I am 'A', the First". In these statements there is a clear equation between this sound and God.

---

[13] "Akaramudala veluttellām ādibhagavanmudaṭrē yulagu". Tirukkural I, 1, 1.

[14] अक्षराणामकारोऽस्मि &c. gita X, 33.

The sound 'a' being the first of the alphabet is the simplest, the most elementary, the most perfect and independent of all the letters to utter. It is uttered without any special effort even by the new born infant. The breathing of a sleeping person also resolves itself into the short and long pronunciations of this letter. The sound that for some reason involuntarily proceeds from the mouth of man is 'a'. Nay, the very motion of the vital air inside the body, if heard by shutting the ears to outer sound, is nothing but this 'a'. Most animals also utter this. The patter of rain, the blowing of wind, the flow of water all approximate to this sound. In a solitary place when no animal, no bird is out, when Nature herself is in deep repose, if one were to listen attentively, one would invariably perceive the gentle but grave, and slow but continuous utterance of this sound. This sound is the first to be uttered by the human being and forms the basis of all human speech. As such it is called 'Nāda' and is coeternal with knowledge, with the Veda and with creation. In music also this sound has a very important place. It is a subtle sound unlike the others and is found in most of them. It is also independent in its utterance requiring no help from any other letter for its manifestation. When added to a consonant, it merges in it and makes it audible but, unlike the other vowels it does not in any way transform the consonant. The other vowels make their presence felt by a very perceptible change in the consonant. God is present everywhere but is not perceptible A real philanthropist does an act of kindness but does not make himself protuberant, but on the other hand, hides his own identity. Such also is the nature of the sound 'a'. Being a perfect sound, though it hides its identlty, it never loses it. The other vowels lose it sometimes even dwindling into consonants. Thus 'i' becomes[15] 'y' and 'u', 'v' but 'a' always remains the same, so much so that when 'e' formed of 'a' + 'i' happens to undergo a change owing to contact with another vowel, this sound separates itself and reveals its own independence and perfectly immutable identity. Being the first of the alphabet it proceeds from the first place of utterance, viz., the throat and 'm' proceeds from the lips, the last place. But it must be understood that the initial effort towards the pronunciation of a letter is made in the abdomen by forcing the vital air up which passing through the chest and throat gets itself modulated according to the wish of the utterer by a conscious movement of some place of utterance[16]. This latter serves as a sort of hindrance to the escaping air which would otherwise have produced 'a' and which now expresses itself as something else. But it must not be forgotten that all along the vital air has moved up, the sound of 'a' also, though suppressed, has been present with it.

Hence the sound 'a' is equal to God—free from change or corruption—and the same under all circumstances.

The sound 'u' is different from 'a'. It is not simple, elementary or perfect Its pronunciation is more elaborate and grosser than that of 'a'. But it is, like 'a', an independent sound in as much as it does not stand in need of any other letter for its pronunciation. Unlike 'a', 'u' when followed by a dissimilar vowel is changed into the consonant 'v'[15]. Hence as an inde-

---

15 इग्यणः सम्प्रसारणम्, P. I, 1, 45.

16 आकाशवायुप्रभवः शरीरात्समुच्चरन्वक्त्रमुपैति नादः । स्थानान्तरेषु प्रविभज्यमानो वर्णत्वमागच्छति यः स शब्दः ॥ आत्मा बुद्ध्या समेत्यार्थान्मनो युङ्क्ते विवक्षया । मनः कायाग्निमाहन्ति स प्रेरयति मारुतम् ॥ मारुतस्तूरसि चरन्मन्द्रं जनयति स्वरम् ॥ वर्णोच्चारणशिक्षायाम्॥

pendent vowel it is like the liberated soul and when it becomes a consonant it is like the soul that has fallen from the state of liberation into the trammels of births and deaths.

As for 'm', it is a consonant produced in the last place of utterance. It is pronounced by joining the lips together and then opening them simultaneously with the expulsion of the breath. In all its stages it depends upon a vowel for its pronunciation. The stages in its pronunciation, joining the lips and then opening them, represent the two stages of the primordial matter. Sometimes the universe marches towards a subtle state and merges in the primordial matter and sometimes the latter assumes a gross form and appears as the visible universe. The two states of the soul are liberation from and entanglement in the cycle of births and deaths, whereas in the case of the primordial matter they are the subtle and gross states. All these are eternal in their succession. In their mutation the supervision, that is, a designed disposal on the part of the Supreme Being, is the efficient cause so that there may be a just allotment of fruit of actions for the enjoyment of the souls.

The vocal form of 'm' is a dot placed above the vowel concerned. This is invariably associated with an independent vowel and never with a consonant. Prakṛti also can never be made to change her state by souls fettered by the residua of their past actions. Nor can the liberated souls who enjoy unlimited bliss constrain her to change. Primordial matter does not sever its connection with a fettered soul, nor does it force itself upon a liberated soul, for a relation between the two then is futile. Hence it is that in ancient treatises elementary matter has been called Prakṛti, Pradhāna, Avyakta, Māyā, &c., all of which are synonymous terms to describe the incomprehensible power of the Supreme Being.

So much about the Sacred Symbol 'Aum'.

There are other and very good names of the Supreme Being, but before this 'Aum' they pale into insignificance. For example 'Rāma' is derived from the root 'rama' to sport with the suffix 'ghañ' or 'ṇa' and means One Who is the cause of the world's rejoicing. So also 'Kṛṣṇa' from the root 'kṛś' and termination 'nuk' means One Who attracts all the worlds and all beings towards Himself. Each of these, therefore, connote only one of the attributes of God, hence their use as meditative, ejaculatory prayers, can yield only partial fruit. The devotee, through such imperfect devotion will only attain to one of the attributes of God, whereas, the utterance of and contemplation on 'Aum' will provide the pious soul eighty-seven[17] names of God at one utterance and place before him all His attributes, deeds and nature. Hence the recitation of such partial names is not to be recommended; nay, it is strictly to be prohibited as a substitute for the glorious 'Aum'.

To put any other name before 'Aum' is a sacrilege, hence 'Harih Aum' and such other expressions are to be condemned. It should also be borne in mind that words like 'Hari', 'Rāma', 'Kṛṣṇa', though names of the Supreme Being have been polluted by Puranic association, being names of good and great men disreputed by profane sectarian writers.

The recitation of 'Aum' must always be accompanied by contemplation which itself should be connected with practice in daily life. Any other method would simply result in waste of time.

---

[17] Vide frontispiece.

A consideration of the written character representing this sacred symbol 'Aum is also replete with interest. The simplest and the oldest way of writing 'Aum' was ओँ, and fully grammatically developed, ओ३म् or ओ३ँ. This last while writing hastily (?) gave rise to the beautiful form ॐ. This is a wonderful letter combining in itself all the principal elements of all the Nāgarī vowels and consonants. Its curious and universal, formation is such as to adapt it to the alphabet of any language in use in the world. How old this written symbol is, has not, it seems, yet been decided by scholars. The Swastikā as well as the Cross are both developed from ॐ.

Nay, the image of Ganēśa, the elephant-headed god of the Purāṇas is clearly a manipulation of this letter. The Ganēśapurāṇa is witness to this, for, it says:—"The majestic Lord in the form of the Auṃkara established in the beginning of the Vedas is always borne in their hearts by Indra and all the gods and by sages. This Lord in the form of the Auṃkāra is called Gaṇanāyaka the leader (lord?) of hosts, and as he is invoked with reverence in all works, he is called Vināyaka (true guide)[18]".

Some say that the symbol ॐ is a short-hand representation of the Sacred Gāyatrī. Whatever it may be, it is a very artistic symbol and India seems to be the only country that can boast of such a beautiful and unique one-lettered symbol to represent the most important name of the Supreme Being. Just as God is unique and outside the universe though the whole universe is sheltered in Him, this symbol also is unique and outside the alphabet, though all the letters of the

[18] ओंकाररूपो भगवान्यो वेदादौ प्रतिष्ठितः । यं सदा मुनयो देवा स्मरन्तीन्द्रादयो हृदि ॥ ओंकाररूपो भगवानुक्तस्तु गणनायकः । यथा सर्वेषु कर्मेषु पूज्यते सो विनायकः ॥ गणेशपुराणे ॥

alphabet are made of elements which can easily be derived from it

The second interpretation of the verse alludes to a number of texts from the Yajurvêda condemning idolatry or use of images for the purpose of mental concentration. These are Yajurvêda XXV, 10-13 of which 10, 11 and 13 are the same as Nos. 2-4 of the stanzas given under the heading 'Prayers and Exhortations' in the beginning of this work. The twelfth when translated means :—

"Oh men ! let us offer all worship to that All-blissful, Glorious Being through Whose Majesty these snow-covered mountains are standing and to Whom belongs the intermediate region which the waters, held together by their viscous nature, fill. Indeed these vast quarters of the universe are His arms, so to say, embracing the whole cosmos"[19].

The 102nd verse of the 12th chapter says :—

"May the Lord of Truth and Righteousness, Creator of the earth Who has also created the heavens and pervades all these and Who, the Unborn, having brought into being waters and the luminous bodies like the (sun), moon &c., (sustains them), not inflict upon us (punishment in the form of) unbearable suffering (brought about by being estranged from Him through evil company). Let us, with heart and soul, offer all worship to that Glorious, All-blissful God (and none else)"[20].

The two stanzas 36 and 37 of Chapter VIII are as follows :—

---

[19] यस्येमे हिमवन्तो महित्वा यस्य समुद्रं रसया सहाहुः। यस्येमाः प्रदिशो यस्य बाहू कस्मै देवाय हविषा विधेम ॥ य० २५ । १२ ॥

[20] मा मा हिंसीज्जनिता यः पृथिव्या यो वा दिवं सत्यधर्मा व्यानट्। यश्चापश्चन्द्राः प्रथमो जजान कस्मै देवाय हविषा विधेम ॥ य० १२ । १०२ ॥

"That Supreme Being than Whom no other and greater is born, Who pervades the whole universe and Who, being the Lord of creatures remains and sports with them, creates (and imparts lustre to) the three luminaries (the sun, fire and electricity). From Him originate the sixteen digits (life or breath, faith, ether, air, light, water, earth, the senses, desire, food, seed, powers, the Vedas (right knowledge and revelation), action, place and name (individual) [21] which he unites with embodied beings."[22]

"A very powerful sovereign ruler and a prince-general possessing justice and other great qualities, protect you, oh people, for the peaceful enjoyment of life. After these, should I (your preceptor) myself enjoy of the good things of the world and help you also to do so. Thus may we all (the leaders and the led) leading honest lives in accordance with the teachings of the Vedas—the word of God—the source of all true learning, acquire vital vigour and attain to happiness."[23]

According to these seven verses the reasons against idolatry can be given roughly, as follows :—

(1) God is the Creator of all planets and He sustains them also. This attribute cannot be reproduced in any 'likeness' of God, however skilfully made. (Y. V. XXV, 10).

(2) Man cannot represent in any image His Most Awful Majesty which the high mountains, the

---

[21] पिप्पलाद says to सुकेशा—इहैवान्तः शरीरे सोम्य स पुरुषो यस्मिन्नेताः षोडश-कलाः प्रभवन्तीति । स प्राणमसृजत । प्राणाच्छ्रद्धां खं वायुर्ज्योतिरापः पृथिवीमिन्द्रियं मनः । अन्नमन्नाद्वीर्यं तपो मंत्राः कर्म लोका लोकेषु नाम च ॥ प्र० ६ । २ ; ४ ॥

[22] यस्मान्न जातः परो अन्योऽस्ति य आविवेश भुवनानि विश्वा । प्रजापतिः प्रजया संरराणस्त्रीणि ज्योतींषि सचते स षोडशी ॥ ८ । ३६ ॥

[23] इन्द्रश्च सम्राड्वरुणश्च राजा तौ ते भक्षं चक्रतुरग्र एतम् । तयोरहमनु भक्षं भक्षयामि वाग्देवी जुषाणा सोमस्य तृप्यतु सह प्राणेन स्वाहा ॥ य० ८ । ३७ ॥

unfathomable sea and the meandering rivers so wonderfully declare. (Y. V. XXV, 11).

(3) The knowledge of the Supreme Being as well as the individual soul and strength physical, mental and spiritual, are His gifts which cannot be got from any idol as it is an inanimate object made by man. (Y. V. XXV, 12).

(4) He rules over all which no idol can do. If some, through foolishness worship idols, there are others who break them. But all adore God under some name or other. (Y. V. XXV, 13).

(5) He is the Creator of the universe and all the elements but is Himself Unborn. Besides this, a devotee of the True God when he falls into bad company and forgets Him, feels unhappy and repents ; but an idolator changes his idols with an easy conscience and commits all sorts of sins along with his idol-worship. Hence an idol cannot be a true representation of God. (Y. V. XII, 102).

(6) He is the Greatest of all. Among beings that are born or known, none is so great as He. He pervades the whole universe and all beings. It is He that by His Omnipotent Holy Will puts together all tha ingredients of which beings embodied are framed and it is He also, that gives light and heat to the sun, electricity and fire. No idol has ever been made having these qualities and powers. (Y. V. VIII, 36).

(7) The Vedas—the source of all right knowledge—according to which all great kings, generals, leaders and teachers of men guide themselves, are revealed by Him. All true and useful knowledge is imparted to human beings by Him. An idol cannot do this. (Y. V. VIII, 37).

(३४) एषो ह देवः प्रदिशोऽनु सर्वाः पूर्वो ह जातः स उ गर्भे अन्तः। स एव जातः स जनिष्यमाणः प्रत्यङ् जनास्तिष्ठति सर्वतोमुखः ॥४॥

पदपाठः—एषः। ह। देवः। प्रदिशऽइति प्रऽदिशः। अनु। सर्वाः। पूर्वः। ह। जातः। सः। ऊँऽइत्यूँ। गर्भे। अन्तरित्यन्तः। सः। एव। जातः। सः। जनिष्यमाणः। प्रत्यङ्। जनाः। तिष्ठति। सर्वतोमुख इति सर्वतःऽमुखः ॥

अन्वयः—हे जना एषो ह देवः सर्वाः प्रदिशोऽनुव्याप्य स उ गर्भेऽन्तः पूर्वो ह जातः स एव जातः स जनिष्यमाणः सर्वतोमुखः प्रत्यङ् तिष्ठति स युष्माभिरुपासनीयो वेदितव्यश्च ॥

Word-meaning &c. :—एषः=this Supreme Being. (In this form the termination of Nom. sing. has not been elided as usual). ह=well-known. प्रदिशः (प्र + √दिश अतिसर्जने + क्विन् P. III, 2, 59)=the intermediate quarters; all the quarters अनु=pervading. सर्वाः=all. पूर्वः=before the primordial creatiod. जातः=manifested Himself. गर्भे=in the heart. अन्तः=in the innermost recesses. जनिष्यमाणः (√जनी प्रादुर्भावे + स्य + शानच् P. III, 1, 33; 2, 127 and 3, 14)=wlll manifest Himself in the coming ages or creations. प्रत्यङ् (प्रतिपदार्थमञ्चतीति प्रति + √अञ्चू गतिपूजनयोः + क्विन् P. III, 2, 59; VI, 4, 24 and VIII, 2, 62)= occupying, pervading or being immanent in every object. (हे) जनाः=oh wise men ! तिष्ठति=He is everywhere immovable. सर्वतोमुखः (सर्वतः मुखादयः अवयवाः यस्य) Whose limbs, viz., mouth &c., are everywhere, that is, Who everywhere accomplishes the work which can be done by the mouth and other limbs.

Translation :—Oh men ! this Supreme Being, indeed, pervades all the quarters. Verily He resides in the heart of all creatures. He manifested Himself before the first creation and will manifest Himself in all the future creations. Himself without limbs, He accomplishes everywhere the work assigned to the limbs (and senses), and is firmly established (by His Immanence) in every object. It is He Whom you should know and adore.

Purport :—God Almighty manifests Himself before all the creations, that is He is ever manifest, or ever the same, whereas matter is not so, assuming as it does sometimes the form of gross evolutes and sometimes the atomic primordial state. Most subtle Himself and not pervaded by anything, He pervades all. Himself without the motor and sense organs, He does everywhere the work for which they are adapted. Though transcending space itself, His place is in the innermost recesses of the hearts of all creatures. None but the thoughtful, therefore, can realise Him.

(३५) यस्माज्जातं न पुरा किं च नैव य आबभूव भुवनानि विश्वा । प्रजापतिः प्रजया संरराणस्त्रीणि ज्योतींषि सचते स षोडशी ॥५॥

पदपाठः—यस्मात् । जातम् । न । पुरा । किम् । चन । एव । यः । आबभूवेत्याऽबभूव । भुवनानि । विश्वा । प्रजापतिरिति प्रजाऽपतिः । प्रजया । संरराण इति सम्ऽरराणः । त्रीणि । ज्योतींषि । सचते । सः । षोडशी ॥

अन्वयः—हे मनुष्या यस्मात्पुरा किञ्चन न जातं यस्सर्वत आबभूव यस्मिन्विश्वा भुवनानि वर्तन्ते स एव षोडशी प्रजया सह संरराणः प्रजापतिस्त्रीणि ज्योतींषि सचते ॥

Word-meaning &c.:—यस्मात्=the Supreme Being. जातम्=born; produced. न=not. पुरा=before. किम् चन=anything. आबभूव=Who exists everywhere. विश्वा (P. VI, 1, 70)=all. भुवनानि=the worlds which support all things. प्रजापतिः=the Protector or Controller of all creatures प्रजया=with the creatures. सम् रराणः (√रमु+कानच् P. III, 2, 106; the final म् is irregularly dropped; or √रा दाने or √रै शब्दे+कानच्)=sporting well; imparting or bestowing benefits on all; revealing the Vedas. त्रीणि ज्योतींषि=the three luminous objects, fire, electricity and the sun. सचते=unites. षोडशी (षोडश+इनि P. V, 2, 115 षोडश कला यस्मिन्सन्ति सः)= Master of the sixteen digits i. e., the 16 items mentioned on page 97 paragraph 1 and in footnote 21, which He unites while creating finite beings.

Translation :—Oh men! than Whom nothing can be said to have come into being earlier in time and Who is Immanent everywhere in the universe, that Lord of creatures remains sporting with the created beings uniting with them the three luminaries (the sun, electricity and fire) and the sixteen digits.

Purport :—God is Unborn and Eternal. Therefore nothing can be older than He in time. It is He that assigns to all souls fruit according to their actions. For the rest see page 97 and footnote No. 21.

(३६) येन द्यौरुग्रा पृथिवी च दृढा येन स्वः स्तभितं येन नाकः। यो अन्तरिक्षे रजसो विमानः कस्मै देवाय हविषा विधेम ॥६॥

पदपाठः—येन। द्यौः। उग्रा। पृथिवी। च। दृढा। येन। स्वरिति स्वः। स्तभितम्। येन। नाकः। यः। अन्तरिक्षे। रजसः। विमानऽइति विऽमानः। कस्मै। देवाय। हविषा। विधेम ॥

अन्वयः—हे मनुष्या येनोग्रा द्यौः पृथिवी च दृढा येन स्वः स्तभितं येन नाकः स्तभितो योऽन्तरिक्षे वर्तमानस्य रजसो विमानोऽस्ति तस्मै कस्मै देवाय वयं हविषा विधेम ॥

Word-meaning &c. :—द्यौः=luminaries like the sun and other planets. उग्रा (√उच समवाये+रन्+टाप् U. II,

28 and P. IV, 1, 4)=formidable, giving out strong light. पृथिवी (√प्रथ प्रख्याने+षिवन्+ङीष् U. I, 150 and P. IV, 1, 41)=the earth and other planets. दृढा=firmly established in their orbits. स्वः=happiness falling to the share of each soul. स्तभितम्=established or declared on a just and firm basis. नाकः (न कम्—अकम्, न अकम्—नाकम्* P. VI, 3, 75 or √णीञ् प्रापणे+आक U. IV, 13 and 15)=emancipation, final beatitude.‡ अन्तरिक्ष (अन्तर्+√ईक्ष दर्शने+घञ् P. III, 3, 19 or अन्तर्मध्ये ऋक्षाणि नक्षत्राणि यस्य P. VI, 3, 109 or अन्तरा इमे क्षयो यस्य or शरीरेषु अन्तर् अक्षयम्) the intermediate region. रजसः§ (√रञ्ज रागे+असुन् U. IV, 189 and 217)=worlds, planets. विमानः वि+√माङ् माने ल्युट्)=Creator, Disposer, Measurer.

For translation see page 2.

Purport :—Human beings should adore only that God Who is the Supporter of the whole universe, the Bestower of all bliss including that of emancipation and is infinitely more pervasive than space (ether) itself.

(३७) यं क्रन्दसी अवसा तस्तभाने अभ्यैक्षेतां मनसा रेजमाने । यत्राधि सूर उदितो विभाति कस्मै देवाय हविषा विधेम आपो ह यद्बृहतीर्यश्चिदापः ॥७॥

पदपाठः—यम् । क्रन्दसीऽइति क्रन्दसी । अवसा । तस्तभाने ऽइति तस्तऽभाने । अभि । ऐक्षेताम् । मनसा । रेजमानेऽइति रेजमाने । यत्र । अधि । सूरः । उदितऽइत्युत्ऽइत । विभातीति विऽभाति ।

---

* नाक आदित्यो भवति । नेता रसानां । नेता भासां । ज्योतिषां प्रणयः । अथ द्यौः । कमिति सुखनाम तत्प्रतिषिद्धं प्रतिषिध्येत ॥ नि० २ । १४ ॥

‡ अन्तरिक्षं कस्मादन्तरा क्षान्तं भवति । अन्तरेमे इति वा । शरीरेष्वन्तरक्षयमिति वा ॥ नि० २ । १० ॥

§ रजो रजतेर्ज्योती रज उच्यते । उदकं रज उच्यते । लोका रजांस्युच्यन्ते । असृगहनी रजसी उच्येते ॥ नि० ४ । १६ ॥

कस्मै । देवाय । हविषा । विधेम । आपः । ह । यत् । बृहतीः । यः । चित् । आपः ॥

अन्वयः—यं परमात्मानं प्राप्ते तस्तभाने रेजमाने क्रन्दसी अवसा सर्वं धरतो यत्र सूरोऽध्युदितो यद् बृहतीरापो ह यश्चिदापः सन्ति ताश्चिदपि विभाति तं तौ चाध्यापकोपदेशकौ मनसाऽभ्यैक्षेतां । तस्मै कस्मै देवाय वयं हविषा विधेम ॥

Word-meaning &c. :—क्रन्दसी (√क्रदि आह्वाने रोदने च or irregularly क्रमु पादविक्षेपे+असुन् U. IV, 189+ङीप् P. IV, 1, 6)=the earth and the sun. अवसा (√अव रक्षणे &c. +असुन्)=protection or support. तस्तभाने (√ष्टभि प्रतिबन्धे +कानच् P. III, 1, 106)=that uphold all. अभि ऐक्षेताम्= both the preceptor and the preacher should look up to. मनसा (√मन ज्ञाने+असुन्)=by means of special or right knowledge. रेजमाने (√रेजृ कम्पने+शानच्)=moving. यत्र= in Whom. अधि उदितः=risen up. विभाति=shines well; thrives; becomes manifest. हविषा=by means of spiritual discipline worth undergoing. विधेम=we should serve or adore. बृहतीः (√बृह्+शतृ+ङीप्)=great. आपः waters; atmosphere; vital air*; space (ether). यः चित् whatever,

Translation :—In Whom the earth and the sun moving in their fixed orbits support all creatures, Wherin the sun rises and fully shines forth, the vital air thrives and space becomes manifest, Him should the preceptors and guides of mankind by means of right knowledge look up to. Let us all, undergoing fitting spiritual discipline adore that All-blissful God with heart and soul.

Purport :—Man should adore only tnat Supreme Being Who is Immanent in all, in Whom the revolving sun, earth and other planets have their stability and by Whom vital air and space are pervaded.

---

* प्राणा वा आपः ॥ तै० ३ । २ । ५ । २ ॥ तां० ६ । ६ । ४ ॥ आपो वै प्राणः ॥ श० ३ । ८ । २ । ४ ॥

(३८) वेनस्तत्पश्यन्निहितं गुहा सद्यत्र विश्वं भवत्येकनीडम्। तस्मिन्निदꣳ सं च वि चैति सर्वꣳ स ओतः प्रोतश्च विभूः प्रजासु ॥८॥

पदपाठः—वेनः। तत्। पश्यत्। निहितमिति निऽहितम्। गुहा। सत्। यत्र। विश्वम्। भवति। एकनीडमित्येकऽनीडम्। तस्मिन्। इदम्। सम्। च। वि। च। एति। सर्वम्। सः। ओत इत्याऽउतः। प्रोतऽइति प्रऽउतः। च। विभूरिति विऽभूः। प्रजास्विति प्रऽजासु॥

अन्वयः—यत्र विश्वमेकनीडं भवति तद्गुहा निहितं सद्वेनः पश्यत्। तस्मिन्निदं सर्वं समेति च व्येति च स विभूः प्रजास्वोतः प्रोतश्चास्ति॥

Word-meaning &c. :—वेनः (√अज गतिक्षेपणयोः+न U. III, 6 or √वेनति कान्तिकर्मा* +घ P. III, 3, 118)=a wise or enlightened person (Nig. II, 15). तत्=that Supreme Being. पश्यत्=sees with his mental eye. निहितम् (नि√डुधाञ् धारणपोषणयोः+क्त P. III, 2, 102 and VII, 4, 42)= existing, being; established. गुहा (√गुहू संवरणे+क+टाप् P. III, 1. 135; IV, 1, 4 and VII, 1, 39,=in the intellect or mind; in the unmanifest cause of the universe. सत्=eternal. यत्र=wherein. विश्वम्=the whole universe. भवति=is, becomes. एकनीडम् (एकम् नीडम् यस्य तत्)=having one refuge or shelter. सम् एति=comes together in its subtle form at the time of dissolution वि एति=gets separated into gross forms at the time of creation. ओतः आ+वेञ् तन्तुसन्ताने+क्त P III, 2, 102 and VI, 1, 16)=(vertically) like the warp. प्रोतः=(horizontally) like the woof. ओतश्च प्रोतश्च=pervading through and through by His Providence and Immanence. विभू (वि√भू सत्तायाम्+क्विप्) =All-pervading.

* वेनो वेनतेः कान्तिकर्मणः॥ नि० १०। १८॥

Translation :—The enlightened man perceives in his (own) mind that Supreme Being in Whom the whole universe has its one refuge. The whole universe (with all the objects in it) comes together at the time of dissolution, in its subtle form in Him, and becomes separated into gross forms at the time of creation. He pervades all beings through and through like the warp and woof of a piece of cloth.

Purport :—Only the wise man knows that Being the Refuge of all beings in Whom the whole universe, so to say, merges at the time of dissolution and from Whom it proceeds at the time of creation and without Whom nothing exists. He alone should be adored and none else.

(३६) प्र तद्वोचेदमृतं नु विद्वान्गन्धर्वो धाम विभृतं गुहा सत्। त्रीणि पदानि निहिता गुहास्य यस्तानि वेद स पितुः पितासत् ॥६॥

पदपाठः—प्र । तत् । वोचेत् । अमृतम् । नु । विद्वान् । गन्धर्वः । धाम । विभृतमिति विऽभृतम् । गुहा । सत् । त्रीणि । पदानि । निहितेति निऽहिता । गुहा । अस्य । यः । तानि । वेद । सः । पितुः । पिता । असत् ॥

अन्वयः—यो गन्धर्वो विद्वान्गुहा विभृतममृतं धाम तत्सन्नु प्रवोचेद्यान्यस्य गुहा निहितानि पदानि त्रीणि सन्ति तानि च वेद स पितुः पिताऽसत् ॥

Word-meaning &c. :—प्र वोचेत् (P. III, 1, 86 and VII, 4, 20)=teaches about (the attributes, actions and nature of). तत्=that Supreme Being. अमृतम् (नञ्+मृङ् मरणे=क्त P. III, 2, 102 or तन् U. III, 88)=imperishable. नु=quickly ; at once ; surely. विद्वान् (√विद ज्ञाने+वसु P. III, 2, 124 and VII, 1, 36)=wise, learned, enlightened. गन्धर्वः (गां वेदवाचं धरति—गो+√धृञ् धारणे+व U. I, 155 and P. VI, 3, 109)=Who supports, that is, protects by learning and propagating. धाम (√डुधाञ् धारण पोषणयोः+मनिन् U. IV, 145)=state or abode of emancipation. विभृतम् (वि √भृञ् भरणे or √डुभृञ् धारण-पोषणयोः+क्त P. III, 2, 102)=well supported, preserved or protected. गुहा=in the intellect. सत्=eternal. त्रीणि=the three states of creation, continuity in existence and dissolution; the three divisions of time, viz., the past, the present and the future. पदानि (√पद गतौ +अच्)=states or positions (of the universe) worth knowing. वेद=knows. पितुः=of the father or elder; of God the Father of all. पिता=protector, supporter by a faithful practice and propagation of the Vedic teachings. पितुः पिता असत्=will be respected even among elderly and experienced people.

Translation :—That wise man the protector of the revealed Vedas (by practice and propagation) who forthwith teaches mankind about the Eternal and Imperishable Supreme Being, the Abode of emancipation well borne (understood or realised) by the rational faculty and who understands the three states (creation, continuance and dissolution or past, present and future) of the universe (which are worth knowing and are) established in His mind, deserves to be respected even among the elderly and experienced.

Purport :—Wise men who realise that aspect of the Supreme Being which is the basis of the emancipation of the individual soul and which is stationed in our rational faculty, and who accurately understand the attributes, actions and nature of things and God Almighty are worthier of respect than even the aged. Manu says :—"An ignorant person is like a child and he who is able to interpret vedic statements is like a father. Hence the wise call him who is lacking in knowledge a child and him who can explain the Vedas 'father'."*

(४०) स नो बन्धुर्जनिता स विधाता धामानि वेद भुवनानि विश्वा। यत्र देवा अमृतमानशानास्तृतीये धामन्नध्यैरयन्त ॥१०॥

पदपाठः—सः। नः। बन्धुः। जनिता। सः। विधातेति विऽधाता। धामानि।। वेद। भुवनानि। विश्वा। यत्र। देवाः। अमृतम्। आनशानाः। तृतीये। धामन्। अध्यैरयन्तेत्यधिऽऐरयन्त॥

अन्वयः—यत्र तृतीये धामन्नमृतमानशाना देवा अध्यैरयन्त यो विश्वा भुवनानि धामानि च वेद स नो बन्धुर्जनिता स विधाताऽस्ति॥

Word-meaning &c. :—सः=that Supreme Being. नः=our. बन्धुः (√बन्ध बन्धने+उ U. I, 7 and 10)=Brother; Well-wisher. जनिता (√जनी प्रादुर्भावे or √जन जनने+णिच्+तृच् P. III, 1, 26 ; 133 and VI, 4, 53)=Producer. विधाता (वि+√डुधाञ् धारणपोषणयोः+तृन् P. III, 2, 135)=Supporter; Who impels by imparting motive force. धामानि= source, place and name. वेद=knows (by direct contact). भुवनानि=the worlds. विश्वा (for विश्वानि according to P. VI, 1, 70)=all. यत्र=in Whom. देवाः= the enlightened. अमृतम्=the bliss of emancipation. आनशानाः (√अशू व्याप्तौ+कानच् P. III, 2, 106)=attain, acquire, obtain. तृतीये=third ; different from the primordial matter and the individual soul. धामन् (धामनि P. VII, 1, 39)=place ; source. तृतीये धामन्=source of final beatitude ; Who is the source of final beatitude and is quite different from the primordial matter and the individual soul. अध्यैरयन्त (अधि+√ईर)= move about according to wish.

---

* अज्ञो भवति वै बालः पिता भवति मन्त्रदः। अज्ञं हि बालमित्याहुः पितेत्येव तु मन्त्रदम्॥ म० २। १५३॥

For translation see page 3.

Purport :—We should bear in mind that that God alone is Omniscient, Omnipotent and the Help of all at all times in Whom the enlightened and those who have undergone spiritual discipline obtain emancipation and rejoice.

(४१) परीत्यं भूतानिं परीत्यं लोकान्परीत्य सर्वाः प्रदिशो दिशंश्च । उपस्थायं प्रथमजामृतस्यात्मनात्मानं-मभि संविवेश ॥११॥

पदपाठः—परीत्येतिं परिऽइत्यं । भूतानिं । परीत्येतिं परिऽइत्यं । लोकान् । परीत्येतिं परिऽइत्यं । सर्वाः । प्रदिशऽइतिं प्रऽदिशः । दिशः । च । उपस्थायेत्युंपऽस्थायं । प्रथमजामितिं प्रथमऽजाम् । ऋतस्यं । आत्मनां । आत्मानंम् । अभि । सम् । विवेश ॥

अन्वयः—यो भूतानि परीत्य सर्वाः प्रदिशो दिशश्च परीत्य ऋतस्यात्मानमभिसंविवेश तं जन एव प्रथमजामुपस्थायात्मना प्राप्तुं शक्नोति ॥

Word-meaning &c. :—परीत्य (परि+√इण गतौ+ल्यप् P. VII, 1, 37)=having pervaded from all sides. भूतानि creatures. लोकान् (√लोक दर्शने+घञ् P. III, 3, 19)=the earth, the sun and other planets that can be seen. सर्वाः=all. दिशः=the four principal cardinal points. प्रदिशः=the intermediate quarters. उपस्थाय (उप+√ष्ठा गतिनिवृत्तौ+ल्यप्)=having studied ; having well utilised or practised. प्रथमजाम् (प्रथममुत्पन्नाम्—प्रथम+आ—√जनी+विट् P. III, 2, 67 ; VI, 4, 41)=the Vedic law or the four Vedas revealed at the first creation. ऋतस्य (√ऋ गतौ+क्त P. III, 2, 1C2)=of the truth. आत्मना (√अत सातत्यगमने +मनिण् U. IV, 153)=by means of his heart and soul. आत्मानम्=the essence or source. अभिसंविवेश=pervades by His Immanence. ऋतस्य आत्मानम्=the very essence of truth in thought word and deed.

Translation :—Only an enlightened person can, after studying the eternal Vedic law (and living up to it), realise by a sincere endeavour from his heart and soul that Supreme Being Who encompasses all the creatures and all the worlds, pervades all the quarters of the universe and is Immanent in the very essence of truth (in thought, word and deed).

Purport :—By a righteous living, study of the Vedas, practice of the Yogic spiritual discipline and by associating with the virtuous one should strengthen one's body, educate one's mind and purify one's soul after which it is not difficult to enjoy the bliss of the realisation of God for He is present everywhere.

(४२) परि द्यावापृथिवी सद्य इत्वा परि लोकान्परि दिशः परि स्वः । ऋतस्य तन्तुं विततं विचृत्य तद- पश्यत्तदभवत्तदासीत् ॥१२॥

पदपाठः—परि । द्यावापृथिवीऽइति द्यावापृथिवी । सद्यः । इत्वा । परि । लोकान् । परि । दिशः । परि । स्वरिति स्वः । ऋतस्य । तन्तुम् । विततमिति विऽततम् । विचृत्येति विऽचृत्य । तत् । अपश्यत् । तत् । अभवत् । तत् । आसीत् ॥

अन्वयः—यो द्यावापृथिवी सद्य इत्वा पर्यपश्यद्यो लोकान्सद्य इत्वा पर्यभवद्यो दिशः सद्य इत्वा पर्यासीद्यः स्वः सद्य इत्वा पर्यपश्यद्य ऋतस्य विततं तन्तुं विचृत्य तत्स्थोऽपश्यद्येन तत्स्थोऽभवद्यतस्ताद्विज्ञान- मासीत्तं परमेश्वरं मनुष्या यथावद्विज्ञायोपासीरन् ॥

Word-meaning &c. :—परि=all round. द्यावापृथिवी (द्यौश्च पृथिवी च P. II, 4, 14 and VI, 3, 29)=the sun and the earth. सद्यः (समाने अहनि—स+द्यस् P. V, 3, 22 and Vartika समानस्य सभावो द्यस् चाहनि)=at once, quickly, soon (after creation). इत्वा (√इण् गतौ+क्त्वा P. III, 4, 21) =having come up to, pervaded, occupied, encompassed, surmounted. लोकान्=the different planets, worlds, things which can be seen. स्वः (सु+√ऋ गतौ+विच् or √स्वृ शब्दोपतापयोः+विच् P. III, 2, 75 or सु+√ईर गतौ कम्पने च Nir. II, 14*)=mundane and supra-mundane happiness; bliss. तन्तुम् (√तनु विस्तारे+तुन् U. I. 69)=the cause (which when expanded, yields effects); string, cord. विततम् (वि+√तनु+क्त P. III, 2, 102 and VI, 4, 37) =expanded, spread. विचृत्य (वि+√चृती हिंसाग्रन्थनयोः +ल्यप् P. III, 4, 21 & VII, 1, 37)=having woven or threaded in various ways. ऋतस्य तन्तुं विततं विचृत्य= having strung (the whole cosmos) on the expanded string of the eternal law of truth, i. e., the eternal moral order. तत्=that happiness or bliss. अपश्यत् (√दृशिर् प्रेक्षणे P. VII, 3, 78 & III, 4, 6)=sees; oversees; smiles on; looks on; shines on. Here supply येन or यतः by whom or from whom as its source. तत् अभवत्= that bliss springs. Supply again येन or यतः as before. तत् आसीत्=that is; that knowledge leading to true happiness is available to mankind.

N. B.—The prefix परि in this verse isto connected with each of the verbs अपश्यत्, अभवत, आसीत् & then once again with अपश्यत् to complete the four items. If connected with इत्वा this verse would be a repetition of the previous one. This stanza seems to be an instance of something like the 'parisaṃkhyā alaṃkāra' of the Classical Sanskrit rhitoricians or the aphorism यथासंख्यमनुदेशः समानाम्, P. I, 3, 10, i. e., "when two sets of an equal number things is referred to, each

---

* स्वरादित्यो भवति । सु अरणः सु ईरणः स्वृतो रसान्स्वृतो भासं ज्योतिषां स्वृतो भासेति वा ॥ नि० २ । १४ ॥ स्वरादित्यः । कस्मात् । सु अरणं गमनं तत्सुखाय हिताय वा शोभनं यस्य । सुखप्रतिपत्त्यर्थो विसन्धि पाठः । सर्वत्र शोभनं वा प्रेरणं तमसां यस्य । सुष्ठु वा ऋतो गतो रश्मिभी रसानादातुम् । भासं वा ज्योतिषां नक्षत्रादीनाम् । स्वृतो भासेति कर्मणि क्त इति विशेषः । पूर्वत्र कर्तरि ॥ स्क० भा० ॥

thing from the one set should be taken along with the one which is in the corresponding order in the second." The word तद् is formed from the root √तनु विस्तारे by adding to it the Uṇadi termination अदि (U. I. 130 and 132). Etimologically, therefore, it can be taken to stand either for God, the individual soul or the primordial matter, all concerned in the expansion of atomic matter into the form of creation. It may also mean final beatitude, towards which all the expanse of creation or of human efforts tends ; or it may signify right knowledge the essence of all action either in the shape of creation or human effort. Hence it is related here to the most important word in the verse, viz., √स्वः which means the highest type of happiness, or right knowledge which is essential† and which properly leads to it (सुष्ठु इयर्ति—गच्छति—इति स्वः).

E. g. Sahitya Darpaṇa say :—"When in answer to a question or by a mere assertion when question is put, a number of things from a group mentioned are eliminated as bearing no resemblance to the thing declared and when such elimination is rendered possible either by the mere form of a word used or by the sense it bears, the figures of speech involved is called 'enumeration'—parisaṃkhya."*

A simple instance of this occurs in the Bhagavadgita‡ :—

---

† वेदाहमेतं पुरुषं महान्तमादित्यवर्णं तमसः परस्तात् । तमेव विदित्वाति मृत्युमेति नान्यः पन्था विद्यतेऽयनाय ॥ य० ३१ । १८ ॥

* प्रश्नादप्रश्नतो वाऽपि कथितादस्तुनो भवेत् ॥ तादृगन्य व्यपोहश्चेच्छाब्द आर्थोऽथवा तदा । परिसङ्ख्या——॥ S. D., S. V. Press Bombay II. p. 288.

‡ नैनं छिन्दन्ति शस्त्राणि नैनं दहति पावकः । न चैनं क्लेदयन्त्यापो न शोषयति मारुतः ॥ अच्छेद्योऽयमदाह्योऽयमक्लेद्योऽशोष्य एव च । नित्यः सर्वगतः स्थाणुरचलोऽयं सनातनः ॥ B. G. II, 23 and 24.

" 'T is not Him that thy weapons wound,
'T is not Him that the fire consumes ;
'T is not Him that the Waters wet,
or that Wind's scorching breath dries up.
Safe from wound, He, safe from fire, He,
safe from moisture and drought alike,
Constant, all-pervading, fixéd,
past all motion, He, eternal."

In each of the first four lines of this quotation one thing is mentioned corresponding to which and in the same order, each half of the fifth and sixth lines mentions another thus making the enumeration complete. The first line says—" 't is not Him Thy weapons wound" in answer to which the first half of the fifth line says—"safe from wound, He," and so on.

Translation :—Man should (try to) know in reality and adore that Supreme Being Who having pervaded the earth at once (after creation)* oversees all (in it), Who (just then) reaching all the other worlds (by His immanence) surrounds them all, Who (at the same time) encompassing all the quarters fully occupies them, Who (in the meanwhile) surmounting (the sphere of) mundane and supra-mundane happiness, smiles on all, Who having (forthwith) strung the whole cosmos on the string of the eternal law of truth, surveys all, from Whom true happiness† is sprung and by Whose grace true knowledge leading to it is available to mankind.

Purport :—Only by adoring the True God and utilising the universe created by Him for one's own and others' just enjoyment, men can forthwith attain to mundane and supramundane happiness as well as

---

* स तपस्तप्त्वेदं सर्वमसृजत यदिदं किञ्च। तत्सृष्ट्वा तदेवानुप्राविशत् ॥तै॰उ॰२।६॥

† तदेतदिति मन्यन्तेऽनिर्देश्यं परमं सुखं । कथं नु तद्विजानीयां किमु भाति विभाति वा ॥ क॰ ५ । १४ ॥

the bliss imparted by right knowledge and rejoice all through their life.

(४३) सद॑सस्पति॒मद्भु॑तं प्रि॒यमिन्द्र॑स्य॒ काम्य॑म्। स॒निं मे॒धाम॑यासि॒षं॒स्वाहा॑ ॥१३॥

पदपाठः—सद॑सः। पति॑म्। अद्भु॑तम्। प्रि॒यम्। इन्द्र॑स्य। काम्य॑म्। स॒निम्। मे॒धाम्। अ॒या॒सि॒षम्। स्वाहा॑ ॥

अन्वयः—हे मनुष्या अहं स्वाहा यं सदसस्पतिमद्भुतमिन्द्रस्य काम्यं प्रियं परमात्मानमुपास्य सनिं मेधामयासिषं तं परिचर्यैतां यूयमपि प्राप्नुत ॥

Word-meaning &c :—सदसः (√षद्लृ विशरणगत्यवसादनेषु+असुन् U. IV, 189)=of the assembly, wisdom, justice, sanction. **पतिम्**=lord, protector. **अद्भुतम्** (√अत सातत्यगमने+क्विप्=अत् or अद् [=अकस्मात् indeclinable]+√भू सत्तायाम् or √भा दीप्तौ+डुतच् U. V. 1)=of wonderful attributes, action and nature. **प्रियम्** (√प्रीञ् प्रीतौ+क P. III, 1, 135 & VI, 4, 77)=beloved; he who pleases or satisfies. **इन्द्रस्य** (√इदि परमैश्वर्ये+रन् U. II, 28)=the individual soul * the lord of the sense organs†. **काम्यम्** (√कमु कान्तौ+ण्यत्, P. III, 1, 124)=desirable, longed for. **सनिम्**

---

* इन्द्रियमिन्द्रलिङ्गमिन्द्रदृष्टमिन्द्रसृष्टमिन्द्रजुष्टमिन्द्रदत्तमिति, P. V, 2, 93. On this the Kasikakara says इन्द्रशब्दात्षष्ठी समर्थाल्लिङ्गमित्येतस्मिन्नर्थे घच्प्रत्ययो भवति। इन्द्रस्य लिङ्गमिन्द्रियम्। इन्द्र आत्मा स चक्षुरादिना करणेनानुमीयते ॥

† Yaska gives 15 derivations of the word Indra among which one means the soul :—१) इन्द्र इरां दृणातीति वा। २) इरां ददातीति वा। ३) इरां दधातीति वा। ४) इरां दारयत इति वा। ५) इरां धारयत इति वा। ६) इन्दवे द्रवतीति वा। ७) इन्दौ रमत इति वा। ८) इन्धे भूतानीति वा। ९) तद्यदेनं प्राणैः समैन्धंस्तदिन्द्रस्येन्द्रत्वमिति विज्ञायते। १०) इदं करणादित्याग्रयणः। ११) इदं दर्शनादित्यौपमन्यवः। १२) इन्दतेर्वैश्वर्यकर्मणः। १३) इन्दञ्छत्रूणां दारयिता वा। १४) द्रावयिता वा। १५) आदरयिता च यज्वनाम् ॥ नि० १०। ८ ॥

No. 9 in the above means the soul which is glorified through the senses (and the vital air) by the enlightened. The other derivations mean, lightening, king &c.

(√षत्र संमर्द्धो+इः U. IV, 140)=by which truth and untruth can be properly distinguished. मेधाम् (√मिधृ or √मेधृ संगमे च+घञ्+टाप्) excellent intellegence. भयासिषम् May I attain to. स्वाहा§ (सु+आह्+ √ह्वेञ् आह्वाने or सु+√ब्रूञ् व्यक्तायां वाचि+घञ्+डा P. III, 3, 18; 4, 84, & VII, 1, 39 all cases) maintaining truth in thought word and deed .(परिचर्य=serving; adoring).

Translation :—May I, by maintaining truth in thought, word and deed and adoring that Supreme Being the Lord of wisdom, the Wonderful, the Beloved and Desired of my soul, attain to that excellent intellect which is always successful in distinguishing between right and wrong. Oh men! you also should act likewise and obtain such wisdom.

Purport :—Those who resort to God Almighty by sincerely living righteous lives, are blessed with all true knowledge and a clear understanding of things which secure them all happiness in life.

(४४) यां मेधां देवगणाः पितरश्चोपासते । तया मामद्य मेधयाग्ने मेधाविनं कुरु स्वाहा ॥१४॥

पदपाठः—याम् । मेधाम् । देवगणा इति देवऽगणाः । पितरः । च । उपासत इत्युपऽआसते । तया । माम् । अद्य । मेधया । अग्ने । मेधाविनम् । कुरु । स्वाहा ॥

अन्वयः—हे अग्ने देवगणाः पितरश्च यां मेधामुपासते तया मेधया मामद्य स्वाहा मेधाविनं कुरु ॥

Word-meaning &c:—मेधाम्=right knowledge, discriminative knowledge. देवगणाः (देवानां गणाः P. II, 2, 8)= numbers of the enlightened or wise. पितरः=those good and wise people who protect others. उपासते= obtain and utilise or enjoy. मेधाविनम् (मेधा+विनि P. V.

§ Yaska's explanation is as follows :—स्वाहेत्येतत्सु आहेति वा स्वा वागाहेति वा स्वं प्राहेति वा, स्वाहुतं हविर्जुहोतीति वा ॥ नि० ८ । २० ॥

2, 121)=he who possesses superior discriminative understanhing. स्वाहा=by truthfulness in speech.

Translation :—Oh Effulgent God! make me a possessor of superior discriminative understanding by bestowing on me through truthful conduct that wisdom which the enlightened and the protectors of society, by Thy grace, attain to and utilise.

Purport :—All men should, by adoring God and associating with the enlightened acquire knowledge and wealth, help others also to do so and serve humanity.

(४५) मेधां मे वरुणो ददातु मेधामग्निः प्रजापतिः।
मेधामिन्द्रश्च वायुश्च मेधां धाता ददातु मे स्वाहा ॥१५॥

पदपाठः—मेधाम् । मे । वरुणः । ददातु । मेधाम् । अग्निः । प्रजापतिरिति प्रजाऽपतिः । मेधाम् । इन्द्रः । च । वायुः । च । मेधाम् । धाता । ददातु । मे स्वाहा ॥

अन्वयः—हे मनुष्या यथा जगदीश्वरो वरुणः स्वाहा मे मेधां ददातु यथाग्निः प्रजापतिर्मे मेधां ददातु यथेन्द्रो मे मेधां ददातु यथा वायुश्च मे मेधां ददातु यथा धाता च मे मेधां ददातु तथा युष्मभ्यमपि ददातु ॥

Word-meaning &c:—मेधा=wisdom; right understanding; quickness of intellect &c. वरुण (√वृञ् वरणे + उनन् U. III, 53)=God the Just (Who elects His devotees or is elected by them). ददातु=May He give, favour with, confer, bestow &c. अग्नि=God the Illuminator of all. प्रजापतिः=The Lord of all creatures. इन्द्रः=God the Omnipotent, the most Opulent. वायुः=God the Source of vitality and strength. धाता=God the Supporter of the cosmos. स्वाहा=Through righteous acts.

Translation :—May God the Just, the Elected of His devotees grant me wisdom through righteous deeds. May God the Effulgent, the Lord of all creatures favour me with right understanding. May God the Omnipotent, the Source of all vitality and strength confer on me the faculty to discriminate between right and wrong.

Purport :—All men should adore the True God and pray to Him to grant to them as well as others discriminative understanding. Mere praying will not do; there should be proper righteous deeds to back it. Prayer heartens one and is an incentive to action. Whenever one prays to God or associates with the wise or learned one should invariably pray for or enquire about one's own as well as others' moral and intellectual advancement which is the very foundation of all progress, social, moral or spiritual.

(४६) इदं मे ब्रह्म च क्षत्रं चोभे श्रियमश्नुताम् ।
मयि देवा दधतु श्रियमुत्तमां तस्यै ते स्वाहा ॥१६॥

पदपाठः—इदम् । मे । ब्रह्म । च । क्षत्रम् । च । उभेऽइत्युभे । श्रियम् । अश्नुताम । मयि । देवाः । दधतु । श्रियम । उत्तमामित्युत्ऽतमाम । तस्यै । ते । स्वाहा ॥

अन्वयः—ईशकृपया विदुषां पुरुषार्थेन च स्वाहा ममेदं ब्रह्म च क्षत्रं चोभे श्रियमश्नुतां यथा देवा मय्युत्तमां श्रियं दधतु तथाऽन्येष्वपि । हे जिज्ञासो ते तस्यै वयं प्रयतेमहि ॥

Word-meaning &c:—इदम् (√इदि परमैश्वर्ये + कमिन् U. IV, 157)=this. ब्रह्म (√बृह or √बृहि वृद्धौ + मनिन् U. 146)=the Vedas, the knowledge revealed by God; the person who is learned in the Vedas. क्षत्रम् (√क्षद भक्षणे + त्र U. IV, 167 or √क्षणु वधे + क्विप् + √त्रैङ् पालने + ड, P. III, 2, 178; Vartika गमादीनामिति वक्तव्यम्; डप्रकरणेऽन्येष्वपि

इष्यते and II, 2, 19 or √क्षणु+क्त+ √त्रैङ्+ड)=kingdom, royalty; the art and science of warfare; the warrior class. उभे=both. श्रियम् (√श्रिञ् सेवायाम्+क्विप् U. II, 57)= splendour, wealth, glory. अश्नुताम्=May both enjoy, attain to, obtain. मयि=on me. देवाः=The enlightened, learned, wise, the beneficent forces of nature. दधतु= may support, bestow on, strengthen with. उत्तमाम् (उत् +तमप् P. V, 3, 55; or उत्+√तमु इच्छायाम्+अच् P. III, 1, 134)=excellent, best. तस्यै=for (the acquisition of) that splendour, greatness or wealth &c. ते=for thee, for you. स्वाहा=by righeons conduct or deeds. (ईशकृपया=by the grace of God. पुरुषार्थेन=by effort or endeavour. प्रयतेमहि= we shall try, make efforts. जिज्ञासो=oh seeker after Truth).

Translation :—By the grace of God and the efforts of the learned, may I, along with those members of my community who are learned in the Vedic law and those who are proficient in the art of war attain to excellent prosperity through rectitude of life. May the enlightened help me as well as others to advance towards such prosperity. Oh seeker after Truth! may we make all efforts that thou be blessed with such prosperity.

Purport :—Those men deserve to be respected by all, who act according to the commandments of God, associate with the enlightened, and help others to advance higher in their status in life by good education, thus regarding others as their own selves.

Chapter IV.

Man's Endeavour after Perfection.

Atharvaveda Book V, Hymn 16.

Subject:—The powers of the individual soul and advice to man to endeavour after perfection.

Metre:—Verses 1-10 jagatī and verse 11 śiscaikapat-triṣṭubh.

(४७) ओ३म् ॥ यद्येकवृषोऽसि सृजारसोऽसि ॥

अथर्ववेदे ५ । १६ । १ ॥

पदपाठः—यदि । एकऽवृषः । असि । सृज । अरसः । असि ॥

अन्वयः—(हे मनुष्य) यदि (त्वम्) एकवृषः असि (तर्हि) सृज (यदि न सृजसि तर्हि) त्वं अरसः असि ॥

N. B.—The anvaya—prose order of each verse till the 10th inclusive will be similar to this, only the numeral द्वि, त्रि &c., as need be, taking the place of एक.

Word-meaning &c.:—यदि=if. एकवृषः (एकेन परमेश्वरेण सह एकस्य परमात्मनः ज्ञानेन वा वृषः अथवा आत्मनः एकस्याः शक्तेः उत्कर्षेण उन्नत्या वा वृषः इति एक+√वृष शक्तिबन्धने वा √वृषु सेचन-मैश्ययोः+क । P. II, 1, 4 and वा० कप्रकरणे मूलविभुजादिभ्य उपसंख्यानम्)=powerful through union with and knowledge of the One (God) ; possessing one of the faculties of the soul or person well developed. असि=thou art. सृज =create ; do some constructive work. अरसः (न विद्यते रसः यस्य इति अरसः P. II, 2, 24 वा० नञोऽस्त्यर्थानां बहुव्रीहिर्वा चोत्तरपदलोपश्च वक्तव्यः)=useless, good for nothing, milk and water, void of essential features.

Translation:—Oh man! if you have acquired power through your union with the Supreme One, do something useful, otherwise you are useless.

Purport :—The special feature of human life is, that every person young or old according to his or her light should, through prayer and contemplation try to know God and by union with Him serve humanity. Shorn of this characteristic, man is nothing but a rational beast.

Comment :—The word **एक** is often used to denote God and indicates His simple and Unitary Nature. E. g. "that Supreme *One* then, with His (great subtle) 'material energy' &c."* in the Nāsadīya hymn (q. v.); "Who is *One* and Colourless", Śvētāśvatarōpaniṣad‡. **वृष** is derived from the root **वृष** meaning to shower or be powerful &c., and hence signifies power.

The Person Who gives this good advice is God Himself, and the medium through whom He delivers it in the primeval creation is the Ṛṣi Angiras. No effort has been made to determine the seer or interpreter of this hymn. This hymn is made up of eleven short and easy mnemonic verses in ten of which the same words occur except a numeral which varies between one and ten both inclusive. Yet each word serves as a mere index to great philosophical truths ushered in by the numeral. Hence, great caution, study and meditation is necessary to interpret or understand the hymn.

The term **एकवृष** has been translated by some into 'one bull'. This is entirely wrong since the word vṛṣa meaning 'bull' bears the 'udātta' or acute accent on the fist syllable§ whereas the word here has it on the last syllable being formed from the root √vṛṣa or √vṛṣu by the addition of the 'mūlavibhujādi' suffix 'ka' the acute accent of which survives according

* आनीदवातं स्वधया तदेकम् ॥ ऋ० १० । १२६ । २ ॥

‡ य एकोऽवर्णः ॥ श्वे० ४ । १ ॥

§ वृषादीनां च ॥ पा० ६ । १ । २०३ ॥

to rules of grammar*. This fact has not been noticed by most scholars which negligence has landed them into a very serious blunder, nay, they have been forced to give up this hymn as meaningless.

(४८) यदिं द्विवृषोऽसिं सृजारसोंऽसि ॥ २ ॥

पदपाठः—यदिं । द्विऽवृषः । असिं । ० ॥

Word-meaning &c.:—द्विवृषः (द्वाभ्यां—परमात्मना आत्मना च द्वयोः—परमात्मनः आत्मनः च ज्ञानेन अथवा आत्मनः द्वयोः शक्त्योः उत्कर्षेण उन्नत्या वा वृषः P. II, 1, 4)=possessing power through true knowledge of the two i. e., God and the soul; powerful through the development of two of the powers of the soul.

Translation:—Oh man! if you have attained to power through true knowledge of God and your own soul do something for the good of humanity, or else, you are good for nothing.

Comment:—Indian Philosophy acknowledges twentyfive† categories the highest of which are the Supreme Being and the human soul. Hence the word द्वि here must be taken to mean the two highest knowing which all others can be known‡. A story is told

---

* Vide P. III, 1, 2; VI, 1, 158 and the interpretation of it in the Mahābhaṣya:—"आगमस्य विकारस्य प्रकृतेः प्रत्ययस्य च । पृथक्स्वरनिवृत्त्यर्थमेकवर्जं पदस्वरः ॥" and the Vartika सतिशिष्टस्वरबलीयस्त्वञ्च and the explanation thereof in the same work, which determines that that acute accent alone remains which is ordained the last, the remaining changing into grave.

† सत्वरजस्तमसां साम्यावस्था प्रकृतिः प्रकृतेर्महान्महतोऽहङ्कारोऽहङ्कारात्पञ्चतन्मात्राण्युभयमिन्द्रियं तन्मात्रेभ्यः स्थूलभूतानि पुरुष इति पञ्चविंशतिर्गणः ॥ सां० १ । १ । ६१ ॥

‡ आत्मनो वा अरे दर्शनेन श्रवणेन मत्या विज्ञानेनेदं सर्वं विदितम् ॥ बृ० २।४।५॥ Also see Br. IV, 5, 6 and Mu. V, 1, 1.

that the great Athenian Teacher Socrates was once delivering a discourse on the nature of the human soul in which he happened to remark "man, know thyself". The story goes on that a Brahman, who was passing that way, heard this statement and told one of Socrate's disciples that a man cannot know himself without first knowing God. One may call this "Theism with a vengeance", but it should be borne in mind that the knowledge of the highest does include knowledge of the lower ones. To reach the highest rung one has to step upon and cross all the lower ones. But supposing one stops in the midway and sits on one of the lower rungs, he may be comfortable, but surely he cannot rise to the top of the ladder. Ancient Indian philosophical treatises especially the Upaniṣads* recommended a man the process of elimination to arrive at a correct knowledge of God and the soul, as in such a process one does necessarily come to know what and why one eliminates. Even if a sound knowledge of these two supreme categories may not equip a man witn all the preparation necessary to prosper in the world, a man who cares for God and his own soul and acts up to his lights is far superior to the scientist who may have made several discoveries, invented motor cars, æroplanes and poisonous gases but neglected his own God and soul. Following the former the world will find peace but under the guidance of the latter its very bowels will be torn asunder with dissensions and strife†. In spiritual

* अथात आदेशो नेति नेति नह्येतस्मादिति नेत्यन्यत्परमस्त्यथ नामधेयं सत्यस्य सत्यमिति ॥ बृ० २ । ६ । ३ ॥ स एष नेति नेत्यात्माऽगृह्यो नहि गृह्यतेऽशीर्यो नहि शीर्यते ॥ बृ० ४ । २ । ४ ॥

† अन्धं तमः प्रविशन्ति येऽसम्भूतिमुपासते । ततो भूय इवते तमो य उ सम्भूत्यां रताः ॥ य० ४० । १२ ॥

and moral life faith in and knowledge of the individual soul as well as the Supreme Being is essential*.

(४६) यदिं त्रिवृषोऽसिं सृजारसोंऽसि ॥ ३ ॥

पदपाठः—यदिं । त्रिऽवृषः । शेषं पूर्ववत् ॥

Word-meaning &c. :—त्रिवृषः (त्रयाणाम् गुणानाम् सत्त्वरजस्तमसाम् सम्यग्ज्ञानेन वृषः P. II, 1, 4)=powerful on account of knowledge of the three attributes sattva, rajas and tamas.

Translation :—Oh man! if thou dost possess power acquired by a right knowledge of the three attributes sattva, rajas and tamas, do something for the good of the world, else thou art a milk and water man.

Comment :—All composite beings are the effects of the 'mixing' of these three ingredients in varying proportions. These three are the essential ingredients in the nature of all beings. The first manifests itself through peacefulness, clear understanding, honesty, brightness and such qualities, the second gives rise to restlessness, activity, ambition, strife and the third produces dullness, inactivity, stupidity &c. Hence, there can be no doubt that a sound knowledge of them would enable a man, through efficient handling to turn material objects to great advantage. But it should be remembered well that these three ingredients are found together only in composite beings having a material part in their formation. God is a Simple Being, is Sat—being, Cit—intelligence and Ananda—bliss; the human soul is sat and cit, and

---

* ऋचो अक्षरे परमे व्योमन्यस्मिन्देवा अधि विश्वे निषेदुः । यस्तन्न वेद किमृचा करिष्यति य इत्तद्विदुस्त इमे समासते ॥ ऋ० १ । १६४ । ३९ ॥ वेदाहमेतं पुरुषं महान्तमादित्यवर्णं तमसः परस्तात् । तमेव विदित्वाऽतिमृत्युमेति नान्यः पन्था विद्यतेऽयनाय ॥ य० ३१ । १८ ॥

elementary (primordial) matter* 'Prakrti' is simply sat. These three words sat, cit and ānanda ought not to be confused with sattva, rajas and tamas, for the ideas connoted by the two sets of expressions are quite distinct. Cit and ānanda are entirely spiritual and sat means existence—*esse*—whereas sattva means the "light" ingredient in the formation of composite beings. Though ānanda is an ever-existent feature in the nature of God it is also enjoyed by tha individual soul in the state of samādhi and final beatitude. When in a spiritual-material composite being, like man, sattva gets purified by the removal of all blemishes†, and cit —'mind-stuff' is developed the material ingredients rajas and tamas get diminished until they entirely cease for the time being when ānanda comes in.

The Supreme Being is perfect, and unlimited Sat, Cit and Ānanda whereas the soul is an imperfect and dependent sat and cit and Prakṛti, imperfect and dependent sat. These two latter, however, like the Supreme Being, are eternal. Hence, if a material scientist, engaged in investigating the structure, nature and utility of material objects, were to prosecute his researches a little further, he would sooner or later tumble upon hard spiritual facts leading to a knowledge of the Soul and God as well. Knowledge is relative, surely, but that idea has not prevented our scientists from constructing machine-guns, dreadnaughts, submarines and aeroplanes in preference to ordinary arms and ships. If our scientists were to scare away the ghost of the relativity of knowledge

* Also called 'Sāmarthya', God's Omnipotence in the form of material energy.

† व्याधिस्त्यानसंशयप्रमादालस्याविरतिभ्रान्तिदर्शनालब्धभूमिकत्वानवस्थितत्वानि चित्तविक्षेपास्तेऽन्तरायाः ॥ दुःखदौर्मनस्याङ्गमेजयत्वश्वासप्रश्वासा विक्षेपसहभुवः ॥ यो० १ । ३० ॥ ३१ ॥

and proceed further in the right direction, they will have followed the good advice given in this sacred text.

(५०) यदि॑ चतुर्वृ॒षोऽसि॑ सृ॒जा॒रसोऽसि ॥ ४ ॥

पदपाठः—यदि॑ । चतुरऽवृषः । ० ॥

Word-meaning &c. :—चतुर्वृषः (चतुर्णाम् धर्मार्थकाममोक्षाणाम् सम्यग्ज्ञानेन चतुर्णाम् वेदानाम् आश्रमाणाम् वर्णानाम् वा सम्यग्ज्ञानेन परिपालनेन वा वृषः P. II, 1, 4)=powerful through knowledge of the four ideals of human life, धर्म= righteousness, अर्थ=wealth, काम=fulfilment of one's desires and मोक्ष=final beatitude.

Translation :—Man, if thou hast, goaded on by the four ideals of human life, progressed and attained to power, do something for the good of thy fellow-beings, if not thou art worthless.

Comment :—Of the four things hinted at in this text the first namely, धर्म—the cultivation of righteousness is the most important as without it the next and surely the last and the highest can never be attained. This dharma, to speak the truth, is the basis of all human development in the right direction. The ancient Indian jurist Manu* describes it as possessing ten distinguishing features, namely, contentment, forgiveness, firmness of mind, honesty, purity or cleanliness, control of the senses, development of one's intellect, acquisition of correct knowledge, truthfulness and freedom from anger. This falsifies the idea which some entertain that dharma is, what is commonly called, religion. This latter word has, now-a-days a very limited signification, viz., conforming to certain views which may not connote

* धृतिः क्षमा दमोऽस्तेयं शौचमिन्द्रियनिग्रहः । धीर्विद्या सत्यमक्रोधो दशकं धर्मलक्षणम् ॥ म० ६ । ९२ ॥ See Comment on the 56th verse.

even one of the features described by Manu. Hence, the word dharma has here been translated by 'righteousness' which is its most approximate English equivalent.

The next is अर्थ which means wealth, property, prosperity &c.

Kāma means fulfilment of one's wishes whatever they may be. But in conformity with धर्म they must be legitimate. It is wrong to translate the word kāma everywhere by 'sexual desire', for this latter is only one of the many significations which that word bears. In the Nāsadīya Sūkta, Kāma stands for the Universal Ego, and in any good Sanskrit dictionary "the Supreme Being" also, will be one of the meanings given. Here, in our hymn, however, it means only the fulfilment of all man's legitimate wishes.

The last, but the greatest of these four is Mōkṣa, final beatitude. To attain this, the former three and especially the first must, in one or more lives, be first acquired, as without these it cannot be reached. Five of the six ancient Indian philosophical systems and many Upaniṣad texts give principles for a man's training only in the first three of these categories, the last being left to most of the Upaniṣads and the Brahma sūtras. But the Holy Vēdas set forth rules and describe the means to attain all the four. In fact, the Upaniṣads and the six systems are simply human attempts to interpret the statements of the Divine Śrutis.

Another interpretation of this and the previous verse should also be noted. The Vēdas are, from time immemorial called त्रयी (trayī) i. e., the triad which expression means the Ṛgvēda, the Yajurvēda and the Sāmavēda, the Atharvavēda to which this hymn belongs being merged in the Ṛgvēda on account of its dealing mostly with scientific truths after the manner of many of the hymns of the former. But they are also said to be four in as much as they were revealed by God in the minds of the four great Ṛṣis, Agni, Vāyu, Sūrya and Angiras at the first creation. Moreover, it should be noted that the purport of the last, the Atharvavēda is to supplement the first three and hence it is rightly taken to be distinct from them.

Hence the purport of this and the previous verse of our hymn would be that a man, who has studied the (three or four) Vēdas and developed his soul's powers should exhibit his fitness by doing something to advance human welfare, failing which he will be considered no good. A study of the Vedas shorn of all practical use of their teachings cannot serve any useful purpose. Therefore the shortcomings of a bookish Vedic student do not indicate that the Vedic teachings are behind time or useless for human life in modern times. "The goodness of the cake consists in the eating thereof" and not in only having it. One should study the Vedas, try to understand them well, and test the principles inculcated in them in practical life. Before this nobody has any right to condemn them.

Another interpretation of this stanza will be according to the four āśramas "stages of man's earthly life". The first brahmacarya, is the stage of preparation and development all round. During this stage man is prohibited from under-taking any task that would involve expense of his physical, mental, moral or spiritual powers. He has simply to store up his resources till no more accumulation is possible. This period in ancient India extended from the 8th year to the 25th and in some cases even to the 48th year of a man's life according as he undertook to study one Veda or more.

Then came the householder's stage गृहस्थाश्रम when he entered into the world, got married and began life as an earner by honest means according to his qualifieations and 'varṇa'*. When his sons and daughters themselves were also blessed with offspring. the time came for him to retire to a lonely place for the study of the Upniṣads and Āraṇyakas and contemplate on God and the soul.

Completing this stage he became a sannyāsin and went about preaching and teaching. This was a period of very intensive activity and not of retirement and idling solely as it is now-a-days supposed to be.

Hence God says, that a man who has gone through the three āśramas or stages of life and is now in the fourth or he who knows the importance of the four stages of man's life must show his worth to the world by doing something for the good of humanity.

Finally this sacred mnemonic reminds us of the division of human society into four classes—a division entirely based on the needs of organised human life. The four āśramas mentioned above and these four divisions—varṇas—do exist in every human society in some form or other, for it is not possible under any circumstances to get rid of them. Knowing this fact it will be the duty of every sensible person to encourage the maintenance of this two fold order by himself following the calls of his own class and order and helping others also to do so.

* This word has nothing to do with the so-called 'caste' now-a-days and simply connotes a class division according to division of labour. The word 'caste' is of Portuguese origin and cannot with fairness be used to designate the Vedic system of class division.

(५१) यदि पञ्चवृषोऽसि सृजारसोऽसि ॥ ५ ॥

पदपाठः—यदि । पञ्चऽवृषः । ० ॥

Word-meaning &c. :—पञ्चवृषः (पञ्चानाम् महाभूतानाम् सम्यग्ज्ञानेन वृषः P. II, 1, 4)=powerful through right knowledge and use of the five great physical elements, viz., earth, water, light (or heat), air and ether.

Translation :—Oh man ! if you are powerful through right knowledge and use of the five great physical elements namely, earth, water, light, air and ether then do something for the good of your fellow beings, else you are good-for-nothing.

Purport :—Every person should make it his duty to understand rightly and turn to good account the physical world.

Comment :—No comment is necessary on this. The present material advancement of Europe is a proof of the truth of this sacred text revealed to humanity millions and millions of years ago. But Prof. Einstein's theory of "relativity ought not to keep our European scientists within the limits of the knowledge of the physical world. Our physical knowledge embraces an infinitesimal particle of the infinite universe, the manifestation of the Power of the Great Almighty Being Whom we call God. For example, the all-pervading ether which extends all over space simply transcends our senses. A powerful and ever-present material substance, the very sustenance of our earthly life, in which we "live, and move and have our being," is so subtle that, we have, in spite of all the progress we have made in physical sciences, to be satisfied with a very poor logical inference of it. In fact, our inference of ether is not less funny than Descartes' "*Cogito, ergo sum*", "I think, therefore, I am" !

Indian philosophy severely condemns all one-sided development. From the physical it asks man to proceed to the spiritual. The fourth and the last stage of man's life (सन्यासाश्रम) is intended for this spiritual training, the consummation of human life. Sanyasa does not mean donning the saffron robe ; but connotes a certain stage of mental development qualifying a man for spiritual training and has very little to do with "uniform".

(५२) यदि षड्वृषोऽसि सृजारसोऽसि ॥ ६ ॥

पदपाठः—यदि । षट्ऽवृषः । ० ॥

Word-meaning &c. :—**षड्वृषः** (षण्णाम्—मदकामक्रोध लोभमोहमात्सर्याणाम् जयेन वृषः P. II, 1, 4)=having power or control over the six passions, **मद**=vanity **काम**=Lust, **क्रोध**= anger, **लोभ**=greed, **मोह**=infatuation and **मात्सर्य**=envy.

Translation :—Man, if thou hast power over thy six passions, viz., lust, anger, greed, foolish attachment and vanity, then do some constructive work for the good of thy fellow-beings, otherwise thou art good-for-nothing.

Purport :—Every person should subdue his or her passions and engage himself or herself in the service of others.

Comment :—In the 8th book of the Atharvaveda the king is advised to suppress those people who live the life of certain beasts and birds. The infatuated are there likened to owls, the wrathful to wolves, the envious to dogs, the lustful to sparrows, the vain to the eagle and the greedy to the vulture. They are also called 'rakṣas' in that text, which term, from its peculiar use in the hymns on medicine in Atharvaveda seems to mean disease germs. If this view be correct then those people who allow themselves to be ruled over by their passions are here considered to be the germs that carry disease into the system of human society and are hence to be destroyed by the government*.

Normal passions are essential for human life whereas abnormal passions are signs of an ill-regulated life. Regulation and control are the methods by which even bad things can be so directed as to become beneficial. A man entirely bereft of passions can be of no use to society. Manu the Indian law-giver says that just as being entirely engrossed in kāma is not commendable so also being void of it is impossible in this existence in as much as Vedic study and the performance of the duties prescribed by the Vedas themselves are objects of kāma† i. e., desire. The same can be asserted of the other five passions. Who is there in the whole world that will condemn a righteous ambition? Who can find fault with the indignation of a just man? Can even saints condemn a Śivaji's or a Cromwell's love for his country? Is not a man bound to have a legitimate affection for his family? All these feelings are in some way possessed even by the lower animals and are coextensive with higher organic life of every type.

"The deep affections of the breast
 That Heaven to living things imparts
Are not exclusively possessed
 By human hearts." (Campbell).

But in "human hearts", under certain circumstances, they get lifted so high up as to become sacred and adorable. A martyr's love for the truth, a virgin's

---

* उलूकयातुं शुशुलूकयातुं जहि श्वयातुमुत कोकयातुं । सुपर्णयातुमुत गृध्रयातुं दृषदेव प्रमृण रक्ष इन्द्र ॥ ऋ० ८ । ४ । २२ ॥

† कामात्मता न प्रशस्ता न चैवेहास्त्यकामता । काम्यो हि वेदाधिगमः कर्मयोगश्च वैदिकः ॥ म० २ । २ ॥

self-sacrifice to preserve her chastity, a patriot's laying down his life for his father-land, a scientist's self-immolation at the altar of a dangerous scientific investigation are all cases in point, proving to what lengths a right attachment (mōha) will carry noble souls. Though the high-souled lady Sita's attachment to her chastity is highly praised, the mad Rāvaṇa's violent passion for women is to be severely condemned. So also earth-hunger, an abnormal symptom of ill-regulated ambition and one-sided, Godless patriotism which may fitly be called "nation-worship", is sinful and deserving of condemnation.

The principle which the verse lays down is that the six passions are a necessity of human life, hence one should regulate and turn them to good account. With this point in view, the Holy Atharvavēda has devoted a long text consisting of several stanzas in the 11th book* to describe the powers good and evil that entered man's body when it was prepared.

"Who knows not Poise is blind within ;
Who knows not poise cannot create ;
Man, uncreative finds no peace ;
Who finds no peace what joy knows he ?
Whichever pow'r is left to roam
While mind, like slackened rein, obeys,
Soon wafts the man's will out from Poise,
As gale wafts out a ship to sea.
Therefore, [on this ascetic path]
The man whose pow'rs are one and all
Held back from their objective field,—
Of him alone the mind is poised."†

---

* Atharvavēda, XI, 8, 18-32.

† नास्ति बुद्धिरयुक्तस्य न चायुक्तस्य भावना । न चाभावयतः शान्तिरशान्तस्य कुतः सुखम् ॥ इन्द्रियाणां हि चरतां यन्मनोऽनुविधीयते । तदस्य हरति प्रज्ञां वायुर्नावमिवाम्भसि ॥ तस्माद्यस्य महाबाहो निगृहीतानि सर्वशः । इन्द्रियाणीन्द्रियार्थेभ्यस्तस्य प्रज्ञा प्रतिष्ठिता ॥ अ० २ । ६६-६८ ॥

(५३) यदि सप्तवृषोऽसि सृजारसोऽसि ॥ ७ ॥

पदपाठः—यदि । सप्तऽवृषः । ० ॥

Word-meaning &c. :—सप्तवृषः (सप्तानाम्—सप्तर्षीणाम् सम्यक्प्रयोगेण वृषः P. II, 1, 4)=having power through or over the seven. The 'seven' here indicates the famous सप्तर्षयः*=seven sages, viz., the five intellectual organs and 'manas' mind and 'buddhi' will.

Translation :—If thou, oh man! hast acquired power through mastery over thy five senses, mind and will, do something for the world at large, if not, thou art no good.

Purport :—Man should control his five senses mind and will and thereby acquire power.

Comment :—The mechanism of the human body is made up of the following six divisions :—

1. The internal sense consisting of manas "mind", cit "estimative faculty and memory", buddhi —"determinative faculty or will" and ahaṃkāra—"the arrogative faculty or ego". Some ancient Indian philosophers admit all these four, but the Saṃkhyas acknowledge only two† merging the 2nd and 3rd in the first. Western philosophers seem to posit a separate estimative faculty distinct from memory, but both of these are taken to be the acts of cit by Indian philosophers.

2. The five intellectual senses viz., cakṣuh—sight; śrōtra—hearing; ghrāṇa—smell; rasana—

---

* सप्त ऋषयः प्रतिहिताः शरीरे सप्तरक्षन्ति सदमप्रमादम् । सप्तापः स्वपतो लोकमीयुस्तत्र जागृतो अस्वप्नजौ सत्रसदौ च देवौ ॥ य० ३४ । ५५ ॥

† महदाख्यमाद्यं कार्यं तन्मनः ॥ चरमोऽहङ्कारः ॥ सां० १ । ७१ । ७२ ॥ Here—'carama' means 'dvitīya'—second. These two alone are the direct evolutes of Prakṛti all the rest emanating from these two and their evolutes.

taste ; and sparśa—touch. These five together form the afferent apparatus directly in contact with the subtle mind on one side and the gross motor organs as well as the objective world, on the other.

3. The five motor organs, the mouth (vāk), hands (pāṇi), feet (padau), anus (payu), the genitals (upastha), forming the efferent apparatus to carry out the behests of the will, before or after intellection, by a positive act.

4. The golaka—seats of these intellectual and motor organs with which the anatomist is more concerned than the philosopher.

5. The digestive apparatus and the circulatory system are also topics for anatomy.

6. The controlling apparatus or the nervous system the central power-house of which is located in the brain is also a subject for the anatomist.

The relation in which the external objects, the senses, the motor organs, the internal sense and the soul stand to one another and the process of intellection is described by a beautiful simile in the Kathopaniṣad :—"The spirit is the charioteer, the body the chariot, the intellect the driver, and the will the reins of horses. The senses are the horses, and the objects of the senses are their paths. Philosophers call that in which the spirit is associated with the senses and the will the enjoyer." The senses of intellection first come into contact† with external objects and carry the report to the mind which by means of its citta cogitates over it,

* आत्मानं रथिनं विद्धि शरीरं रथमेव तु । बुद्धिं तु सारथिं विद्धि मनः प्रग्रहमेव च ॥ इन्द्रियाणि हयानाहुर्विषयांस्तेषु गोचरान् । आत्मेन्द्रियमनोयुक्तं भोक्तेत्याहुर्मनीषिणः ॥ क० १ । ३ । ४ ॥

† इन्द्रियार्थसन्निकर्षोत्पन्नं ज्ञानमव्यपदेश्यमव्यभिचारि व्यवसायात्मकं प्रत्यक्षम् ॥ न्या० १ । १ । ४ ॥ आत्मा मनसा संयुज्यते मन इन्द्रियेणेन्द्रियमर्थेन ॥ वा० भा० ॥

refers to the impressions if any left of such past experiences and then the will intervenes and gives its decision one way or the other. The decision is then laid before the soul who then through the ego arrogates it to himself and if necessary the same process takes place conversely making the motor organs take necessary action. It must be noted in this process that the manas of the mantra includes citta, though to make the matter clear it is mentioned separately. The ego, ahaṃkāra is not counted in the seven, for its function is subsequent to that of buddhi. Manas and buddhi are, therefore, the most important ingredients of the internal sense—antaḥkaraṇa.

The manas or citta, whatever it may be called, comes subsequent to the senses justifying the maxim of the pre-Reformation Scholastics of Europe "*nihil est in intellectu quod non prius fuit in sensu*" i. e., there can be nothing in the mind which has not previously been in the senses. Hence lack of the senses would result in lack of impressions. A blind man has no idea of colour. For preception, therefore, we require an object to perceive, the sense organ with which it should be perceived, the medium through which it is to be perceived i. e., light in the case of visual perception, attention of the mind and finally proximity in time and place of all these and their fitness for perception. Lacking any of these there will be no sense-perception at all. If these factors are present, there will be a corresponding cittavṛtti—modification of the mind which is the concept or idea to be presented to the soul.

From the explanation given above—it will be seen that the senses are responsible for the relation of the soul with external objects. As such they are capable of immense mischief. In fact all woes physical, mental and moral are due to the unregulated dealings of these seven factors. What has been said in the Comment on the previous (6th) mantra regarding the six passions is equally applicable to these seven. The six passions are entirely dependent upon these, manifesting themselves when these run amoc and receding into the back-ground when these are controlled. If one subdues the eye and the mind, lust disappears. If the tongue and mind is subdued gluttony and the desire to eat rich foods will vanish. Thus, if the senses and the mind and intellect are regulated life will surely become pleasant and useful and man will attain to great powers. This is the cittavṛtti-nirōdha* of the laudable Indian science of yoga.

The senses are centres of power, hence if they are safeguarded power is apt to accumulate and increase. If the senses are let loose the power gets dissipated the result of which will be violent passions. Subdued passions are a sure sign of a regulated will and controlled senses. The same Upaniṣad beautifully explains this point thus:—"He is ignorant who is always associated with the uncontrolled will, and whose senses are not mastered over like a charioteer's unbroken horses. But he is wise, who is always associated with the controlled will, and whose senses are mastered over like a charioteer's broken horses. He who is ignorant, always frivolous, and unchaste, does not attain to that Divin Plane, but goes down to the world. But he who is wise, always serene and chaste attains to that Divine Plane, from which there is no return to earthly life. He, whose driver is the spiritual knowledge, (including austerity, judgment and reason) and whose will is under his control, reaches the termination of the worldly journey. That is the supreme

* योगश्चित्तवृत्तिनिरोधः ॥ यो०-१ । २ ॥

region of the Omnipresent God—Viṣṇu".*

(५५) यद्यंष्टवृषोऽसि सृजारसोऽसि ॥ ८ ॥

पदपाठः—यदि । अष्टऽवृषः । ० ॥

Word-meaning &c. :—अष्टवृषः (अष्टानाम् योगाङ्गानाम् सम्यग्ज्ञानेन वृषः P. II, 1, 4)=one who has achieved ability in the eight means of yoga—the science of spiritual and mental discipline.

Translation :--If thou, oh man, hast developed thy powers by the practice of the eight means of yoga spiritual discipline, do something useful for thy fellow-beings, otherwise thout art a failure in life.

Purport :—It is the duty of every person to follow the exercises of the yogic science and develop his or her powers.

Comment :—In the two previous verses the Holy Teacher has advised man to subdue his passions by controlling and directing his senses and mind. In the present text the means for achieving this most desirable aim are given. They are the eight divisions of the Yoga philosophy current in India from time immemorial. They are called in technical language 'aṣṭau angani'—the eight limbs. The available text book on the subject is the Yoga Sūtra of the renowned Sage Patanjali the author of the Great Commentary

---

§ यस्त्वविज्ञानवान्भवत्ययुक्तेन मनसा सदा। तस्येन्द्रियाण्यवश्यानि दुष्टाश्वा इव सारथेः ॥ यस्तु विज्ञानवान्भवति युक्तेन मनसा सदा। तस्येन्द्रियाणि वश्यानि सदश्वा इव सारथेः ॥ यस्त्वविज्ञानवान्भवत्यमनस्कः सदाऽशुचिः। न स तत्पदमाप्नोति संसारं चाधिगच्छति ॥ यस्तु विज्ञानवान्भवति समनस्कः सदा शुचिः। स तु तत्पदमाप्नोति यस्माद्भूयो न जायते ॥ विज्ञानसारथिर्यस्तु मनःप्रग्रहवान्नरः। सोऽध्वनः परमाप्नोति तद्विष्णोः परमं पदम् ॥ क० ३ । ५-६ ॥ In the above verses there is a clear reference to the following stanza from the Ṛgvēda :—
तद्विष्णोः परमं पदं सदा पश्यन्ति सूरयः। दिवीव चक्षुराततम् ॥ ऋ० १ । २२ । २० ॥

—Mahābhāṣya on the grammar of Pāṇini. The most sceptical of critics have admitted the time to be not later than the 2nd century before the Christian era when he flourished, though it has, by others, been proved to be very much earlier. Patanjali says that "by the practice of the different parts of Yoga the impurities being destroyed, knowledge becomes effulgent up to discrimination."* These divisions are eight in number viz:—yama=abstentions, and niyama=observances, and āsana=postures, and prāṇāyāma=regulations-of-the breath, and pratyāhāra=with-drawal of-the-senses, and dhāraṇā=fixed-attention, and dhyāna=contemplation, and samādhi=concentration.†

Of these the first viz., the Yamas or abstentions are five, viz., ahiṃsā=abstinence-from-injury, satya=abstinence-from-falsehood, astēya=abstinence from theft, brahmacarya=abstinence from incontinence, and aparigraha=abstinence from acceptance of gifts.‡ All these have to be practised without reservation in thought, word and deed.

The observances also are five, e. g., śauca=internal and external purification, santōṣa=contentment, tapas=mortification, svādhyāya=study-of-the-Veda, and Īśvarapraṇidhāna=the worship of God.§ These also, it may be observed here, are to be practised in thought word and deed.

The formula regarding āsana is 'sthirasukham-āsanam',|| i. e., a posture should be firm and pleasant.

With regard to prāṇāyāma the sage Patanjali, says that "the controlling the motion of the exhala-

* योगाङ्गानुष्ठानादशुद्धिक्षये ज्ञानदीप्तिराविवेकख्यातेः ॥ यो० २ । २८ ॥

† यमनियमासनप्राणायामप्रत्याहारधारणाध्यानसमाधयोऽष्टावङ्गानि ॥ २९ ॥

‡ अहिंसासत्यास्तेयब्रह्मचर्यापरिग्रहा यमाः ॥ ३० ॥

§ शौचसन्तोषतपःस्वाध्यायेश्वरप्रणिधानानि नियमाः ॥ ३२ ॥

|| स्थिरसुखमासनम् ॥ ४६ ॥

tion and the inhalation follows after this (that is after attaining firmness of posture)."*

Dharaṇa—fixed attention is cittasya dēśabandhah =holding the mind on to some particular object,† and an unbroken flow of knowledge in that object is dhyāna‡=contemplation. Finally this same (contemplation), shining forth (in consciousness) as the intended object and nothing more, and, as it were, emptied of itself, is concentration.§

Out of the 195 short and sweet aphorisms of the beautiful treatise on Yoga by the Great Patanjali only nine have been utilised in this Comment so far and it will be no exaggeration to say that these give the whole science of Yoga in a nutshell. As a full explanation of these topics is necessary for a clear understanding of the sacred text being dealt with, short notes culled from the remaining aphorisms of the treatise on Yoga and other works as well as some Vedic texts will not be out of place here.

The first item to be considered is śaūca—purification or cleanliness. It is a well known fact that cleanliness indicates, carefulness, agility, good taste, respectability and many other things on the part of a person who keeps himself or herself clean. Taking only the question of clothing and the body, it is next to impossible that a lazy dolt will keep them clean. The idea of bathing and washing his clothes or even of changing them, will be painful to him. Once a rich man accompanied by his servant went to a river and had a dip in it. He finished his bath and came ashore but in the meanwhile, his servant had left for a few

---

* तस्मिन्सति श्वासप्रश्वासयोर्गतिविच्छेदः प्राणायामः ॥ यो० २ । ४९ ॥

† देशबंधश्चित्तस्य धारणा ॥ ३ । १ ॥

‡ तत्र प्रत्ययैकतानता ध्यानम् ॥ २ ॥

§ तदेवार्थमात्रनिर्भासं स्वरूपशून्यमिव समाधिः ॥ ३ ॥

minutes just to attend to something urgent. The gentleman kept standing without wiping his body shivering in the cold breeze. Some minutes passed and passers by out of curiosity asked him why he did not wipe his damp hair and person. He curtly replied that he was waiting for his servant to come and do the thing for him. That man was really a lazy man. Such a man can never be a fit subject for the teaching of Yoga. Laziness is the greatest obstacle to the practice of Yoga and the sign by which it can be detected is an unkempt, dirty, jumbled up look of the clothing and body of a man. Moreover, external cleanliness is a means to acquire and maintain physical health. Side by side with the cleanliness of attire and person one should have cleanliness of speech as well. A correct deliberate, matter-of-fact, and parsimonious way of speaking is just the manner for a yogi and this also is external cleanliness. All do not have a good voice, but it is within the reach of all to think before speaking and to utter words correctly and avoid bad and unpleasant expressions. Abusive language, sarcasm and prevarication are curtains through which a mean, dirty mind peeps. Cleanliness of speech is the sign of a mind fit for concentration.

Internal cleanliness depends entirely upon one's thoughts. If one could keep one's thoughts pure one's mind and soul would always be clean and this supreme achievement will beam through the whole person. The principles enunciated by the great Indian law giver Manu on this subject have been given on pp. 64 and 65. Plain living and high thinking is exactly the way for a yogi.

The famous Roman Emperor Marcus Aurelius' mother Aurelia, had once told her son, that his thoughts should always be such as he would never be ashamed of acknowledging before others. If some body were to question one as to what one was thinking at the time, one ought to be able to tell him or her all the contents of one's mind. That is the way of a yogi. Cleanliness of attire and person, and purity of speech and thought, are essential for a yogi.

The regulation of breathing is the next topic. From time immemorial the prāṇa or breath has engaged the attention of Indian asceticism. There is such an intimate connection between breath and mind that if one of these two is controlled the other of itself becomes regulated. Breathing invariably becomes slow and noiseless when a man's mind is deeply occupied with some high and difficult question. Those who can apply their mind to serious meditation should contemplate on God with special attention to breathing and they will have achieved success in prāṇāyāma. Those who cannot concentrate their mind should try to regulate their breathing by easy and slow steps and their mind will lose its fickleness. This inter-relation of breath and mind, was, thousands of years ago, discovered by Indian scientists.

Āsana or posture is such a method of excercise as will keep the body fit for Yoga. Any exercise, such as Sandow's is quite enough to make the body agile, light, and of moderate bulk and it is exactly such a body that is required for a yogi. To attain this, healthy and simple fare and good anatomical exercise are necessary. But at the time of the yogic exercise there is another sort of āsana required, which is simply a comfortable way of sitting. This posture should be such as would keep the body of the exercitant firm and comfortable. Failing this the exercitant will find no pleasure in his exercise. Hence it is that yogis always advise their pupils to "acquire" this posture first. What is to be noted is that the body should not shake or otherwise attract the attention of the exercitant. With this proviso any manner of sitting at exercise will do. In walking, standing and kneeling a good deal of exertion is necessary which pulls away the mind from the exercise. Hence sitting or if this is inconvenient owing to fatigue or sickness, the corpse posture—śavasana—lying flat on one's back like a dead body, is the most suitable.

And when the Man draws back all round
(like tortoise gathering in its limbs)
His sense-powr's from their object-field,—
His will abides in perfect Poise.*

This is pratyahara, described by Patanjali as "the withdrawal of the senses which is as it were imitation of the mind-stuff itself on the part of the organs by disjoining themselves from their objects",† as a result of which there is complete mastery of the sense organs.

The Commentator Vyāsa says on this :—"There are those who think 1. that the mastery of the organs is a lack of desire for the various things, sounds and so forth. Longing (vyasana) is attachment in the sense that it puts him a long way from (vy-asyati) a good. 2. [Others think that] unforbidden experience is legitimate. 3. Others, that there may be conjunction [of the organs] with the [various things] sounds and so forth as one desires. 4. Others think that there is a subjugation of the senses when there is no passion or aversion after the thinking of the various things is without pleasure or pain. 5. Jaigīṣavya

* यदा संहरते चायं कूर्मोऽङ्गानीव सर्वशः । इन्द्रियाणीन्द्रियार्थेभ्यस्तस्य प्रज्ञा प्रतिष्ठिता ॥ भ० २ । ५८ ॥

† स्वविषयासम्प्रयोगे चित्तस्य स्वरूपानुकार इवेन्द्रियाणां प्रत्याहारः ॥ ततः परमा वश्यतेन्द्रियाणाम् ॥ यो० २ । ५४ ॥ ५५ ॥

thinks that it is refusal to perceive [the various things beginning with sound] as a result of the mind-stuff's (cittasya) singleness-of-intent. And as a result of this when [the yogin's] mind-stuff is restricted, the organs are restricted, [and] there is not as in the case of the subjugation of the other organs, any further need of means performed with effort. But this mastery which is this singleness-of-intent is the complete [mastery]".*

This withdrawal of the organs from their objects should be gradually developed till it is complete. Illegitimate objects must at once be given up at whatever cost to one's sensitiveness and ill-regulated will; then unnecessary objects such as luxuries be reduced and finally entirely given up. At a further stage the legitimate and necessary objects themselves such as food and clothing be gradually reduced till the very least minimum is attained which should be retained just for the sake of keeping body and soul together in order to be able to do one's God-ordained duties. This process must be pursued in thought, word and deed, at the same time.

"As for the fool who sits apart,
his active powers held in check,
While sense-things occupy his mind,—
a hypocrite is that man called."†
But who controlling sense by mind,
O Arjuna, fears not to ply

---

* शब्दादिष्वव्यसनमिन्द्रियजय इति केचित्। सक्तिर्व्यसनं व्यस्यत्येनं श्रेयस इति। अविरुद्धा प्रतिपत्तिर्न्याय्या। शब्दादिसंप्रयोगः स्वेच्छयेत्यन्ये। रागद्वेषाभावे सुखदुःखशून्यं शब्दादिज्ञानमिन्द्रियजय इति केचित्। चित्तैकाग्र्यादप्रतिपत्तिरेवेति जैगीषव्यः। ततश्च परमा त्वियं वश्यता यच्चित्तनिरोधे निरुद्धानीन्द्रियाणि नेतरेन्द्रियजयवत्प्रयत्नकृतमुपायान्तरमपेक्षन्ते योगिन इति॥ व्या० भा०॥

† कर्मेन्द्रियाणि संयम्य य आस्ते मनसा स्मरन्। इन्द्रियार्थान्विमूढात्मा मिथ्याचारः स उच्यते॥ भ० ३। ६॥

His active powers, heart-detached,
in Karma-yoga,—he excells."*

The inimitable Jesus also, in his Sermon on the Mount, teaches the same principle. "Ye have heard that it was said by them of old time, Thou shalt not commit adultery. But I say unto you, That whosoever looketh on a woman to lust after her hath committed adultery with her already in his heart."†

The result of the withdrawal of the organs is that they become the willing, obedient, servants of man and not his masters.

Ahiṃsā, abstinence from inflicting injury on others and even on one's own self is also tc be practised. Unpleasant speech hurting the feelings of others and angry thoughts are as bad as killing.

The same can be said of continence (brahmacarya) and truthfulness (satya). These also have to be practised in thought word and deed, without any reservation or restriction. Lies told in jest have a pernicious effect on man's character. They slacken his mind and make him a regular liar afterwards. Incontinence in thought as well as deed has the same effect viz., loss of vīrya=semen-virile, the preservation of which is extremely necessary for a yogi. Bad thoughts affect the whole atmosphere and thereby a large number of beings, by whirling injurious subtle currents in the all-pervading ether which injuriously affect man's mind. The flood of such infected ether survives for a long time till some high-souled being comes at a later stage and sets a flood of virtuous ideas afloat to the cleansing of the former. Till then the poor world has to suffer all sorts of ills. Rasputin

* यस्त्विन्द्रियाणि मनसा नियम्यारभतेऽर्जुन । कर्मेन्द्रियैः कर्मयोगमसक्तः स विशिष्यते ॥ भ० ३ । ७ ॥

† Gospel of Matthew V, 27 and 28.

the notorious Russian priest, a monstrous fornicator propagated his horrid ideas of adultery or rather "free-love" till he was done away with by the hand of an assassin. But his horrible ideas continued after him with the result that a few years back a bishop was found to be continuing his mission.

So also angry and abusive language, lies uttered intentionally or in joke as well as prevarication or mental restriction injure others by setting loose, false, unhealthy and abnormal thought-currents in the mind of others which generally terminate in false and illegitimate acts injurious both to the individual concerned as well as society.

Killing animals for food also is a sin. In the beginning of the Bible we have the following statement:—"So God created man in his own image, in the image of God created he him; male and female created he them. And God blessed them, and God said unto them, Be fruitful, and multiply, and replenish the earth, and subdue it: and have dominion over the fish of the sea, and over the fowl of the air, and over every living thing that moveth upon the earth. And God said, Behold, I have given you every herb bearing seed, which is upon the face of the earth, and every tree, in the which is the fruit of a tree yielding seed; to you it shall be for meat. And to every beast of the earth, and to every foul of the air, and to every thing that creepeth upon the earth, wherein there is life, I have given every green herb for meat: and it was so".* In this text there is a clear injunction that God has allotted vegetables to be the diet of all "living things".

Paul in his Espistle to the Romans delivers himself thus:—"Him that is weak in the faith receive ye,

* Genesis I, 27-30.

but not to doubtful disputations. For one believeth that he may eat all things: another, who is weak, eateth herbs. Let not him that eateth despise him that eateth not; and let not him which eateth not judge him that eateth: for God hath received him."*

The following unstinted condemnation of an attitude to injure others in any way as well as of killing for food is noteworthy:—"Oh ye who take pleasure in killing, who spoil others' happiness, ye pests, ye mean ones, may your weapons of killing revert and attack you! Eat them whose ye are! Eat him who has sent you! Eat your own flesh."†

The Holy Atharvavēda has this injunction, "let not the teeth of a child (even) injure his parents, but let them eat rice, barley, black pulses, sesamum (and such other cereals) which are allotted to man for his food and which will fetch him immense wealth."‡

The sage Kaṇāda also sets down these rules:—"Duties prescribed by the Vedas cannot produce their fruit, if the man performing them subsists on evil diet. Diet becomes evil when it involves injury (to others). The taint of such diet affects them also who come in contact with the eater thereof. This evil consequence does not arise in the case of good (harmless) diet. Therefore man should endeavour to subsist on such harmless food."§

A man who has attained these stages can easily proceed to dhāraṇā—fixed attention, thence to dhyāna

* Paul's Epistle to the Romans XV, 1-30.

† शरभक शेरभ पुनर्वो यन्तु यातवः पुनर्हेतिः किमीदिनः। यस्य स्थ तमत्त यो वः प्राहैत्तमत्त स्वा मांसान्यत्त ॥ अ० २ । २४ । १ ॥

‡ व्रीहिमत्तं यवमत्तमथो माषमथो तिलम्। वां भागो निहितो रत्नधेयाय दन्तौ मा हिंसिष्टं पितरं मातरं च ॥ अ० ६ । १४० । २ ॥

§ तद्दुष्टभोजने न विद्यते ॥ दुष्टं हिंसायाम् ॥ तस्य समभिव्याहारतो दोषः ॥ तददुष्टे न विद्यते ॥ पुनर्विशिष्टे प्रवृत्तिः ॥ वै० ६ । १ । ६-१०॥

—contemplation and samādhi—concentration which leads to the bliss of emancipation—mōksha.

(५५) यदि नवृषोऽसि सृजारसोऽसि ॥ ६ ॥

पदपाठः—यदि । नवऽवृषः । ० ॥

Word-meaning &c. :—नववृषः (नवद्वारवतः शरीररूपिणः मन्दिरस्य दुर्गस्य पुरस्य राज्यस्य वा स्वामित्वेन वृषः P. II, 1, 4)= powerful by the possession of a splendid temple, fort, city or kingdom with-nine-gates in the shape of the body.

Translation :—If thou, oh man ! art really powerful by means of the possession of a wonderful temple (of the eternal soul) with nine doors use it profitably to thee and to others, or else thou art worth nothing.

Purport:—The human person is a rare possession, the means of salvation. Every person should utilise it to advantage.

Comment :—The human body is the most wonderful of God's creations. It is a grand temple in which its Deity, the soul, nay God Himself is enshrined.

In Vedic poetry it has been variously described now as a chariot now a city &c. A fine passsage from the Kathōpaniṣad has already been quoted in the Comment on verse 53 p. 133.

The following are from the Atharvavēda :—

"Oh man ! may onward progress be for ever thine and never lagging behind. I equip thee with strength for thy life's pilgrimage. Come, mount thou this *chariot* in the *shape of thy body* that will carry thee on to deathless bliss, and when thou wilt be hoary with age and experience, place thou thy knowledge at the service of other travellers."*

"There is an impregnable *city (in the shape of the human body)* with nine portals (=seven apertures in the head and two below) and eight circles† in which dwell celestial (=very powerful) beings (the mind, the will, the ego, the five senses &c.) and in which there is a celestial (=leading those to beatitude who utilise it properly) golden (=precious and glorious) treasure-chest (=heart) surrounded by luster."‡

In point of its marvellous construction it surpasses any mechanism divine or human. Its internal structure is so fine and complicated that many of its parts are still a problem to the anatomist. Within its small compass it holds such a vast and variegated structure, that it has rightly been likened, by ancient Indian philosophers, to the universe itself and called Kṣudra-brahmāṇḍa—the little universe or Piṇḍa-brahmāṇḍa—the universe in the form of the body. It is considered by Indian philosophers to be composed of the three bodies 'sthūla'—gross, 'sūkṣma'—fine, and 'linga'—subtle and of five sheaths|| viz., annamayakōśa—the sheath composed of food, prāṇamaya kōśa—the sheath composed of the vital airs, manōmaya kōśa—the sensorial sheath, vijñānamaya kōśa—the cognitional sheath, and ānandamaya kōśa—the sheath of bliss.

---

* उद्यानं ते पुरुष नावयानं जीवातुं ते दक्षतातिं कृणोमि । आ हि रोहेममृतं सुखं रथमथ जिर्विर्विदथमावदासि ॥ अ० ८ । १ । ६ ॥

† Vide p. 37. The sun—'sūrya' should be inserted between 'manipūraka' and 'anāhata' to make th total eight.

‡ अष्टाचक्रा नवद्वारा देवानां पूरयोध्या । तस्यां हिरण्ययः कोशः स्वर्गो ज्योतिषावृतः ॥ अ० १० । २ । ३१ ॥

See also the Gita V, 13 :—सर्वकर्माणि मनसा संन्यस्यास्ते सुखं वशी । नवद्वारे पुरे देही नैव कुर्वन्न कारयन् ॥

|| तै० उ० १ । १० । ६ ॥

The gross body is made of the annamaya kōśa and takes in the daily supply of material and ejects waste. It is this body that is built up by proteins and kept going by vitamines. The middling or fine body sūkṣma śarīra, is a composite of seventeen elements, viz., the five intellectual and five motor organs, the five vital airs and the mind and will. It is the means of perception, and contains within itself the subtle body the vesture of the three sheaths, viz., the sheath of the vital airs, the sensorial sheath and the cognitional sheath. The last viz., the sheath of bliss is a vehicle enabling the soul to enjoy final beatitude which is acquired when man has done all that is necessary and after which nothing remains to be done.

This is the wonderful body which we look down upon with such disgust that Kabīra calls it dirty,* and St. Francis of Assissi, "my brother ass". Anyhow, there is one side of it, viz., its being a means of attaining final beatitude which brings before our mind its supreme importance.

This body is endowed with 9 doors, viz., two eyes, two ears, two nostrils, one mouth, one opening for urinating and another for voiding excrements. These are its entrances and exits through which food, air, and impressions enter in and waste matter escapes out, both processes quite necessary to keep it fit. The Atharvavēda calls these "the nine keepers that God has disposed in different ways for the support of the body".† He who knows the use of these openings will keep them clean, and take great care of them as objects of very great worth. Such a man will not fall

---

* जा रे गन्दे काया तेरा गुण गाया=Oh dirty body! get you gone, much have I extolled thy attributes. A hortatory song said to be composed by Kabīra.

† तस्येमे नव कोशा विष्टम्भा नवधा हिताः ॥ अ० १३ । ४ । १० ॥

into the temptations of incontinence, hearing profane music, looking at exciting sights, eating and drinking delicious and harmful things, talking too much, smelling perfumes, touching soft and ticklish things and taking breeze just for enjoyment. His body is intended for a higher use, hence he will keep it clean, pure and healthy. He will consider his body a field to cultivate and sow good seeds of spiritual knowledge in—seeds which will later give a harvest of bliss lasting for aeons and aeons.

"The 'field', Oh Kunti's son, is but
another term for this thy form:
The Being who (within) surveys
is called Field-Know'r by them that know".*

Hence the sacred text we are dealing with orders us to keep this physical body clean and holy as the fitting temple of the eternal soul and God himself and attain to such powers as will enable us to earn salvation.

(५६) यदि दशवृषोऽसि सृजारसोऽसि ॥ १० ॥

पदपाठः—यदि । दशऽवृषः । ० ॥

Word-meaning &c. :– दशवृषः (दशलक्षणकं धर्मं सम्यग्ज्ञात्वा पूर्णतया संसेव्य च वृषः P. II, 1, 4)=powerful by having understood well and fully lived up to the Law of Righteousness distinguished by its ten features.

Translation :—If thou art powerful by having understood well and fully lived up to the Law of Righteousness distinguished by its ten features, do something for the good of thy fellow-beings, else thou art good-for-nothing.

Purport :—Having utilised all the means mentioned in the previous nine verses a man should follow the Law of Righteousness which is the goal of human life.

---

* इदं शरीरं कौन्तेय क्षेत्रमित्यभिधीयते । एतद्यो वेत्ति तं प्राहुः क्षेत्रज्ञ इति तद्विदः ॥ भ० १३ । १ ॥

Comment :—About this 'Dharma' or the Law of Righteousness Manu lays down the following injunctions :—

"Contentment, forgiveness, firmness of mind, non-interference with others' rights to property, cleanliness (or purity), control over the senses, right understanding of the principles according to which human society thrives, right knowledge of the soul (and the Supreme Being), truthfulness and freedom from anger these are the ten-fold distinguishing features of (the Law of) Righteousness."*

"All persons belonging to these four orders of human society should, invariably and without sparing any pains, resort to this Law of Righteousness with ten features."†

"Those enlightened persons who study well these ten features of this Law and live up to them attain to the highest state (final beatitude)."‡

The Sage Kaṇāda begins his treatise on the Vaiśeṣika philosophy by a description of Dharma. He says:—"We shall now describe 'Dharma'." " 'Dharma' is that (means) by which one can attain to prosperity in life and to emancipation after". Again, "the Vedas are authoritative because they tell about this 'Dharma'."§

The Mahābhārata also extolls 'Dharma' in these words :—"Desistance from injuring others, truthful-

---

* धृतिः क्षमा दमोऽस्तेयं शौचमिन्द्रियनिग्रहः । धीर्विद्या सत्यमक्रोधो दशकं धर्मलक्षणम् ॥ म॰ VII, 92.

† चतुर्भिरपि चैवैतैर्नित्यमाश्रमिभिर्द्विजैः । दशलक्षणको धर्मः सेवितव्यः प्रयत्नतः ॥ Ibid, 92.

‡ दशलक्षणानि धर्मस्य ये विप्राः समधीयते । अधीत्य चानुवर्तन्ते ते यान्ति परमां गतिम् ॥ Ibid' 93.

§ अथातो धर्मं व्याख्यास्यामः ॥ यतोऽभ्युदयनिःश्रेयससिद्धिः स धर्मः ॥ तद्वचनादाम्नायस्य प्रामाण्यम् ॥ वै॰ १ । १ । १-३ ॥

ness, freedom from anger, firmness of mind and straight-forwardness, this (five-fold) oh lord of kings, is the certain distinguishing feature of Dharma".* In these five the above ten are somehow included.

Elsewhere in the same work it is said :—

"Dharma is one's father and mother, Dharma is one's lord and well-wisher, Dharma is one's brother and friend and Dharma is one's master, oh tormentor of foes !"†

"From Dharma spring wealth and the fulfilment of one's wishes, from Dharma originate all enjoyments and all sorts of happiness. From Dharma arises power that is in the forefront and from Dharma it is that celestial (=highest worldly) happiness and the supreme stage (of emancipation) arise."

"When this holy Dharma is resorted to, it saves one from great fear, for man by it attains to the position of the twice-born and becomes enlightened as it sanctifies him."

"Oh Yudhiṣṭhira ! the will to follow Dharma is produced in man only when by lapse of time the effects of sin are wiped out."

"Birth in the human frame is difficult to secure even after thousands of lives, hence he deceives himself who being born as man does not practise Dharma."‡

---

* अहिंसा सत्यमक्रोध आनृशंस्यं दमस्तथा । आर्जवं चैव राजेन्द्र निश्चितं धर्मलक्षणम् ॥ अनु० ६० । १९ ॥

† धर्मः पिता च माता च धर्मो नाथः सुहृत्तथा । धर्मो भ्राता सखा चैव धर्मः स्वामी परंतप ॥ आश्व० ६९ । १२ ॥

‡ धर्मादर्थश्च कामश्च धर्माद्भोगाः सुखानि च । धर्मादैश्वर्यमेवाग्र्यं धर्मात्स्वर्गो गतिः परा ॥ धर्मोयं सेवितः शुद्धस्त्रायते महतो भयात् । धर्माद्द्विजत्वं देवत्वं धर्मः पावयते नरम् ॥ यदा च क्षीयते पापं कालेन पुरुषस्य तु । तदा संजायते बुद्धिर्धर्मं कर्तुं युधिष्ठिर ॥ जन्मान्तरसहस्रैस्तु मनुष्यत्वं हि दुर्लभम् । तद्गत्वापीह यो धर्मं न करोति स्ववञ्चितः ॥ आश्व० ६९ । ११-१६ ॥

In the Bible (Psalm CVI, 3) we read :—"Blessed are they that keep judgment, and he that doeth righteousness at all times."

Jesus in his wonderful Sermon on the Mount (Matt. V, 6 said :—"Blessed are they which do hunger and thirst after righteousness: for they shall be filled."

The triple armour extolled in Atharvaveda IX, 2, 16* is really an armour fitted by righteousness and not merely of physical elements along with the soul. Almost the same idea is voiced by Manu in the following lines :—"As white ants construct the ant-hill, a man should, by alleviating the sufferings of all creatures and through rectitude of conduct, go on gradually accumulating Merit that it may stand him in good stead in his life after death. For there, neither can father and mother be of any service to man, nor his family and relatives; Dharma alone will aid him. Man is born alone, dies alone, enjoys the good or evil consequences of his actions also alone. When a man dies, casting away the corpse as if it were a clod of earth or a log of wood, all relatives walk off with their faces turned away, but the Merits of his righteous life follow him beyond the grave. Hence one should invariably accumulate Merit through rightoous living, for by its aid one can surmount insurmountable darkness† (in the shape of birth in the lower animals). A man whose life is most distinguished by Righteousness and whose demerits are wiped off by an austere living is forthwith conveyed with an earthly body refulgent

* See the Kāmasūkta given elsewhere.

† असुर्या नाम ते लोका अन्धेन तमसा वृताः । तांस्ते प्रेत्याभिगच्छन्ति ये के चात्महनो जनाः ॥ य० ४० । ३ ॥

with luster, to the world of Divine bliss by Dharma."*

This is the consummation of human life for which the whole life is merely a preparation. This done nothing more remains to be done.

(५७) यद्येकादशोऽसि सोपोदकोऽसि ॥११॥

पदपाठः—यदि । एकादशः । असि । सः । अपऽउदकः । असि ॥

अन्वयः—(हे नर) यदि एकादशः असि (तर्हि) स (त्वम्) अपोदकः असि ॥

Word-meaning &c. :—यदि=if. एकादशः=eleventh, i. e., somethiug other than what has been said in the previous ten verses ; making no endeavour to attain any of the perfections and powers described in the ten verses before this, or doing nothing even having developed one or more of his powers.

Translation :—Oh man, if thou hast not endeavoured to attain any of the powers so far described or having attained one or more of them dost nothing and art therefore, so to say, the eleventh, then I say, such a one as thou is useless, since he has not himself progressed in the right direction and cannot therefore help humanity towards its goal.

Purport :—Man as such, is bound to better his own, and then help in the betterment of his fellowmen's, physical, mental and spiritual prospects, by whole-hearted endeavours in the right direction.

---

* धर्मं शनैः सञ्चिनुयाद्वल्मीकमिव पुत्तिकाः । परलोकसहायार्थं सर्वभूतान्यपीडयन् ॥२३८॥
नामुत्र हि सहायार्थं पिता माता च तिष्ठतः । न पुत्रदारा न ज्ञातिर्धर्मस्तिष्ठति केवलः ॥२३९॥
एकः प्रजायते जन्तुरेक एव प्रलीयते । एकोऽनुभुङ्क्ते सुकृतमेक एव च दुष्कृतम् ॥२४०॥
मृतं शरीरमुत्सृज्य काष्ठलोष्ठसमं क्षितौ । विमुखा बान्धवा यान्ति धर्मस्तमनुगच्छति ॥२४१॥
तस्माद्धर्मं सहायार्थं नित्यं सञ्चिनुयाच्छनैः । धर्मेण हि सहायेन तमस्तरति दुस्तरम् ॥२४२॥
धर्मप्रधानं पुरुषं तपसा हतकिल्बिषम् । परलोकं नयत्याशु भास्वन्तं खशरीरिणम् ॥२४३॥

Comment :—This beautiful discourse on 'Man's Endeavours after Perfection", has come to an end. Step by step, the Holy Teacher led us on through nine stages and in the tenth, brought us face to face with what may be called the consummation of human progress. The marvellous point to be noted in this discourse is that, the Preacher does not say that it is possible for some or even all to rise to such heights, but he orders us to exert ourselves for such achievements and if we do not act up to his advice condemns us as "juiceless", "pithless" void of all that makes a man a man. Hence the question of possibility does not arise. When a Higher Power that knows all about us and has at His back and call, all that we may need, commands us to do a certain thing it is not fair that we should deliberate over the why and how of it or question whether it is possible to carry out the order or not. We must at once obey the order and start to work with the very first step.

We have also to bear in mind that God does not say that we must achieve all these stages at once. He simply asks us to start with one step first, and then having attained perfection in it, to proceed to the next. There is, it should be noted, no time limit set to this work. It may take a day, some years, a life time, or even hundreds of years. It all depends upon how the soul is disposed. Therefore, time does not matter; what matters is the achievement itself. Achieve, and achieve, and achieve. Go on achieving. Do not stop to rest or think, for your duty is to work your own salvation which is the necessary ultimate goal of your life, to neglect which at any stage of your life will be a sin. This goal according to the dispositions of the soul, will be achieved soon or late, but achieved it must be. It is in the very nature of the soul to attain salvation. What is required, is a whole-hearted endeavour.

There is, however, no short cut to this all round progress. In the beginning of the beautiful Mundakopaniṣad* we are told that "Śaunaka possessing big houses, having respectfully approached Angiras, asked, "Sire, what is it, that being known, all else is known?" The account eontinues, "he said, 'you should know that there are two kinds of knowledge, which the divine sages call the Parā (esoteric) and Aparā (exoteric)'." The sage then proceeds to mention the four Vedas, and the ancillary sciences. This is a clear indication that the easy method of which Śaunaka was in search does not exist. The great sage Śrī Kṛṣṇa also in the Gītā says to Arjuna :—

"I'll teach thee now without reserve
 this Wisdom matched with science true,
Which having mastered, naught remains
 for thee in earthly life to learn."†

and then lays down elaborate instructions on jñāna-yōga—atonement by means of knowledge. The gist of Śrī Kṛṣṇa's discourse is that all subsists in God, and to know God one has to investigate into the whole universe. The knowledge of God as already stated somewhere in the Comment on one previous verses, is got by elimination. Hence the sacred text prefers to mention all the items, fifty-four in number, in detail, to show the long journey man has to make. Emancipation, surely, comes at the end, but from the first step till reaching the goal it will be, for the progressing soul, a life of peace end happiness.

---

* कस्मिन्नु भगवो विज्ञाते सर्वमिदं विज्ञातं भवतीति ॥ तस्मै स होवाच द्वे विद्ये वेदितव्ये इति ह स्म यद्ब्रह्मविदो वदन्ति परा चैवापरा च ॥ मु० १ । ३-४ ॥

† ज्ञानं तेऽहं सविज्ञानमिदं वक्ष्याम्यशेषतः । यज्ज्ञात्वा नेह भूयोऽन्यज्ज्ञातव्यमवशिष्यते ॥ गी० ७ । २ ॥

In such a long and difficult process it is but natural that failures would often confront a man. At such a time despondency would be one's worst foe. To desist from attempting further at such a time would simply mean a horrible, irretrievable, downfall. Hence the only course left for the aspirant is to persevere in spite of all odds. Against despondency Manu says :—"One should not look down upon oneself on account of failures, but persevere in one's attempts towards progress till death, never for a moment thinking that one would not attain the goal."*

Every failure, one must know, is a stepping stone to success. The aspirant, it mnst be noted, should remember that he has, in his attempts towards progress, to remember three things, namely to *hope* for success, to *bear* all his troubles patiently and go on achieving with a heart disposed to *love* all creatures. In the charming words of Adelaide Anne Proctor he should say to himself :—

"Be strong to *hope*, oh Heart !
Though day is bright,
The stars can only shine
In the dark night.
Be strong, oh Heart of mine,
Look towards the light !

Be strong to *bear*, oh Heart !
Nothing is vain :
Strive not, for life is care,
And God sends pain,
Heaven is above, and there
Rest will remain !

Be strong to *love*, oh Heart !
Love knows not wrong,
Didst thou love—creatures even,
Life were not long ;

---

* नात्मानमवमन्येत पूर्वाभिरसमृद्धिभिः। आमृत्योः श्रियमन्विच्छेन्नैनां मन्येत दुर्लभाम् ॥ म० ४ । १३७ ॥

Didst thou love God in Heaven
Thou wouldst be strong !"*

King Robert Bruce of Scotland had, after long fighting with the English, almost lost heart. Taking shelter in a deserted church building he saw a spider attempting to climb by its string to the very dome above. It slipped and fell down many times but kept on persevering till in the end it succeeded. Robert took a lesson from this incident, himself persevered and was, as a result of his resoluteness, elevated to the throne of Scotland.

In the Ṛgvēda it is said :—"All the enlightened, all beneficent forces of Nature long for him who is persevering and have no regard for him who "sleeps". Him, who blunders, they crush forsooth."†

II. Another and simpler interpretation of the Vṛṣa Sūkta is also possible The word वृष in this interpretation denotes the power in the form of any of the ten senses and motor organs man is naturally endowed with. The function of each of these is a great force to be utilised by man in the profitable regulation, and direction of his life. The five sense organs are a great asset in our life's journey and so are the five motor organs. But if these ten faculties are not controlled and properly exercised they do not develop, nay, they deteriorate and make life a burden, a failure. By ordinary care and use they retain just the minimum amount of utility and help man somehow to pass his life. Such a mediocre man cannot be of any special use to the world beyond occupying some space, consuming some victuals and at the most propagating

* Legends and Lyrics and Other Poems by Adelaide Anne Proctor, Everyman's Library, p. 42 and 43.

† इच्छन्ति देवाः सुन्वन्तं न स्वप्नाय स्पृहयन्ति । यन्ति प्रमादमतन्द्राः॥ ऋ० ८।२।१८ ॥

his species. But a man of undeveloped and unregulated organs is mostly a burden to the earth, a drain on society's resources and a bad example to the posterity. It was not of such that Gray sang :—

"Full many a gem of purest ray serene
The dark unfathom'd caves of ocean bear :
Full many a flower is born to blush unseen,
And waste its sweetness on the desert air."*

Therefore, in order to spend his life profitably to himself and to his fellowmen man has to pay special attention to the regulation and development of these ten faculties of his. But it is not possible for a very large majority of men to develop all these ten. According to one's bent of mind one should select and specialise the particular faculty that one can most successfully develop and set about one's task at once in right earnest. Suppose a man determines to exercise his hands. The wrist, the fingers and their tips, and the joints of the hand will require full care to exercise and develop them properly. It will take a good time, perhaps the best part of his life, for the man to develop the powers of his hands and utilise them profitably. If successful, he may become a skilful artizan or artist, living a happy and honest life, helping others to live and thus prove a good citizen and an ideal member of human society.

It must however be noted that the special training and development of any one or more of his faculties does not mean that the man should neglect his other organs and let them go their own way. It is his sacred duty to guard all the other organs with the greatest care, failing to do which he will not succeed in his attempt of developing his powers. Hence the conclusion is that every man should try to develop

* Gray's "Elegy Written in a Country Churchyard."

one or more of his powers and at the same time protect the others with great care. With this proviso, every man can reasonably be expected to specialise himself at least in one of his personal powers.

Hence the hymn lays down that:—

A man who has attained power through the proper regulation and development of even one of his faculties should do some constructive work for his own and society's benefit. This is the only way in which his worth can be known. Otherwise people will call him worthless.

A man is answerable to God and society even if he develops more than one or all of his faculties. He who has specialised in two has the same responsibility as the man who has developed all his ten faculties. Even the man who has developed all his faculties is responsible to God and humanity. The greater one's qualifications the greater also one's responsibilities. A rich man owning crores cannot whistle away his time, saying "I am amply provided for, I need not do anything", for, his responsibilities are very great. Just in the same way a man who has developed all his ten faculties has to do more of constructive work to discharge his duty towards humanity. Failure to do so, would result in the ignominy of the man, his family and even the society to which he belongs.

The hymn does not stop here. In the 11th stanza it enunciates a very serious principle about success in life. A man may be very learned, proficient rich or virtuous, but if he is not, at the same time, ambitious and pushing, he will be no good to society. It is therefore necessary that every man should try to come forward and be the first. Such an ambition, is not sinful, nay it is a necessity, a duty. The Vedic scriptures do not condemn the right sort of ambition, they encourage it. In the Atharvaveda we read :—

"I am the centre of riches. Fain would I be the centre of mine equals."*

Again :—

"I am the head of riches. Fain would I be the head of mine equals."†

The following passages from the same Veda advise man to advance before others as he is endowed with various powers :—

"Thou art wise, thou art the protector of a body. Attain supreme bliss and surpass thy equals."‡

"Thou art power, thou art enlightener, thou art bliss, thou art light. Attain to supreme bliss and surpass all thy equals."§

"Oh man, I endow thee with a mind that knows not weariness, such a mind as is possessed by the man who is always foremost. Be thou, therefore, the pilot of thy followers carrying them up towards the upper shore, and leading them uphill run thou (forward) with confidence."||

In the same Veda XI chapter hymn 8th vv. 18 to 27 describe the various powers that entered the mortal frame of man after his creation. The first$ of these

---

* नाभिरहं रयीणाम् नाभिः समानानां भूयासम् ॥ अ० १६ । ४ । १ ॥

† मूर्धाहं रयीणाम् मूर्धा समानानां भूयासम् ॥ अ० १६ । २ । १ ॥

‡ सूरिरसि वर्चोधा असि तनूपानोऽसि । आप्नुहि श्रेयांसमति समं क्राम ॥ अ० २ । ११ । ४ ॥

§ शुक्रोऽसि भ्राजोऽसि स्वरसि ज्योतिरसि । आप्नुहि श्रेयांसमति समं क्राम ॥ अ० २ । ११ । ५ ॥

|| अश्रान्तस्य त्वा मनसा युनज्मि प्रथमस्य च । उत्कूलमुद्वहो भवोदुह्य प्रति धावतात् अ० १९ । २५ । १ ॥

$ यदा त्वष्टा व्यतृणत्पिता त्वष्टुर्य उत्तरः । गृहं कृत्वा मर्त्यं देवा पुरुषमाविशन् ॥ अ० ११ । ८ । ४ ॥

verses calls man a "little artizan" the son of the "Greater Artizan" God, the maker of the universe.

Hence endowed with such faculties a man must not allow himself to be idle but develop his powers and endeavour his utmost to rise high above others. Such an ambition is legitimate, nay, it is the very essence of life. For this purpose, a man need not be perfect every way, but specialisation in only one field is quite enough. So much, every man or woman can reasonably be expected to do. It is not also necessary that one should try to become a great religious or political leader, or the leader of a country or community. Our humble society or family is a miniature world where a full excercise of all our faculties is always in demand.

Hence the last verse of the hymn :—"यद्येकादृशोऽसि &c.," says that though a man may or may not have specialised in one or more of his faculties, he must have the ambition to be foremost among his equals. Such an ambition will compel him to regulate his forces and advance forward. But if on the other hand, even having developed all one's faculties, one remains in the back-ground on account of false modesty, laziness or any other cause—is satisfied, so to say, with being the eleventh when ten others join one in some undertaking—never oneself takes the initiative or lead and is hence quite contented with giving one's assenting vote, such a one is good for nothing. The text advises :—"Be not a life-less bag of bones; take courage in both hands and act like a man."

It is true, this interpretation does not differ much from the first. It is almost a summary of the first which gives many more and varied details. The special feature of this interpretation is the stress it lays on the idea of pushing to the front.

III. Lastly our hymn gives us the scale of numeration and notation. Along with the beautiful advice on endeavour after perfection and pushing to the front it tells us that the principal numbers are only ten and that the successive numbers are got by putting together ten and any other number in the scale. Along with numeration it gives us an idea of addition and subtraction as well, for, these two processes give all the numbers but 'one', by adding 'one' to any successive number in the upward scale or by subtracting 'one' from the higher number in the downward scale. To go back to the primeval creation mentally and observe the Divine Teacher instructing the earliest human race through its great Rsis (seers), is necessary to realise the significance of these Vedic texts. There are many more hymns on this subject which cannot be dealt with here since this is not a text book on mathematics. We refer the curious reader to Maharṣi Dayananda's "Introduction to the Commentary on the Vedas" and the "Light of Truth" for these and other questions relevant for the understanding of what is here said on the "Vṛṣa-sūkta."

Concluding remarks:—The etymologies of the compounds एकवृष, द्विवृष &c., given in the explanatory notes on this hymn are entirely in conformity with Pāṇini's Aṣṭadhyayī. A careful search is necessary to pick out from this difficult and voluminous work that exact rule that would satisfy a particular case. Most European scholars and their Indian followers seize any rule that comes handy and explain away even the most difficult formation. Griffith committed this mistake for, his translation of the hymn runs :—

"Bull, if thou art the single bull, beget. Thou hast no vital sap." This is due to his deep-rooted prejudice that the Atharvaveda is an ordinary book, far inferior perhaps, to a third rate English poet's writing. His footnote, therefore, tries to enlighten the curious leisure-hour reader as follows :--"The hymn, which is *a charm for the increase and prosperity of cattle,* contains ten other similar lines, the only difference being that in the place of ēkavṛṣah, single bull, dvivṛṣah double bull, or, two bulls,—trivṛṣah triple bull, or, worth three bulls, and so on follow in regular order up to ekādaśah, eleven-fold, in stanza 11 in which apōdakah, waterless, stands instead of the arasah sapless, of the preceding lines." From this irrelevant note only this much can be gathered that Griffith failed to grasp the 'in-lying' signification of this hymn of mnemonics. He did not however confess his inability to do so, but like the fox who called the grapes sour because she could not get at them, he tried to represent the hymn itself to be meaningless.

Whitney in his translation of the Atharvavēda comes out thus :—"(1) If thou art sole chief, let go, sapless art thou." He then adds that द्विवृष &c. are expressions "*not admitting of real translation.*" He further says "Perhaps the hymn is directed against insect pests, through their leaders, whether few or many." His "translation" of the remaining verses is as follows :—(2) "If thou art twice chief &c. Or rather perhaps double chief ; triple chief &c., or 'one of two' 'one of three' &c. (3) If thou art thrice———. (4) If thou art four times———&c. (11) If thou art eleven fold, then thou art waterless." Whitney also, has failed to explain this hymn, for his statements are incoherent and self-contradictory. To understand and represent anything correctly one ought to approach the subject in a spirit of humility—with fear and trembling. Only a sceptic determined to misrepresent things about others would assume any other attitude. It is regrettable our European savants do not seem to have this trait so essential for good scholarship.

It is this unsympathetic fault-finding attitude that has made Winternitz, in his "History of Indian Literature" page 155, scoff at Deussen for having taken "endless trouble to *discover* sense and meaning in the "philosophical" hymns of the Atharvavēda, and to *establish certain coherent ideas* in them." He is not pleased with Deussen's finding in Atharvavēda X, 2 and XI, 8 "the idea that deals with the 'realisation of Brahman in man'." He finds in them '*pseudophilosophy*' and not true philosophy. He complains that "while in a celebrated hymn of the Ṛgvēda X, 121, a *deep-thinker* and *a true poet* refers in bold words to the splendour of the cosmos and *sceptically asks about the creator*, in Atharvavēda X, 2 a *verse-maker enumerates one after the other all the limbs of man*, and asks who has created them." He thinks "one would be honouring this kind of verses too much by seeking deep wisdom." A stray idea of true philosophy here and there makes no difference at all, for "just as the *liar*" (sic !) "must sometimes speak the truth, in order that one may believe his lies, so the pseudophilosopher, too, must introduce here and there into his fabrications a real philosophical idea which he has '*picked up*' *somewhere or other*, in order that one may take his *nonsense* for the height of wisdom."

This ungenerous attitude has originated from the writer's prejudice. He maintains that the Vēdas are written by men, that the Atharvavēda is much later than and mostly a copy of, the Ṛgvēda and so on and so forth. Now when the markets are flooded with attractive books of poetry and on science, when Roentgen rays and Radio are ordinary things, 'a catalogue' of the limbs of the human body or an account of the merits of herbs in a poetic style can appeal to very few minds. But to the man who believes in the existence of the primitive revelation from which all current arts and sciences have directly or indirectly sprung, there is no 'pseudophilosophy' no 'lies' no 'picked up ideas' and no 'nonsense' here, but serious instruction, the basis of all human development, without which man would have been no better than beast.

Such raving remarks as those of Winternitz cannot discourage us from honouring the oldest scientific, poetical and philosophical records of humanity of which Indians are the proud possessors.

Chapter V.

Praise of the Soul.

Ṛgvēda X, 119.

Seer :—The Sage Lava, the son of Indra.

Subject :—Powers of the soul visualised through spiritual discipline.

Metre :—Stanzas 1-5 and 7-10 gayatrī, 6, 12 and 13 nicṛd-gayatrī and verse 11 viraḍ-gayatrī.

Tone :—Ṣaḍja.

(५८) ओ३म् ॥ इति वा इति मे मनो गामश्वं सनुयामिति । कुवित्सोमस्यापामिति ॥ १ ॥

पदपाठः—इति । वै । इति । मे । मनः । गाम् । अश्वम् । सनुयाम् । इति । कुवित् । सोमस्य । अपाम् । इति ॥

अन्वयः—इति वै इति मे मनः अस्ति गाम् अश्वम् सनुयाम् इति सोमस्य अहम् कुवित् अपाम् इति ॥

Word-meaning &c. :—इति (√इण् गतौ+क्तिच् P. III, 3, 1 and 174)=thus ; that ; for ; because ; as ; that is all ; enough &c. वै=surely (or an expletive). मनः= mind ; resolution ; decision ; determination. गाम् अश्वम् =all worldly possessions consisting of cows, horses &c. सनुयाम (√षणु दाने)=that I should give away in charity. सोमस्य (√षु प्रसवैश्वर्ययोः+मन U. I, 140)=of the world ; joys of a devotional or spiritual life ; advantages of yogic discipline. कुवित् (Nig. III, 1)=much;

कुवित् सोमस्य अपाम्=oft have I enjoyed the advantages of spiritual discipline; many times; enough; ample. अपाम् =I have enjoyed. I have often drunken of the pleasures of the world to intoxication.

Translation :—(The spiritually advanced man having enjoyed the world's happiness to his satisfaction is ardently inclined to renounce everything and so says to himself or addressing God as the witness of his resolve :—) Thus and surely thus does my mind propose that I should give away in charity all my worldly possessions including cows, horses, etc., for many a time have I enjoyed of the advantages of the 'Yogic Spiritual Discipline'.

Purport :—Man must not be immersed all his life in the enjoyment of worldly pleasures. He should always aim at the topmost step of spiritual advance and when by devotion to God and the practice of Yōga he feels a strong desire for renunciation, assign enough of his property to his family, give away the rest in charity and become a vānaprasthī or sanyāsin.

Comment:—'Sanuyām' is the first person singular potential mood form of the √सन् give, given in the Dhātupātha as ṣaṇu, dānē, i. e., 'to give'. Macdonell in his 'Vedic Grammar for Beginners' p. 426 gives "san, gain, VIII, P," which interpretation has no trustworthy authority to support it and must therefore be rejected as unwarranted. The form 'apām' is the aorist of the √पा to drink given in the dhātupātha as 'pā pānē' i. e., to drink. Here it means to get disgusted of the world after the enjoyment of the superior pleasures of the spiritual life the result of yogic discipline and devotion to God, or to become senseless by frequent enjoyment of worldly pleasure just as a man by taking liquor gets drunk. The idea of enjoyment resulting in the disgust of something or the loss of discretion is involved in every stanza of the hymn. In English also 'drunken' means intoxicated but a very great similarity between two languages so far apart in age cannot be expected,

Having failed to realise the true spirit of the hymn, European savants have construed it to mean the 'self-praise' of Indra drunken with Sōma juice. The subject (devatā) of the hymn is ātmastuti, i. e., 'laudation of the soul' and not 'Indra'. The sage of the hymn is 'Lava' 'Aindra', i. e., Lava a descendent of Indra or the subtle individual soul (Indrasya apatyam or Indrah ēva), since Indra means, God, the sun, lightening, &c. as well as the individual soul. 'Indra' is still in use in India as an individual name, and the word 'Lava' also is famous in Indian history as the name of one of the sons of the illustrious Rāma. Hence it is quite probable that the interpreter of this hymn is a sage named 'Lava' the son of Indra a human being."

In the Muṇḍakōpaniṣad there is a comment on R. V. I, 164, 20, as follows:—"Attaching itself through ignorance to the same tree on which it and the Supreme Being are both resident, the human soul caught in the snares of infatuation laments on account of its incapacities (in its worldly life). But when it sees its companion the Supreme Being commanding all power then it knows that every thing is the sport of His Glorious Majesty and is freed from its sorrows."*

This is exactly the state of the man pictured in this hymn.

The expression 'kuvit' many times, signifies the idea of transmigration, which is another point European scholars deny, contending that this doctrine is not to be found in the Vedas.

---

* समाने वृक्षे पुरुषो निमग्नोऽनीशया शोचति मुह्यमानः । जुष्टं यदा पश्यत्यन्यमीशमस्य महिमानमिति वीतशोकः ॥ मु॰ ३ । १ । २ ॥

(५९) प्र वाता इव दोधत उन्मा पीता अयंसत ।
कुवित्सोमस्यापामिति ॥ २ ॥

पदपाठः—प्र । वाताःऽइव । दोधतः । उत् । मा । पीताः । अयंसत । ० ॥

अन्वयः—प्रदोधतः वाताः इव इमे पीताः मा अधुना उदयंसत अहम् सोमस्य कुवित् अपाम् इति ॥

Word-meaning &c. :—वाताः (√वा सुखाप्तिगतिसेवासु + तन् U. III, 86)=winds. प्रदोधतः (√दोध क्रुध्यतिकर्मा Nig. II. 12)=extremely agitated i. e., blowing a very strong gale. पीताः (√पा पाने + क्त)=these worldly pleasures that I have been enjoying; the advantages of yogic discipline I have enjoyed. मा=me. उदयंसत (उत् + √यम्)= pull away ; blow away.

Translation :—I feel that these blessings of the spiritual advancement that I have been enjoying, do now, like fiercely blowing tempestuous winds pull me away from the enjoyments of the world.

Purport :—The nature of worldly pleasures is such that they restrain a man and keep him tethered down to a limited scope. Hence a man of spiritual development feels his movements fettered by them. But advancement in spiritual life through devotion and yogic discipline has such force that it pulls him off and severs all his undue connection with the world. Every man or woman must contemplate on the nature and effects of worldly happiness and try to escape their evil influence through devotion to God and spiritual discipline.

(६०) उन्मा पीता अयंसत रथमश्वा इवाशवः ।
कुवित्सोमस्यापामिति ॥ ३ ॥

पदपाठः—उत् । मा । पीताः । अयंसत । रथंम् । अश्वाःऽइव । आशवः । ० ॥

अन्वयः—यथा आशवः अश्वाः रथम् उदयंसत तथा इमे पीताः मा इदानीम् उदयंसत, कुतः अहम् सोमस्य कुवित् अपाम् इति ॥

Word-meaning &c. :—आशवः (√अशूङ् व्याप्तौ संघाते च + उण् U. I, 1)=fleet ; swift.

Translation :—Nay, like swift horses that pull off a chariot, these powers of the spiritual discipline I have attained carry me away from the pleasures of the world that have long fettered me.

Purport :—Enjoyed too long, these worldly pleasures will fetter down a man against his will, and render him entirely helpless to save himself from their pernicious effect, utter ruin being the final result. But a pious and righteous life will bestow on him such power as will help him to tear himself off from them.

(६१) उपं मा मतिरस्थित वाश्रा पुत्रमिंव प्रियम् ।
कुवित्सोमस्यापामिति ॥ ४ ॥

पदपाठः—उपं । मा । मतिः । अस्थित । वाश्रा । पुत्रम्ऽइव । प्रियम् ॥ ० ॥

अन्वयः—वाश्रा प्रियम् पुत्रम् इव मदीया मतिः इदानीम् मा उपास्थित, कुवित् अहम् सोमस्य अपाम् इति ॥

Word-meaning &c.:—मतिः (√मन बोधे + क्तिच् P. III, 3, 174)=understanding ; reason. उप अस्थित=to stand near; to serve, wait upon, attend, take care of. वाश्रा (√वाश्टृ शब्दे + रक् + टाप् U. II, 13 and P. IV, 1, 4)=a cow bellowing for its calf. पुत्रम्=calf.

Translation :—Just as the mother cow stands near her dear calf (and protects it) so has my reason strengthened by the spiritual training I have erstwhile had, stood me in good stead now.

Purport :—At critical times it is only one's mind that helps one in one's difficulties, hence one should habituate it to incline God-ward through devotion and spiritual discipline.

(६२) अहं तष्टेव बन्धुरं पर्यचामि हृदा मतिम् ।
कुवित्सोमस्यापामिति ॥ ५ ॥

पदपाठः—अहम् । तष्टाऽइव । बन्धुरम् । परि । अचामि । हृदा । मतिम् । ० ॥

अन्वयः—तष्टा बन्धुरम् इव अहम् मे मतिम् हृदा पर्यचामि, कुतः अहम् सोमस्य कुवित् अपाम् इति ॥

Word-meaning &c. :—तष्टा (√तक्ष्+तृच्)=carpenter. बन्धुरम् (√बन्ध बन्धने+उरच् U. I, 41)=crooked. हृदा (√हृञ् हरणे+तुक्+क्विप् P. III, 2, 178 and VI, 1, 71)=by means of the conscience. पर्यचामि=I bend down and straighten i. e., regulate.

Translation :—For, just as the carpenter bends down and straightens a crooked 'wood' so have I regulated my understanding through my conscience, by long undergoing spiritual discipline.

Purport :—Every person should subject his or her understanding to the voice of conscience and thus escape from the snares of the world.

Comment :—The beautiful description of 'mati'—understanding or discretion in both the 4th & 5th stanzas and of 'hṛd' in the latter which has been translated by conscience, conclusively falsifies the contention of European scholars that the hymn is a song of drunken Indra's self-praise. A drunken person's mind cannot take care of him as the mother cow does of her calf, nor can the drunkard straighten his mind with his conscience, for intoxication is the name of a change produced in the mind and not on the stomach. A toper's limbs may be all in order but his intellect must be affected if he is to be called intoxicated.

The dictionary meaning of the word 'paryac' is to bend by tying round with cloth &c. A bandhura, 'crooked' stick is straightened by bending it in the opposite direction where it is crooked by means of weight or pressure exerted on it somehow. Applied to mind it means the subjection of the intellect or understanding (or better still reason) to the conscience, which is not at all possible for the drunkard to do as long as he is intoxicated, for it is only when he regains consciousness that he will be able to listen to the voice of his conscience. The remorse that will set in after the intoxication is over will lead to his turning a new leaf in life. In physical intoxication though the body may be sound the mind ceases to work in an orderly manner, but in moral intoxication the mind gets a wrong direction in which it does work quite satisfactorily. It is this moral intoxication that the hymn treats of. All worldlings, engrossed in money-making or hunting after high positions and lime-light are morally intoxicated. The mind and conscience of such a man do work all right in a particular groove according to his occupation, except during some lucid moments when his mental faculty gets a contrary impulse from the conscience in the right direction which leads to the man's improvement. This is the lesson the hymn teaches by describing the grandeur of the soul.

(६३) नहि मे अक्षिपच्चनाच्छान्त्सुः पंच कृष्टयः ।
कुवित्सोमस्यापामिति ॥ ६ ॥

पदपाठः—नहि । मे । आक्षिपत् । चन । अच्छान्त्सुः । पंच । कृष्टयः । ० ॥

अन्वयः—पंचकृष्टयः एनाम् मे मतिम् न अच्छान्त्सुः नहि सा अक्षिपत् चन, कुतः अहम् सोमस्य कुवित् अपाम् इति ॥

Word-meaning &c. :—अक्षिपत्=shake; waver. नहिचन=never. अच्छान्त्सुः (Ved. aor. of √छदु or छन्द 10th conj)=prevail upon; persuade. पंच=five. कृष्टयः (√कृष विलेखने+क्तिच् P. III, 3, 174)=which attract or pull, i. e., the senses that draw the mind and the soul towards the world.

Translation:—My mind is now so firm that the five senses cannot draw it towards the enjoyments of the world for I have been strengthened by the nectar of spiritual discipline I have erstwhile drunken.

Purport :—Only a man of determined and well-grounded resolute will, can overcome the allurements of worldly pleasures. An ordinary weak-minded man will drift along as they carry him. Hence every man or woman should try to discipline his or her mind so as to make it strong and discrete.

Comment :—'Acchāntsuh' is an aorist third person plural form of the √छदु or छन्दु 10th conj., meaning to cover, prevail upon or persuade; but unfortunately Macdonell in his Vedic Grammar for Beginners p. 382 gives 'chad or chand *seem*, II': According to him—and perhaps also the St. Petersburg Lexicon it is a verb of the 2nd (adādi) conjugation and means 'to seem'. This information however has absolutely no foundation. The roots √छदु and √छन्दु have according to the dhātupātha current in India from time immemorial, the following significations:—(1) √छदि भ्वादिः ऊर्जने=chad 1st conj.=to nourish, or strengthen. (2) √छदि चुरादिः आच्छादने=chad 10th conj.=to conceal, cover. (3) √छदि (छादृ) भ्वादिः संवरणे=chad or chand 1st conj.=to cover. (4) √छदि (छन्दृ) चुरादिः संवरणे =chad or chand 10th conj. to cover, please, persuade. The signification "to seem" given by Macdonell seems to be a mere presumptuous conjecture from such formations as छद्मन् (U. IV, 144) meaning trick, deception, disguise &c., in which there is something which *seems*, but this is no plea at all since the idea of something concealed or covered is more important. The other meaning of the root viz., to please or persuade is entirely lost sight of by Macdonell. The mistake is, unfortunately copied by Dr. Lakshmaṇa Svarūpa in his Index to the edition of the Nirukta with the Scholia of Mahēśvara and Skandasvamin p. 42 col. 2nd first line where it is said 'अच्छान् Ao. S. of √छद्, it has appeared, 9.8.' Skandasvami's remarks are "अच्छान् छादयन्ति। किम्? सामर्थ्यान्मनः। अत्यन्तं प्रीतिं करोतीत्यर्थः।" Another older and reputed commentator Durgacarya says:— "स एव विस्मोदक एवंप्रकारो महाममवच्छदत्। स्नेन फलशब्देन सत्त्वार्थिषु पुनः पुनः भृशं वा मनश्छादयित्वा देवन एवैकस्मिन्मम मन उत्साहयति।" Both these scholiasts mean by छद् or छाद् here, 'to overpower the mind and make the person do something which he would never otherwise have done.'

In the face of these great and ancient authorities to whom Sanskrit was their 'lingua franca', Macdonell's imaginary and wrong ieterpretation can carry no weight.

(६४) नहि मे रोदसी उभे अन्यं पक्षं चन प्रति।
कुवित्सोमस्यापामिति ॥ ७ ॥

पदपाठः—नहि। मे। रोदसी इति। उभे इति। अन्यम्। पक्षम्। चन। प्रति। ०॥

अन्वयः—उभे रोदसी मे अन्यं पक्षं चन प्रति नहि, अहम् सोमस्य कुवित् अपाम् इति॥

Word-meaning &c. :—रोदसी (√रुद्+असुन् U. IV, 189)=the earth and the heavens. उभे=both. अन्यम्=one; a part or division. पक्षम् (√पण व्यवहारे स्तुतौ च+स U. III, 62 and 69)=power; strength. चन=not; not at all; not even. प्रति=as compared with.

Translation:—Both the earth and the heavens together cannot be compared to a part of my powers which fact I know having many a time enjoyed the advantages of spiritual discipline.

Purport: —It is very necessary for spiritual advance that the devotee should at times institute a thorough-going comparison between his soul and his material possessions and environments which will convince him of the real worth of his soul. In fact, excepting God, there is nothing greater, nay, even equal to the soul in power and grandeur. He or she who knows this will never fall into evil ways.

(६५) अभि द्यां महिना भुवमभीऽइमां पृथिवीं महीम् । कुवित्सोमस्यापामिति ॥ ८ ॥

पदपाठः—अभि । द्याम् । महिना । भुवम् । अभि । इमाम् । पृथिवीम् । महीम् । ० ॥

अन्वयः—अभि द्याम् अभि इमाम् महीम् पृथिवीम् च अहम् महिना भुवम्, हि अहम् सोमस्य कुवित् अपाम् इति ॥

Word-meaning &c. :—अभि=as compared with; set face to face with, (आभिमुख्यम् Vide Gaṇaratnamahodadhi). द्याम् (√द्युत दीप्तौ+डा U. II, 67 and P. VII, 1, 90) =the heavens. महीम् (√मह पूजायाम्+अच+ङीष् P. III, 1, 134 and IV, 1, 41)=spacious, vast. पृथिवीम् (√प्रथ प्रख्याने+षिवन्+ङीष् U. I, 150 and P. IV, 1, 41)=earth. महिना (√मह पूजायाम्+इनण् U. II, 56 and P. VII, 1, 39)=with glory. भुवम्=I am. अभि भुवम्=I surpass.

Translation :—Set face to face with the heavens or this earth, my glory is greater, which I have realised while often times enjoying the advantages of spiritual discipline.

Purport :—The earth and the heavens, nay, the whole universe, is created for the benefit of the soul. This fact is a proof of the truth mentioned in the stanza that man's soul is more glorious than the heavens and the earth together. In fact it is second in glory only to God. Oh could men and women think over and realize this great truth in their lives !

Comment :—In the 7th and 8th verses of the hymn is depicted the surprise of the man of spiritual advancement when he realises the true nature of his soul as compared with the trivial worldly possessions that had kept him chained down to the earth. He realises, and marvels at the unexpected realisation, that the earth and the heavens are very small* as compared to the powers and glory of his soul. This knowledge dawns upon the man only when the intoxication of worldly pleasures is over. As long as this lasts it is not possible for any man, however, rich† and learned‡ he may be, to perceive and be convinced of the great powers of the soul. For, this cannot be accomplished by book-reading—a mere theoretical knowledge—but requires patient and long practice of spiritual discipline.§

---

* यं यं लोकं मनसा संविभाति विशुद्धसत्त्वः कामयते यांश्च कामान् । तं तं लोकं जयते तांश्च कामांस्तस्मादात्मज्ञं ह्यर्चयेद्भूतिकामः ॥ मु० ३ । १ । १० ॥

† अमृतत्वस्य तु नाशास्ति वित्तेन ॥ बृ० २ । ४ । २ ॥

‡ नायमात्मा प्रवचनेन लभ्यो न मेधया न बहुना श्रुतेन । यमेवैष वृणुते तेन लभ्यस्तस्यैष आत्मा वृणुते तनूं स्वाम् ॥ क० २ । २३ ॥

§ नाविरतो दुश्चरितान्नाशान्तो नासमाहितः । नाशान्तमानसो वापि प्रज्ञानेनैनमाप्नुयात् ॥ २४ ॥

न चक्षुषा गृह्यते नापि वाचा नान्यैर्देवैस्तपसा कर्मणा वा । ज्ञानप्रसादेन विशुद्धसत्त्वस्ततस्तु तं पश्यते निष्कलं ध्यायमानः ॥ मु० ३ । १ । ८ ॥

(६६) हन्ताहं पृथिवीमिमां नि दंधानीह वेह वा ।
कुवित्सोमस्यापामिति ॥ ६ ॥

पदपाठः—हन्त । अहम् । पृथिवीम् । इमाम् । नि । दधानि । इह । वा । इह । वा । ० ॥

अन्वयः—हन्त अहम् इमाम् पृथिवीम् इह वा इह वा निदधानि, सोमस्य कुवित् अपाम् इति ॥

Word-meaning &c. :—हन्त=well; very well; well then. निदधानि=I will or should relinquish; I will sever all my attachments to. इह वा इह वा=here and here alone; here and now.*

Translation:—Well then, here and now I will sever all my attachments to this earth for, erstwhile have I enjoyed the pleasures of spiritual advance and am now satisfied.

(६७) ओषमित्पृथिवीमहं जङ्घनानीह वेह वा ।
कुवित्सोमस्यापामिति ॥ १० ॥

पदपाठः—ओषम् । इत् । पृथिवीम् । अहम् । जंघनानि । इह । वा । इह । वा । ० ॥

अन्वयः—अहम् पृथिवीम् इह वा इह वा ओषम् इत् जङ्घनानि यतः अहम् सोमस्य कुवित् अपाम् इति ॥

Word-meaning &c, :—ओषम् (√उष दाहे+घञ् P. III, 3, 18)=quickly; at once. इत्=indeed. जङ्घनानि (यङ् लुक् of √हन हिंसागत्योः)=I will renounce; let me renounce, sever all connection with. पृथिवीम्=the earth; earthly possessions.

Translation :—Let me, therefore, here and now indeed, sever all my connection with earthly possessions at once, for I have in many a life enjoyed enough of them.

---

* वा is here used in the sense of deliberation. वेति विचारणार्थो हन्ताहं पृथिवीमिमां निदधानीह वेह वेति ॥ पा० १ । ४ ॥

Purport :—In this and the previous stanza the earnestness of the attitude of the person who is bent upon renouncing the world is succinctly but clearly depicted. Only that man can truly renounce the world who feels and realises fully that the earthly enjoyments he has been enjoying are trite in comparison with his vast spiritual prospects extended all over the future. Such a feeling inclines a man to make all efforts to hasten the liberation of his soul from the obstructions of worldly possessions. The sooner he takes the step the better he thinks.

Comment :—The knowledge of the powers of his soul that has dawned upon the exercitant of spiritual discipline persuades him to renounce his worldly possessions immediately. This is what the sage Patanjali says in his treatise on Yoga :—

"That effect which comes to those who have given up their thirst after objects either seen or heard and which wills to control the objects, is non-attachment."* Here begins the upward movement of the soul of the exercitant. He however does not stop here. He rises still higher and attains to what the next aphorism says :—

"That is extreme non-attachment which gives up even the qualities (sattva, rajas and tamas), and comes from the knowledge of (the real nature of) the Puruṣa."† This means that the exercitant becoming aware of the real nature of his own soul as well as of the Supreme Being severs his connection with all that is endowed with the three forces (attributes=guṇas) of nature (primordial matter=Prakṛti) the subtlest of which is his own mind (buddhi). When this also is given up there arises what is called

* दृष्टानुश्रविकविषयवितृष्णस्य वशीकारसंज्ञा वैराग्यम् । यो० १ । १५ ॥

† तत्परं पुरुषख्यातेर्गुणवैतृष्ण्यम् ॥ १६ ॥

Kaivalya i. e., perfect isolation from all material connections.

(६८) दिवि मे अन्यः पक्षोऽधो अन्यमचीकृषम् ।
कविरसोमस्यापामिति ॥ ११ ॥

पदपाठः—दिवि । मे । अन्यः । पक्षः । अधः । अन्यम् । अचीकृषम् । ० ॥

अन्वयः—अन्यः मे पक्षः दिवि आसीत् अन्यम् पक्षम् अहम् अधः अचीकृषं, हि, अहम् सोमस्य कुवित् अपाम् इति ॥

Word-meaning &c. :—पक्षः (√पच्+सुट्+असुन् U. IV, 189 and 220)=side, part. दिवि=in the heavens i. e., the region excluding the earth and the atmosphere surrounding her; in light spiritual. अधः=below, on the earth; in earthly life or existence; in darkness i.e., matter. अचीकृषम्=I have pulled, that is, brought down.

Translation :—One side of my life (my soul) I have in the world (=sphere) of light (where there is no hindrance in the shape of matter and ignorance) and only one part have I brought down here in the darkness (of the material world) for in many a life have I enjoyed the pleasures of both.

Purport :—Roughly speaking there are three regions, the earthly, the atmospheric and the heavenly. The soul, itself a lustrous being roams about in all these when it is unfettered but gets confined to one particular earthly region when it is encased in a body. A contemplation of this fact will convince man of the necessity of renunciation of worldly possessions at a certain stage in his mundane existense—the region where darkness in the shape of material attachments fetters his soul.

(६९) अहमस्मि महामहोऽभिनभ्यमुदीषितः ।
कुवित्सोमस्यापामिति ॥ १२ ॥

पदपाठः—अहम् । अस्मि । महाऽमहः । अभिऽनभ्यम् । उत्ऽईषितः । ० ॥

अन्वयः—अहम् महामहः, अभिनभ्यम् उदीषितः अस्मि, सोमस्य अहम् कुवित् अपाम् इति ॥

Word-meaning &c. :—अस्मि=I am i. e., I feel I am. महामहः (महताम् महः)=great among the great; being spiritually advanced he is regarded with respect even among men considered great and noble owing to their wealth and high station. अभिनभ्यम् (अभि+नभि+यत् P. V, 1, 2)=upto the intermediate regions; from the earth to the heavens. उदीषितः (उत्+√ईष गति हिंसादर्शनेषु+क्त)=elevated; raised; going up; extended.

Translation :—Having many a time enjoyed the pleasures of the world and being now released from their fetters I now feel that I am great among the great and that my soul's powers are extended beyond the intermediate regions.

Purport :—Real greatness consists not in wealth or high station but in a true mental and spiritual development. A man who is mentally and spiritually great is highly respected even by the rich. When such a man realising the vanity or worldly riches and the greatness of his own soul severs his connection with the world and day and night meditates on God, he feels even in his bodily life the bliss of liberation. This should be the aim of every man and woman.

Comment :—The 11th and 12th verses still further and in more forcible language depict the glory of the soul. What is said here is far beyond the power of the sense organs, even above the capacity of the material mind. It is only the soul as isolated from material fetters, in spite of bodily life continuing, that can realise this wonderful truth. The powers of the soul are in these two stanzas described in very attractive colours which some may think exaggerated. But European writers also testify to the truth of the statement made in these stanzas. A French novelist Flammarion tells that the soul of a man who died in the last quarter of the 19th century, no sooner it left the body, flew to a very far star and from their witnessed Napoleon still on the field of Waterloo. The battle of Waterloo was fought in 1815.* This means that the soul of the man had in a second transferred itself to a star so far situated from the earth that the light proceeding from the battle field when the war was still raging had taken more than sixty years to reach it. What a tremendous leap† when we remember that light travels at the rate of 1,86,000 miles per second ! But yet, let us remember that Flammarion's estimate‡ is very very low and his statement not very scientific.

(७०) गृहो याम्यरंकृतो देवेभ्यो हव्यवाहनः ।
कुवित्सोमस्यापामिति ॥ १३ ॥

पदपाठः—गृहः । यामि । अरंऽकृतः । देवेभ्यः । हव्यऽवाहनः । ० ॥

अन्वयः—अहम् देवेभ्यः गृहः अरंकृतः हव्यवाहनः यामि हि सोमस्य कुवित् अपाम् इति ॥

Word-meaning &c. :—गृहः (√गृह ग्रहणे+घ P. III, 3, 118)=a companion; an assistant; an attendant. यामि= I go. अरंकृतः=adorned with true knowledge through

* Green's 'History of the English People' (1909) p. 835.
† 347,122,640,000,000 miles per second.
‡ The Outline of Science.

renunciation of the world. देवेभ्यः=for the liberated* souls now in the beatific state. हव्यवाहनः (हव्यं वहतीति हव्य + √वह प्रापणे + ल्युट् P. III, 2, 69)=possessing qualifications enabling one to associate with them on a footing of equality.

Translation :—During many lives have I enjoyed the happiness of worldly possessions and now, adorned with true knowledge through renunciation of the world, and becoming a fitting companion for liberated souls in their beatific state I shall go to associate with them on terms of equality.

Purport :—There are innumerable liberated souls moving near and around us but their sphere of existence being very subtle we are not able to perceive them. That man however, who shakes off self, severs all his connection with the world, meditates on God and attains true knowledge, does, either in yogic trance or after casting off the body, join them and become one of them.

Comment :—The powers described in this hymn are those of the soul either emancipated or being still in the body released from the encumbrances of material connection through unexhausted residua of past actions. The migrating soul does possess these powers but they are suppressed by material encumbrances brought about by the fruits of past actions still to be enjoyed. Of the liberated soul the Maharṣi Dayānanda in his Light of Truth p. 284 says:—"The (emancipated) soul enjoys the bliss of emancipation through God in the same way as it enjoys the worldly pleasures through the body. The emancipated soul roams about in the Infinite All-pervading God as it desires, sees all nature through pure knowledge, meets other emancipated souls, sees all the laws of nature in

* देवा महिमानः ॥ श० १०।२।२।२॥ अमृता देवाः ॥ श० २।१।३।४॥

operation, goes about all the worlds visible, and invisible, sees all objects that come within its knowledge, the more its knowledge increases the happier it feels. Being altogether pure, the soul acquires perfect knowledge of all hidden things in the state of emancipation."*

These are the powers of the soul released from all its earthly shackles, but it should not be understood that its powers are infinite. The same writer on page 278 of the book* says :—"The soul is finite in knowledge and powers. It is not the seer of the three periods of time—the past, the present and the future, it cannot therefore recall its past. Besides, the manas —the principle of thought and attention—by means of which the soul knows, cannot have two ideas—i. e., of the past as well as of the present—at the same time. Let alone things that happened in the previous life of the soul, why cannot a man remember what happens in this very life from the time of conception till, say, the age of five. We see and hear so many different things while we are awake, and dream of so many different things while in slumber, why can we not recall all those things when we are in deep sleep. You could never tell, if you were asked, for example, what you were doing on the ninth day of the fifth month of the thirteenth year of your life exactly at ten in the morning; which way you were looking; what the position of your head and hands was; whether your mouth was open or shut; and what you were then thinking of. When such is the case even in this life, how absurd then to question the validity of the previous existence of the soul simply because it cannot recall what happened in that life ? It is a

---

* Dr. Chiranjiva Bharadwāja's translation, Lahore (1927) edn.

good thing too that the soul cannot remember its past, otherwise there would have been no happiness for it. It would have died of sheer pain and mental anguish brought on by brooding over the terrible sufferings and sorrows of its past lives. No man can ever know what happened in his past lives even if he were to try to do so, because the soul's power and knowledge are limited. God alone can know that."

The passage quoted above refers to the ordinary embodied soul, that is, a common human being as we see him or her in our daily life—one like ourselves. those whose vision has been purified and broadened by the yogic spiritual discipline of whom Maharṣi Dayānanda himself was one, the Yōga treatise of the Sage Patanjali II chapter, aphorism 39, thus describes :—"When he is fixed in non-receiving, he becomes aware of the nature of his life."* On this the commentator Vyāsa says :—"the Yogi becomes aware of what he was in his past life, of what nature and what will he be and of what nature in the future."† In III chapter again we are told that :—"By perceiving the impressions, (comes) the knowledge of past life."‡ On this the late Swāmi Vivēkananda thus comments :—"Each experience that we have, comes in the form of a wave in the citta, and this subsides and become finer and finer, but is never lost. It remains there in minute form, and if we can bring this wave up again, it becomes memory. So if the yogi can make a saṃyama on these past impressions in the mind, he will begin to remember all his past lives."§

* अपरिग्रहस्थैर्ये जन्मकथंतासम्बोधः ॥ यो० २ । ३९ ॥

† कोऽहमासं कथमहमासं किंस्विदिदं कथंस्विदिदं के वा भविष्यामः कथं वा भविष्याम इत्येवमस्य पूर्वान्तपरान्तमध्येष्वात्मजिज्ञासा स्वरूपेणावर्तते ॥ व्या० भा० ॥

‡ संस्कारसाक्षात्करणात्पूर्वजातिज्ञानम् ॥ यो० ३ । १८ ॥

§ Complete Works 5th edn. Vol. I, p. 276.

The next aphorism further states that :—"By making saṃyama on the signs in another's body, knowledge of his mind comes."*

The passages quoted above help us to draw the conclusion that the accomplished yogi can, if he concentrates his mind on his 'impressions' and on the corporal signs and impressions of others, come to know much about his own life and the life of others. But from this, it should not be thought that man can become omniscient. The correct definition of the soul as given by the Maharṣi Dayānanda is :—"The soul is an immortal, invisible principle, which is endowed with thought and judgment, desire and passion, pleasure and pain, and so forth."†

The same great writer paraphrasing(?) a passage from the XIV book of the Śatapatha Brahmaṇa as follows :—शृण्वन् श्रोत्रं भवति, स्पर्शयँस्त्वग् भवति, पश्यँश्चक्षुर्भवति, रसयन् रसना भवति, जिघ्रन् घ्राणं भवति, मन्वानो मनो भवति, बोधयन् बुद्धिर्भवति, चेतयँश्चित्तं भवति, अहं कुर्वाणोऽहंकारो भवति,‡ thus comments :—"the physical body or the organs of the senses do not accompany the soul in the state of salvation; but she retains her pure essential qualities. In plain words, the soul in salvation turns, by virtue of

---

* प्रत्ययस्य परचित्तज्ञानम् ॥ १९ ॥

† Light of Truth—Beliefs 4. Durga Prasada's translation.

‡ This seems to be a paraphrase of Br. U. I, 4, 17:—अकृत्स्नो हि सः प्राणन्नेव प्राणो नाम भवति वदन्वाक्पश्यंश्चक्षुः शृण्वञ्छ्रोत्रं मन्वानो मनस्तान्यस्यैतानि कर्मनामान्येव ॥ "The soul is incomplete. Hence, while breathing it, indeed, assumes the form of the vital air, while speaking that of the organ of speech, while seeing that of the eye, while hearing that of the ear and while thinking that of the mind for all these are names given to the soul from its actions." The application of the passage to the liberated soul is really very intelligent and not at all far-fetched.

her power, into the ear in order to hear, the skin to touch, the eye to see, the tongue to taste, the nose to smell, the will to desire or imagine, the intellect to determine, the memory to remember, and the consciousness to know her individuality. Her body is ideal depending upon her will-power. Just as the soul does her duties in the world by means of the organs of sense fixed in the body, so does she enjoy happiness of all kinds by means of her powers in the beatific state." By ear, skin &c., are meant the faculties of hearing, touch &c., and not particular parts of the physical body.

It is exactly this type of soul that is described in the hymn. The hymn advises all men and women to elevate their souls by discrimination through renunciation to this high state.

Chapter VI.

Faith in the Unseen God.

Ṛgvēda X, 151.

Seer:—Śraddha Kamayanī.

Subject:—Faith i. e. Firm Adherence to Truth.

Metre:—Verses, 1, 4, 5 anuṣṭubh; 2, viraḍanuṣṭubh; 3, nicṛdanuṣṭubh.

Key:—Gandhara.

ओ३म् ॥ श्रद्धयाग्निः समिध्यते श्रद्धया हूयते हविः । श्रद्धां भगस्य मूर्धनि वचसा वेदयामसि ॥१॥

पदपाठः—श्रद्धया । अग्निः । सम् । इध्यते । श्रद्धया । हूयते । हविः । श्रद्धाम् । भगस्य । मूर्धनि । वचसा । आ । वेदयामसि ॥

अन्वयः—श्रद्धया अग्निः (साधु) समिध्यते । श्रद्धया हविः (साधु) हूयते । (अतः वयम्) श्रद्धाम् भगस्य मूर्धनि (वर्तमानाम्) वचसा (अन्यान्) आवेदयामसि ॥

Word-meaning &c. :—श्रद्धया*=by faith, faith in the Unseen (God); firmness in truth. अग्निः=God the Self-refulgent, Omniscient, Omnipresent, Illuminator of all; sacrificial fire; the soul; the sacrifice; a good deed; the year; light; heat; initiation; mortification; life; purity; semen virile; virile power; the special features

* श्रत् सत्यम् अस्याम् धीयते इति—श्रत् + √डुधाञ् धारणपोषणयोः + अङ् + टाप् according to P. III, 3, 104 षिद्भिदादिभ्योऽङ् and IV, 1, 4 अजाद्यतष्टाप्—श्रद्धा.

of womanhood &c.* समिध्यते†=is well lighted, illuminated, kindled, maintained, strengthened, advanced &c. हूयते=pervaded by faith and sanctified by the grace of God; is well offered; performed, accomplished. हविः$=oblation; transactions of human life; giving and taking; mutual dealings; routine transactions of daily life. श्रद्धाम्=of faith. भगस्य=of fortune, riches, great virtues or powers. मूर्धनि‡=at the head, foremost, best, highest. वचसा§=by word, oral instruction. आवेदयामसि||=we inform, teach, instruct, establish, &c.

Translation :—The soul of a man engaged in righteous works is strengthened by a strong faith in the Unseen God and, his dealings with his fellows are sanctified by an attitude firmly established in truth. Hence we (all) should know faith in God to be at the head of all great virtues, teach others accordingly and help them have such faith.

---

* (धर्मः, अर्कः, शुक्रः, ज्योतिः, सूर्यः) अग्नेर्नामानि । श॰ ६ । ४ । २ । २५ ॥ आत्मा वा अग्निः । श॰ ७ । ३ । १ । २ ॥ अग्निर्वै रेतोधा । तै॰ २।१।२।११। इयं (पृथिवी) अग्निः । श॰ ६ । १ । १ । १४ ॥ वागेवाग्निः । ३ । ५ । ४ । ८ ॥ तै॰ ३ । ६ । ५ । २ ॥ तपो वाऽअग्निः । श॰ ३ । ४ । ३ । २ ॥ पुरुषोऽग्निः । श॰ १४ । ६ । १ । १५ ॥ योषा वाऽअग्निः । श॰ १४ । ६ । १ । १६ ॥ अग्निर सर्वे कामाः । श॰ १० । २ । ४ । १ ॥ मन एवाग्निः । श॰ १० । १ । २ । ३ ॥ प्राणो वा अग्निः । श॰ ६ । ५ । १ । ६८ ॥ वीर्यं वा अग्नि । तै॰ १ । ७ । २ । २ ॥ गो॰ २ । ६ । ७ ॥ अग्निर्मेधाधिपतिः । श॰ ३ । २ । २ । ७ ॥ पर्जन्यो वाऽअग्निः । श॰ १४ । ६ । १ । १३ ॥ अग्निर्वोऽस्मद्‌: श॰ ३ । ४ । ४ । १५ ॥ दिशोऽग्निः । श॰ ६ । २ । ३ । ३४ ॥ आयुर्वा अग्निः । ६ । ७ । ३ । ७ ॥ अग्निर्वो दाता । श॰ ५ । २ । ५ । २ ॥ अग्निर्वा अर्वा । तै॰ १ । ३ । ६ । ४ ॥

$ √हु दानादनयोः आदाने चेत्यंके + इसि U. II, 108.

† सम् + √ञिइन्धी दीप्तौ + यक् + ते, P. III, 1, 67 सार्वधातुके यक् .

‡ √मुर्वी बन्धने + कनिन् according to U. I, 159 श्वनुक्षन्पूषन्प्लीहक्लेदन्स्नेहन्मज्जन्नर्यमन्विश्वप्सन्परिज्मन्मातरिश्वन्मघवन्निति—मूर्धन् .

§ √वच परिभाषणे + असुन् according to U. IV, 189 सर्वधातुभ्योऽसुन्—वचस् .

|| आ + √विद ज्ञाने or √विद सत्तायाम् or √विद विचारणे or √विद्लृ लाभे or √विद चेतनाख्याननिवासेषु + णिच् by P. III, 1, 26 हेतुमति च .

Comment :—This verse contains a metaphor and allows an infinite number of renderings according to the various significations of the words 'agni', 'hūyatē' and 'havih'. The plainest and the most 'literal' translation that would suggest itself to the reader will be as follows :—"Through faith in the Unseen God it is that the sacrificial fire is well kindled (by the sacrificer) and if there is such faith, the oblation is properly offered into it. Hence, knowing a strong faith in the Supreme Being to be at the head of all great powers, we should teach all people to trust in God."

The metaphor in the stanza applies a general law obtaining in the physical world to the spiritual. A scientist who knows of the properties of fire or electricity and believes in its utility can himself derive great advantage from it and help others also to do so. A devotee who has a strong and active faith in the Unseen God, the Self-refulgent, Omniscient, Omnipotent, Omnipresent, Illuminator of all, will have his own inner self filled with Divine luster by the grace of God. A man knowing of the uses of fire can purify the air by kindling it in a particular place and burning in it material possessing disinfecting and nourishing properties. This act also requires a sound knowledge of and belief in, the utilities of fire. The devotee also, who is actuated by an active faith in God, will carry on all his transactions with his fellowmen with perfect honesty, for his faith in God will pervade all departments of his life. A sincere faith in God will always be practical and entirely transform the life of the devotee. A scientist also who possesses a sound knowledge of and believes in, the utilities of fire or electricity can, by using it advantageously win honour, acquire wealth and popularity, and become a source of great influence for himself and others. Just in the same way, a pious man, by his sincere faith in God, can attain to great powers such as persuading the rich to do works of utility, reclaiming the fallen, curing the sick &c. But it must be borne in mind, these powers can come only in their due order. First a strong and sincere faith in God, then a thorough reform of life, and at the third stage of themselves the powers will manifest themselves; there is no shortcut. It is only a sincere devotee like an able scientist, that is expected to teach others about faith.

Faith, or a grounding in truth must be at the root of all human actions, though its intensity and features may vary according to various persons. Things are not done for their own sake but rather with some ulterior motive. As Yājñavalkya advised Maitreyī * (vide Br. U. II, 4,5). "Anything cannot be desirable simply for its own sake but rather because it serves some purpose of his own self. Therefore, one should try to visualise one's own self by hearing about it from the wise, thinking and deeply contemplating over it, for by hearing about, deliberating over and rightly understanding the soul (or self) the whole world can be known."

The gulf between this ulterior motive and the object desired or effort put forth is bridged over by that faculty of the soul which is commonly called 'faith'. This word according to Western notions denotes a system of beliefs or religious or other doctrines. It is in this sense that the word is used in such phrases as 'the Christian faith', 'the Muslim faith' &c., in which it is taken simply as a synonym of "religious beliefs or doctrines." The word 'persuasion' also is

* न वा अरे सर्वस्य कामाय सर्वम् प्रियम् भवत्यात्मनस्तु कामाय सर्वं प्रियं भवत्या-त्मा वा अरे द्रष्टव्यः श्रोतव्यो मन्तव्यो निदिध्यासितव्यो मैत्रेय्यात्मनो अरे दर्शनेन श्रवणेन मत्या विज्ञानेनेदं सर्वं विदितम् ॥ बृ० २ । ४ । ५ ॥

used almost in the same sense. In the New Testament of the Bible, in the discourses delivered by Christ, and in the writings of his Apostles this word is used to mean a belief in God as the Father, Creator and Punisher of the human soul, and in Christ as the only-be-gotten son of God the saviour of mankind from the wrath of God by arbitrating between Him and mankind and by taking the responsibility of the sin of all mankind for all time by dying on the cross. To this, later on it seems, the belief in the Holy Ghost or Spirit of God as an altogether separate entity was added which has come down to many of the Christian sects. The Christian Doxology, *Gloria Patri, et Filio, et Spiritui Sancto; Sicut erat in principio et nunc et semper, et in Saecula saeculorum,*" i. e., 'Glory be to the Father and to the Son and to the Holy Ghost, as it was in the beginning, is now and ever shall be," gives this doctrine in a nutshell.

Generally, faith is the attitude of propriety or truthfulness in dealing. A 'faithless' person and such other expressions support this sense of the word. It is in this sense that Tennyson has used the word in his poem 'Lancelot and Elaine' where he speaks of the illegitimate love of Lancelot for King Arthur's queen Guinevere, when he says :—

"His faith unfaithful kept him falsely true,
His honour rooted in dishonour stood."

But in this stanza the word Śraddha' is used in a broader sense. It means a faith in the Unseen God leading to a firm adherence to Truth in our daily dealings in life. It has nothing to do with set doctrines or beliefs having a restricted sphere. This idea has been clearly stated in R. V. VIII, 1, 31, and Y. V. XIX, 77 thus:—"When the righteous man actuated by faith in Me, entreats Me to bestow on Him virility and power for the control and use of his restless sense and motor organs which like horses yoked to his mind that like a chariot affords his soul to take a journey to the objects of the senses, and when I occupy such mental faculty of his, he comes to know (acquire) all means required for a peaceful and contented life and the soul that is in the cavity of his heart gets an opportunity to enjoy all things that are worthy of enjoyment."*

God, the Protector of all mankind, finding out His perfect understanding, truth and untruth as determined by their different characteristics, clearly teaches us about them in various ways and directs us to treat untruth with scorn and put faith in truth. He has, for this end, blessed us with the mental faculty, pure (and simple in itself), endowed with various potencies to ward off evil, the means to attain to righteousness the most potent force of human life, bliss-imparting, keeping off sickness and death, fit to be known and the medium of right knowledge. All should adore only that Almighty God Who has conferred on mankind this great favour."†

This aspect of the question about faith will become clear when the reader goes through all the Vedic stanzas collected on the subject.

Such faith, the verse says is at the head of all great powers. The word भग does not simply mean wealth or fortune, but indicates, as the notes on the word given on p. 50 must have shown, all great powers or virtues that man can aspire after through a strict self-discipline. Riches as well as virtues and

---

* आ यदश्वान्वनन्वतः श्रद्धयाहं रथे रुहम्। उत वामस्य वसुनश्चिकेतति यो अस्ति याद्वः पशुः॥ ऋ० ८ । १ । ३१॥ These words are addressed by God to the devotee through the original Ṛṣi.

† दृष्ट्वा रूपे व्याकरोत्सत्यानृते प्रजापतिः। अश्रद्धामनृतेऽदधाच्छ्रद्धां सत्ये प्रजापतिः। ऋतेन सत्यमिन्द्रियं विपानं शुक्रमन्धसऽइन्द्रस्येन्द्रियमिदं पयोऽमृतं मधु॥ यजुर्वेदे १९ । ७७।

powers are only a means and not the end. Ultimately the end of human life resolves itself into something unseen and this calls for faith.

Those who have attained to such faith should make it a point to lay their own experience before their fellowmen and thus prevent them from being carried away by worldly things or powers into infidelity.

The interpretations of the word श्रद्धा given in ancient Indian works are interesting. In the Taittirīya Brāhmaṇa Faith is called the "mother of (all righteous) desires."[1] The Śatapatha Brāhmaṇa referring to the ceremony of initiation says:—"What gives form to this ceremony of initiation is faith."[2] Elsewhere in the same work faith is called "luster" or rather "what imparts luster."[3] "It is faith only that does not allow to be destroyed what is once piously desired, hence the sacrificer who performs a religious sacrifice with a firm faith does not lose the fruit of his act,"[4] says the Śānkhāyana Brāhmaṇa. In the Taittirīya Brāhmaṇa again we are told that "by faith the *waters* are meant,"[5] i. e., just as water pervades the whole place where it is collected, so faith should pervade through and through the whole work a man undertakes. His attitude towards it should be one of implicit and unconditional faith. The Śatapatha Brāhmaṇa elsewhere refers to faith as the "duhitā" of "Sūrya" i. e., that attitude of a devotee's mind which enables him to attain all his desired objects from God

---

[1] श्रद्धां कामस्य मातरम् हविषा वर्धयामसि ॥ तै० २ । ८ । ८ । ८ ॥

[2] एतद्दीक्षायै रूपं यच्छ्रद्धा ॥ श० १२ । ८ । २ । ४ ॥

[3] तेज एव श्रद्धा ॥ श० ११ । ३ । १ । १ ॥

[4] श्रद्धैव सकृदिष्टस्याक्षितिः । स यः श्रद्दधानो यजते तस्येष्टं न क्षीयते ॥ शां० ७।४॥

[5] श्रद्धा वा आपः ॥ तै० ३ । २ । ४ । १ ॥

the Creator."[6] In the Aitarēya Brahmaṇa faith is called the 'wife'[7] and truth the 'husband', i. e., faith in the validity of the act done is essential for success. Having through examination found out that an undertaking is right one should, with trust in God engage oneself in it and this attitude will crown one's efforts with success.

(७२) प्रियं श्रद्धे ददतः प्रियं श्रद्धे दिदासतः ।
प्रियं भोजेषु यज्वस्विदं म उदितं कृधि ॥२॥

पदपाठः—प्रियम् । श्रद्धे । ददतः । प्रियं । श्रद्धे । दिदासतः । प्रियम् । भोजेषु । यज्वऽसु । इदम् । मे । उदितम् । कृधि ॥

अन्वयः—हे श्रद्धास्पद जगदीश्वर श्रद्धे (=श्रद्धया) ददतः प्रियं (कृधि) दिदासतः (च) प्रियं (कृधि) । भोजेषु यज्वसु (च प्रियं कृधि) मे (अपि) इदम् उदितम् कृधि ॥

Word-meaning &c. :—प्रियम्*=good. प्रियम् कृधि=do good to, bless him or her with happiness. ददतः†=who actually gives out of faith. दिदासतः‡=who, unable to

---

[6] श्रद्धा वै सूर्यस्य दुहिता ॥ श॰ १२ । ७ । ३ । ११ ॥

[7] श्रद्धा पत्नी सत्यं यजमानः ॥ ऐ॰ ७ । १० ॥

* √प्रीञ् प्रीतौ+क by P. III, 1, 135 इगुपधज्ञाप्रीकिरः कः The ञ् is an indicatory letter as laid down in P. I, 3, 8 लशक्वतद्धिते, only क being the termination. The former is dropped by P. I, 3, 9 तस्य लोपः and before the latter which remains the final ई of the root is changed इय् by P. VI, 4, 77 अचि श्नुधातुभ्रुवां य्वोरियङुवङौ ।

† √डुदाञ् दाने श्लु+शतृ P. III, 2, 124 लटः शतृशानचावप्रथमासमानाधिकरणे and reduplication according to P. II, 4, 75 जुहोत्यादिभ्यः श्लुः and VI, 1, 10 श्लौ.

‡ √डुदाञ् दाने+सन्+शतृ. The desiderative termination सन् is added according to P. III, 1, 7 धातोः कर्मणः समानकर्तृकादिच्छायां वा. The reduplication is in accordance with P. VI, 1, 9 सन्यङोः .

give for some reason, entertains a sincere wish to give when able to do so. भोजेषु§=on them that feed or protect. यज्वसु$=on those who do good works. इदम्=in this case; this. मे=for me, mine. उदितम्||=advancement, progress, noble thoughts aspirations or pursuits; what is uttered. इदम् मे उदितम् कृधि=bless me that I also may advance in all these cases or (myself) doing all these things; may my words be fulfilled or come true.

Note:—By ददतः and दिदासतः is meant the giving of charity, paying of tribute to the ruler, sustaining the learned who teach or imparting education to the pupil. On this point vide the दानसूक्त R. V. X, 119 given elsewhere in this book.

Translation:—Oh Lord of the Universe, Receptacle of our faith ! bless him with happiness that actuated by faith in Thee, gives of his possessions to the deserving and bless him also, that unable to give, entertains a pious and sincere wish to give when possible. Bless them that devote themselves to the protection of mankind and those that do good works. May, I, with such faith in Thee as my guide, rise high among all these.

Comment:—Faith purifies the soul of the dross of untruth in thought, word and deed and helps it to develop its powers. As such, it is absolutely necessary that all who are engaged in the battle of life should have a vigorous faith without which it is impossible

---

§ √भुज पालनाभ्यवहारयोः + अच् by P. III, 1, 134 नन्दिग्रहिपचादिभ्यो ल्युणिन्यचः.

$ √यज देवपूजासंगतिकरणदानेषु + क्वनिप् P. III, 2, 103 सुयजोर्ङ्वनिप्.

|| उत् + √इण् गतौ or √इङ् अध्ययने or √इक् स्मरणे + क्त P. III, 2, 102 निष्ठा, Or √वद व्यक्तायां वाचि + क्त. The samprasārana takes place by P. VI, 1, 15 वचिस्वपियजादीनां किति.

to succeed. Faith in one's own powers enables one to resist all odds and faith in the Unseen brings untold peace and endurance. It should be noted that the Holy Vedas do not promise any such magic results to faith as compelling the sycamine tree to get itself uprooted and replanted in the sea.$

The effect of faith, the text says, is to advance the peace and happiness of the soul practising it. A faithful desire, like a faithful deed, has the same result, but such faith has to be implemented by an effort towards its fulfilment. He who advises others about faith must himself be an advanced example of it.

(७३) यथा देवा असुरेषु श्रद्धामुग्रेषु चक्रिरे । एवं भोजेषु यज्वस्वस्माकमुदितं कृधि ॥ ३ ॥

पदपाठः—यथा । देवाः । असुरेषु । श्रद्धाम् । उग्रेषु । चक्रिरे । एवम् । भोजेषु । यज्वऽसु । अस्माकम् । उदितम् । कृधि ॥

अन्वयः—हे श्रद्धास्पद जगदीश्वर ! यथा श्रद्धे (=त्वयि श्रद्धया प्रतिष्ठिताः) देवाः उग्रेषु असुरेषु श्रद्धाम् चक्रिरे एवम् अस्माकम् भोजेषु यज्वसु (च सदा) उदितम् कृधि ॥

Word-meaning &c. :—यथा=just as. देवाः*=the wise or high-souled men. (Vide not on देव elsewhere in this book.) असुरेषु†=in those who are prepared even to offer their lives. उग्रेषु‡=in the brave. श्रद्धाम् चक्रिरे=have in all ages put faith or confided in each other. एवम्=thus. भोजेषु§=in those who have the

$ The Gospel of Luke XVII, 6.

* See page 3 .

† See Comment .

‡ √उच समवाये + रक् U. II, 28 ऋज्रेन्द्राग्रवज्रविप्रकुब्जचुब्जक्षुरखुरभद्रोग्रभेरभेलशुक्रशुक्लगौरवम्रेरामालाः.

§ See p. 195

means to enjoy and impart happiness to others. **यज्वसु**|| =in the wise who do good works—viz., worshipping God and honouring the righteous, associating with the good and, imparting food or learning to the deserving or supporting those who do good to society. **अस्माकम् उद्दितम् कृधि**=help us to advance forward.

Translation :—Even as the wise have in all ages trusted in the brave prepared even to sacrifice their lives for the good of mankind, so, oh God of our faith! through mutual confidence grounded in faith in Thee, may we advance forward—those of us who wield power to enjoy and impart worldly happiness to others trusting in and being trusted by the heroic and wise prepared even to offer their lives for the good of mankind.

Comment :—Society has two sorts of people who advance its welfare, those learned and wise men who live a life of sacrifice propagating learning and doing works of philanthropy and piety, and those who have all material and political power in their hands and on whom the physical well-being of Society depends. There should be cooperation through mutual trust and faith in the Unseen between these two if the society is to live and prosper. Given this mutual understanding and faith in the Unseen the Society or Nation would acquire wonderful power and rise to high eminence among the nations of the world.

Hence faith has been extolled in the Vedas in very glowing terms. For example according to verse No. 2 of the 102nd hymn of the first book of the Ṛgvēda the sublime and incomprehensible nature of the visible universe is said to engender faith:—"Oh learned

|| √यज देवपूजासंगतिकरणदानेषु+ङ्वनिप् by P. III, 2. 103 सुयजो ङ्वनिप्—यज्वन्. See also note at the end of the Comment on the hymn.

preceptor! through whom we attain to wealth and knowledge, your abilities and the Omnipotence of God Who is the Source of all wealth and knowledge; the seven types of rivers carrying sweet waters assuming a form and volume fit to be seen and requiring to be crossed over by various means of conveyance such as boats etc., the heavens and earth; the vast intermediate region; and the sun and moon endowed with forms charming to look at as well as supporting and imparting happiness to us; all these visibly moving before us inspire us with faith (in the power of God)."*

In Ṛgvēda II, 26, 3, corporate activity under the lead of great men is said to fructify only when the deed is inspired by faith in God :—"Oh learned man! that man alone acquires strength of body and soul and attains to happiness who, with his heart filled with faith and with a courteous attitude, serves in every way (a righteous man) the keeper of Vedic knowledge and saviour of the learned, and who supports (shares) his knowledge along with the common folk, with his own race as well as his own sons by birth, and holds his riches in common with men endowed with the virtues of leadership."†

In a beautiful prayer in Yajurvēda faith is reckoned as second after truth and a precious boon (among many others to be asked of God:—"My truthful transactions and the benefit that others may derive from them; my faith in God and the things that lead to its fulfilment; my offspring and movable belongings including

---

* अस्य श्रवो नद्यः सप्त बिभ्रति द्यावाक्षामा पृथिवी दर्शतं वपुः । अस्मे सूर्याचन्द्रमसाभिचक्षे श्रद्धे कमिन्द्र चरतो वितर्तुरम् ॥ ऋग्वेदे, १, १०२, २ ॥

† स इज्जनेन स विशा स जन्मना स पुत्रैर्वाजं भरते धना नृभिः । देवानां यः पितरमाविवासति श्रद्धामना हविषा ब्रह्मणस्पतिम् ॥ ऋग्वेदे, २, २६, ३ ॥

all things reckoned as such; my money and valuables along with cereals; all my possessions coupled with the good of all; anything great and worthy I may be having in my possession as well as the welcome I extend to the learned and righteous; my recreation and the means therefor; my joy and jubilation; the things that I have achieved, am achieving, shall achieve hereafter and everything relating thereto; my good utterances, well weighed thoughts, deeds nobly done and, the means therefor; vouchsafe, I beseech Thee oh God Almighty, that all these be endowed by Thy grace with such edifying force as will influence others to advance in truthfulness and righteousness."*

In Yajurvēda XX, 24 the devotee just entering upon the threshold of his vows for initiations prays :—"Oh Self-refulgent God, Saviour of all righteous deeds (like truthspeaking &c.), vouchsafe, I beseech Thee, that being established in Thee (true knowledge about Thee), I may kindle in my soul the flame of Thy devotion by meditation and thereby accomplishing my vows (of truth-speaking, continency &c.) secure a firm hold on those principles the following of which helps one to maintain an unflinching faith in Thee. Having by this process become an initiate, may I, by Thy grace, reveal the secrets of Thy glory to others."†

In R. V. VII. 32, 14 a righteous king is said to be the guardian of faith :—

"Oh most righteous and powerful king, what mortal man entertains a wish to scorn him who has

---

* सत्यं च मे श्रद्धा च मे जगच्च मे धनं च मे विश्वं च मे महश्च मे क्रीडा च मे मोदश्च मे जातं च मे जनिष्यमाणं च मे सूक्तं च मे सुकृतं च मे यज्ञेन कल्पन्ताम् ॥ यजुर्वेदे, १८ । ५ ॥

† अभ्यादधामि समिधमग्ने व्रतपते त्वयि । व्रतं च श्रद्धां चोपैमीन्धे त्वा दीक्षितो अहम् ॥ यजुर्वेदे ॥२० । २४ ॥

secured wealth (and position) at thy hands, and in the light diffused by thy protective reign ? What learned man wishes to usurp the knowledge and faith of others."*

In Yajurvēda XIX, 30 faith is said to be essential for emancipation.

"That person (boy, girl, man or woman) who adopting the vow of truthspeaking, continency &c., becomes initiated, attains, by such initiation, (fame and) prosperity and thereupon advances to faith. Proceeding thus, he then attains through faith to God (and righteousness) and is blessed with happiness."†

Formed according to U. I, 42 by adding the suffix उरन् to the root अस् meaning 'to throw', the word असुर means (अस्यति शत्रून्दुरितं वा)'he who throws' (or vanquishes) the foe or evil ? This is, probably the earliest signification of the word when it was equivalent to राक्षस or रक्षस् (from √रक्ष to protect+असुन् U. IV, 189) meaning those who protect others. In this good sense it was applied to the king and the warrior class whose duty it was to protect all the members of society. In this sense it can be sublimated to designate God Himself the Protector of all and Vanquisher of all evil.

But when that class of men in society whose duty consisted in protecting others even at the cost of their own lives (असून् राति), deteriorated into a gang of selfish power-seekers and hardened sensualists sacrificing the welfare and lives of others for their own enjoyment, both the words असुर and राक्षस or रक्षस् came

* कस्तमिन्द्र त्वावसुमा मर्त्यो दधर्षति । श्रद्धा इत्ते मघवन्पार्ये दिवि वाजी वाजं सिषासति ॥ ऋग्वेदे ७ । ३२ । १४ ॥

† व्रतेन दीक्षामाप्नोति दीक्षयाप्नोति दक्षिणाम् । दक्षिणा श्रद्धामाप्नोति श्रद्धया सत्यमाप्यते ॥ यजुर्वेदे १९ । ३० ॥

to bear a contrary signification in which they are used in later Vedic and classical Sanskrit literature. Used in the Vedas as they are in both the senses, more often in a good sense, they now, in modern and classical Sanskrit, have entirely lost their better import and invariably bear the worse. In both the sense, however, the idea of protection is prominent. In the better sense it means he who protects others at the sacrifice of even his own interests and life, while in the worse it would mean he who protects himself and his own interests at the sacrifice of even others' lives. Hence there seems to be no need to assume any historical background behind the 'deterioration' of the sense of this word.

Commenting on Ṛgveda III, 55, 19 Yāska (Nir. X, 34) remarks:—"Among the beneficent forces of nature. (**देवानाम्**) God has bestowed a very great one on this air viz., 'asuratva' which means the possession of right understanding (**प्रज्ञावत्त्वम्**) or vitality (**अनवत्त्वम्**). The word **असुः** is a name for right understanding, since it wards off calamities (**अस्यति अनर्थान्**) or because the ideals ~~of~~ human life (**अर्थाः**) are included in it (**अस्याम् अस्ताः**)." √**असु**+**उ** U. I, 10=**असु**+**र** in the sense of **मतुप्**. "Or the word 'asura' is formed from 'vasu' by dropping its initial 'va' (**असुरत्वमादिलुप्तं**)."* **वसु**+**र**=**असु**+**र**

---

* महच्चास्मै देवानामसुरत्वमेकं प्रज्ञावत्त्वं वानवत्त्वं वा । अपि वा सुरिति प्रज्ञानाम । अस्यत्यनर्थान् । अस्ताश्चास्यामर्थाः । असुरत्वमादिलुप्तम् ॥ नि० १० । ३४ ॥
On this Durgācārya comments:—असुरिति प्रज्ञानाम । तया तद्वत्त्वम् । तया महत्या प्रज्ञया उदकेन साधनेन सर्वमिदं जनयति पुष्णाति वर्धयति च । अप्रज्ञो हि साधनसंपत्तावपि किं कुर्यात् । अथवा । अनवत्त्वम् । असुः प्राणस्तेन तद्वत्त्वम् । एवमपि सति प्राणेनैव शक्यते एतत्सर्वं कर्तुम् । अप्राणो हि किं कुर्यात् । अन्नवत्त्वमिति केचित् । तेषामन्न-हेतुनोदकेन तद्वत्त्वम् । तथापि योज्यम् । असुरिति प्रज्ञानाम । तस्करमात् । अस्यत्यनर्थान् । प्रज्ञैव हि प्रज्ञावतोऽस्यति क्षिपत्यनर्थान्नाशयति । अस्ताश्चास्यामर्थाः । न हि तदस्ति व्यक्तेर्यत्सर्वं प्रज्ञावतां प्रज्ञायां नास्ति । एतावांस्तु विशेषोऽभिव्यक्तमनभिव्यक्तमिति । अथवा । यदेतदसुरत्वं असुमतो भावो वसुरत्वमेतत् । रोमत्वर्थे । वकारलोपश्च । वसुनोदकेन तद्वान् ॥

as above. This latter would mean he who bestows wealth or means of living on man. If 'vasu' means water the term असुर would signify the cloud.

Yāska in another place in his work (Nir. III, 18) interprets the word असुर in a different way. There he says while explaining the verse R. V. X, 53, 4 :—"The word 'asurāh' means those who do not remain peacefully at a place स्थानेषु अ-सु-रताः [=नञ् + सुष्ठु + √रमु क्रीडायाम् + क्त]), i. e., the restless. Or it means those who are thrown down (=deposed) from their high positions (अस्ताः स्थानेभ्यः [=√असु + उरन् U. I, 42]). Or it may be taken to be formed from the word असु meaning 'vital air' with the termination र in the sense of possession affixed to it (अपि वासुरिति प्राणनाम), since it is extended all over inside the body of a creature (अस्तः शरीरे भवति). Those who possess such vital air are called 'asurāh' (तेन तद्वन्तः)."* असुः अस्य अस्ति इति=असु + र. "Another interpretation is: God created (असृजत) good beings (देवान्) from good forces (सोः), hence they have been called 'surāh' (तत्सुराणां सुरत्वम्). He created evil beings (असुरान्) from the evil forces (असोः) from which the evil nature (असुरत्वम्) of evil beings (असुराणाम्) is understood (विज्ञायते) ....Some explain the word पञ्चजनाः occurring in the verse to stand for गन्धर्व, पितृ, देव असुर and रक्षस्."†

असुषु प्राणेषु रमते (Svāmi Dayananda Sarasvati on R. V. I. 35, 7) which sports in the vital air of creatures i. e., endows them with life, (the sun) according to Vārtika कप्रकरणे मूलविभुजादिभ्य उपसंख्यानम् P. III, 2, 5; Mahābhāṣya. असून् प्राणान् राति ददाति इति=असु + √रा + क

* असुरा असुरताः स्थानेष्वस्ताः स्थानेभ्य इति वा । अपि वासुरिति प्राणनाम । अस्तः शरीरे भवति । तेन तद्वन्तः ॥ नि॰ ३ । ८ ॥

† सोऽदेवानसृजत तत्सुराणां सुरत्वमसोरसुरानसृजत तदसुराणामसुरत्वमिति विज्ञायते । पञ्चजनाः—गन्धर्वाः पितरो देवा असुरा रक्षांसीत्येके ॥ Ibid.

P. III, 2, 3=असुरः. As the giver of life, it means God also. This sense is clearly brought out in the verse from the Ṛgvēda referred to above:—"Where (क) is that sun (सूर्यः) now (इदानीम्) [at this time of night], which gives life, as it were, to all creatures (असुरः) [that lie lifeless during night time, by awakening them with its light in the morning], which possessed of beautifully projecting rays (सुपर्णः) leading all beings in the right path (सुनीथः) exerting a subtle force that sets the planets in motion (गभीरवेपाः) diffuses light (व्यख्यत्) all over the worlds situated in the celestial regions (अन्तरिक्षाणि)? who (कः) knows (चिकेत)? Which of the many (कतमाम्) shining regions (द्याम्) do its (अस्य) rays (रश्मिः) pervade (आततान) [at this time]?"*

'Asu' is a synonym for प्राण†—the vital air and प्राण means आपः‡—waters. Hence असुर would mean असून्=अपः राति=ददाति इति असुरः मेघः i. e., the cloud which yields water. For example the devotee prays in R. V. 51, 11§ saying:—"May nourishing objects (like milk &c.) and the cloud—असुरः (by showering rain) impart happiness to us." In R. V. V, 83, 6$ the cloud—असुर—is said to protect man by showering down waters.

'Asura' itself means air, e.g., in R. V. III, 29, 14|| fire is said to be produced from the midst of the (formless) air. Hence all the meanings of वायु—air, would also be the meanings of असुर.*

---

* विसुपर्णो अन्तरिक्षाण्यख्यद्गभीरवेपा असुरः सुनीथः । केदानीं सूर्यः कश्चिकेत कतमां द्यां रश्मिरस्याततान ॥ ऋ० १ । ३५ । ७ ॥

† प्राणो वा असुः ॥ श० ६ । ६ । २ । ६ ॥

‡ प्राणा वा आपः ॥ तै० ३ । २ । ५ । २ ॥ तां० ९ । ९ । ४ ॥

§ स्वस्ति पूषा असुरो दधातु नः ॥ ऋ० ५ । ५१ । ११ ॥

$ अपो निषिञ्चन्नसुरः पिता नः ॥ ऋ० ५ । ८३ । ६ ॥

|| यदसुरस्य जठरादजायत ॥ ऋ० ३ । २९ । १४ ॥

* वायुर्वै प्राणः ॥ शां० ८।४॥ जै०उ० ४।२२।११॥ ऐ० २।२६॥३।२॥ तां० ४।६।८॥ श० ४।४।१।१५॥ गो० २।१।१६॥ स (वायुः) यत्पुरस्ताद्वाति । प्राण एव भूत्वा पुरस्ताद्वाति । तस्मात्पुरस्ताद्वान्तं सर्वाः प्रजाः प्रतिनन्दन्ति ॥ तै० २।३।९।४।५॥ वायुप्राणेत्रा वै पशवः। श० ४।४।१।१५॥ यत्पशुंपतिर्वायुस्तेन ॥ शां० ६ । ४॥

In R. V. III, 53, 7; 56, 8 and similar passages the word असुर denotes a commander, general or king who invariably vanquishes his foes.*

In R. V. II, 27, 10† 'asura' is a negative Bahuvrihi compound formed with नञ् and सुरा—न विद्यते सुरा यस्य—who is not addicted to drinking intoxicating drinks.

In A. V. XX, 91, 2 the word 'asura' means a wise man, while in XX, 36, 4 it signifies the evil, wicked &c.‡

The following passage from Devaraja Yajvan's scholion on the Nighantu p. 73 gives two more etymologies of the word:—'असु गतिदीप्त्यादानेषु' भौवादिकः स्वरितेत् पूर्वस्मादेव सूत्रात् [असिमसोरुरन् U. I, 42-43] उरन्। असति गच्छत्यन्तरिक्षे, दीप्यते स्वयम्, आदत्ते वा जलं वर्षितुं। यद्वा; 'सुर ऐश्वर्ये (तुदा० प०)', इगुपधलक्षणः कः (P. III, 1, 135) सुरतीति सुर ईश्वरः, स्वतन्त्र इत्यर्थः, असुरः अनीश्वरः, इन्द्रादिपरतन्त्र इत्यर्थः। "दिवःश्येनासो असुरस्य नीळयः (ऋ० सं० ८, ४, २४, १)"—"दीर्घाधियो रक्षमाणा असुर्यम् (ऋ० सं० २, ७, ६, ४)"—इति च निगमौ ॥

The above passage is taken in toto from the Asiatic Society of Bengal, Calcutta's edition of the book printed in 1882, prepared by the late Pandita Satyavrata Samaśrami, Bhattacarya. It is a pity that this great scholar thought it necessary to utilise English punctuation marks in a purely Sanskrit work. He has overlooked the euphonic changes also in several places, a blunder which cannot be excused in a scholar of such repute.

'Asuṣu prāṇeṣu ramata ityasuram'§ in the neuter gender means the mind since it sports in the vital airs.

* दिवस्पुत्रासो असुरस्य वीराः ॥ ऋ० ५।५३।६॥ राजन्त्यसुरस्य वीराः ॥ ५६।५।८॥

† त्वं विश्वेषां वरुणासि राजा ये च देवा असुर ये च मर्ताः ॥ ऋ० २।२७।१०॥

‡ दिवस्पुत्रासो असुरस्य वीराः ॥ अ० २० । ९१ । २ ॥ पुरुहूत पुरूवसोऽसुरघ्नः ॥ अ० २० । ३६ । ४ ॥

§ मनो वा असुरम् । तध्यसुषु रमते । जै० उ० ३ । ६ । ७ । १ ॥

(७४) श्रद्धां देवा यजमाना वायुगोपा उपासते ।
श्रद्धां हृदय्य१याकूत्या श्रद्धया विन्दते वसु ॥ ४ ॥

पदपाठः—श्रद्धाम् । देवाः । यजमानाः । वायुऽगोपाः । उप । आसते । श्रद्धाम् । हृदय्यया । आऽकूत्या । श्रद्धया । विन्दते । वसु ॥

अन्वयः—देवाः यजमानाः वायुगोपाः श्रद्धाम् उपासते । हृदय्यया आकूत्या श्रद्धाम् (विन्दते) श्रद्धया (च) वसु विन्दते ॥

Word-meaning &c. :—देवाः=the wise who have advanced in spiritual life. यजमानाः*=who do righteous works. वायुगोपाः†=those who perform yoga, i. e., the regulation of breathing. उपासते=resort to faith, do all these things through faith. हृदय्यया‡=heart-felt. आकूत्या§ =by determination. विन्दते=obtains. वसु=means to attain firmness in life.

Translation :—Those who by good works have risen high in spiritual life and have advanced in spiritual disciplinə by the practice of the regulation of breathing, take recourse to faith in God. A heart-felt firm resolve disposes one to attain faith in God and through such faith one attains a firm hold on life.

---

* √यज देवपूजासंगतिकरणदानेषु + मुक् + शानच् according to P. VII, 2, 82 आने मुक् and III, 2, 124 लटः शतृशानचावप्रथमासमानाधिकरणे—यजमान. See also note at the end of the hymn.

† वायुः गोपः=(रक्षकः) येषां ते by P. II, 2, 24 अनेकमन्यपदार्थे—वायुगोपाः. गोपः is formed according to P. II, 2, 19 उपपदमतिङ् and III, 2, 3 आतोऽनुपसर्गे कः ।

‡ हृदये भवति इति—हृदय + यत् according to P. III, 3, 53 तत्र भवः and 55 शरीरावयवाच्च ।

§ आ + √कूङ् शब्दे + क्तिन् according to P. III, 3, 94 स्त्रियां क्तिन् ।

Comment:—This verse states the necessity of yogic spiritual discipline including **प्राणायाम**=regulation of breathing. Of 'prāṇayāma' the Yōgasūtra II, 52[1] says:—"Thereby (by the regulation of breathing) the covering on the light of the mind (citta) is attenuated," and thereafter[2], (II, 53) "The mind becomes fit for a steady contemplation (of the Unseen)."

Manu in the 6th chapter of his code says[3]:—"A right performance of the three types of prāṇayāma (**रेचक, पूरक, कुम्भक**) along with the mental recitation of (and meditation on the name of God 'Aum' and the seven vyāhṛtis (sacred syllables) becomes in the case of the Brāhmaṇa (=man devoted to God) performing it the highest type of religious austerity." "Just as by smelting all the dross of metals is burnt away so all the defects of the sense (and motor) organs are burnt off by the restraining of breath." "By the regulations of breathing one should burn off the defects of the organs and by a steady contemplation (of God) one should destroy the stain of sin (on the soul). By withdrawing the senses from their objects one should cut off the connection between these two and by meditating on (the attributes of) God all characteristics of weakness should be annihilated."

The Bhagavadgita Ch. IV, 29[4] has a very beautiful description of this exercise to lay before us:—

---

[1] ततः क्षीयते प्रकाशावरणम् । यो० २।५२॥

[2] धारणासु च योग्यता मनसः ॥५३॥

[3] प्राणायामा ब्राह्मणस्य त्रयोऽपि विधिवत्कृताः । व्याहृतिप्रणवैर्युक्ता विज्ञेयं परमं तपः । म० ६।७०॥ दह्यन्ते ध्मायमानानां धातूनां हि यथा मलाः । तथेन्द्रियाणां दह्यन्ते दोषाः प्राणस्य निग्रहात् ॥७१॥ प्राणायामैर्दहेद्दोषान्धारणाभिश्च किल्बिषम् । प्रत्याहारेण संसर्गान्ध्यानेनानीश्वरान्गुणान् ॥७२॥

[4] अपाने जुह्वति प्राणं प्राणेऽपानं तथापरे । प्राणापानगती रुद्ध्वा प्राणायामपरायणाः ॥

"Others merge 'on-breath' (prāṇa) in off-breath (apāṇa)
and off-breath in on-breath as well,
Checking the dual vital tide,
On mastery of Life (prāṇāyāma) intent."

This yogic exercise, nay, the entire system of spiritual discipline calls for a steady faith in the Unseen, to acquire which a concentrated mind is essential. A fickleminded person cannot have faith. The mind must be firm and well-disposed that faith may strike root in it. 'Vasu in the stanza means 'shelter' or 'residence'. It may also denote the abode of the soul and the Supreme Being in the cavity of the heart which is perceived by the mind's eye rendered fit by discipline.

(७५) श्रद्धां प्रातर्हवामहे श्रद्धां मध्यन्दिनं परि ।
श्रद्धां सूर्यस्य निमृचि श्रद्धे श्रद्धापयेह नः ॥ ५ ॥

पदपाठः—श्रद्धाम् । प्रातः । हवामहे । श्रद्धाम् । मध्यन्दिनम् । परि । श्रद्धाम् । सूर्यस्य । निऽम्रुचि । श्रद्धे । श्रत् । धापय । इह । नः ॥

अन्वयः—(वयम्) श्रद्धाम् प्रातर्हवामहे, मध्यन्दिनम् परि श्रद्धाम् (हवामहे), सूर्यस्य निम्रुचि श्रद्धाम् (हवामहे) । हे श्रद्धे ! इह नः श्रद्धापय ॥

Word-meaning &c. :—श्रद्धाम्* (श्रद्धया)=through faith. प्रातर्†=in the morning. हवामहे‡ (आह्वयामः)=we invoke upon God. मध्यन्दिनम्परि=at midday. निम्रुचि§ =setting. नः श्रद्धापय=give us faith.

---

* The accusative is here used in place of the instrumental according to P. VII, 1, 39 सुपां सुलुक्पूर्वसवर्णाच्छेयाडाड्यायाजालः.

† See p. 49.

‡ Here samprasāraṇa has taken place in the root √ह्वेञ् स्पर्धायां शब्दे च according to P. VI, 1, 34 बहुलं छन्दसि, and the verb is conjugated like one of the 1st conjugation ending in ह.

§ नि+√म्रुचु गतौ+क्विप् according to P. I, 2, 178 अन्येभ्योऽपि दृश्यते—निम्रुच्.

Translation :— Through faith do we invoke upon God early in the morning, at midday and at the setting of the sun. Oh Lord ! fill us with faith in Thee.

Purport :— Faith is necessary in all actions and for all people, even the saints. Man should early in the morning renew his faith and resolve to abide by it. At midday he should see whether he has been acting up to his resolution. At the end of the day in the evening, he should examine himself and try to find out the reason for his failures if any. This method should be followed everyday and a confidential diary kept to mark the progress or otherwise.

The Devatā as well as the Ṛṣi of this beautiful hymn is Sraddhā. By devatā, the subject of the hymn is meant and by Ṛṣi, the sage who interpreted it. The reason for the evincidence of the name of both is that the sage whose real name was something else (his patronymic is Kāmāyanē) but lost to history, so consummately practised the truth set forṭh in this hymn that he became well known among his contemporaries as a specialist on faith. Hence people for brevity's sake called him Śraddhā.

Griffith and Wilson seem to have failed to see in this hymn the beautiful teaching—Indian scholars from time immemorial, have found. Their translation of the verses is slipshod, insipid and void of any moral. Wilson, to make matters worse leaves the words Śraddhā, Bhaga, Asura and Vāyu untranslated, so that his imperfect translation can very well vie with a schoolboy's rough work. It is an expression of the intention of these scholars and their modern Indian and European followers to fight tooth and nail for the invidious principle of the mythological interpretation of Vedic texts. They mean that here Śraddhā is the name of an imaginary goddess whom the Vedic singer conceived. It is very strange that the well-known rhetorical rule of the personification of abstract ideas and virtues in European languages, should not, according to these scholars, be applicable to Vedic Sanskrit. From the expressions, 'dadatah,' 'didāsatah,' 'bhōjeṣu,' 'yajvasu' and 'yajamāna' our scholars have taken certain parts of the hymn to be at best a beggar's calls for alms, or the money-grabbing lazy priest's droll, lip-deep praise of his donors intended to wheedle the latter into giving him something! To those who seriously intend to understand Vedic teachings, the imperfect and prejudiced translations and notes of most European scholars and their Indian followers can be of very little use.

In the Chāndōgyōpaniṣad faith is said to be quite essential, not only knowledge and application,* to achieve success and that everyone should try to understand† what it consists in.

In the other upaniṣads too, faith is extolled in various ways. The Bṛhadāraṇyakōpaniṣad says that faith is to be put only in what is seen‡ and not in mere hearsay. It also says in another place that only a righteous man actuated by genuine faith will engage himself in a sacrifice or some such religious undertaking and spend money over it.§ If religion seems to have lost its hold over man's mind in the whole world today it is firstly, because most of the religions prevailing in the world now are man-made and secondly, because man has no faith. In the very beginning of the Kaṭhōpaniṣad faith is said to be the cause which

---

* यदेव विद्यया करोति श्रद्धयोपनिषदा तदेव वीर्यवत्तरं भवति ॥ छां० १।१।१०॥

† यदा वै श्रद्दधात्यथ मनुते । नाश्रद्दधन्मनुते । श्रद्दधदेवमनुते । श्रद्धात्वेव विजिज्ञासितव्येति ॥ ७ । १९॥

‡ कस्मिन्नु यज्ञः प्रतिष्ठित इति दक्षिणायामिति । कस्मिन्नु दक्षिणा प्रतिष्ठितेति श्रद्धायामिति । यदा ह्येव श्रद्धत्तेऽथ दक्षिणां ददाति ॥ बृ० ३ । ९ । २१ ॥

actuated Naciketā in questioning his father.* In the Muṇḍakōpaniṣad faith is said to originate from the Supreme Being Himself†, while in the Praśnōpaniṣad faith is considered to be as essential as brahmacarya (=continence) and tapas‡ (=austerity) and in another place that God has created faith from the universal vital breath.

The Bhagavadgītā describes faith in the following strains:—

"The Sons of MAN who take their stand
 on this, My View, that alters not,
In guileless, unsuspecting *Trust*,—
 they, too, are loosed from bonds of act."‖

"The *faithful*, heart-whole Devotee,
 sense held by Will, finds Wisdom His.
Once Wisdom has been found (within,)
 He swiftly wins to Final Peace."§

"He that *has faith*, but no control,
 Whose mind from Yōga goes astray,
Whose bid for Yōga fails at last,—
 What path, O Kṛṣṇa treads that man"?

"O Pārtha, neither here nor there
 does ruin lie in wait for him.
In sooth, no man of handsome deeds,
 O dearest, treads the Path of Woe."*

---

§ चक्षुर्हि वै सत्यम् । तस्माद्यदिदानीं द्वौ विवदमानावेयातामहमदर्शमहमश्रौषमिति य एवं ब्रूयादहमदर्शमिति तस्मा एव श्रद्दध्याम ॥ ५ । १४ । ४॥

* तं ह कुमारं सन्तं दक्षिणासु नीयमानासु **श्रद्धा**विवेश ॥ क० १ । १ । २॥

† तस्माच्च देवा बहुधा संप्रसूताः साध्या मनुष्याः पशवो वयांसि । प्राणापानौ व्रीहियवौ तपश्च **श्रद्धा** सत्यं ब्रह्मचर्यं विधिश्च ॥ मु० २ । १ । ७ ॥

‡ तपसा ब्रह्मचर्येण **श्रद्धया** विद्यया ॥ प्र० १ । २ । १० ॥ स तत्र तपसा ब्रह्मचर्येण **श्रद्धया** संपन्नो महिमानमनुभवति ॥ ५ । ३ ॥ स प्राणमसृजत । प्राणाच्छ्रद्धां ॥ ६ । ४ ॥

‖ ये मे मतमिदं नित्यमनुतिष्ठन्ति मानवाः । **श्रद्धा**वन्तोऽनसूयन्तो मुच्यन्ते तेऽपि कर्मभिः ॥ भ० ३ । ३१ ॥

§ श्रद्धावाँल्लभते ज्ञानं तत्परः संयतेन्द्रियः । ज्ञानं लब्ध्वा परां शान्तिमचिरेणाधिगच्छति ॥ ४ । ३९ ॥

* अयतिः **श्रद्धयोपेतो** योगाच्चलितमानसः । अप्राप्य योगसंसिद्धिं कां गतिं कृष्ण गच्छति ॥ भ० ६ । ३७ ॥ योगिनामपि सर्वेषां मद्गतेनान्तरात्मना । श्रद्धावान्भजते यो मां स मे युक्ततमो मतः ॥ ४७ ॥

"They who, discarding Scripture-Law,
with *heart of faith* make sacrifice,—
What is their state, O Krsna, say,
pure *Sattva*, *Rajas*, *Tamas* dark"?

"Threefold in kind is such faith
in man incarnate, nature-sprung;
Pure, *Rajas*-stained, and tamasic—
lend ear while I descant thereon.

The *faith* of every man depends
on what he feels himself to be,
Faith-wrought is man, O Bharata,—
whate'er his *faith*, the same is he."†

"Sweet peace and loveliness of mind,
restraint of tongue and thought control,
Heart's purity,—these are, O Friend,
[by sages] mental penance called.

This triple penance, if performed
by men with utter *Faith* endowed,
At One expecting naught for self,—
as *Sattvic Penance* is proclaimed."‡

"Yea, e'en the man who merely hears
with faith, and pure uncarping mind;—
That man shall enter, when set free,
the radiant spheres where dwell the just."§

In the Manusmrti also man is advised to resort to works of public utility with faith and it is also said that food given with faith is holy and that given without it is impure.*

---

† ये शास्त्रविधिमुत्सृज्य यजन्ते श्रद्धयान्विताः । तेषां निष्ठा तु का कृष्ण सत्त्वमाहो रजस्तमः ॥ **त्रिविधा भवति श्रद्धा** देहिनां सा स्वभावजा । सात्त्विकी राजसी चैव तामसी चेति तां शृणु ॥ **सत्त्वानुरूपा** सर्वस्य **श्रद्धा** भवति भारत । श्रद्धामयोऽयं पुरुषो यो यच्छ्रद्धः स एव सः ॥ भ० १७ । १-३ ॥

‡ मनः प्रसादः सौम्यत्वं मौनमात्मविनिग्रहः । भावसंशुद्धिरित्येतत्तपो मानसमुच्यते ॥ श्रद्धया परया तप्तं तपस्तत्त्रिविधं नरैः । अफलाकांक्षिभिर्युक्तैः सात्त्विकं परिचक्षते ॥ १६ ॥ १७ ॥

§ **श्रद्धावाननसूयश्च** शृणुयादपि यो नरः । सोऽपि मुक्तः शुभाँल्लोकान्प्राप्नुयात्पुण्यकर्मणाम् ॥ १८ । ७१ ॥

* **श्रद्धयेष्टं च पूर्तं च** नित्यं कुर्यादतन्द्रितः । **श्रद्धाकृते ह्यक्षये** ते भवतः स्वागतैर्धनैः ॥ म० ४ । २२६ ॥ श्रद्धापूतं वदान्यस्य हतमश्रद्धयेतरम् ॥ २२५ ॥

The Mahābhārata also expatiates on faith in the following words:—"Lack of Faith is the greatest sin for it is Faith that releases one from sin. The man of Faith throws off sinfulness just like a snake discarding its slough." Śāntiparvan 270, 15.

"The cessation from sinning of the saintly is nobler on account of their Faith. That man of Faith who is freed from the blemishes of his character is really purified." 16.

'Of what use are austerities, worldly life and (even) self to a man? Man is constituted of his Faith, for to what he has pinned his Faith that he becomes." 17.

"Thus has Righteousness been fully described by the virtuous who have an insight into its implications. By a vision of this Righteousness have we also truly become seekers after Truth." 18.

"Oh wisest of men have Faith, thereby shall you attain the highest." 19.

"The characteristics of a wise man are that he always resorts to praiseworthy actions and not censurable ones, believes in the Unseen and has faith." Viduraprajāgaraparvan 33, 16.

अश्रद्धा परमं पापं श्रद्धा पापप्रमोचनी ।
जहाति पापं श्रद्धावान्सर्पो जीर्णामिव त्वचम् ॥
महाभारते शान्तिपर्वणि २७० । १५ ॥
ज्यायसी या पवित्राणां निवृत्तिः श्रद्धया सह ।
निवृत्तशीलदोषो यः श्रद्धावान्पूत एव सः ॥ १६ ॥
किं तस्य तपसा कार्यं किं वृत्तेन किमात्मना ।
श्रद्धामयोऽयं पुरुषो यो यच्छ्रद्धः स एव सः ॥ १७ ॥
इति धर्मः समाख्यातः सद्भिर्धर्मार्थदर्शिभिः ।
वयं जिज्ञासमानास्तु संप्राप्ता धर्मदर्शनात् ॥ १८ ॥
श्रद्धां कुरु महाप्राज्ञ ततः प्राप्स्यसि यत्परम् ॥ १९ ॥
निषेवते प्रशस्तानि निन्दितानि न सेवते ।
अनास्तिकः श्रद्दधान एतत्पण्डित लक्षणम् ॥
विदुरप्रजागरपर्वणि ३३ । १६ ॥

To understand fully the Vedic teaching on faith it is essential to know something about truth and righteousness. About the latter enough has been said in the Comment on Stanza No. 56, pages 149-153. With regard to truth the following verses Nos. 12 to 16 from the last hymn of the 7th book of Ṛgvēda should be carefully noted:—"It is well-known (सु विज्ञानं) to the intelligent (चिकितुषे) person (जनाय) that truthful (सत् च) and untruthful (असत् च) utterances (वचसी) are directly opposed to each other (पस्पृधाते). Of these two (तयोः) that which (यत्) is truthful (सत्यम्) and that which (यतरत्) is more straightforward (ऋजीयः) does God the Inner Vital Force of the whole universe (सोमः) save (अवति) and completely destroy (आहन्ति) what is untruthful (असत्)."*

The next stanza still more forcibly describes God's displeasure at untruth:—"God the Moving Force of the universe (सोमः) does not thatwise (न वै उ) punish (हिनोति) the wicked (वृजिनम्) or those whose duty it is to protect others (क्षत्रियम्) but who bear their power (धारयन्तम्) in vain (मिथुया), as He does punish (हन्ति) those who delight in injuring others (रक्षः), and as He thoroughly chastises (आ हन्ति) the speaker (वदन्तम्) of untruth (असत्). For both these (उभौ) lie (शयाते) in the bonds of the power (प्रसितौ) of Almighty God (इन्द्रस्य)."†

The remaining three verses picture the agony of the penitent soul at God's disregard of her and the strong hatred she has for untruth and the attitude to wilfully harm others:—"Oh Most Refulgent God! (अग्ने) if (यदि वा) I (अहम्) have made untruth my divinity (अनृतदेवः आस) or (वा) if I falsely (मोघम्) make to myself

* सुविज्ञानं चिकितुषे जनाय सच्चासच्च वचसी पस्पृधाते । तयोर्यत्सत्यं यतरदृजीयस्तत्सोमोवति हन्त्यासत् ॥ ऋ० ७ । १०४ । १२ ॥

† न वा उ सोमो वृजिनं हिनोति न क्षत्रियं मिथुया धारयन्तम् । हन्ति रक्षो हन्त्यासद्वदन्तमुभाविन्द्रस्य प्रसितौ शयाते ॥१३॥

(अप्यूहे) other gods (देवान्) [then surely I am a sinner deserving of Thy wrath]. But Oh Thou Knower of all creatures (जातवेदः) [knowing as Thou dost of our innocense] why (किम्) dost Thou get angry (हृणीषे) with us (अस्मभ्यम्) ? May the lie-utterers (द्रोघवाचः) come into contact (सचन्ताम्) with Thy chastisement (निः ऋथम्)."†
"Oh Lord if I am a tormentor of others (यातुधानः अस्मि) or (वा) if (यदि) I have ruined (ततप) the life (आयुः) of any man (पुरुषस्य) may I be chastised (मुरीय) this very day (अद्या). But (अध) may he (सः) who (यः) falsely (मोघम्) accuses (आह) me (मा) of being an injurer of others (यातुधानः इति) be separated (वियूया) from his ten (दशभिः) offspring (वीरैः)."‡ "May Almighty God (इन्द्रः) destroy (हन्तु) him (तम्) with a great (महता) destruction (वधेन) and may that meanest (अधमः) of all (विश्वस्य) creatures (जन्तोः) be ruined for ever (पदीष्ट) who calls (आह) me (मा) a tormentor of others (यातुधान इति) though I am not such (अयातुम्) or (वा) who (यः) himself being an injurer of others (रक्षाः) says (आह) that (इति) he is pure (शुचिः अस्मि)."||

The Mahabharata praises Truth in the following words:—"Better than a hundred wells is a tank, and superior to a hundred tanks is a sacrifice. Better than a hundred sacrifices is a son but *Truth is preferable even to a hundred sons.*" Adiparvan 99, 30.

वरं कूपशताद्वापी वरं वापीशतात्क्रतुः ।
वरं क्रतुशतात्पुत्रः सत्यं पुत्रशताद्वरम् ॥
महाभारत आदिपर्वणि ९९ । ३० ॥

---

† यदि वाहमनृतदेव आस मोघं वा देवां अप्यूहे अग्ने । किमस्मभ्यं जातवेदो हृणीषे द्रोघवाचस्ते निर्ऋथं सचन्ताम् ॥१४॥

‡ अद्या मुरीय यदि यातुधानो अस्मि यदि वायुस्ततप पूरुषस्य । अधा स वीरैर्दशभिर्वियूया यो मा मोघं यातुधानेत्याह ॥१५॥

|| यो मायातुं यातुधानेत्याह यो वा रक्षाः शुचिरस्मीत्याह । इन्द्रस्तं हन्तु महता वधेन विश्वस्य जन्तोरधमस्पदीष्ट ॥१६॥

"If a thousand 'aśvamedha' sacrifices and Truth were to be weighed in a balance, *Truth indeed will weigh more than the former.*" 31.

"A study of all the Vedas and washing oneself in all sacred reservoirs *are not equal to a sixteenth part of Truth-fulness.*" 32.

"*There is no righteousness equal to Truthfulness and there is nothing which can surpass it, and there is no sin more fearful than untruth.*" 33.

"Among the virtuous Truthfulness is ever considered to be a righteous duty for Truth is the eternal Righteousness. Therefore *all should revere Truth* for Truth itself is the highest state man can attain." Śantiparvan 160, 4.

"*Truth is Righteousness, Truth is power, Truth is spiritual discipline and Truth is the Eternal Brahma. Truth is the highest act of Righteousness and everything is established in Truth.*" 5.

" ....
Truth, oh descendent of Bharata! is thirteenfold as admitted by the whole world." 7.

अश्वमेधसहस्रं च सत्यं च तुलया धृतम् ।
अश्वमेधसहस्राद्धि सत्यमेव विशिष्यते ॥ ३१ ॥
सर्ववेदाधिगमनं सर्वतीर्थावगाहनम् ।
सत्यस्यैव च राजेन्द्र! कलां नार्हन्ति षोडशीम् ॥ ३२ ॥
नास्ति सत्यसमो धर्मो न सत्याद्विद्यते परम् ।
नहि तीव्रतरं पापमनृतादिह विद्यते ॥ ३३ ॥
सत्यं सत्सु सदा धर्मः सत्यं धर्मः सनातनः ।
सत्यमेव नमस्येत सत्यं हि परमा गतिः ॥
महाभारते शान्तिपर्वणि १६० । ४ ॥
सत्यं धर्मस्तपो योगः सत्यं ब्रह्म सनातनम् ।
सत्यं यज्ञः परः प्रोक्तः सर्वं सत्ये प्रतिष्ठितम् ॥ ५ ॥
....
सत्यं त्रयोदशविधं सर्वलोकेषु भारत ! ॥ ७ ॥

"*Truth speaking, equanimity, firmness of mind, undoubtedly freedom from jealousy, forgiveness, modesty, forbearance, freedom from malice.*" 8.

"*Renunciation, thoughtfulness, nobility of behaviour, contentment (or patience), being always charitably disposed towards others, abstinence from injuring others, these oh lord of kings, are the thirteen aspects of Truth*". 9.

"Truth is imperishable and indeed, likewise beyond change. It is also in full harmony with all types of Righteousness and can be attained only through spiritual discipline." 10.

"Equanimity is that attitude of the mind towards what is desirable or undesirable to one's self as well towards one's foe wherein desire and hatred diminish, longing and anger also wear away." 11.

"Firmness of mind consists in freedom from coveting what is another's, gravity, fortitude, freedom from vileness, and suppression of anger, all of which can be attained only through right understanding." 12.

"The wise say freedom from jealousy consists in control of oneself even in acts of charity and righteousness. A man attains it when he becomes established in Truthfulness." 13.

सत्यं च समता चैव दमश्चैव न संशयः ।
अमात्सर्यं क्षमा चैव ह्रीस्तितिक्षानसूयता ॥ ८ ॥
त्यागो ध्यानमथार्यत्वं धृतिश्च सततं दया ।
अहिंसा चैव राजेन्द्र ! सत्याकारास्त्रयोदश ॥ ९ ॥
सत्यं नामाव्ययं नित्यमविकारि तथैव च ।
सर्वधर्माविरुद्धं च योगेनैतदवाप्यते ॥ १० ॥
आत्मनीष्टे तथानिष्टे रिपौ च समता तथा ।
इच्छाद्वेषक्षयं प्राप्य कामक्रोधक्षयं तथा ॥ ११ ॥
दमो नान्यस्पृहा नित्यं गाम्भीर्यं धैर्यमेव च ।
अशाठ्यं क्रोधदमनं ज्ञानेनैतदवाप्यते ॥ १२ ॥
अमात्सर्यं बुधाः प्राहुर्दाने धर्मे च संयमः ।
अवस्थितेन नित्यं च सत्येनामत्सरी भवेत् ॥ १३ ॥

"(Forgiveness is that attitude in which) a virtuous person puts up with all occurrences bearable or unbearable, agreeable or disagreeable and thence attains Truth." 14.

"A modest person is indefatigable in doing good and is peaceful in speech and thought. This attitude is attainable through dutifulness." 15.

"Forbearance is an excellent virtue. A man ought to be forbearant for the sake of righteousness and his means as well as for the guidance of others by setting a good example. This attitude arises from fortitude." 16.

"As for freedom of malice it consists in gravity of attitude and is attainable through charitableness."

"Renunciation is that attitude of the man who sheds off his attachment to the objects of the senses. Accordingly this takes place only when a man is bereft, of likes and dislikes and not otherwise." 17.

"Thoughtfulness is a type of skilfulness (?) which is attainable through silence. Nobility of conduct is

---

अक्षमायाः क्षमायाश्च प्रियाणीहाप्रियाणि च ।
क्षमते सर्वतः साधुस्ततः प्राप्नोति सत्यताम् ॥ १४ ॥
कल्याणं कुरुते बाढं धीमान्न ग्लायते क्वचित् ।
प्रशान्तवाङ्मना नित्यं ह्रीस्तु धर्मादवाप्यते ॥ १५ ॥
धर्मार्थहेतोः क्षमते तितिक्षा धर्म उत्तमः ।
लोकसंग्रहणार्थं वै सा तु धैर्येण लभ्यते ॥ १६ ॥
अनसूया तु गाम्भीर्यं दानेनैतदवाप्यते ।
त्यक्तस्नेहस्य यस्त्यागो विषयाणां तथैव च ।
रागद्वेषप्रहीणस्य त्यागो भवति नान्यथा ॥ १७ ॥
ध्यानं च शाठ्य*मित्युक्तं मौनेनैतदवाप्यते ।
आर्यता नाम भूतानां यः करोति प्रयत्नतः ।
शुभं कर्म निराकारो वीतरागस्तथैव च ॥ १८ ॥

---

* The word शाठ्य here is unjustifiable and inappropriate in the extreme. This is the Kumbhakoṇam text. The translation follows the etymology of the word and is only approximate.

the disposition of the man who does good to creatures without any show and bereft of any attachment." 18.

" Firmness of mind is that virtue by means of which a man remains unmoved whether in happiness or misery. The wise man who aspires after the advancement of his soul should always resort to this virtue." 19.

" A man should always be forgiving and attached to Truth. A wise man free from exultation and anger attains to firmness of mind." 20.

" Freedom from malice towards any creature in deed, thought and word, kindness and a disposition to help the needy—this is the time-honoured Law of Righteousness for all the virtuous." 21.

" These thirteen are distinct in form but they have all Truth as their one common characteristic. They depend upon Truth, Oh descendent of Bharata, and advance it." 22.

" It is not possible to exhaust the list of the merits of Truth, Oh king! and it is for this reason that the wise, the protectors of human society and the enlightened—all—praise it." 23.

" There is no righteousness surpassing Truthfulness and there is no sin greater than untruth. The

---

धृतिर्नामसुखेदुःखे यया नाप्नोति विक्रियाम् ।
तां भजेत सदा प्राज्ञो य इच्छेद्भूतिमात्मनः ॥ १९ ॥
सर्वथा क्षमिणा भाव्यं तथा सत्यपरेण च ।
वीतहर्षभयक्रोधो धृतिमाप्नोति पण्डितः ॥ २० ॥
अद्रोहः सर्वभूतेषु कर्मणा मनसा गिरा ।
अनुग्रहश्च दानं च सतां धर्मः सनातनः ॥ २१ ॥
एते त्रयोदशाकाराः पृथक्सत्यैकलक्षणाः ।
भजन्ते सत्यमेवेह बृंहयन्ते च भारत ॥ २२ ॥
नान्तः शक्यो गुणानां च वक्तुं सत्यस्य पार्थिव ।
अतः सत्यं प्रशंसन्ति विप्राः सपितृदेवताः ॥ २३ ॥
नास्ति सत्यात्परो धर्मो नानृतात्पातकं परम् ।
स्थितिर्हि सत्यं धर्मस्य तस्मात्सत्यं न लोपयेत् ॥ २४ ॥

basis of all righteousness is Truth. Hence man must never violate Truth." 24.

"Through Truthfulness does a man secure good gifts and also ability to do righteous works with good consequences attendant thereon. The use of the three luminous phenomena of nature (fire, electricity and the sun), intelligence to grasp Vedic truths and all other determinative features of righteousness does a man obtain only through Truthfulness." 25.

"In conformity with Truth (=its true and immutable attribute) does the sun shine, the fire burn and the wind (?) blow, for all is established in Truth." Asvamēdhika parvan 110, 30."

"The enlightened, the protectors of human society and Vedic scholars are pleased with Truth. Truthfulness is considered to be the highest type of righteousness, hence man must never violate Truth." 31.

"The ancient sages were attached to Truth for their prowess was for Truth and their vows were always Truthful, hence *Truthfulness surpasses all other virtues.*" 32.

"*Truth alone is the* Supreme *Being, Truth alone is the highest power, Truth alone is the greatest righteous*

उपैति सत्याद्दानं हि तथा यज्ञाः सदक्षिणाः ।
त्रेताग्निहोत्रं वेदाश्च ये चान्ये धर्मनिश्चयाः ॥ २५ ॥
सत्येन सूर्यस्तपति सत्येनाग्निः प्रदीप्यते ।
सत्येन महतो* वान्ति सर्वं सत्ये प्रतिष्ठितम् ॥
महाभारत आश्वमेधिकपर्वणि ११० । ३० ॥
सत्येन देवाः प्रीयन्ते पितरो ब्राह्मणास्तथा ।
सत्यमाहुः परो धर्मस्तस्मात्सत्यं न लोपयेत् ॥ ३१ ॥
मुनयः सत्यनिरता मुनयः सत्यविक्रमाः ।
मुनयः सत्यशपथास्तस्मात्सत्यं विशिष्यते ॥ ३२ ॥

---

* महतो वान्ति perhaps means 'all great beings go according to'. Cf. महाजनो येन गतः स पन्थाः ।

work and Truth alone is the highest learning." Santiparvan 197, 70.

"Truth awakens when one acts up to the teachings of the Vedas and the fruit of Truthfulness is said to be very sublime. Power, righteousness and detachment of the senses from their objects all these are established on Truthfulness." 71.

"*The end of Vedic study is Truthfulness, and the end of the study of all the ancillary lores also. The end of all sacrifices (=great deeds) and all the Principles (=Law) thereof, the fruit of the observance of vows and the Sacred Name of God, 'Aum', are Truth itself.*" 72.

"The creation of all (finite) beings is in conformity with Truth and the continuance of their species also, for even the wind blows and the sun shines in accordance with Truth." 73.

"Fire also burns (only) in conformity with Truth and celestial (=the highest worldly) happiness is established in Truth. Truth is righteous deeds, Truth is austerity, Truth is the Vedas, the hymns of the praise of God, and the Highest Wisdom. 74.

"It is said that once Righteousness and Truthfulness were put in the two pans of a balance severally

---

सत्यमेकं परं ब्रह्म सत्यमेकं परं तपः ।
सत्यमेकं परो यज्ञः सत्यमेकं परं श्रुतम् ॥
महाभारते शान्तिपर्वणि १९७ । ७० ॥
सत्यं वेदेषु जागर्ति फलं सत्ये परं स्मृतम् ।
तपो धर्मो दमश्चैव सर्वं सत्ये प्रतिष्ठितम् ॥ ७१ ॥
सत्यं वेदास्तथाङ्गानि सत्यं यज्ञास्तथा विधिः ।
व्रतचर्या तथा सत्यमोंकारः सत्यमेव च ॥ ७२ ॥
प्राणिनां जननं सत्यं सत्यं सन्ततिरेव च ।
सत्येन वायुरभ्येति सत्येन तपते रविः ॥ ७३ ॥
सत्येन चाग्निर्दहति स्वर्गः सत्ये प्रतिष्ठितः ।
सत्यं यज्ञस्तपो वेदाः स्तोभा मन्त्राः सरस्वती ॥ ७४ ॥
तुलामारोपितो धर्मः सत्यं चैवेति नः श्रुतम् ।
समां कक्षां धारयतो यतः सत्यं ततोऽधिकम् ॥ ७५ ॥

and weighed but as equilibrium was maintained Truthfulness must be acknowledged to be the greater." 75.

"Dharma is protected by Truthfulness, learning is protected by application, complexion is preserved by ablutions and family honour by good behaviour." Viduraprajāgaraparvan 34, 39.

"Washing oneself in all the sacred reservoirs or straightforwardness towards all beings are both equal, if not, the latter is superior to the former." 35, 2.

"Oh mighty one ! be straightforward in your dealings with your sons. You will thereby acquire great fame in this life and supreme happiness after." 3.

"It is said that to say nothing is superior to say something. To utter the truth is the second mode of speaking, to say something pleasant the third mode and to say what is right is the fourth." 36, 12.

"He is the best type of man who being gentle, selfcontrolled and truthful in speech always takes things about others in the right way (=as they are) and never in a contrary manner (=as they are not)." 16.

सत्येन रक्ष्यते धर्मो विद्या योगेन रक्ष्यते ।
मृजया रक्ष्यते रूपं कुलं वृत्तेन रक्ष्यते ॥
महाभारते विदुरप्रजागरपर्वणि । ३४ । ३९ ॥

सर्वतीर्थेषु वा स्नानं सर्वभूतेषु चार्जवम् ।
उभे त्वेते समे स्यातामार्जवं वा विशिष्यते ॥ ३५ । २ ॥

आर्जवं प्रतिपद्यस्व पुत्रेषु सततं विभो ।
इह कीर्तिं परां प्राप्य प्रेत्य स्वर्गमवाप्स्यसि ॥ ३ ॥

अव्याहृतं व्याहृताच्छ्रेय आहुः सत्यं वदेद्व्याहृतं तद्द्वितीयम् ।
प्रियं वदेद्व्याहृतं तत्तृतीयं धर्म्यं वदेद्व्याहृतं तच्चतुर्थम् ॥ ३६ । १२ ॥

भावमिच्छति सर्वस्य नाभावे कुरुते मनः ।
सत्यवादी मृदुर्दान्तो यः स उत्तमपूरुषः ॥ १६ ॥

"He is a middling type of man who notes others' weaknesses, and does not appease another in vain words but if he promises something, does give it." 17.

"He who being suspicious on his own account has no confidence even in something beneficial that may proceed from others and discards his friends, is, indeed, the lowest type of man." 19.

"Oh king ! men who constantly speak what is pleasant are easily available, but of what is salutary and at the same time unpleasant both the speaker and listener are rare." 37, 15

"A king has a true helper in that man who regardless of what is pleasant or unpleasant to his master sticks to his duty and tells him things unpleasant but salutary." 16.

The Manusmṛti describes Truth as follows:—"A witness who speaks the truth in his evidence, gains (after death) the most excellent regions (of bliss) and here below unsurpassable fame, for Truthfulness of speech is revered in the Vedas." 8, 81.

नानर्थकं सान्त्वयति प्रतिज्ञाय ददाति च ।
रन्ध्रं परस्य जानाति यः स मध्यमपूरुषः ॥ १७ ॥

न श्रद्दधाति कल्याणं परेभ्योऽप्यात्मशङ्कितः ।
निराकरोति मित्राणि यो वै सोऽधमपूरुषः ॥ १९ ॥

सुलभा पुरुषा राजन्सततं प्रियवादिनः ।
अप्रियस्य तु पथ्यस्य वक्ता श्रोता च दुर्लभः ॥ ३७ । १५ ॥

यो हि धर्मं समाश्रित्य हित्वा भर्तुः प्रियाप्रिये ।
अप्रियाण्याह पथ्यानि तेन राजा सहायवान् ॥ १६ ॥

सत्यं साक्ष्यं ब्रुवन्साक्षी लोकानाप्नोति पुष्कलान् ।
इह चानुत्तमां कीर्तिं वागेषा ब्रह्मपूजिता ॥ म० ८ । ८१ ॥

"He who gives false evidence is firmly bound* by the fetters of Varuṇa (=God the Just) and suffers during one hundred existences; let man therefore give true evidence." 82.

"As the Brāhmaṇa (=man learned in the Vedas) is superior among men, as the sun is the most lustrous of all the luminaries in the planetary region and as the head is the most important of all the parts of the body, so is Truthfulness the greatest type of righteousness." 1.

"There is no righteousness surpassing Truthfulness and there is no sin greater than untruth, especially in the conduct of a witness. Hence Truthfulness is the greatest (of all virtues)." 2.

"Truth is one without a second A man speaking it will, therefore, never be confounded (as to what to say and how to say it at any time). Truth is the ladder to supreme bliss and like a boat carries one safe beyond to emancipation)." 3.

साक्ष्येऽनृतं वदन्पाशैर्बध्यते वारुणैर्भृशम् ।
विवशः शतमाजातीस्तस्मात्साक्ष्यं वदेदृतम् ॥ ८२ ॥

The following three verses are found in some editions :—

ब्राह्मणो वै मनुष्याणामादित्यस्तेजसां दिवि ।
शिरो वा सर्वगात्राणां धर्माणां सत्यमुत्तमम् ॥ १ ॥
नास्ति सत्यात्परो धर्मो नानृतात्पातकं परम् ।
साक्षिधर्मे विशेषेण तस्मात्सत्यं विशिष्यते ॥ २ ॥
एकमेवाऽद्वितीयं तु प्रब्रुवन्नावबुध्यते ।
सत्यं स्वर्गस्य सोपानं पारावारस्य नौरिव ॥ ३ ॥

---

* सहस्रधार एव ते समस्वरन्दिवो नाके मधुजिह्वा असश्चतः । तस्य स्पशो न निमिषन्ति भूर्णयः पदे पदे पाशिनः सन्ति सेतवे ॥ अ० ५ । ६ । ३ ॥

"In that God Himself, in Whom there is no suffering, Who supports luster in a thousand ways (=imparts luster to all beings in innumerable ways viz., reason, sun, electricity, fire &c.) do the sweet-tongued (righteous men) of unwavering lives rightly sound (their warning) 'His frowning watchmen never close their eyes ; possessed of snares they are present at every step to bind (the wicked)". A. V. V, 6, 3.

"By Truthfulness a witness is purified, through Truthfulness his merit grows; truth must, therefore, be spoken by witnesses of all classes of society." 83.

"The soul herself is the witness of man's good or bad deeds and man is his own refuge in time (of trouble). Despise not they own soul, the supreme witness of man." 84.

"The wicked, indeed, say in their hearts, 'Nobody sees us'; but all beneficient beings (mentioned in the following verse) distinctly see them and the Perfect Being that is in their own breasts." 85.

"The sky (=ether and space), the earth, the waters, the heart, the moon, the sun, the fire, observance (of vows), the wind, the night both the (morning and evening) twilights and one's duty (in life) these are the knowers of the conduct of all corporeal beings." 86.

"If thou thinkest, O good man, with respect to thyself, 'I am alone' (know that) that Sage who witnesses all virtuous and sinful acts, ever resides in thy heart." 91.

सत्येन पूयते साक्षी धर्मः सत्येन वर्धते ।
तस्मात्सत्यं हि वक्तव्यं सर्ववर्णेषु साक्षिभिः ॥ ८३ ॥

आत्मैव ह्यात्मनः साक्षी गतिरात्मा तथात्मनः ।
मावमंस्थाः स्वमात्मानं नृणां साक्षिणमुत्तमम् ॥ ८४ ॥

मन्यन्ते वै पापकृतो न कश्चित्पश्यतीति नः ।
तांस्तु देवाः प्रपश्यंति स्वस्यैवान्तरपूरुषः ॥ ८५ ॥

द्यौर्भूमिरापो हृदयं चन्द्रार्काग्नियमानिलाः ।
रात्रिः संध्ये च धर्मश्च वृत्तज्ञाः सर्वदेहिनाम् ॥ ८६ ॥

एकोऽहमस्मीत्यात्मानं यत्त्वं कल्याण मन्यसे ।
नित्यं स्थितस्ते हृद्येष पुण्यपापेक्षिता मुनिः ॥ ९१ ॥

"Headlong, in utter darkness shall the sinful man tumble into hell, who being interrogated in a judicial inquiry answers one question falsely." 94.

"The enlightened do not consider any man better in this world than him, of whom his conscious soul has no distrust, when he gives evidence." 96.

"He (=the witness) kills (=incurs guilt equal to killing ?) five (of his relatives), by false testimony regarding small cattle, he kills ten by false testimony regarding kine, he kills a hundred by false evidence concerning horses, and a thousand by false evidence concerning men." 98.

"By speaking falsely in a cause regarding gold, he kills the born and the unborn; by false evidence concerning land, he kills everything; beware, therefore, of false evidence concerning land." 99.

"Let no wise man swear an oath falsely, even in a trifling matter; for he who swears an oath falsely is lost in this world and after death." 111.

"Whenever false evidence has been given in any suit, let the judge reverse the judgment, and whatever has been done must be (considered as) undone." 117.

अवाक्शिरास्तमस्यन्धे किल्बिषी नरकं व्रजेत् ।
यः प्रश्नं वितथं ब्रूयात्पृष्टः सन्धर्मनिश्चये ॥ ९४ ॥
यस्य विद्वान्हि वदतः क्षेत्रज्ञो नाभिशङ्कते ।
तस्मान्न देवाः श्रेयांसं लोकेऽन्यं पुरुषं विदुः ॥ ९६ ॥
पञ्च पश्वनृते हन्ति दश हन्ति गवानृते ।
शतमश्वानृते हन्ति सहस्रं पुरुषानृते ॥ ९८ ॥
हन्ति जातानजातांश्च हिरण्यार्थेऽनृतं वदन् ।
सर्वं भूम्यनृते हन्ति मा स्म भूम्यनृतं वदीः ॥ ९९ ॥
न वृथा शपथं कुर्यात्स्वल्पेऽप्यर्थे नरो बुधः ।
वृथा हि शपथं कुर्वन्प्रेत्य चेह च नश्यति ॥ १११ ॥
यस्मिन्यस्मिन्विवादे तु कौटसाक्ष्यं कृतं भवेत् ।
तत्तत्कार्यं निवर्तेत कृतं चाप्यकृतं भवेत् ॥ ११७ ॥

"Let him (=who desires prosperity) say what is true, let him say what is pleasing, let him utter no disagreeable truth, let him utter no agreeable falsehood; that is the eternal Law of Righteousness." 4, 138.

"What is well, let him call well, or let him say 'well' only; let him not engage in a useless enmity or dispute with any body." 139.

"Let him always delight in Truthfulness, (obedience to) the Law of Righteousness; conduct worthy of a respectable person, and purity; let him govern his pupils according to the sacred law; let him keep his speech, his arms, and his belly under control." 175.

"He who describes himself to virtuous (men), in a manner contrary to truth, is the most sinful (wretch) in this world; he is a thief who makes away with his own self." 255.

"All things (have their nature) determined by speech; speech is their root, and from speech they proceed; but he who is dishonest with respect to speech, is dishonest in everything." 256.

सत्यं ब्रूयात्प्रियं ब्रूयान्न ब्रूयात्सत्यमप्रियम् ।
प्रियं च नानृतं ब्रूयादेष धर्मः सनातनः ॥ ४ । १३८ ॥

भद्रं भद्रमिति ब्रूयाद्भद्रमित्येव वा वदेत् ।
शुष्कवैरं विवाद च न कुर्यात्केनचित्सह ॥ १३९ ॥

सत्यधर्मार्यवृत्तेषु शौचे चैवारमेत्सदा ।
शिष्यांश्च शिष्याद्धर्मेण वाग्बाहूदरसंयतः ॥ १७५ ॥

योऽन्यथा सन्तमात्मानमन्यथा सत्सु भाषते ।
स पापकृत्तमो लोकें स्तेन आत्मापहारकः ॥ २५५ ॥

वाच्यर्था नियताः सर्वे वाङ्मूला वाग्विनिःसृताः ।
तान्तु यः स्तेनयेद्वाचं स सर्वस्तेयकृन्नरः ॥ २५६ ॥

The etymology of the word यज्ञ is fully explained on pp. 5 and 11. Primarily it is formed from the root √यज देवपूजासङ्गतिकरणदानेषु by adding the suffix नङ् in conformity with P. III, 3, 90 यजयाचयतविच्छप्रच्छरक्षो नङ् i. e., 'the suffix नङ् is added to the roots √यज, √याच, √यत, √विच्छ, √प्रच्छ and √रक्ष in the sense of any case except the nominative and connotes the idea of some action indicated by the verb.' The word thus formed must, if the derivation is scientific, import all the ideas involved in the expressions देवपूजा, सङ्गतिकरण and दान. For example, देव is derived from the root √दिवु in the sense of क्रीड़ा, विजिगीषा, व्यवहार, द्युति, स्तुति, मोद, मद, स्वप्न, कान्ति and गति (see pp. 5 and 10) and पूजा from the root √पूज in the sense of पूजा, worship, honour, receiving with respect. Hence देवपूजा would mean honouring, respecting or satisfying anything or anybody characterised by the 'doing' or 'being' indicated by the ten significations of the verb दिवु i. e., a playful child (क्रीड़ा), a merchant or lawyer (व्यवहार), a needy or poor person (कान्ति) &c. सङ्गतिकरण means associating with, uniting with or joining something to something else, communicating with, conveying to, piecing together, construing in harmony with, &c. In this sense यज्ञ would, along with other significations, also mean any means of conveyance which helps a man to move from one place and reach another. दान is derived from the root √डुदाञ् दाने, giving or imparting, such as alms, learning &c.

From the above explanation it should not be considered impossible or far-fetched to take यज्ञ to mean any righteous or good work in which the above mentioned acts are involved. In this sense any good and legitimate act of philanthropy, done with a view to derive some benefit oneself or to impart it to others would be called a yajña. In the Śatapatha Brahmaṇa a yajña is called adhvara, i. e., an act involving no harm or injury to any being.[1] Haling, saluting or speaking respectfully to, a worthy person is called a yajña.[2] Hence a lecture, a discourse, a sermon or a speech delivered, an address or ovation given to a deserving person or a debate held on some topic would also be a yajña. Fortune[3] virtue or power, and glory or greatness[4] are also yajña. A wise or great[5] and learned man is also called yajṇa (=yajanīya=deserving of respect). Wealth or means[6] of happiness, the sun or celestial regions[7], a great deed,[8] the general public,[9] the Vedas,[10] the portion of the sacrificer,[11] the sacrificer himself,[12] the soul,[13] a man,[14] animals,[15] the universe,[16] the waters,[17] semen virile,[18] an offering,[19] &c., &c., are all called yajña in the Brahmaṇa literature. This word is so important that it denotes God as well.[20] Hence to confine it to some religious sacrifice exclusively is to betray ignorance of the methods of Vedic exegesis.

---

[1] अध्वरो वै यज्ञः ॥ श० १ । २ । ४ । ५ ॥ ४ । १ । ३८ ॥ ३९ ॥ &c. see p. 17. [2] येभ्य एतन्नमस्करोति नमो नम इति । यज्ञो वै नमः । यज्ञेनैवैनांस्तन्नमस्कारेण नमस्यति तस्मादु ह नायज्ञियं ब्रूयान्नमस्त इति यथा हैनं ब्रूयाद्यज्ञस्त इति तादृक्तत् श० ७ । ४ । १ । ३० ॥ [3] यज्ञो वै भगः ॥ श० ६ । ३ । १ । १९ ॥ [4] यज्ञो वै महिमा ॥ श० ६ । ३ । १ । १८ ॥ [5] ये वै ब्राह्मणाः शुश्रुवांसोऽनूचानास्ते विप्रास्तानेवैतदभ्याह बृहतो विपश्चित इति । यज्ञो वै बृहन्विपश्चित् ॥ श० ३ । ५ । ३ । १२ ॥ [6] यज्ञो वै वसुः ॥ श० १ । ७ । १ । ९ ॥ [7] यज्ञो वै स्वः ॥ श० १ । १ । २ । २१ ॥ [8] यज्ञो वै श्रेष्ठतमं कर्म ॥ श० १ । ७ । १ । ५ ॥ तै० ३ । २ । १ । ४ ॥ [9] यज्ञो वै विट् ॥ श० १४ । ३ । १ । ६ ॥ [10] सैषा त्रयीविद्या यज्ञः ॥ श० १ । १ । ४ । ३ ॥ [11] यज्ञो वै यजमानभागः ॥ ऐ० ७ । २६ ॥ [12] यजमानो वै यज्ञः ॥ ऐ० १ । २८ ॥ [13] आत्मा वै यज्ञः ॥ श० ६ । २ । १ । ७ ॥ [14] पुरुषो वै यज्ञः ॥ शां० १७ । ७ ॥ गो० २ । ५ । ४ ॥ श० १ । ३ । २ । १ ॥ तै० ३ । ८ । २३ । १॥ जैउ० ४ । २ । १ ॥ &c., &c. [15] पशवो यज्ञः ॥ श० ३ । २ । ३ । ११ ॥ &c. [16] यज्ञो वै भुवनम् ॥ तै० ३ । ३ । ७ । ५ ॥ [17] आपो वै यज्ञः ॥ ऐ० २ । २० ॥ श० ३ । ८ । ५ । १ ॥ [18] रेतो वाऽअत्र यज्ञः ॥ श० ७ । ३ । २ । ३ ॥ [19] आहुतिर्हि यज्ञः ॥ श० ३ । १ । ४ । १ ॥ [20] विष्णुर्यज्ञः ॥ गो० २ । १ । १२ ॥ तै० ३ । ३ । ६ ॥ यज्ञः प्रजापतिः ॥ श० ११ । ६ । ३ । ९ ॥ &c.

In the Chāndōgyōpaniṣad yajña is said to be an essential element supporting the Sacred Law of Righteousness—Dharma.[1] In the same work yajña is said to be the name of the all-purifying air,[2] and elsewhere again brahmacarya[3]—continence is called yajña. In the Bṛhadāraṇyakōpaniṣad in the 'Sampratti' rite the father is directed[4] to call his son yajña. Later on God—Prajāpati[5] also is called yajña, and in another place yajña is said to be essential for the Brāhmaṇa to know the Great Ātman[6] (=God). In the Taittiriyōpaniṣad a highly advanced intellect[7] is said to be necessary to perform yajña

The following points are noteworthy in what the Gītā teaches about yajña. (1) The householder should first feed the respectable guest and then himself eat his food. (2) Yajña is essential for rain. (3) The Supreme Being is ever present in a yajña. (4) Work done for yajña does not fetter the doer. (5) There are several types of yajña as detailed below:

"*When* Brahma-*priest* to Brahma-*fire*
throws Brahma-*offering*, Brahma-*ghee*,—
To none but Brahma *shall he go*
Who merges every deed in Brahma. 4, 24.

---

[1] त्रयो धर्मस्कन्धा यज्ञोऽध्ययनं दानमिति प्रथमः ॥ छां० १ । २३ । १ ॥ [2] एष ह वै यज्ञो योऽयं पवत एष ह यन्निदं सर्वं पुनाति । यदेष यन्निदं सर्वं पुनाति तस्मादेष एव यज्ञस्तस्य मनश्च वाक् च वर्तनी ॥ ४ । १६ । १ ॥ [3] अथ यद्यज्ञ इत्याचक्षते ब्रह्मचर्यमेव तद्ब्रह्मचर्येण ह्येव यो ज्ञाता तं विन्दते ॥ ८ । ५ । १ ॥ [4] अथातः सम्प्रत्तिर्यदा प्रैष्यन्मन्यतेऽथ पुत्रमाह त्वं ब्रह्म त्वं यज्ञस्त्वं लोक इति ॥ बृ० १ । ५ । १७ ॥ [5] यज्ञः प्रजापतिरिति ॥ ३ । ९ । ६ ॥ [6] तमेतम् (महान्तमात्मानम्) देवानुवचनेन ब्राह्मणा विविदिषन्ति यज्ञेन दानेन तपसाऽनाशकेन ॥ ४ । ४ । २२ ॥ [7] विज्ञानं यज्ञं तनुते ॥ तै० उ० २ । ५ । १ ॥

(1) यज्ञशिष्टाशिनः सन्तो मुच्यन्ते सर्वकिल्बिषैः । भुञ्जते ते त्वघं पापा ये पचन्त्यात्मकारणात् । भ० ३।१३॥ (2) यज्ञाद्भवति पर्जन्यः ॥ १४ ॥ (3) ब्रह्म नित्यं यज्ञे प्रतिष्ठितम् ॥ १५ ॥
(4) यज्ञार्थात्कर्मणोऽन्यत्र लोकोऽयं कर्मबन्धनः ॥ ९ ॥

(5) ब्रह्मार्पणं ब्रह्महविर्ब्रह्माग्नौ ब्रह्मणा हुतम् ।
ब्रह्मैव तेन गन्तव्यं ब्रह्मकर्मसमाधिना ॥ भ० ४ । २४ ॥

"Some yogis offer sacrifice
in worship to [His] Powers Bright;
While some, their mere lives Sacrifice,
rain offerings into Brahma-Fire. 25.

"Some pour sense-powers—hearing first—
into the Fires of sense-restraint;
Some pour sense-things—sound and the rest—
into bright sense-perception Fires. 26.

"Yet others offer sacrifice
of every Act of sense and life
Into the Wisdom-kindled Fire
of Yoga wrought by Self-control. 27.

"Yet others pour in their offerings
of wealth, asceticism, training,
of sacred study and knowledge,—
Self-mastered men of steadfast vows. 28.

"Others merge 'on-breath' in 'off-breath'
and 'off-breath' in 'on-breath' as well,
Checking the dual vital tide,
on Mastery of Life intent. 29.

"Others, eating with self-control,
offer up to their life-breaths, Lives;—
All these have mastered Sacrifice;
in them its Power starves out sin. 30.

दैवमेवापरे यज्ञं योगिनः पर्युपासते ।
ब्रह्माग्नावपरे यज्ञं यज्ञेनैवोपजुह्वति ॥ २५ ॥

श्रोत्रादीनीन्द्रियाण्यन्ये संयमाग्निषु जुह्वति ।
शब्दादीन्विषयानन्य इन्द्रियाग्निषु जुह्वति ॥ २६ ॥

सर्वाणीन्द्रियकर्माणि प्राणकर्माणि चापरे ।
आत्मसंयमयोगाग्नौ जुह्वति ज्ञानदीपिते ॥ २७ ॥

द्रव्ययज्ञास्तपोयज्ञा योगयज्ञास्तथापरे ।
स्वाध्यायज्ञानयज्ञाश्च यतयः संशितव्रताः ॥ २८ ॥

अपाने जुह्वति प्राणं प्राणेऽपानं तथापरे ।
प्राणापानगती रुध्वा प्राणायामपरायणाः ॥ २९ ॥

अपरे नियताहाराः प्राणान्प्राणेषु जुह्वति ।
सर्वेऽप्येते यज्ञविदो यज्ञक्षपितकल्मषाः ॥ ३० ॥

"Their food Sacrifice-Leavings, They,
ambrosia-fed, reach deathless Brahma.
The Sacrifice-less holds no claim
on *this* World—whence then on the next? 31.

"Thus many kinds of sacrifice
for Brahma's consumption are laid out,
Know these all sprung of [His one] Act
thus knowing *Thou* shalt be set free. 32.

"Better than object-sacrifice
the Sacrifice of *consciousness* :—
The whole-sale cycle of Cosmic Act
is rounded out when Self knows self." 33.

(6) yajña, charity—dāna and austerities—tapas can never be given up; but on the contrary must always be practised. (7) Yajña is as essential as Vedic study, and self-control.

In short, what the Gītā teaches about yajña is the same as what is laid down in the Brāhmaṇas viz., **यज्ञो वै श्रेष्ठतमं कर्म.**

Yajvan or yajamāna used in the hymn being dealt with, will also allow as many interpretations. A Yajamāna is a man of Faith who undertakes to do some great deed for the benefit of one's own self and the world at large, undergoing all the '*sacrifice*' involved. Such undertaking necessarily calls for faith, since without Faith in the Unseen, it is impossible for a man

---

यज्ञशिष्टामृतभुजो यान्ति ब्रह्म सनातनम् ।
नायं लोकोऽस्त्ययज्ञस्य कुतोऽन्यः कुरुसत्तम ॥ ३१ ॥

एवं बहुविधा यज्ञा वितता ब्रह्मणो मुखे ।
कर्मजान्विद्धि तान्सर्वानेवं ज्ञात्वा विमोक्ष्यसे ॥ ३२ ॥

श्रेयान्द्रव्यमयाद्यज्ञाज्ज्ञानयज्ञः परंतप ।
सर्वं कर्माखिलं पार्थ ज्ञाने परिसमाप्यते ॥ ३३ ॥

(6, यज्ञदानतपःकर्म न त्याज्यं कार्यमेव तत् ॥ १८ । ५ ॥ यज्ञे तपसि दाने च स्थितिः सदिति चोच्यते ॥१६। २७ ॥ (7) वेदेषु यज्ञेषु तपःसु चैव दानेषु यत्पुण्यफलं प्रदिष्टं ॥ ८ । ४८ ॥ दानं दमश्च यज्ञश्च स्वाध्यायस्तप आर्जवम् ॥ १ । १६ ॥

to go beyond his daily routine and self.* It must be borne in mind that a yajña is not exactly a great deed like the conquest of a country or a wonderful scientific discovery or giving away of millions in charity. Every good deed engendered by faith however humble, is a yajña and every man who does it however lowly in human society he may be, is a yajamāna.

Jesus in the famous Parable of the Good Samaritan really explained what a yajña or a yajamāna should be. The passage is charming and deserves to be quoted here:—"And, behold a certain lawyer stood up, and tempted him, saying, Master, what shall I do to inherit eternal life? He said unto him, What is written in the law? how readest thou? And he answering said, "Thou shalt love the Lord thy God with all thy heart, and with all thy soul, and with all thy mind; and thy neighbour as thyself." And he said unto him, Thou hast answered right: this do, and thou shalt live. But he, willing to justify himself, said unto Jesus, And who is my neighbour? And Jesus answering said, A certain *man* went down from Jerusalem to Jericho, and fell among thieves, which stripped him of his raiment, and wounded *him*, and departed leaving *him* half-dead. And by chance there came down a certain priest that way; and when he saw him, he passed by on the other side. And likewise a Levite, when he was at the place, came and looked *on him*, and passed by on the other side. But a certain Samaritan, as he journeyed, came where he was: and when he saw him, he had compassion *on*

* Du musst glauben du musst wagen,
den die Gotter lein kein pfand,
Nur ein Wunder Kan dich tragen
in das schone Wunder-land.
Schiller.

"Thou must believe and thou must risk, it is only then that God will bestow His promise on thee; but the wonder of it all will be waiting for thee in that beautiful Wonderland!"

him. And went to *him*, and bound up his wounds, pouring in oil and wine, and set him on his own beast, and brought him to an inn, and took care of him. And on the morrow when he departed, he took out two pence and gave *them* to the host, and said unto him. Take care of him; and whatsoever thou spendest more, when I come again, I will repay thee. Which now of these three, thinkest thou, was neighbour unto him that fell among the thieves? And he said, He that shewed mercy on him. Then said Jesus unto him, Go, and do thou likewise."*

In the following tale, Whittier, in his beautiful style, lays bare the heart of a true yajamāna :—

The Brother of Mercy.

Piero Luca, known of all the town
As the gray porter by the Pitti wall
Where the noon shadows of the gardens fall,
Sick and in dolor, waited to lay down
His last sad burden, and beside his mat
The barefoot monk of La Certosa sat.
Unseen, in square and blossoming garden drifted,
Soft sunset lights through green Val d'Arno sifted;
Unheard, below the living shuttles shifted
Backward and forth, and wove in love or strife,
In mirth or pain, the mottled web of life;
But when at last came upward from the street
Tinkle of bell and tread of measured feet,
The sick man started, strove to rise in vain,
Sinking back heavily with a moan of pain.
And the monk said, "Tis but the Brotherhood
Of Mercy going on some errand good:
Their black masks by the palace-wall I see'
Piero answered faintly, 'Woe is me!
This day for the first time in forty years
In vain the bell hath sounded in my ears,
Calling me with my brethren of the mask,
Beggar and prince alike to some new task
Of love or pity,—haply from the street
To bear a wretch plague-stricken, or with feet

* The Gospel of Luke X, 25-37.

Hushed to the quickened ear and feverish brain,
To tread the crowded lazaretto's floors,
Down the long twilight of the corridors,
Midst tossing arms and faces full of pain.
I loved the work: it was its own reward.
I never counted on it to offset
My sins, which are many, or make less my debt
To the free grace and mercy of our Lord;
But somehow, father, it has come to be
In these long years so much a part of me,
I should not know myself, if lacking it,
But with the work the worker too would die,
And in my place some other self would sit
Joyful or sad,—what matters, if not I?
And now all's over. Woe is me!'—'My son'
The monk said soothingly, 'thy work is done;
And no more as a servant, but the guest
Of God thou enterest thy eternal rest.
No toil, no tears, no sorrows for the lost,
Shall mar thy perfect bliss. Thou shalt sit down
Clad in white robes, and wear a golden crown
Forever and forever'—Piero tossed
On his sick-pillow: 'Miserable me!
I am too poor for such grand company;
The crown would be too heavy for this gray
Old head; and God forgive me if I say
It would be hard to sit there night and day,
Like an image in the Tribune, doing naught
With these hard hands, that all my life have wrought,
Not for bread only, but for pity's sake.
I'm dull at prayers: I could not keep awake,
Counting my beads. Mine's but a crazy head.
Scarce worth the saving, if all else be dead.
And if one goes to heaven without a heart,
God knows he leaves behind his better part.
I love my fellow-men; the worst I know
I would do good to. Will death change me so
That I shall sit among the lazy saints,
Turning a deaf ear to the sore complaints
Of souls that suffer? Why, I never yet
Left a poor dog in the *strada* hard beset,
Or ass o'erladen! Must I rate man less
Than dog or ass, in holy selfishness?
Methinks (Lord, pardon, if the thought be sin!)
The world of pain were better, if therein

One's heart might still be human, and desires
Of natural pity drop upon the fires
Some cooling tears.'

Thereat the pale monk crossed
His brow, and muttering, 'Madman! thou art lost!'
Took up his pyx and fled; and, left alone,
The sick man closed his eyes with a great groan
That sank into a prayer, 'Thy will be done!'

Then was he made aware, by soul or ear,
Of somewhat pure and holy bending o'er him
And of a voice like that of her who bore him,
Tender and most compassionate: 'Never fear!
For heaven is love, as God himself is love;
Thy work below shall be thy work above.'
And when he looked, lo! in the stern monk's place
He saw the shining of an angel's face!" *

Adalaide Anne Proctor in two of her charming poems has drawn a beautiful pen-picture of the true yajamāna endowed with perfect śraddhā. Both the pieces are subjoined for the enlightenment of the reader :—

The Three Rulers.

I saw a ruler take his stand
And trample on a mighty land;
The People crouched before his beck
His iron heel was on their neck,
His name shone bright through blood and pain,
His sword flashed back their praise again.

I saw another Ruler rise—
His words were noble, good and wise;
With the calm sceptre of his pen
He ruled the minds and thoughts of men:
Some scoffed, some praised—while many heard,
Only a few obeyed his word.

Another Ruler then I saw—
Love and sweet Pity were his law:
The greatest and the least had part
(Yet most the unhappy) in his heart—

* The Poetical Works of John Greenleaf Whittier, The Oxford University Press edition 1898, pp. 272, 273.

The People, in a mighty band,
Rose up, and drove him from the land.'*

A Knight Errant.

Though he lived and died among us,
Yet his name may be enrolled
With the Knights whose deeds of daring
Ancient chronicles have told.

Still a stripling he encountered
Poverty, and struggled long,
Gathering force from every effort,
Till he knew his arm was strong.

When his heart and life he offered
To his radient mistress—Truth;
Never thought, or dream, or faltering,
Marred the promise of his youth.

So he rode forth to defend her,
And her peerless worth proclaim;
Challenging each recreant doubter
Who aspersed her spotless name:

First upon his path stood Ignorance,
Hideous in his brutal might;
Hard the blows and long the battle
Ere the monster took to flight.

Then, with light and fearless spirit,
Prejudice he dared to brave;
Hunting back the lying craven
To her black sulphureous cave.

Followed by his servile minions,
Custom, the old Giant rose;
Yet he, too, at last was conquered
By the good Knight's weighty blows.

Then he turned, and, flushed with Victory,
Struck upon the brazen shield
Of the world's great king, Opinion,
And defied him to the field.

Once again he rose a conqueror,
And, though wounded in the fight,
With a dying smile of triumph
Saw that Truth had gained her right.

---

* Legends & Lyrics & Other Poems by Adelaide Anne Proctor, Everyman's Library Series, p. 21.

On his failing ear re-echoing
Came the shouting round her throne;
Little cared he that no future
With her name would link his own.

Spent with many a hard-fought battle,
Slowly ebbed his life away,
And the crowd that flocked to greet her
Trampled on him where he lay.

Gathering all his strength, he saw her
Crowned and reigning in his pride:
Looked his last upon her beauty,
Raised his eyes to God, and died.*

* Ibid pp. 25 and 26.

Chapter VII.

Succouring the Needy or Charity.

Ṛgvēda X, 117.

Seer :—Bhikṣu.

Subject :—Praise of the opulent man (Indra) and advice to help with money and food the needy and to impart learning to the deserving.

Metre :—Stanza 1 nicṛj-jagatī; 2 padanicṛj-jagatī; stanzas 3, 7 and 9 nicṛt-triṣṭubh; 4 and 6 triṣṭubh; stanza 5 virāt-triṣṭubh; and 8 bhurik-triṣṭubh.

Tone :—Dhaivata.

(७६) ओ३म् ॥ न वा उं देवाः क्षुधमिद्वधं ददुरु-
ताशितमुप गच्छन्ति मृत्यवः । उतो रयिः पृणतो नोप-
दस्यत्युताऽपृणन्मर्डितारं न विन्दते ॥ १ ॥

अन्वितपदपाठः—देवाः क्षुधम् इत् वधम् ददुः न वै उ अशितम् उत मृत्यवः उप गच्छन्ति । उतो पृणतः रयिः न उप दस्यति उत अपृणन् मर्डितारम् न विन्दते ॥

Word-meaning &c.:—वै=surely. उ=an expletive. देवाः=the force of nature that sustain creatures. क्षुधम्*=hunger, a hungry man. इत्—only. वधम्=death. ददुः=

---

* √क्षुध बुभुक्षायाम् + क्विप् by P. III, 2, 76 क्विप् च, i. e., 'the termination क्विप् is added to all verbs whether alone or preceded by some prefix whether in Vedic or ordinary Sanskrit.'

have assigned. उत=even. अशितम्*=him who has enough to eat. उप गच्छन्ति=go near; approach. मृत्यवः†=various types of death. उत=certainly. पृणतः‡=of him who gives charity, helps or supports the needy. रयि$ः= wealth. उप दस्यति=exhausts; is finished. उत=but; on the other hand. अपृणन्=who does not help others. मार्डितारम्§=a friend to console.

Translation:—Providence has not surely ordained death only for the hungry and ill-fed, for death in various forms does make short work even of such as have enough to eat. It is also certain that the wealth of him who (out of his resources) helps the needy does

---

* √अशु भोजने+इट्+क्त according to P. VII, 2, 35 आर्धधातुकस्येड्वलादेः and III, 3, 114 नपुंसके भावे क्तः The termination क्त is here added in the abstract sense of feeding or eating and the augment इट् is inserted between it and the root as the former is nonconjugational and begins with त (क् being indicatory), a consonant of the वल् प्रत्याहार. The word metaphorically means one well-fed &c.

† √मृङ् प्राणत्यागे+त्युक् by U. III, 21 भुजिमृङ्भ्यां युक्त्युकौ—'to the roots भुज् and मृ the terminations युक् and त्युक् are to be added.'

‡ √पृण प्रीणने+शतृ by P. III, 2, 124, लटः शतृशानचावप्रथमासमानाधिकरणे, 'the terminations शतृ and शानच् are added to verbs instead of those of लट्—present-tense terminations—and the resulting form is not used with a noun in the nominative case as its subject.'

$ √रीङ् गतौ+इ U. IV, 139 अच इः, 'to roots ending in vowels the termination इ is added, or √रा दानग्रहणयोः+युक्+इ according to P. VII, 3, 33 आतो युक् चिण्कृतोः, 'to a base ending in आ the augment युक् is added before चिण् and कृत् terminations.' The final आ is here irregularly shortened.

§ √मृड सुखे+तृच् P. III, 1, 133 ण्वुल्तृचौ, 'the terminations ण्वुल् and तृच् are added to all verbs in the sense of the agent' (P. III, 4, 67).

not get exhausted, whereas he who does not succour the poor has none to console him in time of trouble.

(७७) य आध्राय चकमानाय पित्वोऽन्नवान्त्सन् रफितायोप जग्मुषे । स्थिरं मनः कृणुते सेवते पुरोतो चित्स मर्डितारं न विन्दते ॥ २ ॥

अन्वितपदपाठः—यः अन्नऽवान् सन् पित्वः चकमानाय रफिताय उपऽजग्मुषे आध्राय मनः स्थिरं कृणुते उतो पुरा सेवते सः चित् मर्डितारम् न विन्दते ॥

Word-meaning &c.:—**आध्राय***=to the needy, poor, indigent. **चकमानाय**†=longing (for food). **रफिताय**‡=reduced to straits. **उप जग्मुषे**§=approaching for help. **स्थिरम् कृणुते**=makes hard, hardens. **मनः**=heart. **सेवते**=eats; enjoys. **पुरा**=in his very sight. **उतो**=but. **चित्**=surely. **पित्वः**||=of food. **अन्नवान्**$=having plenty of food.

Translation:—That man, surely, will have no one to console him in time of trouble who, having plenty to eat, does not give a morsel to the indigent person that reduced to straits and, oppressed with hunger, comes to him for help, but hardens his heart and eats in the very sight of the poor man.

---

*आ + √डुधाञ् धारणपोषणयोः + रक् U. II, 13, or आ + √धृञ् धारणे + क Vartika कप्रकरणे मूलविभुजादिभ्य उपसंख्यानम् or आ + √ध्यै तृप्तौ + क by P. III, 1 136, आतश्चोपसर्गे कः applied irregularly.

†√कमु कान्तौ + कानच् by P. III, 106 लिटः कानज्वा.

‡√रफि गतौ + क्त P. III 2, 102, निष्ठा and VII, 2, 35.

§उप + √ गम्लृ गतौ + क्वसु by P, III, 2, 107 क्वसुश्च.

||√पा रक्षणे or √पा पाने or √ओप्यायी वृद्धौ + तु by U. I, 71 कमिमनिजनिगाभायाहिभ्यश्च.

$ अन्न + मतुप् by P. V, 2, 94 तदस्यास्त्यस्मिन्निति मतुप् and VII, 2, 94 मादुपधायाश्च मतोर्वोऽयवादिभ्यः

(७८) स इद्भोजो यो गृहवे ददात्यन्नकामाय चरते कृशाय । अरमस्मै भवति यामहूता उतापरीषु कृणुते सखायम् ॥ ३ ॥

अन्वितपदपाठः—यः कृशाय अन्नकामाय चरते गृहवे ददाति सः इत् भोजः । अस्मै यामऽहूतौ अरम् भवति उत अपरीषु सखायम् कृणुते ॥

Word-meaning &c :—इत्=alone; verily. भोजः*=(√भुज) =an eater; one who eats. गृहवे†=one who begs for alms. ददाति=gives. अन्नकामाय‡=one who longs for food. चरते= going about. कृशाय§=lean; emaciated. अरम्=plenty; enough (food wealth &c). अस्मै=for him. भवति=there will be. यामहूतौ||=as a result of such philanthropic deeds. अपरीषु$=in time of distress, lack of completion or sufficiency, occasions of want, another, other, adjective of यामहूतिषु understood. सखायं कृणुते=it will secure him friends.

Translation:—That man really enjoys his food who feeds also the poor emaciated beggar that goes about oppressed with hunger begging from door to door. He will have plenty of wealth as a result of such philanthropic deeds and his charity will secure him friends in his own need.

---

* √भुज पालनाभ्यवहारयोः + अच् by P. III, 1, 134 नन्दिग्रहिपचादिभ्यो ल्युणिन्यचः.

† गृह् ग्रहणे + कु U. I, 23.

‡ अन्नं कामयते इति अन्न + काम by P. II, 2, 19 उपपदमतिङ्.

§ √कृश तनूकरणे + क P. III, 1, 135 इगुपधज्ञाप्रीकिरः कः.

|| √या प्रापणे + मन् U. I, 140 अर्तिस्तुसु &c. + √ह्वेञ् + क्तिन् P. III, 3, 94 स्त्रियां क्तिन् ।

$ नञ् + √पॄ पालनपूरणयोः + इ U. IV, 139 अच इ + ङीप् by P. IV, 1, 45, बह्वादिभ्यश्च applied irregularly or अपर + ङीप् by P. IV, 1, 30 केवलमामकभागधेय &c.

(७६) न स सखा यो न ददाति सख्ये सचाभुवे सचमानाय पित्वः । अपास्मात्प्रेयान्न तदोको अस्ति पृणन्तमन्यमरणं चिदिच्छेत् ॥ ४ ॥

अन्वितपदपाठः—पित्वः सचमानाय सचाऽभुवे सख्ये यः न ददाति स सखा न । अस्मात् अप प्र इयात् तत् ओकः न अस्ति । पृणन्तम् अन्यम् अरणम् चित् इच्छेत् ॥

Word-meaning:—सचाभुवे*=to him who is of the same persuasion; to a member of the same society. सचमानाय†=to him who wishes for. पित्वः= of food. अप प्रेयात्=one should go away from. ओकः‡=human dwelling पृणन्तम्=one who helps. अरणं§=who gives readily. चित्=if. इच्छेत्=wishes.

Translation:—He is not a true friend who does not feed a man of his own persuasion who, oppressed with hunger, goes to him for help. One must not go to such a one but leave him forthwith for, his house is really not a human dwelling. One should go to some other person who can be more easily approached if one wishes to get help without much bother.

(८०) पृणीयादिन्नाधमानाय तव्यान् द्राघीयांसमनुपश्येत पंथाम् । ओ हि वर्तन्ते रथ्येव चक्राऽन्यमन्यमुप तिष्ठन्त रायः ॥ ५ ॥

---

* √षच समवाये + क्विप् P. III, 2, 76=सच् + टा the instrumental singular termination + √भू सत्तायाम् + क्विप् by the above rule. The compound is formed either according to P. II, 2, 29 उपपदमतिङ् or II, 1, 4 सह सुपा.

† √षच + शानच् P. III, 2, 124 & VII, 2, 82.

‡ √अव रक्षणगतिकान्ति &c. (see p. 84 f. n. 10) + कक् by U. III, 41 सृवृभूशुषिमुषिभ्यः कक्.

§ √ऋ गतौ + ल्यु by P. III, 1, 134 नन्दिग्रहिपचादिभ्यो ल्युणिन्यचः.

अन्वितपदपाठः—तव्यान् नाधमानाय पृणीयात् इत् द्राघीयांसम् पन्थाम् अनु पश्येत । रथ्याऽइव चक्रा ओ हि रायः वर्तन्त अन्यम्ऽअन्यम् उप तिष्ठन्त ॥

Word-meaning &c.:—**पृणीयात्**=should help; should feed. **इत्**=surely. **नाधमानाय***=to one seeking for help. **तव्यान्**†=strong. **द्राघीयांसम्**‡=longer; further. **अनुपश्येत**=he should see. **पंथाम्**§=road; way. **द्राघीयांसम् पंथाम् अनुपश्येत**=he should cast a glance on the long journey-in-life he has still to finish, during which, who knows what may happen. **उ हि**=for surely. **आ वर्तन्ते=(आ+√वृत्)**=go on revolving. **रथ्या**||=pertaining to a chariot. **चक्रा**=wheels. **अन्यम् अन्यम्**=from one another; one after the other. **उप तिष्ठन्त**=take recourse to. **रायः**¶=riches.

Translation:—A strong man who can afford to help the weaker seeking for help, should surely succour the latter. He should, in doing so, look to the long road he has still to cross on the journey of life during which, no one is sure what may happen, for; riches go on revolving like the wheels of a chariot—now going to one owner now to another.

(८१) मोघमन्नं विन्दते अप्रचेताः सत्यं ब्रवीमि वध इत्स तस्य । नार्यमणं पुष्यति नो सखायं केवलाघो भवति केवलादी ॥ ६ ॥

---

* √नाधृ याच्ञोपतापैश्वर्याशीःषु+शानच् P. III, 2, 124 & 82.

† तव बलनाम Nig. II, 9+ईयसुन् P. V, 3, 57 द्विवचनविभज्योपपदे तरबीयसुनौ the initial ई being irregularly dropped.

‡ दीर्घ+ईयसुन् as above and P. VI, 4, 157 प्रियस्थिरस्फिरोरु &c.

§ √पत्लृ गतौ+स्थ+इनि U. IV, 12 पतः स्थ च and 6 गमेरिनिः.

|| रथ+यत् P. IV, 4, 76 तद्वहति रथयुगप्रासङ्गम्.

¶ √रा दाने+डै U. II. 66 रातेर्डैः.

अन्वितपदपाठः—यः अर्यमणम् न पुष्यति नो सखायम्, (सः) केवलऽआदी केवलऽअघः भवति । सत्यम् ब्रवीमि (सः) अप्रचेताः अन्नम् मोघम् विन्दते । सः तस्य वधः इत् ॥

Word-meaning &c.:—मोघम्*=in vain. अन्नम्=food. विन्दते (√विद्)=gets. अप्रचेताः†=an evil intentioned person; a wicked person. सत्यम्=truth. ब्रवीमि=I say. वधः=death, अर्यमणम्‡=a noble or respectable person. पुष्यति=nourishes; feeds. नो=nor केवलाघः§=who has only sin to his credit. केवलादी‖=who eats alone.

Translation:—He who does not feed either a respectable guest or a (poor) friend in distress, but eats all alone, has only sin to his credit. To speak the truth, that wicked man gets his food in vain. It is not food, but it is his death.

(८२) कृषन्नित्फाल आशितं कृणोति यन्नध्वानमप वृङ्क्ते चरित्रैः । वदन्ब्रह्माऽवदतो वनीयान् पृणन्नापिरपृणन्तमभिष्यात् ॥ ७ ॥

अन्वितपदपाठः—फालः कृषन् इत् आशितम् कृणोति । वदन् ब्रह्मा अवदतः वनीयान् । पृणन् आपिः अपृणन्तम् अभि ष्यात् । यन् अध्वानम् चरित्रैः अपवृङ्क्ते ॥

---

* √मुह अविवेके+घञ् P. III, 3, 18 भावे irregularly applied and the final ह् of the root is changed to घ्.

† √अज गतौ+यत् P. III. 1, 97 अचो यत् irregularly applied, and 103 अर्यः स्वामिवैश्ययोः+√माङ् माने+कनिन् U. I, 159 श्वनुक्षन्पूषन्प्लीहन् &c.

‡ केवलम् अघम् यस्य केवल+अघ P. II, 2, 24 अनेकमन्यपदार्थे. अघ is formed from √अघ पापकरणे+(in the causal sense) णिच् P. III 1, 26 हेतुमति च+अच् P. III, 1, 134.

§ केवलआसौ आदी च—केवल+आदी P. II, 1, 57 विशेषणं विशेष्येण बहुलम्. आदी is formed from √अद भक्षणे+णिनि by P. III, 2, 78 सुप्यजातौ णिनिस्ताच्छील्ये.

Word-meaning &c.:—कृषन्*=ploughing. इत्=only. फालः†=who wields the plough; the peasant. आशितम्‡=food. कृणोति=makes; provides. यन्§=who performs his journey of life. अध्वानम्$=the road; journey. अपवृङ्क्ते (√वृज्)=finishes. चरित्रैः||=by righteous deeds. वदन्¶=speaking; teaching. ब्रह्मा=a learned man अवदतः=than him who does not speak or teach वनीयान्£=better; superior. आपिः$=a friend; a man of charitable disposition. अपृणन्तम्=who does not give or help. अभि स्यात्=surpasses.

Translation:—The peasant provides himself and others with food only by cultivating the soil. A man learned in the sacred scriptures who teaches is superior to him that does not teach. A person of charitable disposition and ready to succour one in need, is superior to him who does not help. Therefore, every man should make it his duty to perform his journey in life only by means of daily righteous dealings with all.

(८३) एकपाद्भूयो द्विपदो वि चक्रमे द्विपात्त्रिपादमभ्येति पश्चात्। चतुष्पादेति द्विपदामभिस्वरे सम्पश्यन्पंक्तीरुपतिष्ठमानः ॥ ८ ॥

---

* √कृष विलेखने+शतृ.

† √फल विदारणे+घञ् P. III. 3, 16 अकर्तरि च कारके संज्ञायाम्+अच् (फाल: अस्य अस्ति इति) P. V, 2, 127 अर्शआदिभ्योऽच्.

‡ √इण् गतौ+शतृ.

§ √अद भक्षणे+क्वनिप् U. IV, 116 अदेर्धंच, or √अत सातत्यगमने+क्वनिप् as above, or √आध (Vedic) गतौ+वनिप् U. IV, 113,

|| √चर गतौ भक्षणे च+इत्र U. IV, 173 अशित्रादिभ्य इत्रोत्रौ.

¶ √वद व्यक्तायां वाचि+शतृ.

£ वन+ईयसुन् P. V, 3, 57.

$ √आप्लृ व्याप्तौ+इण् V. इणजादिभ्यः on P. III, 3, 108.

अन्वितपदपाठः— एकऽपात् भूयः द्विपदः विचक्रमे । द्विऽपात् त्रिपादम् पश्चात् अभिएति । चतुःऽपात् द्विऽपदाम् अभिऽस्वरे उपऽतिष्ठमानः पङ्क्तीः समऽपश्यन् एति ॥

Word-meaning &c.:—**एकपात्***=having a certain amount of wealth. **द्विपदः**†=who has twice the amount or more than what the former has; the second class bourgeos. **भूयः**=more often; specially. **वि चक्रमे**= cross; transgress; walk upon. **त्रिपादम्**‡=him who has thrice as much wealh as the first or more than the second. **अभि एति**=goes; approaches. **पश्चात्**=behind; after. **अभि स्वरे**§=invocation; praise. **द्विपदाम् अभिस्वरे**=connotes the idea that when a very rich or highly placed person comes on the scene the second class bourgeoisie leave their superiors behind and take to cringing before him. **सम् पश्यन्**$=looking down upon patronisingly, **पङ्क्तीः**||=lines, rows or groups of men less wealthy than himself. **उपतिष्ठमानः**¶=being regarded with respect.

Translation:—A rich man tries to walk on the same path as he who has twice as much wealth and the latter wishes to run after him who has thrice as much. When a still wealthier man appears on the scene the second class bourgeoisie leave both their superiors and inferiors behind and cringe before him and laud him.

---

*एकः पादः यस्य इति एक+पात् P. II, 2, 24.

†द्वौ पदौ or पादौ यस्य इति द्वि+पद् as above. पद्—√पद गतौ+क्विप्.

‡त्रयः पादाः यस्य इति as above पाद is derived from √पद् by adding the termintion घञ् by P. III, 3, 16 पदरुजविश &c.

§अभि+स्वृ शब्दे+अप् P. III, 2, 57 ऋदोरप् or √स्वर आक्षेपे+अच् III, 1, 134.

$√दृशिर् प्रेक्षणे+शतृ.

||उप+√ष्ठा गतिनिवृत्तौ+शानच्.

¶√पचि व्यक्तीकरणे विस्तारे वा+क्तिन् P. V, 1, 59 पङ्क्तिविंशतित्रिंशत् &c. In this case the termination is said to be ति in the Madhaviya Dhatūvṛtti as well as the Kaśika.

He, being thus regarded by all of them with respect and awe, passes his way looking down patronisingly upon these small fry.

(८४) समौ चिद्धस्तौ न समं विविष्टः सम्मातरा चिन्न समं दुहाते। यमयोश्चिन्न समा वीर्याणि ज्ञाती चित्सन्तौ न समं पृणीतः ॥ ६ ॥

अन्वितपदपाठः—समौ हस्तौ चित् समम् वि विष्टः । समऽमातरौ चित् समम् दुहाते । यमयोः चित् न समा वीर्याणि । ज्ञाती सन्तौ चित् न समम् पृणीतः ॥

Word-meaning &c.:—**समौ**=both equal. **चित्**=though even. **हस्तौ***=the two hands of a person. **समम्**=equal in every way. **विविष्टः**†=perform. **सम् मातरौ**‡=two cows born of the same mother. **दुहाते**=both give milk. **यमयोः**§ of two persons who are twins. **वीर्याणि**||=powers; prowess. **ज्ञाती**£=two persons belonging to the same family. **पृणीतः**=both give charity.

Translation:—The two hands of a person are equal, but both of them do not do the same amount of work. Two cows born of the same mother do not yield an equal amount of milk. Two persons may be twins but their powers will be different. In the same

* √हसे हसने+तन् U. III, 86 हसिमृग्रिण्वामि &c.

† वि+√विष (Vedic) करणे+क्त.

‡ समा माता ययोः ते P. II, 2, 24.

§ √यम उपरमे+अप् or घञ् P. III, 3, 63 यमः समुपनिविषु च or अच् by P. III, 1. 134.

|| √अज गतिक्षेपणयोः+रक् U. II 13 स्फायितञ्चिवञ्चिशकिक्षिपि &c; (वी is substituted for the root according to P. II, 4, 56 अजेर्व्यघञपोः) or √वीर विक्रान्तौ+अच् P. III, 1, 134, or वि+√ईर गतौ+क P. III, 135 इगुपधज्ञाप्रीकिरः कः+यत् P. V, 1, 119 तस्य भावस्त्वतलौ or IV, 4, 98 तत्र साधुः or V. I, 5, तस्मै हितम्.

£ √ज्ञा अवबोधने+क्तिन्.

way two persons though born in the same family cannot be opulent to the same extent.

Comment:—The futility of wealth hoarded and idly kept is hinted at in the very first stanza. Death is the leveller; it has no regard for the rich, nor any special hostility towards the poor though these latter may succumb to it earlier through starvation. He who gives out of his store to the indigent will not himself be reduced to straits, hence let him not fear lest, by giving charity he should exhaust all his riches. He who keeps his wealth hidden will not be able to save it for time and tide wait for no man. An unforeseen calamity may sweep off all his possessions and leave him a beggar to thank Providence that his person at least is safe.

The main purpose of this beautiful hymn is to extol charity and disparage stinginess and disregard of the poor. The expressions used to describe the latter; अध्र, indigent; रफित, reduced to penury; गृहवे, begging from door to door; कृश, emaciated नाधमान, seeking for help; पित्वः चकमानाय, पित्वः सचमानाय, अन्नकामाय, longing for food; excite pity in the heart of the reader. The hymn draws a full pen-picture of the scene where a rich man hardens his heart and dismissing a poor beggar with mere words, himself eats with relish. Such, the text says, do not eat food but march quickly to meet their death; their abodes, though lofty and splendid mansions, are not human habitations. The poor should never even cast a glance at these but seek for some one more gentle-hearted.

The same idea has been expressed in a somewhat different style in the Manusmriti, the Bhagvad Gita and many other ancient works. Manu says:—

"He who gets his food prepared for himself only and eats alone, does really eat sin and not food. The principle laid down for the righteous is that one should eat after having utilised a portion of the food for some charitable purpose".*

The Bhagvad Gita† also voices the same opinion in the 13th verse of the 3rd chapter.

But the later Indian religious, legal and philosophical works have a view of charity quite different from what is expressed in this beautiful hymn. Their dicta on the subject seem to be less broad-minded though just and true. They maintain that charity should be given only to a

*अघं स केवलं भुङ्क्ते यः पचत्यात्मकारणात् । यज्ञशिष्टाशनं ह्येतत्सतामन्नं विधीयते ॥२।११८॥

†See page 229.

respectable guest, who for example, goes about preaching and teaching. Manu has elaborate rules on the subject of charity as to how, when and where it is to be practised. The best person who deserves charity in his opinion is the Brahmana (a man learned in the Vedas and devoted to God), though he does not exclude others. But Vedic teaching is quite clear on the point. Our hymn mentions three types of persons to whom charity must be given if one wishes to save oneself from sin: (1) The first type is called आध्र, रफित, कृश, गृद्ध and clearly refers to the poor man reduced to abject poverty who goes about begging from door to door to save himself and his family from starvation. Of such a one no caste and creed is to be asked, none of his antecedents and qualifications enquired into, but he should simply be helped for the mere asking. (2) The second, according to the hymn is सचाभू सखा, a friend of one's own persuasion—a member of the same society. If the first excites pity, this has a clear right. To render help to him is to practise the advice given in the principle "charity begins at home." (3) The third group is what is generally called अतिथि, here called अर्यमन्—a respectable person. It refers also to a man of good standing who has been suddenly reduced to straits and who is ashamed of going about begging. To help such is the duty of all respectable people.

The list of the indigent mentioned in our hymn is very exhaustive and at the same time severely exclusive, for, it strictly excludes all professional beggars, who go about collecting money, grain and other things to be sold at the bazaars. They are lazy people deserving no encouragement. They are not indigent but deceitful. The Vedas have no kind words for such cheats.* According to our text, only the genuinely indigent starving folk are worthy of charity and they must be helped under all circumstances.

The seventh stanza praises industry, the idea of "give and take" on which the life of human society depends. Everybody has to work to deserve his food and he who has riches can be worthy of it only if he gives charity. Even the learned man must devote himself to the work of diffusing knowledge if he has to earn his bread. Thus unproductive wealth and dilettantic "unproductive learning", are both condemned in the Vedas.

In the eighth stanza the relativity of riches is spoken of. No man can be absolutely rich. There are only grades of riches, and if

---

* इच्छन्ति देवाः सुन्वन्तं न स्वप्नाय स्पृहयन्ति । यन्ति प्रमादमतन्द्राः ॥ ऋ० ८।२।१८॥ see p. 157. उद्यानं ते पुरुष नावयानं जीवातुं ते दक्षतातिं कृणोमि ॥ अ० ८।१।६॥ see p. 147. कुर्वन्नेवेह कर्माणि जिजीविषेच्छतं समाः ॥ य० ४०।२॥

only wealth were to be the norm of respectability then the world would be nowhere. Hence not the possession of wealth but the use to which it is put, should be the standard by which a man should be judged. He who gives to the needy out of what little he has, is far superior to the millionaire who gives nothing or very little comparatively, if at all he gives.

Like money and food, learning, training, civil and political rights and other advantages, are also objects fit to be imparted in charity to the deserving. These also are the monopoly of no country or nation in as much as they go on changing hands age after age. Hence he who being himself well off in these does not bestow them on those deserving of them is to be condemned in the strongest terms according to the spirit of the hymn. It must be borne in mind that all these benefits when not exchanged with or imparted to, others are lost and become totally 'extinct' in course of time.

In the last stanza we are told that the practising of charity does not depend upon birth. Just as both the hands of a man being equal do not both do an equal amount of work, nor do two cows of the same breed yield the same amount of milk, nor twins possess the same powers because all these are born of the same 'stock', so also the inclination to give alms does not depend upon birth or pedigree. The hymn suggests that this noble trait is got from the residua of the man's past lives, his training and company. But none need be discouraged. To try and acquire this merit of helping the poor is a very noble thing for which every man ought to endeavour.

Chapter VIII.

The Soul of the Universe and His 'Universal' Body.

Yajurvēda Chapter XXXI.

Seer :—Verses 1-16 the Sage Nārāyaṇa, 17-22 the Sage Uttaranārāyaṇa and verse 4, the Sage Mēdhatithi.

Subject :—The order of human society according to God's dispensation. Verses 1, 3, 4, 6, 8-16 treat of God the Soul of the Universe; verse 2, of God the Overlord of the Universe; 5, of God the Creator; 7, of God the Dispenser and Ruler of the Universe; verses 17-19 and 22, of God the Perfect; verse 20, of God the Illuminator of the Hearts of the Righteous and 21 of the Duty of the Enlightened towards Humanity.

Metre :—Verses 1-3, 8-11 and 14, nicṛdanuṣṭubh; 4, 5, 7, 12, 13, 15, 20 and 21, anuṣṭubh; verse 6, virāḍanuṣṭubh; 16, virāt-triṣṭubh; verse 17 and 19, bhurik-triṣṭubh; 18, nicṛt-triṣṭubh; and 22 nicṛdārṣī-triṣṭubh.

Tone :—Stanzas 1-15, 20 and 21 gāndhāra; 16-19 and 22 dhaivata.

N. B.—The following interpretation of the 'Puruṣa-Sūkta' is prepared by collating the two commentaries on the hymn by Maharṣi Svāmi Dayānanda Sarasvatī the one in his scholion on the Yajurvēda, Ch. XXXI and the other in his 'Introduction to the Commentary on the Vedas' viz., the chapter on 'Cosmogony'.

अथ परमात्मन उपासनास्तुतिपूर्वकं सृष्टिविद्याविषयमाह ॥

This hymn, in the light of the Principles of the Science of Cosmogony which it explains, teaches of the Practice of the Presence of God and His Adoration.

(८५) ओ३म् ॥ सहस्रशीर्षा पुरुषः सहस्राक्षः सहस्रपात् । स भूमिं सर्वतः स्पृत्वाऽत्यतिष्ठद्दशाङ्गुलम् ॥१॥

पदपाठः—सहस्रऽशीर्षा पुरुषः सहस्रऽअक्षः सहस्रऽपात् सः भूमिम् सर्वतः स्पृत्वा अति अतिष्ठत् दशऽअङ्गुलम् ॥

भाष्यम्=**Explanation:**—सहस्रशीर्षा०—अत्र मन्त्रे पुरुष इति पदं विशेष्यमस्ति सहस्रशीर्षेत्यादीनि विशेषणानि च ॥

In this verse the word 'puruṣa' is the substantive while the words 'sahasraśīrṣa' &c. are its adjectives.

अत्र पुरुषशब्दार्थे प्रमाणानि । पुरुषं पुरिशयं इत्याचक्षीरन् । नि० अ० १, खं० १३ ॥ पुरि संसारे शेते सर्वमभिव्याप्य वर्तते स परमेश्वरः ॥

The following are the authorities for the interpretation of the word 'puruṣa'. The word 'puruṣa' means God because He pervades the universe 'puri' (Nir. I, 13) or He fills and exists in the entire cosmos.

पुरुषः*—पुरिषादः पुरिशयः पूरयतेर्वा पूरयत्यन्तरित्यन्तरपुरुषमभिप्रेत्य । यस्मात्परं नापरमस्ति किञ्चिद्यस्मान्नाणीयो न ज्यायोऽस्ति किंचित् । वृक्ष इव स्तब्धो दिवि तिष्ठत्येकस्तेनेदं पूर्णं पुरुषेण सर्वमित्यपि निगमो भवति ॥ नि० अ० २, खं० ३† ॥ पुरुषः—पुरि सर्वस्मिन्संसारेऽभिव्याप्य सीदति वर्तत इति ।

---

* पुरुषः—(१) √पुर गमने + कुषन् ॥ उ० ४ । ७४ ॥ (२) पुरि सीदतीति पुरि + √षद्लृ विशरणगत्यवसादनेषु=पुरिषादः—पुरिषः—पुरुषः ॥ (३) पुरि शेते इति पुरि + √शीङ् स्वप्ने=पुरिशयः—पुरुषः ॥ (४) √पूरी आप्यायने + कुषन् ॥ उ० ४ । ७४॥ (५) पूरयत्यन्तो यः=√पॄ पूर्तौ + कुषन् ॥ उ० ४ । ७४ ॥

† पुरुषः पूःशरीरं शद्लृ शातन इत्यस्य शात्यत इति कर्मणि घञ् शादः । पुरि शादो मलसञ्चयः पुरि शादोऽस्यासौ पुरिशादः सप्तम्यलोपोपधाविकारशकारषकारोकाराणां व्यापत्त्यादिना पुरुषः । तथा च वसाः शुक्रमसृगित्यादि द्वादशैते नृणां मला इति स्मरणात् । अथवा शदिर्गत्यर्थः । तस्मात्पुर्शब्दोपपदे डप्रत्ययः । पुरं शरीरं भोक्तृत्वेन गच्छतीति पुरिशः सप्तम्यलुक् शकारषकारव्यापत्त्योकारस्योपजननेन पुरुषः । अस्मिन्पक्षे पुरि शादो गमनमस्येति व्युत्पत्तिवचनम् । पुरि शाद इति तु पाठान्तरं । बहुः पापसञ्चयः शादोऽस्मिन्निति व्युत्पत्तिवचनम् । पुरिशयोऽथवा पुरि पूरयितव्येऽन्नादिना शरीरे शेते तिष्ठत्युपलभ्य इत्यर्थः । तथा च प्रयोगः पुरि पुरुषः शेत इति । पूरयतेर्वा । अस्योपपत्तिवचनं पूरयत्यन्तरित्यन्तरपुरुषमभिप्रेत्य । अन्तरपुरुषः

पूरयतेर्वा०—यः स्वयं परमेश्वर इदं सर्वं जगत्स्वरूपेण पूरयति व्याप्नोति तस्मात्स पुरुषः। अन्तरिति०—यो जीवस्याप्यन्तर्मध्येऽभिव्याप्य पूरयति तिष्ठति स पुरुषः। तमन्तरपुरुषमन्तर्यामिनं परमेश्वरमभिप्रेत्येयमृक् प्रवृत्तास्ति। यस्मात्परमिति—यस्मात्पूर्णात्परमेश्वरात्पुरुषाख्यात्परं प्रकृष्टमुत्तमं किंचिदपि वस्तु नास्त्येव। पूर्वं वा नापरमस्ति यस्मात्परमर्वाचीनं तत्तुल्यमुत्तमं वा किंचिदपि वस्तु नास्त्येव। तथा यस्मादणीयः सूक्ष्मं ज्यायः स्थूलं महद्वा किंचिदपि द्रव्यं न भूतं न भवति नैव च भविष्यतीत्यवधेयम्। यः स्तब्धो निष्कम्पः सर्वस्यास्थिरतां कुर्वन्सन्स्थिरोऽस्ति। क इव वृक्ष इव यथा वृक्षः शाखापत्रपुष्पफलादिकं धारयँस्तिष्ठति तथैव पृथिवीसूर्यादिकं सर्वं जगद्धारयन्परमेश्वरोऽभिव्याप्य स्थितोऽस्तीति। यश्चैकोऽद्वितीयोऽस्ति नास्य कश्चित्सजातीयो विजातीयो वा द्वितीय ईश्वरोऽस्तीति। तेन पुरिषेण—पुरुषेण परमात्मना यत इदं सर्वं जगत्पूर्णं कृतमस्ति तस्मात्पुरुषः परमेश्वर एवोच्यते। इत्ययं मन्त्रो निगमो निगमनं परं प्रमाणं भवतीति वेदितव्यम्॥

The Supreme Lord is so called since He occupies the entire universe or because He pervades it completely with His essence or as He resides within and fills the interior of the soul. The following stanza (Śvetāśvatarōpaniṣad III, 9 and Mahānārāyaṇopaniṣad XVII, 4) describes that Inner Puruṣa, the Supreme Lord, Who

---

क्षेत्रज्ञस्तमभिप्रेत्योच्यते। तेन हीन्द्रियप्राणादिरूपं पुर्यष्टकं स्थूलञ्च धात्वादिरूपं शरीरं यात्रव्याप्तिभूतत्वात्पूरितम्। अथवा पूरयत्यन्तरित्येवमन्तो ग्रन्थः क्षेत्रज्ञाभिप्रायः पूर्ववद्योजनीयः। ततोऽपि पर आत्माऽन्तरोऽन्तर्हिततर आगमगम्यो यः सर्वोपनिषत्सु गीयते। पुरुषः पूरणो विश्वस्य सकलस्य विकारजातस्य संभक्ता पुरुषस्तमभिप्रेत्य निगमोऽपि गीयते—यस्मात्परमिति। यस्मात्परं कारणभूतं तस्य नापरमन्यत्किंचिदस्ति सर्वस्य जगतस्तस्यैव कारणत्वात्। यस्मान्नाणीयो यस्मान्न सूक्ष्मतरं न ज्यायो वृद्धतरञ्च किञ्चिदस्ति। यश्च वृक्ष इव—यथा वृक्षः स्तब्धो निष्क्रिय एवमसंकोचविकासधर्माविविद्योतनस्वभाव आत्मन्येव तिष्ठति। अथवा दिवि द्युलोके। प्रदर्शनञ्च द्युग्रहणम्। दिव्यन्तरिक्षे भुवि च य एक एव तेनेदं चतुर्दशसंस्थं भुवनं पूर्णं पुरुषेण सर्वं कृत्स्नम्॥ स्क० भा०॥

In the above passage the word puruṣa is taken to mean both the individual soul and the Supreme Being, but in the derivation too much stress is laid upon the body as the source of sin and dirt. In contrast with this we have the following commentary on the passage by Durgacārya.

पुरुषः पुरिषादः। पूः शरीरं बुद्धिर्वा। तयोरसौ विषयोपलब्ध्यर्थं सीदतीति पुरिषादः पुरुषः। पुरिशयः। अथवा तयोरसौ शेते विशेषेणास्त इति पुरिशयः सन् पुरुष इत्युच्यते। पूरयतेर्वा। पूर्णमनेन पुरुषेण सर्वगत-

is the in-dwelling Ruler of all. There never was anything superior to or higher than the Supreme Lord the All-pervading-one, Who is called the Puruṣa. There can never be anything equal or superior to Him. There was not, is not and shall never be anything greater than He. He moves and renders all things unstable but Himself remains unmoved, stable and without a tremor. As a tree supports its branches leaves, flowers and fruits so does God uphold this entire universe, from the earth to the sun etc. He is one without a second. There is no second God of the same or of a different class. As the Supreme Lord fills all this (the universe) He is called the Puruṣa. This verse is the highest authority for taking the word puruṣa in the sense of the all-pervading God. (Nir. II, 3).

सर्वं वै सहस्रम् ॥ शतपथ ७ । ५ । २ । १३ ॥ सर्वं—सर्वमिदं जगत्सहस्रनामकमस्तीति विज्ञेयम् । सहस्रशी०—सहस्राण्यसंख्यातान्यस्मदादीनां शिरांसि यस्मिन्पूर्णे पुरुषे परमात्मनि स सहस्रशीर्षा* पुरुषः । सहस्राक्षः† अस्मदादीनां सहस्राण्यक्षीणि यस्मिन्नेवमेव सहस्राण्यसंख्याताः पादाश्च यस्मिन्वर्तन्ते स सहस्राक्षः सहस्रपात्‡ ।

त्वाज्जगदिति पुरुषः । पूरयत्यन्तरित्यन्तरपुरुषमभिप्रेत्य । अन्तरित्यन्तरपुरुषाभिप्रायेणैवमुच्यते प्रासङ्गिकम् । निगमश्च भवति यस्मात्परमित्यादिः । यस्मात्परमपरं वा न किञ्चिदप्यस्ति यस्माच्च न किञ्चिदप्यणीयो नापि ज्यायोऽन्यदस्ति स एव सर्वमित्यभिप्रायः । वृक्ष इव स्तब्धो नित्यमसंकोचविकाशधर्मा दिवि आनन्दति स्वात्मनि सर्वद्विभावेन तिष्ठति यस्तेन पुरुषेणेदं पूर्णं सर्वं जगदिति ॥ दु० ॥

Durgacārya's remarks are really refreshing in contrast with the despondency and disgust caused by Skandasvamin's comment quoted above, but His Holiness Maharṣi Dayānanda Sarasvati surpasses both these in his method of Vedic exigesis.

* सहस्रशीर्षा—सहस्राणि शीर्षाणि यस्मिन्सः । पा० २।२।२४॥ सहस्र—सहस् (बहु० निरं० ३।१॥) + र (मत्वर्थीयः ।) पा० ५।२।१०४॥१०७॥ सहस्—√षह मर्षणे + असुन् । उ० ४।१८९॥ बलम् । निघं० २।९॥ शीर्षन् शीर्षश्छन्दसि॥ पा० ६।१।६०॥

† सहस्राक्षः—सहस्राण्यक्षीणि यस्मिन् । अक्षिन्—√अशू व्याप्तौ + क्सिः । उ० ३।१५६॥ अथवा √अक्ष व्याप्तौ + इन् ॥ पा० ३।४।६७॥

‡ सहस्रपात्—सहस्रा अनन्ताः पादाः यस्मिन्वा अपरिमिता गतिशक्तयो यस्य । पाद्—√पद गतौ स्थैर्ये च + णिच् + क्विप् । पा० ३।१।२६॥३।१७८॥

The word sahasra according to the Satapatha Brahmaṇa VII, 5, 2, 13 is the name of this entire universe. God is the Puruṣa with thousands of (innumerable) heads, because in Him, the All-pervading Supreme Being, there exist thousands of heads of beings like us. He is said to have thousands of (i. e. innumerable) eyes, since the innumerable eyes of beings like us exist in Him. In the same way He in whom thousands or innumerable feet of beings like us exist is said to have innumerable feet.

स भूमि* सर्वतः† स्पृत्वा०‡—स पुरुषः परमेश्वरः सर्वतः सर्वेभ्यो बाह्यान्तर्देशेभ्यो (भूमिरिति भूतानामुपलक्षणं) भूमिमारभ्य प्रकृतिपर्यन्तं सर्वं जगत्स्पृत्वाभिव्याप्य वर्तते ॥

The Supreme Lord fills the earth (which here stands for its denizens also) and the Prakṛti, i. e., the entire universe, from all sides, from within and without.

अत्यतिष्ठत्०—दशाङ्गुलमिति§ ब्रह्माण्डहृदययोरुपलक्षणम्। अङ्गुलमित्यवयवोपलक्षणेन मितस्य जगतोऽत्र ग्रहणं भवति। पञ्च स्थूलभूतानि पञ्च सूक्ष्माणि चैतदुभयं मिलित्वा दशावयवाख्यं सकलं जगदस्ति। अन्यच्च पञ्च प्राणाः सेन्द्रियं चतुष्टयमन्तःकरणं दशमो जीवश्च। एवमेवान्यदपि जीवस्य हृदयं दशाङ्गुलपरिमितं च तृतीयं गृह्यते। एतत्त्रयं स्पृत्वा व्याप्यात्यतिष्ठत्। एतस्मात्त्रयाद्बहिरपि व्याप्तः सन्नवस्थितः। अर्थाद्बहिरन्तश्च पूर्णो भूत्वा परमेश्वरोऽवतिष्ठत इति वेद्यम् ॥

The expression 'daśangulam' is suggestive of the universe and the heart. The word 'angulam' (finger) is here used as a name for limbs or members and, firstly, signifies the finite world. The entire universe is composed of ten parts, viz., the five gross and the five subtle, i.e., altogether ten elements. Secondly, the phrase may also be taken to mean the five vital airs (prāṇas) the four inner senses, the mind (manas) &c., together with the outer senses, and the soul (jīva) as the tenth; or again, finally, it may mean the soul's heart which also measures ten finger-breadths. God pervades these three and transcends them, existing out of or beyond

---

* भूमिम्—√भू सत्तायाम्+मि। उ० ४। ४५ ॥

† सर्वतः—सर्व+तसिल् ॥ सर्वोभयार्थाभ्यामेवेति वार्तिकम् ॥

‡ स्पृत्वा—√स्पृ व्याप्तौ+क्त्वा ॥ पा० ३।४।२१॥

§ दशाङ्गुलम्—दशाङ्गुलानि यस्य स दशाङ्गुलस्तम्। पा० २।२।२४ ॥ दशन् √दशि+कनिन् ॥ उ० १।१५६॥ अङ्गुलम्—√अगि गतौ वा √अङ्क पदे लक्षणे च+उलच्। उ० ५।६॥

these three as well. This means that it should be understood from the passage that God exists pervading the universe from inside as well as outside.

अन्वयः—हे मनुष्या ! यः सहस्रशीर्षा सहस्राक्षः सहस्रपात्पुरुषोऽस्ति स सर्वतो भूमिं स्पृत्वा दशाङ्गुलम् जगदत्यतिष्ठत्तमेवोपासीध्वम् ॥

Translation:—Oh men ! ye should worship that God only Who is the Lord of the whole creation, in Whom the innumerable heads, eyes, feet and other parts and limbs of all creatures exist and through Whose impulse they work. He pervades from all round the earth (and other planets) and completely transcends the whole world of which, the five gross and five subtle elements are the ten limbs.

भावार्थः—हे मनुष्या यस्मिन्पूर्णे परमात्मन्यस्मदादीनामसंख्यातानि शिरांस्यक्षीणि पादादीन्यङ्गानि च सन्ति यो भूम्याद्युपलक्षितं पञ्चभिः स्थूलैर्भूतैः सूक्ष्मैश्च युक्तं जगत्स्वसत्तया प्रपूर्य यत्र जगन्नास्ति तत्राऽपि पूर्णोऽस्ति तं सर्वनिर्मातारं परिपूर्णं सच्चिदानन्दस्वरूपं नित्यशुद्धबुद्धमुक्तस्वभावं परमेश्वरं विहायान्यस्योपासनां यूयं कदाचिन्नैव कुरुत किन्त्वस्योपासनेन धर्मार्थकाममोक्षानलंकुर्यात ॥

Purport:—Oh men you must worship none else but that Omnipresent God in Whom the innumerable heads, eyes, feet and other limbs of ours and all other Creatures exist (and by Whose impulse they function). He pervades the world made up of the ten constituents in the shape of the five gross and five subtle elements, and exists in His perfection even there where there is no world. He is the Creator of all and Perfect; His essence is Being, Intelligence and Bliss and He is by His nature eternal, ever-pure, all-knowing and ever-free. Only by worshipping* Him should you hope to attain to the four ideals of human life, namely righteousness, prosperity, fulfilment of wishes and final beatitude.

---

* स य एतदेवं विद्वानक्षरं प्रणौत्येतदेवाक्षरं स्वरममृतमभयं प्रविशति तत्प्रविश्य यदमृता देवास्तदमृतो भवति ॥ छां० १।४।५॥ "The knower of God who thus knows this Imperishable Supreme Being, enters into Him, the Immortal One in Whom there is no death and no fear, thus described by the Sāmaveda. The enlightened of olden times attained to Him and through Him immortal life : So also will the devotee now become immortal by knowing Him. Ch. I, 4, 5. यथोदकं शुद्धमासिक्तं तादृगेव भवति । एवं मुनेर्विजानत आत्मा भवति गौतम ॥ क० ४।१५॥

(८६) पुरुष एवेदं सर्वं यद्भूतं यच्च भाव्यम्। उतामृतत्वस्येशानो यदन्नेनातिरोहति ॥ २ ॥

पदपाठः—पुरुषः एव इदम् सर्वम् यत् भूतम् यत् च भाव्यम् उत अमृतऽत्वस्य ईशानः यत् अन्नेन अतिऽरोहति ॥

भाष्यम् = **Explanation:**—पुरुषः एतद्विशेषणयुक्तः सत्यैर्गुणकर्मस्वभावैः परिपूर्णः पुरुषः परमेश्वरः ॥

God the Supreme Lord of the universe distinguished by these qualities, i.e., Whose attributes, actions and nature are ever truthful.

इदम्=प्रत्यक्षाऽप्रत्यक्षात्मकं जगत्=the visible and invisible universe. सर्वम्=सम्पूर्णम्=entire, whole. यद्भूतम्=यज्जगदुत्पन्नमभूत्=the universe that came into being. भाव्यम्*=उत्पत्स्यमानम्=that will come into being, that will be created. चकाराद्वर्तमानं च=by 'ca' 'and', that which is in existence is meant. पुरुष एव०=तत्त्रिकालस्थं सर्वं विश्वं पुरुष एव कृतवानस्ति नान्यः। नैवातो हि परः कश्चिज्जगद्रचयितास्तीति निश्चेतव्यम् ॥

Puruṣa i. e., God alone is the maker of the universe past, present and future. Verily there is no other maker of the universe than He.

उत=अपि=also. अमृतत्वस्य=मोक्षभावस्य। अविनाशिनो मोक्षसुखस्य कारणस्य वा=of the state of final beatitude; of the indestructible happiness of salvation or of the indestructible cause. ईशानः†=ईषणशीलः। अधिष्ठाता। सर्वस्येश्वरो दाता च मोक्षस्य। Whose nature is to rule; the Controller; the Supreme Lord of all and the Bestower of final beatitude. यत्=यस्मात्=wherefore. अन्नेन=पृथिव्यादिना जगता सह=along with the universe consisting of the earth &c. अतिरोहति=अत्यन्तं वर्धते। व्यतिरिक्तः सञ्जन्मादिरहितोऽस्ति। तस्मात्स्वयमजः सन्सर्वं जनयति स्वसामर्थ्यादिकारणात्कार्यं जगदुत्पादयति। नास्यादिकारणं किञ्चिदस्ति। किञ्च सर्वस्यादिनिमित्तकारणं पुरुष एवास्तीति वेद्यम् ॥

---

* भाव्यम्—√भू सत्तायाम् + ण्यत् ॥ पा० ३। १। १२३ ॥

† ईशानः—√ईश ऐश्वर्ये + शानच् ॥ पा० ३। २। १२४ ॥

Advances, progresses; He is independent of and distinct from the world—this earth—and is free from birth &c. Though Himself unborn He makes all take birth and produces this cosmos—the effect—with His Sāmarthya—its first material cause. The first cause of Him—the Puruṣa, there is none, but He is the first efficient cause of all.

अन्वयः—हे मनुष्या यद्भूतं यच्च भाव्यमुतापि यदन्नेनातिरोहति तदिदं सर्वममृतत्वस्येशानः पुरुष एव रचयति ॥

Translation:—Oh men! that Supreme Lord alone, the Bestower of final beatitude, fashions this visible and invisible universe past, present and future which, along with this earth endlessly progresses on.

भावार्थः—हे मनुष्या येनेश्वरेण यदा यदा सृष्टिरभूत्तदा तदा निर्मितेदानीं यो धरति पुनर्विनाश्य रचिष्यति यदाधारेण सर्वं वर्तते वर्धते च तमेव परेशं परमात्मानमुपासीध्वं नाऽस्मादितरम् ॥

Purport:—Oh men you should adore none but that Supreme Lord alone by Whom this universe has been brought into being during all its creations, by Whom it is now supported, will be hereafter created and by Whose support everything exists and grows.

(८७) एतावानस्य महिमातो ज्यायांश्च पूरुषः ।
पादोऽस्य विश्वा भूतानि त्रिपादस्यामृतं दिवि ॥ ३ ॥

पदपाठः—एतावान् अस्य महिमा अतः ज्यायान् च पूरुषः पादः अस्य विश्वा भूतानि त्रिऽपात् अस्य अमृतम् दिवि ॥

भाष्यम्=Explanation:—एतावान्*=दृश्यादृश्यं ब्रह्माण्डरूपम्=the visible and invisible universe. अस्य=जगदीश्वरस्य=of that Lord of the universe. महिमा†=माहात्म्यम्=greatness; glory. अस्य पुरुषस्य भूतभविष्यद्वर्तमानस्थो यावान्संसारोऽस्ति तावान्महिमा वेदितव्यः । एतावानस्य महिमास्ति चेत्तर्हि तस्य महिम्नः परिच्छेद इयत्ता जातेति गम्यते ॥

---

* एतावान्—एतद्+वतुप् ॥ पा० ५ । २ । ३९ ॥

† महिमा—महत्+इमनिच् ॥ पा० ५ । १ । १२२ ॥

If it be said that the past, the present and the future universes are the measure of His greatness, it will become finite and something that can be measured.

अत्र ब्रूते। (अतो ज्याया॰ऽ॰) अतः=अस्मात्=than this visible and invisible universe. ज्यायान्*=अतिशयेन प्रशस्तः। महान्=excessively Superior to or greater than पूरुषः=परिपूर्णः=the Perfect One. नैतावन्मात्र एव महिमेति। किं तर्हि। अतोऽप्यधिकतमो महिमानस्तस्यास्तीति गम्यते॥

Hence it is said that His greatness is not so much only. He far exceeds the greatness indicated by them.

अत्राह। It is added. (पादोऽस्य॰) पादः†=एकांशः=a part. अस्य=अनन्तसामर्थ्यस्येश्वरस्य=of God whose power is indefinite. विश्वा=विश्वानि प्रकृत्यादिपृथिवीपर्यन्तानि सर्वाणि भूतान्येकः पादोऽस्त्येकस्मिन्देशांशे सर्वं विश्वं वर्तते=the entire cosmos, from Prakṛti to the earth and all the creatures, are only a fractional part of the greatness of the Almighty Lord. त्रिपात्=त्रयः पादा यस्मिन्=in which three parts exist. (The subtle world of light). अस्य=जगत्स्रष्टुः=of the Creator of the universe. अमृतम्=नाशरहितम्=indestructible. दिवि=द्योतनात्मके स्वस्वरूपे=in His own self-effulgent essence. अस्य दिवि द्योतनात्मके स्वस्वरूपेऽमृतं मोक्षसुखमस्ति। तथाऽस्य दिवि द्योतके संसारे त्रिपाज्जगदस्ति। प्रकाश्यमानं जगदेकगुणमस्ति प्रकाशकं च तस्मात्त्रिगुणमस्ति। स्वयं च मोक्षस्वरूपः सर्वाधिष्ठाता सर्वोपास्यः सर्वानन्दः सर्वप्रकाशकोऽस्ति॥

The bliss of final beatitude is in His own self-effulgence and the three-fourths of the cosmos exists in the regions of light. The portion that illumines the world is three times as much again as the portion that is illumined. He is absolutely free and unhampered, the Ruler of all, adored by all, All-bliss, and the Illuminator of all.

अन्वयः—हे मनुष्या अस्य परमेश्वरस्यैतावान्महिमाऽतोऽयं पूरुषो ज्यायानस्य च विश्वा भूतान्येकः पादोऽस्य त्रिपादमृतं दिवि वर्तते॥

---

* ज्यायान्—वृद्ध=ईयसुन्॥ पा॰ ५। ३। ५७॥ ६२॥

† पादः—√पद गतौ स्थैर्ये च+घञ्॥ पा॰ ३। ३। १६॥

Translation:—Oh men! this visible and invisible world is a mere indication of the greatness of the Lord of the universe, for He is Perfect and infinitely great. The whole gross universe of movable and immovable beings (comprising the earth &c.) make up only a fractional part of His majesty, while the subtle world of light three times as great as the former and the bliss of emancipation, exist in His self-effulgent essence.

भावार्थः—इदं सर्वं सूर्यचन्द्रादिलोकलोकान्तरं चराचरं यावज्जगदस्ति तच्चित्रविचित्ररचनानुमानेनेश्वरस्य महत्त्वं सम्पाद्योत्पत्तिस्थितिप्रलयरूपेण कालत्रये ह्रासवृद्ध्यादिनाऽपि परमेश्वरस्य चतुर्थांशे तिष्ठति नैवास्य तुरीयांशस्याप्यवधिं प्राप्नोति । अस्य सामर्थ्यस्यांशत्रयं स्वेऽविनाशिनि मोक्षस्वरूपे सदैव वर्त्तते नानेन कथनेन तस्याऽनन्तत्वं विहन्यते किंतु जगदपेक्षया तस्य महत्त्वं जगतो न्यूनत्वञ्च ज्ञाप्यते ॥

Purport:—The whole of the present movable and immovable universe comprising the sun, moon and other planets, bears witness to the greatness of God inferred through its multifarious formations. Though continually increasing and decreasing in its form through the three stages of creation, continuous existence and dissolution, it subsists in only a quarter of God's Divine Majesty, nay, it does not come up even to that much of His greatness. Three parts of God's Omnipotence eternally exist in His imperishable beatific state, and by saying so we do not at all diminish His infinite nature, but try to depict, so to say, His infinite greatness as compared with the world and the littleness of the latter in contrast with His Infinite Majesty.

(८८) त्रिपादूर्ध्व उदैत्पुरुषः पादोऽस्येहाभवत्पुनः ।
ततो विष्वङ्व्यक्रामत्साशनानशने अभि ॥ ४ ॥

पदपाठः—त्रिऽपात् ऊर्ध्वः उत् ऐत् पुरुषः पादः अस्य इह अभवत् पुनः ततः विष्वङ् वि अक्रामत् साशनानशने अभि ॥

भाष्यम्—**Explanation**:—त्रिपात्*=त्रयः पादा अंशा यस्य सः । Having three parts. ऊर्ध्वः=सर्वेभ्य उत्कृष्टः संसारात् पृथङ्मुक्ति-

* त्रिपात्—त्रयः पादा यस्य यस्मिन्वा सः ॥ पा० २ । २ । २४ ॥

स्वरूपः । Surpassing all, different from the cosmos and ever free in His essence. अयं पुरुषः परमेश्वरः पूर्वोक्तस्य त्रिपादोपलक्षितस्य सकाशादूर्ध्वमुपरिभागेऽर्थात्पृथग्भूतोऽस्त्येवेत्यर्थः । एकपादोपलक्षितं यत्पूर्वोक्तं जगदस्ति तस्मादपीहास्मिन्संसारे सः पुरुषः पृथगभव व्यतिरिक्त एवास्ति । स च त्रिपात्संसार एकपाच्च मिलित्वा सर्वश्चतुष्पाद्भवति । अयं सर्वः संसार इहास्मिन्परमात्मन्येव वर्तते पुनर्लयसमये तत्सामर्थ्यकारणे प्रलीनश्च भवति ॥

The purport of this stanza is that the Puruṣa (God) is above and beyond and distinct from what has been described above as the three-fourths. He is distinct and separate from this world also which has been described as the one-fourth. The three-fourths cosmos and the one-fourth together make up four portions. The whole of this universe exists in the Supreme Being and is again absorbed in the cause—His Sāmarthya—at the time of the dissolution.

तत्रापि स पुरुषोऽविद्यान्धकाराज्ञानजन्ममरणज्वरादिदुःखादूर्ध्वः परः (उदैत्) उदितः प्रकाशितो वर्तते ॥

Even then the Puruṣa shines above all, free from nescience, darkness, ignorance, birth, death, fever, disease and other suffering.

पुरुषः=पालकः=the Protector (of all). पादः=एको भागः= one part. इह=जगति=in the world or cosmos. अभवत्=भवति=is, comes into being. पुनः* पुनः=again and again. ततः=अनन्तरम्=then. विष्वङ्†=यो विषु सर्वत्राञ्चति प्राप्नोति । Who pervades all, goes everywhere. ततो विष्वङ्=ततस्तत्सामर्थ्यात्सर्वमिदं विश्वमुत्पद्यते । From that Omnipotence of His the cosmos comes into being. किञ्च तत् । What sort of cosmos is it ? साशनानशने‡=यदेकमशनेन भोजनकरणेन सह वर्तमानं

---

* पुनः —पनाय्यते स्तूयत इति √पन स्तुतौ + अर् । पृशोदरादित्वादकारस्योत्वं ॥ पा० ६ । ३ । १०९ ॥

† विष्वङ्—विषु अञ्चतीति—विषु + √अञ्चु गतिपूजनयोः + क्विन् ॥ पा० ३ । २ । ५९ ॥ ६ । ४ । २४ ॥ ८ । २ । ६२ ॥

‡ साशनानशने—साशनञ्चानशनञ्च ॥ पा० २ । २ । २९ ॥ अशनेन सह साशनम् ॥ पा० २ । २ । २८ ॥ न विद्यते अशनं यस्मिँस्तदनशनं ॥ पा० २ । २ । २४ ॥ वा० नञोऽस्त्यर्थानां वाच्यो वा चोत्तरपदलोपः ॥ अशनम्—√अश भोजने + ल्युट् ॥ पा० ३ । ३ । ११७ ॥

जङ्गमं जीवचेतनादिसहितं जगत् । द्वितीयमनशनमविद्यमानमशनं भोजनं यस्मिंस्तत्पृथिव्यादिकं च यज्जडं जीवसम्बन्धरहितं जगद्वर्तते तदुभयं तस्मात्पुरुषस्य सामर्थ्यकारणादेव जायते । यतः स पुरुष एतद्द्विविधं जगद्विविधतया सुष्ठुरीत्या सर्वात्मतयाप्नोति तस्मात् सर्वं द्विविधं जगदुत्पाद्य (अभिव्यक्रामत्) सर्वतो व्याप्तवानस्ति ॥

The animate world, which moves and eats, i. e., the living beings endowed with life and consciousness, and the inanimate world, such as, the earth, &c., which does not eat, i. e., which is devoid of life and consciousness—both, are created with His Sāmarthya. The Puruṣa enters this two-fold world through and through in many and beautiful ways and having created the two-fold universe pervades it altogether and entirely.

अन्वयः—पूर्वोक्तत्रिपात्पुरुष ऊर्ध्वं उदैत । अस्य पाद इह पुनरभवत् । ततः साशनानशने अभि विष्वङ् सन् व्यक्रामत् ॥

Translation :—The tripartite Puruṣa described in the above verse, that is, God the Protector, surpassing all, existing in His beatific state is distinct from the world and rises above all in His Divine Majesty. One quarter of His Omnipotence is manifested in the universe that comes into being again and again in an ever-recurring cycle of creation and dissolution after which His Divine Immanence pervades in a special manner both animate beings consisting of organisms that subsist on food and inanimate things that do not require food.

भावार्थः—अयं परमेश्वरः कार्यजगतः पृथगंशत्रयेण प्रकाशितः सन्नेकांशस्वसामर्थ्येन सर्वं जगत्पुनः पुनरुत्पादयति पश्चात्तस्मिंश्चराचरे जगति व्याप्य तिष्ठति ॥

Purport:—This Supreme Lord being revealed by the three parts of His Majesty distinct from the created world, produces the cosmos again and again by means of the one part, namely, His Sāmarthya and thereupon pervading the movable and immovable world remains in it by His Immanence.

(८९) ततो॒ वि॒राड॑जायत वि॒राजो॒ अधि॒ पूरु॑षः । स जा॒तो अत्य॑रिच्यत प॒श्चाद्भूमि॒मथो॑ पु॒रः ॥ ५ ॥

पदपाठः—ततः विऽराट् अजायत विऽराजः अधि पूरुषः सः जातः अति अरिच्यत पश्चात् भूमिम् अथो पुरः ॥

भाष्यम्=Explanation:—ततो विराडजायत=ततस्तस्माद्ब्रह्माण्डशरीरः सूर्यचन्द्रनेत्रो वायुप्राणः पृथिवीपाद इत्याद्यलङ्कारलक्षणलक्षितो हि सर्वशरीराणां समष्टिदेहो विविधैः पदार्थैं राजमानः सन्विराडजायतोत्पन्नोऽस्ति ॥

From Him was produced Viraṭ—the shining one—the body of all the bodies taken together collectively, resplendent with various objects, which is metaphorically described as one whose body is the universe, whose eyes are the sun and the moon, whose breath is the wind, and whose feet are the earth.

विराजो* अधि पूरुषः=तस्माद्विराजोऽध्युपरि पश्चाद्ब्रह्माण्डतत्त्वावयवैः पुरुषः सर्वप्राणिनां जीवाधिकरणो देहः पृथक्पृथगजायतोत्पन्नोऽभूत् ॥

After Viraṭ were formed the special bodies of all living beings from the elements of the universe.

स जातो अत्यरिच्यत=स देहो ब्रह्माण्डावयवैरेव वर्धते नष्टः संस्तस्मिन्नेव प्रलीयत इति परमेश्वरस्तु सर्वेभ्यो भूतेभ्योऽत्यरिच्यतातिरिक्तः पृथग्भूतोऽस्ति ॥

These bodies derive growth from the elements and after death return to and are absorbed into them. God, however, remains distinct from all created beings.

पश्चाद्भूमिमथो† पुरः=पूर्वं भूमिमुत्पाद्य धारितवांस्ततः पुरुषस्य सामर्थ्यात्स जीवोऽपि देहं धारितवानस्ति। स च पुरुषः परमात्मा ततस्तस्माज्जीवादप्यत्यरिच्यत पृथग्भूतोऽस्ति ॥

He first created the earth and gave it support and then the jīvas (souls), through His might, have supported their corporeal frames on it. The Puruṣa the Supreme Being, is distinct from the jīva also.

अन्वयः—हे मनुष्यास्ततो विराडजायत विराजो अधि पुरुष अथो स पुरो जातोऽत्यरिच्यत पश्चाद्भूमिं जनयति तं विजानीत ॥

Translation:—From the Supreme Being (as the efficient cause) comes into being the entire cosmos

---

* विराट्—वि+√राजृ दीप्तौ+क्विप् ॥ पा० ३।२।१७८ ॥

† पश्चात्—अपर+आति ॥ पा० ५।३।३२ ॥

beaming with objects indefinite in variety and number which He then controls after creation. Being already manifest by His Omnipotence and distinct from the universe He now fashions the earth. Oh men! You should realise Him.

भावार्थ:—परमेश्वरादेव सर्वं समष्टिरूपं जगज्जायते स च तस्मात्पृथग्भूतो व्याप्तोऽपि तत्कल्मषालिप्तोऽस्य सर्वस्याधिष्ठाता भवति । एवं सामान्येन जगन्निर्माणमुक्त्वा विशेषतया भूम्यादिनिर्माणं क्रमेणोच्यते ॥

Purport:—The whole universe as an aggregate originates from the Supreme Lord alone Who, distinct as He is from the former, is not soiled with any of its blemishes though pervading it and, thus does He control it.

Having thus, in general terms, described the creation of the universe, the Veda does now, in a special manner, relate the creation of the earth and other objects in order.

(९०) तस्माद्यज्ञात्सर्वहुतः सम्भृतं पृषदाज्यम् ।
पशूँस्ताँश्चक्रे वायव्यानारण्या ग्राम्याश्च ये ॥ ८ ॥

पदपाठः—तस्मात् यज्ञात् सर्वऽहुतः सम्ऽभृतम् पृषत्ऽआज्यम् पशून् तान् चक्रे वायव्यान् आरण्याः ग्राम्याः च ये ॥

भाष्यम्=Explanation:—तस्मात्=पूर्वोक्तात्=(from the Puruṣa) described above. यज्ञात्=सच्चिदानन्दादिलक्षणात्पूर्णात्= the perfect one as distinguished by the attributes existence, intelligence and bliss. सर्वहुत:*=सर्वहुतात्, सर्वपूज्यात्सर्वोपास्यात्सर्वशक्तिमतः (परब्रह्मणः)=(From the Parabrahman) the Almighty one that is acceptable to all or, worshipped and adored by all. (सर्वैर्हूयत आदीयत इति सर्वहुतः) संभृतं† पृषदाज्यम्‡=पृषु सेचने धातुः । पर्षन्ति सिञ्चन्ति क्षुत्प्रवृत्त्यादि

* सर्वहुत—सर्व + √हु दानादनयोः । आदाने चेत्येके । + क्त ॥ पा० ३।२।१०२॥

† सम्भृतम्—सम् + √भृञ् भरणे + क्त ॥ पा० ३ । २ । १०२ ॥

‡ पृषदाज्यम्—पृषच्चाज्यञ्च पृषदाज्यम् ॥ पा० २ । ४ । ६ ॥ पृषत्—√पृषु सेचने + अति ॥ उ० २ । ८४ ॥ आज्यम्—√अञ्जू व्यक्तिम्रक्षणकान्तिगतिषु + क्यप् ॥ वा० अञ्जेश्चोपसंख्यानं संज्ञायाम् ॥

=पृषु सेचने धातुः । पर्षन्ति सिञ्चन्ति क्षुन्निवृत्त्यादिकारकमन्नादि वस्तु यस्मिंस्तत्पृषत् । आज्यं घृतं मधु दुग्धादिकं च । पृषदिति भक्ष्यान्नोपलक्षणम् । आज्यमिति व्यञ्जनोपलक्षणम् । यावद्वस्तु जगति वर्तते तावत्सर्वं पुरुषात्परमेश्वरसामर्थ्यादेव जातमिति बोध्यम् । तत्सर्वमीश्वरेण स्वल्पं स्वल्पं जीवैश्च सम्यग्धारितमस्ति । अतः सर्वैरनन्यचित्तेनायं परमेश्वर एवोपास्यो नान्यश्चेति ॥

The word pṛṣat in the text comes from the root pṛṣu to moisten or pour and hence it means that by which food, &c., that pacifies hunger, is moistened. Ājyam means ghee, honey, milk &c. Pṛṣat stands for food which is masticated and ājyam for that which is eaten without mastication. All the objects found in the universe were created by God's Samarthya and by Him they are upheld, although to some slight extent the jivas (individual souls) also uphold and maintain them. All should, therefore, worship God alone and none else with an undivided mind.

पशूंस्तांश्चक्रे‡ य आरण्या वनस्थाः पशवो* ये च ग्राम्याः§ ग्रामस्थास्तान्सर्वान्स एव चक्रे कृतवानस्ति । स च परमेश्वरो वायव्यान्† वायुसहचरितान्पक्षिणश्चक्रे चकार । मीनादीनन्यान्सूक्ष्मदेहधारिणः कीटपतङ्गादीनपि कृतवानस्ति ॥

He alone made the beasts of the forest and the animals that live in towns. God alone made the birds of the air and the small living creatures, such as, insects, &c. The conjunction 'ca' (and) implies fish insects, moths &c.

(सम्भृतम्—सम्यक्सिक्तं जातम् । वायव्यान्—वायुवद्गुणान् । आरण्याः—अरण्ये भवाः सिंहादयः । ग्राम्याः—ग्रामे भवा गवादयः ।)

अन्वयः—हे मनुष्यास्तस्मात्सर्वहुतो यज्ञात्सर्वं पृषदाज्यं सम्भृतं य आरण्या ग्राम्याश्च तान्वायव्यान्पशूंश्चक्रे तं विजानीत ॥

Translation:—From that Supreme Being acknowledged and adored by all, all objects of enjoyment

---

* पशून्—√दृशिर् प्रेक्षणे+कु ॥ उ० १ । २७ ॥ पा० ७ । ३ । ७८ ॥

† वायव्यान्—वायु+यत् ॥ पा० ४ । २ । ३१ ॥

‡ आरण्याः—अरण्य+अण् ॥ वा० अरण्याण्णः ॥ अरण्यम्—√ऋ गतौ+अन्य ॥ उ० ३ । १०२ ॥ अथवा नञ्+√रमु क्रीडायाम्+यत् ॥ उ० ४ । ११२ ॥

§ ग्राम्याः—ग्राम+य ॥ पा० ४ । २ । ९४ ॥ ग्रामः—√ग्रस भक्षे+मन् ॥ उ० १ । १३९ ॥ १४३ ॥

such as food to be masticated and that which is used to season such food are produced well formed. From Him also come into being sylvan beasts like the lion and domestic animals like the cow, birds of the air (fish and all small living creatures such as insects &c.). Oh men ! you should know Him.

भावार्थः—येन सर्वैर्ग्रहीतव्येन पूज्येन जगदीश्वरेण सर्वजगद्धिताय पृषदाज्यादि भोग्यं वस्तु ग्रामस्था वनस्था वायव्याश्च पशव अन्ये मीनकीटादयश्च निर्मितास्तं सर्वे उपासीरन् ॥

Purport:—All should adore that Lord of the universe alone who is acknowledged by all and by Whom are created all enjoyable objects as curds &c., all domestic animals, wild beasts, birds of the air, fish and insects &c.

(९१) तस्माद्यज्ञात्सर्वहुत ऋचः सामानि जज्ञिरे ।
छन्दांसि जज्ञिरे तस्माद्यजुस्तस्मादजायत ॥७॥

पदपाठः—तस्मात् यज्ञात् सर्वऽहुतः ऋचः सामानि जज्ञिरे
छन्दांसि जज्ञिरे तस्मात् यजुः तस्मात् अजायत ॥

भाष्यम् = **Explanation**:—तस्माद्यज्ञात्सर्वहुतः=तस्माद्यज्ञात्सच्चिदानन्दादिलक्षणात्पूर्णात्पुरुषात् सर्वहुतात्सर्वपूज्यात्सर्वोपास्यात्सर्वशक्तिमतः परब्रह्मणः । ऋचः*=ऋग्वेदः । यजुः$=यजुर्वेदः । सामानि†=सामवेदः । छन्दांसि‡=अथर्ववेदश्च । जज्ञिरे=चत्वारो वेदास्तेनैव प्रकाशिता इति वेद्यम् ।

The Ṛgvēda, the Yajurvēda the Sāmavēda and the Atharvavēda were produced by the Supreme and perfect Being, Para-brahman who possesses the attributes of self-existence, consciousness and bliss, Who is Omnipotent and universally adored. The meaning is that the four Vedas were revealed by God Himself.

---

* ऋचन्ति स्तुवन्ति यया सा ऋच्—√ऋच् स्तुतौ + क्विप् ॥ उ० २ । ५७ ॥

† सामानि—√षो नाशे + मनिन् ॥ उ० ४ । १५३ ॥

‡ छन्दांसि—√चदि आह्लादने + असुन् ॥ ४ । १८६ ॥ २१९ ॥ छन्दत्यर्चतिकर्मेति निघंटौ ॥ ३ । १४ ॥ छन्दांसि छादनादिति निरुक्ते ॥ ७ । १२ ॥

$ यजुः—√यज देवपूजासंगतिकरणदानेषु + उसि ॥ उ० २ । ११५ ॥

सर्वहुत इति वेदानामपि विशेषणं भवितुमर्हति वेदाः सर्वहुताः । यतः सर्वमनुष्यैर्होतुमादातुं ग्रहीतुं योग्याः सन्त्यतः ।

The word sarvahutah should also be taken as an adjective denoting an attribute of the Vedas because they also are worthy of acceptance by all.

जज्ञिरे अजायतेति क्रियाद्वयं वेदानामनेकविद्यावत्त्वद्योतनार्थम् । तथा तस्मादिति पदद्वयमीश्वरादेव वेदा जाता इत्यवधारणार्थम् । वेदानां गायत्र्यादिच्छन्दोन्वितत्वात्पुनश्छन्दांसीति पदं चतुर्थस्याथर्ववेदस्योत्पत्तिं ज्ञापयतीत्यवधेयम् । यज्ञो वै विष्णुः । शतपथ १ । १ । २ । १३ । इदं विष्णुर्विचक्रमे त्रेधा निदधे पदम् । यजुर्वेद ५ । १५ । इति सर्वजगत्कर्तृत्वं विष्णौ परमेश्वर एव घटते नान्यत्र । वेवेष्टि व्याप्नोति चराचरं जगत्स विष्णुः परमेश्वरः ॥

The two words jajñire and ajayata both meaning 'produced' are used to show that the Vedas teach numerous sciences. Similarly the pronoun tasmat (from Him) is used twice for the purpose of laying stress on the fact that God alone is the Author of the Vedas. The Vedas contain various metres—Gāyatri &c., but not withstanding this, the word chandāṃsi (metres)—is used to indicate that the Atharvaveda also was revealed by God. The word 'Yajña' means 'Viṣṇu' according to Śatap. Br. 1, 1, 2, 13 where it is said 'verily Viṣṇu is Yajña.' Now Viṣṇu means God according to Yajurveda V, 15. The attributes of creating the universe can be applicable to God alone. He is called Viṣṇu because He pervades the animate and the inanimate world.

अन्वयः—हे मनुष्यास्तस्माद्यज्ञात्सर्वहुतः परमात्मनः ऋचः सामानि जज्ञिरे तस्माच्छन्दांसि जज्ञिरे तस्माद्यजुरजायत । युष्माभिः स विज्ञातव्यः ॥

Translation:—Oh men! from the universally Supreme Lord the All-pervading, were produced the Ṛks and the Samans, from Him was produced the Atharvaveda and from Him was the Yajurveda produced. You should know him.

भावार्थः—हे मनुष्या भवन्तो यस्मात्सर्वे वेदा जायन्ते तं परमात्मानमुपासीरन्वेदांश्चाधीयीरंस्तदाज्ञानुकूलं च वर्तित्वा सुखिनो भवन्तु ॥

Purport:—Oh men! You ought to adore that Supreme Being from Whom all the Vedas originate, study the Vedas, act in accordance with His commandments and thus be happy.

(९२) तस्मादश्वा॑ अजायन्त ये के चो॑भयादतः ।
गावो॑ ह जज्ञिरे तस्मात्तस्मा॑ज्जाता अजावयः ॥८॥

पदपाठः—तस्मा॑त् अश्वाः अजायन्त ये के च उभय॑ऽदतः गावः ह जज्ञिरे तस्मा॑त् तस्मा॑त् जाताः अजावयः ॥

भाष्यम्=Explanation:—तस्मादश्वा०=तस्मात्परमेश्वरसामर्थ्यादेवाश्वास्तुरङ्गा अजायन्त । ग्राम्यारण्यपशूनां मध्येऽश्वादीनामन्तर्भावादेषामुत्तमगुणवत्त्वप्रकाशनार्थोऽयमारम्भः ॥

Horses were produced through the Samarthya (might) of the Puruṣa—the Supreme Lord. Although horses &c. are included among 'beasts of the forest' and 'domestic animals' mentioned in one of the foregoing verses, they are again mentioned here in order to emphasize their good qualities.

ये के चोभयादतः*=उभयतो दन्ता येषां त उभयादतः । ये केचिदुभयादत उष्ट्रगर्दभादयस्तेऽप्यजायन्त ॥

(From Him) also were produced animals having two rows of teeth, such as camels, asses &c.

गावो ह जज्ञिरे तस्मात्=तथा तस्मात्पुरुषसामर्थ्यादेव गावो धेनवः किरणाश्चेन्द्रियाणि च जज्ञिरे जातानि ॥

From the might of the Puruṣa were produced cows, the rays of light and the sense organs.

तस्माज्जाता अजावयः†=एवमेव चाजाश्छागा अवयश्च जाता उत्पन्ना इति विज्ञेयम् ॥

---

* उभयादतः—उभयतो दन्ता येषान्ते ॥ पा० ५ । ४ । १४२ ॥ ६ । १ । १३७ ॥ दन्तः—√दमु उपशमे + तन् ॥ उ० ३ । ८६ ॥

† अजाश्चावयश्च ॥पा० २ । २ । २९ ॥ अजा—अजति गच्छतीति √अज गतिक्षेपणयोः + अच् + टाप् ॥ पा० ३ । १ । १३४ ॥ ४ । १ । ४ ॥ अविः—अवति दुग्धादिप्रदानेन रक्षतीति √अव रक्षणगत्यादिषु + इन् ॥ उ० ४ । ११८ ॥

It should be understood that in like manner were produced goats and sheep.

अन्वयः—हे मनुष्या युष्माकमश्वा ये के चोभयादतः सन्ति ते तस्मादजायन्त । तस्माद्गावो ह जज्ञिरे तस्मादजावयो जाता इति वेद्यम् ॥

Translation:—Oh men! your horses and such other animals of yours as have two rows of teeth, were producod from that Supreme Being as the efficient cause. It should also be understood that cows, goats and sheep also were produced from Him.

भावार्थः—हे मनुष्या यूयं गवाश्वादयो ग्राम्याः सर्वे पशवो यस्मात्सनातनात्पूर्णात्पुरुषादेवोत्पन्नास्तस्याज्ञोल्लङ्घनं कदापि मा कुरुत ॥

Purport:—Oh men! you should never transgress the commandments of that Eternal and Perfect Puruṣa (God) from Whom all domestic animals such as cows, horses &c. have come into being.

(९३) तं य॒ज्ञं ब॒र्हिषि॒ प्रौक्ष॒न्पुरु॑षं जा॒तम॑ग्र॒तः ।
तेन॑ दे॒वा अ॑यजन्त सा॒ध्या ऋष॑यश्च॒ ये ॥९॥

पदपाठः—तम् य॒ज्ञम् ब॒र्हिषि॑ प्र औ॒क्ष॒न् पुरु॑षम् जा॒तम् अ॒ग्र॒तः तेन॑ दे॒वाः अ॒यजन्त सा॒ध्याः ऋष॑यः च॒ ये ॥

भाष्यम्=Explanation:—(तं यज्ञं बर्हिषि०)=यमग्रतः सृष्टेः प्राग्जातं प्रादुर्भूतं जगत्कर्तारम् पुरुषं पूर्णं यज्ञं सर्वपूज्यं बर्हिषि* मानसे ज्ञानयज्ञे हृदयान्तरिक्षे वा प्रौक्षन्प्रकृष्टतया यस्यैवाभिषेकं कृतवन्तः कुर्वन्ति करिष्यन्ति चेत्युपदिश्यत ईश्वरेण (तेन देवा०)=तेन परमेश्वरेण पुरुषेण वेदद्वारोपदिष्टास्ते सर्वे देवा विद्वांसः साध्या† ज्ञानिन ऋषयो मन्त्रद्रष्टारश्च ये चान्ये मनुष्यास्तं परमेश्वरमयजन्तापूजयन्त । अनेन किं सिद्धं सर्वे मनुष्याः परमेश्वरस्य स्तुतिप्रार्थनोपासनापुरःसरमेव सर्वकर्मानुष्ठानं कुर्युरित्यर्थः ॥

The learned, the sages, the seers of the Vedic verses and all other men receiving instruction from the Puruṣa (God) through the Vedas worshipped Him (in the past, do worship Him now and shall worship Him in the future) and adore Him in spirit and mind or place Him exalted above all in the space (temple)

---

* बर्हिषि—√बृह √बृहि वृद्धौ + इसि ॥ उ० २ । १०९ ॥ आकाशम् हृदयाकाशम् वा ॥

† साध्याः—साध्यं येषामस्तीति साध्यास्ते—साध्य + अच् ॥ पा० ५ । २ । १२७ ॥

of their heart—yea, Him, the Puruṣa, the perfect Being, manifest from all times, the maker of the universe, the adorable. The instruction conveyed by this verse is that all men should commence all works and undertakings with praise, prayer and worship of God.

अन्वयः—हे मनुष्या ये देवा साध्या ऋषयश्च यमग्रतो जातं यज्ञं पुरुषं बर्हिषि प्रौक्षंस्त एव तेनायजन्त च तं यूयं विजानीत ॥

Translation:—Oh men! you should realise that Lord God, the perfect and adorable Who manifested Himself even before the creation and Whom the learned, the sages and the seers of the Vedic law have in all ages worshipped according to His divine instruction and installed exalted high above all on the throne of their heart.

भावार्थः—विद्वद्भिर्मनुष्यैः सृष्टिकर्त्तेश्वरो योगाभ्यासादिना सदा हृदयान्तरिक्षे ध्यातव्यः पूजनीयश्च ॥

Purport:—The learned should undergo the yogic spiritual discipline and always adore God the Creator of the cosmos in spirit and mind and meditate upon Him.

(९४) यत्पुरु॑षं॒ व्यद॑धुः कति॒धा व्य॑कल्पयन् ।
मुखं॒ किम॑स्या॒सी॒त्किम्बा॒हू किमू॒रू पादा॑ उच्येते ॥१०॥

पदपाठः—यत् पुरु॑षम् वि अद॑धुः क॒ति॒धा वि अ॒क॒ल्प॒य॒न् मुख॑म् किम् अ॒स्य आ॒सी॒त् किम् बा॒हू किम् ऊ॒रू पादौ॑ उ॒च्ये॒ते ॥

भाष्यम्=**Explanation**:—यत्=यम्=whom. एतं पूर्वोक्तलक्षणं पुरुषं=परमेश्वरं=the Puruṣa described already is called the Supreme Lord. कतिधा*=कियत्प्रकारैः=in how many ways. व्यकल्पयन्=तस्य सामर्थ्यगुणकल्पनं कुर्वन्तीत्यर्थः=they explain the multifarious powers of God.

व्यदधुः=तं सर्वशक्तिमन्तमीश्वरं विविधसामर्थ्यकथनेनादधुरर्थादनेकविधं तस्य व्याख्यानं कृतवन्तः कुर्वन्ति करिष्यन्ति च ॥

---

* कतिधा—कति+धा ॥ पा० ५ । ३ । ४२ ॥

They postulate Almighty God as distinguished by various powers, that is, they taught, are teaching and will teach about God in various ways as an Almighty Being having multifarious potencies.

अस्य=पुरुषस्य=by this Puruṣa. **मुखं*=मुख्यगुणेभ्यः किमुत्पन्नमासीत्**=mouth that is what is produced with superior qualities. **किं बाहू†=बलवीर्यादिगुणेभ्यः किमुत्पन्नमासीत्**=what are the two arms, that is what is produced by God with qualities like power, valour &c. ? **किमूरू‡=व्यापारादिमध्यमगुणैः किमुत्पन्नमासीत्**=what is produced by Him as possessing middling qualities like business instincts &c. ? **पादा उच्येते=पादावनर्थान्मूर्खत्वादि नीचगुणैः किमुत्पन्नं वर्तते**=what is created by Him with such low qualities as lack of intelligence &c. ? **अस्योत्तरमाह**=the answer to these questions is given in the following verse.

अन्वयः—हे विद्वांसो भवन्तं यद्यं पुरुषं व्यदधुस्तं कतिधा व्यकल्पयन्नस्य सृष्टौ मुखं किमासीद्बाहू किमुच्येते ऊरूपादौ च किमुच्येते ॥

Translation:—Oh learned men ! in how many ways do you describe the might of Him whom you postulate to be the Puruṣa (God) ? Who in His creation occupy the place of the face, that is, are created by Him with the highest qualities ? Who take the place of the arms that is are endowed with such qualities as strength, valour &c, ? Who hold the position of the thighs, that is, possess such middling qualities as business-instinct &c. ? and finally, who occupy the position of the feet or possess the lowest qualities viz , lack of understanding &c. ?

भावार्थः—हे विद्वांसोऽत्र संसारेऽसंख्यं सामर्थ्यमीश्वरस्यास्ति तत्र समुदाये मुखमुत्तमाङ्गं बाह्वादीनि चाङ्गानि कानि सन्तीति ब्रूत ॥

Purport:—Oh wise men ! in this world innumerable features of the Omnipotence of God are seen. Please say which in this aggregate are equal to the face or are the best and what are like the arms or are the integral parts.

---

* मुखम्—खनत्यन्नादिकमनेनेति √खनु अवदारणे + अच् ॥ उ० ५ । १६ । २० ॥

† बाहू—बाध्यन्ते विलोड्यन्ते पदार्था अनेनेति बाहुस्तौ—√बाधृ विलोडने + कु ॥ उ० १ । २७ ॥

‡ ऊरू—ऊर्णोत्याच्छादयति या सा—√ऊर्णु आच्छादने + कु ॥ उ० १ । २२ ॥ ३० ॥

(९५) ब्राह्मणोऽस्य मुखमासीद्बाहू राजन्यः कृतः।
ऊरू तदस्य यद्वैश्यः पद्भ्यां शूद्रो अजायत ॥११॥

पदपाठः—ब्राह्मणः अस्य मुखम् आसीत् बाहू राजन्यः कृतः ऊरू तत् अस्य यत् वैश्यः पत्ऽभ्याम् शूद्रः अजायत ॥

भाष्यम्=Explanation:—ब्राह्मणोऽस्य मुखमासीत्=अस्य पुरुषस्य मुखं ये विद्यादयो मुख्यगुणाः सत्यभाषणोपदेशादीनि कर्माणि च सन्ति तेभ्यो ब्राह्मण‡ आसीदुत्पन्नो भवति ॥

The Brahmaṇa is said to be produced from the mouth of the Puruṣa, that is, endowed with the best qualities such as, knowledge &c., and with capability for such acts as truthful speech and the vocation of a teacher and preacher.

बाहूराजन्यः* कृतः=बलवीर्यादिलक्षणान्वितो राजन्यः क्षत्रियस्तेन कृत आसीदुत्पन्नो भवति ॥

He made the Kṣatriya (the governing or warrior class) and ordained him to possess the qualities of strength, valour, &c.

ऊरू तदस्य यद्वैश्यः†=कृषिव्यापारादयो गुणा मध्यमास्तेभ्यो वैश्यो वणिग्जनोऽस्य पुरुषस्योपदेशादुत्पन्नो भवतीति वेद्यम् ॥

---

‡ ब्राह्मणः—ब्रह्म वेदः परमेश्वरो वा। तं जानातीति—ब्रह्मन्+अण्॥ पा० ४।२।५६॥

* राजन्यः—√राजृ दीप्तावैश्वर्ये च+अन्य॥ उ० ३।१००॥

† वैश्यः—विड्भ्यः प्रजाभ्यो मनुष्येभ्यो वा हितः—√विश प्रवेशने+क्विप्+ष्यञ्॥ पा० ३।२।१७८॥ ५।१।५॥ If the termination ष्यञ् is added in the sense of स्वार्थ, i. e., in the original sense of the word itself according to the Vartika चतुर्वर्णादीनां स्वार्थ उपसंख्यानम्, the form वैश्य would simply mean "a common subject" or "a member of the general public" and not one given to the advancement of nation-building professions such as trade and agriculture which is the sense required in the stanza. Besides विश् does not belong to the चतुर्वर्णादि group which is not an आकृतिगण. Nor can it be applied by the aphorism गुणवचनब्राह्मणादिभ्यः कर्मणि च P. V, 1, 124 since then it would denote only a quality, state or action, e. g., विशः गुणः भावः

The qualities of agriculture, trade and commerce are of the middling order. The vaiśya or the trader was produced with these qualities by God's command.

पद्भ्यां शूद्रो‡ अजायत=पद्भ्यां पादेन्द्रियनीचत्वमर्थाज्जडबुद्धित्वा-दिगुणेभ्यः शूद्रः सेवागुणविशिष्टः पराधीनतया प्रवर्तमानोऽजायत जायत इति वेद्यम् ॥

कर्म वा विश्+ष्यञ् वैश्यम् and the form would be a neuter abstract noun. But to the form thus evolved the aphorism अर्श आदिभ्योऽच् P. V, 2, 127 can be applied, e. g., विश्+ष्यञ्=वैश्यम् ; वैश्यम् अस्य विद्यते इति वैश्य+अच्=वैश्यः. But this form is futile since it does not give the sense required. Therefore the only course left is to apply the aphorism. तस्मै हितम् P. V, 1, 5.

‡ शूद्रः—शोचनीयः—√शुच शोके+रक् ॥ उ० २ । १९ ॥ This means 'one who ought to be pitied' or 'who is in a miserable state.' It cannot be said a sweeper, or a cook is in 'a pitiable state.' Bhartṛhari says:—निःस्वो वष्टि शतं शती दशशतं लक्षं सहस्राधिपो लक्षेशः क्षितिराजतां क्षितिपतिश्चक्रेशतां वाञ्छति । चक्रेशः सुरराजतां सुरपतिर्ब्रह्मास्पदं वाञ्छति ब्रह्मा विष्णुपदं हरिः शिवपदं तृष्णावधिं को गतः ॥ According to this dictr[illegible] everyone is comparatively miserable. The preceding chapter on Charity ought to be consulted in this connection. This derivation seems to draw attention to the fact that there are always bound to be in human society, for its own good such people as, by their daily life or work, seem unfit or social intercourse, and that they ought to be pitied and treated with kindness and not scorn. The word can be derived from √शुन्धिर् पूतीभावे in the sense of the agent, i. e., 'who cleans or purifies' and in this sense sublimated would mean God Him[illegible]. In Kannada the word 'holeya' means 'holasu te[illegible]yuvava[illegible] - one who removes dirt. The Holeyas are considered to be the lowest 'caste' in Coorg and some other parts of Southern India. The Tamilians have a curious legend (perhaps not yet committed to writing) about the word शूद्र. They say that when the Āryans first invaded the Tamil country they tumbled upon the Tamil Sūtra Literature, e. g., the Agastiyam (now unavailable), and the Tolkāppiyam—both ancient Tamil grammars written in Sūtra style—and such other

The Sūdra, whose differentiating attribute is the service of and dependence on others, was produced with qualities of the lowest order, like feet occupying the lowest place in the body, such as, dulness of intellect &c.

छन्दसि लुङ् लङ् लिटः। अष्टाध्यायी ३।४।६। इति सूत्रेण सामान्यकाले त्रयो लकारा विधीयन्ते।

In this verse the past tense denotes all the tenses because according to the grammatical rule, P. III, 4, 6, in the Vedas, all the tenses, present, past and future, are used interchangeably.

अन्वयः—हे जिज्ञासवो यूयमस्य सृष्टौ ब्राह्मणो मुखमासीद्बाहू राजन्यः कृतो यदूरू तदस्य वैश्य आसीत्पद्भ्यां शूद्रोऽजायतेत्युत्तरांश्च यथाक्रमं विजानीत॥

Translation:—Oh you who are desirous to learn! know that in creation (that is, of the Virat-puruṣa, the body of all the bodies, mentioned in verse five above) the Brahmaṇa (the man knowing God and given to teaching and preaching) occupies the position of the face, that is, being created with the best and the highest qualities of head and heart he is highest in the social scale (according to God's dispensation). The next in order (you should know) is the Kṣatriya (or the governing and warrior class) who can be said to be the arms of this Puruṣa, created as he is, with such qualities as strength, valour &c. The agricultural and commercial class endowed with qualities necessary for farming, business &c., occupying the middlemost position in the scale of human society can be compared to

---

works which they could not understand and to decipher which they had to resort to Tamil scholars. Hence the Aryans began to call the Tamils 'Sūtra' which word in course of time became शूद्र. It is true fragments of the Agustiyam still available, the wonderful Tolkāppiyam, the Kannaḍa शब्दमणिदर्पण, शब्दानुशासन and कर्णाटकभाषाभूषण (a Sanskrit work), the Siṃhalese Sidatsāra-sangarāva are all in Sūtra style. But Sanskrit Sūtra literature is much older. Besides Tolkāppiyar, the author of Tolkāppiyam is reputed to be a direct pupil of Pāṇini. Thus between सूत्र and शूद्र there seems to be no connection.

the thighs of this Virāt-puruṣa. Finally the Sūdra occupies the position of His feet being lowest in the social scale on account of such qualities as lack of intelligence &c. These are the answers to the questions put in the above verse.

भावार्थः—ये विद्याशमदमादिषूत्तमेषु गुणेषु मुखमिवोत्तमास्ते ब्राह्मणाः। येऽधिकवीर्या बाहुवत्कार्यसाधकास्ते क्षत्रियाः। ये व्यवहारविद्याकुशलास्ते वैश्या ये च सेवायां साधवो विद्याहीनाः पादाविव मूर्खत्वादिनीचगुणयुक्तास्ते शूद्राः कार्या मन्तव्याश्च ॥

Purport:—The Brāhmaṇas are those who are exalted like the face in the possession of such superior qualities as learning, peacefulness of disposition and control of the senses. Those who possess more of strength and valour and take an active part in the accomplishment of any task like the arms of a man, are the Kṣatriyas. Those who are proficient in the knowledge of business are the Vaiśyas while those who are void of learning and are distinguished by such qualities as dulness &c., but are capable of serving others should be understood to be the Śūdras and utilised as such.

(९६) चन्द्रमा मनसो जातश्चक्षोः सूर्यो अजायत।
श्रोत्राद्वायुश्च प्राणश्च मुखादग्निरजायत ॥१२॥

पदपाठः—चन्द्रमाः मनसः जातः चक्षोः सूर्यः अजायत श्रोत्रात् वायुः च प्राणः च मुखात् अग्निः अजायत ॥

भाष्यम्=**Explanation**:—चन्द्रमा* मनसो जातः=तस्यास्य पुरुषस्य मनसो मननशीलात्सामर्थ्याच्चन्द्रमा जात उत्पन्नोऽस्ति ॥

The moon was produced from the mind, that is, the reflective element of the Sāmarthya of this Puruṣa.

चक्षोः† सूर्यो अजायत=तथा चक्षोर्ज्योतिर्मयात्सूर्यो अजायत उत्पन्नोऽस्ति ॥

---

* चन्द्रमाः—√चदि आनन्दे+रक् ॥ उ० २ । १३ ॥ चन्द्रम् आनन्दम् मिमीते असौ इति चन्द+म+असि ॥ उ० ४ । २२३ ॥ २२८ ॥

† चक्षुः—√चक्षिङ् दर्शने+उसि ॥ उ० २ । ११६ ॥

The sun was produced from the eyes, that is, the refulgent portion (of this Virat-puruṣa).

श्रोत्रा*द्वायुश्चप्राण†श्च=श्रोत्राकाशमयाद्वाकाशो नभ उत्पन्नमस्ति। वायुमयाद्वायुरुत्पन्नोऽस्ति प्राणश्च सर्वेन्द्रियाणि चोत्पन्नानि सन्ति ॥

The sky was produced from the ears, that is, the akaśiya portion; the atmosphere was produced from the atmospheric portion and also, were produced the vital air and all the sense organs.

मुखान्मुख्यज्योतिर्मयादग्निरजायतोत्पन्नोऽस्ति ॥

Fire was produced from the mouth, i.e., the chief refulgent portion.

अन्वयः—हे मनुष्या अस्य ब्रह्मणः पुरुषस्य मनसश्चन्द्रमा जातश्चक्षोः सूर्योऽजायत श्रोत्राद्वायुश्च प्राणश्च मुखादग्निरजायतेति बुध्यध्वम् ॥

Translation:—Oh men ! You should understand that the moon has originated from the mind or the reflective element of this Supreme Being or the Puruṣa, the sun has been produced from His eyes or the refulgent element; the sky (ether) from His ear or etheric aspect, the atmosphere, the vital air (and the sense organs) from His atmospheric aspect and from His principal refulgent aspect fire has been produced.

भावार्थः—यदिदं सर्वं जगत्कारणादीश्वरेणोत्पादितं वर्तते तत्र चन्द्र-लोको मनःस्वरूपः सूर्यश्चक्षुःस्थानी वायुः प्राणश्च श्रोत्रवन्मुखमिवाग्निर्लोम-वदोषधिवनस्पतयो नाडीवन्नद्योऽस्थिवत्पर्वतादिर्वर्तत इति वेदितव्यम् ॥

Purport:—In the cosmos that has been created by God from the causal element, it should be understood that the moon is of the essence of the mind, the sun is in the place of the eyes, the atmosphere and the vital air are like the ears, the fire is like the mouth, trees and plants like the hair, rivers like the blood-vessels and mountains like the bones and so on.

---

* श्रोतम्—√श्रु श्रवणे+तन् ॥ उ० ४ । १६८ ॥

† प्राणः—प्र+√अन प्राणने+अच् घञ् वा ॥

(९७) नाभ्या॑ आसीद॒न्तरि॑क्षं शी॒र्ष्णो द्यौः सम॑वर्तत । प॒द्भ्यां भूमि॒र्दिशः॒ श्रोत्रा॒त्तथा॑ लो॒काँ२ ॥ अकल्पयन् ॥१३॥

पदपाठः—नाभ्याः॑ आ॒सी॒त् अ॒न्तरि॑क्षम् शी॒र्ष्णः द्यौः सम् अवर्तत पत्ऽभ्याम् भूमिः दिशः श्रोत्रा॒त् तथा॑ लो॒कान् अकल्पयन् ॥

भाष्यम्=Explanation:—नाभ्या* आसीदन्तरिक्षम्†=अस्य पुरुषस्य नाभ्या अवकाशमयात्सामर्थ्यादन्तरिक्षमुत्पन्नमासीत् ॥

The inter-stellar space or intermediate region was produced from the navel, i. e., the power of fixing spatial relations of this Puruṣa.

शीर्ष्णो‡ द्यौः समवर्तत=एवं शीर्ष्णः शिरोवदुत्तमसामर्थ्यात्प्रकाशमयाद्द्यौः§ सूर्यादिलोकः प्रकाशात्मकः समवर्तत सम्यगुत्पन्नः सन्वर्तते ।

The sun &c., were produced from the head, that is, the highest portion of the Samarthya which occupies a place of eminence like the head

पद्भ्यां भूमिः=पृथिवीकारणमयात्सामर्थ्यात्परमेश्वरेण भूमिर्धरित्री उत्पादितास्ति जलं च ॥

God made the earth and waters from the feet, i. e., the terrestrial elements of tho Samarthya.

दिशः* श्रोत्रात्†=शब्दाकाशकारणमयात्तेन दिश उत्पादिताः सन्ति ॥

From the ears, that is, the aural (ākāśiya) elements He produced the directions.

लोकाँ२ ॥ अकल्पयन्=तथा तेनैव प्रकारेण सर्वलोककारणमयात्सामर्थ्यादन्यान्सर्वाँल्लोकांस्तत्रस्थान्स्थावरजङ्गमपदार्थानकल्पयत्परमेश्वर उत्पादितवानस्ति ॥

In like manner God produced all the spheres and the animate and inanimate objects contained therein from the respective elements of His Sāmarthya.

---

* नाभिः—√णह बन्धने+इञ् ॥ उ० ४ । १२५ ॥ १२६ ॥

† अन्तरिक्षम्—see p. 102.

‡ शीर्ष—see footnote* p. 254

§ द्यौः—√द्युत दीप्तौ+डो ॥ उ० २ । ६७ ॥

अन्वयः—हे मनुष्या यथाऽस्य नाभ्या अन्तरिक्षमासीच्छीर्ष्णो द्यौः पद्भ्यां भूमिः समवर्तत श्रोत्राद्दिशोऽकल्पयंस्तथाऽन्यांल्लोकानुत्पन्नानिव जानीत ॥

Translation:—Oh men ! Know that from that element of His Sāmarthya which determines spatial relations and which can be called the navel of this Virāt-puruṣa (the body of all bodies referred to in verse five) the intermediate regions came into being. From His head, that is, the highest portion of His Sāmarthya the celestial regions (consisting of the sun &c.,) were produced. From His feet or the terrestrial elements of the Sāmarthya of God the earth and waters came into being. From the ears, that is, the aural elements of His Sāmarthya He produced the directions. In the same manner, you should know, other spheres and the animate and inanimate objects in them are produced.

भावार्थः—हे मनुष्या यद्यदत्र सृष्टौ कार्यभूतं वस्तु वर्तते तत्तत्सर्वं विराडाख्यस्य कार्यकारणस्याऽवयवरूपं वर्तत इति वेद्यम् ॥

Purport:—Oh men ! it should be understood that whatever created there is in the cosmos, is simply a part of what is called Virāt the cause, itself an effect.

(९८) यत्पुरुषेण हविषा देवा यज्ञमतन्वत ।
वसन्तोऽस्यासीदाज्यं ग्रीष्म इध्मः शरद्धविः ॥१४॥

पदपाठः—यत् पुरुषेण हविषा देवाः यज्ञम् अतन्वत वसन्तः अस्य आसीत् आज्यम् ग्रीष्मः इध्मः शरत् हविः ॥

भाष्यम्=**Explanation:**—यत्पुरुषेण०=देवा विद्वांसः पूर्वोक्तेन पुरुषेण हविषा* गृहीतेन दत्तेन वाग्निहोत्राद्यश्वमेधान्तं शिल्पविद्यामयं च यद्यं यज्ञं प्रकाशितमतन्वत विस्तृतं कृतवन्तः कुर्वन्ति करिष्यन्ति च ॥

The learned extended, do and will extend the yajña (=righteons work) from the agnihōtra to the aśvamedha and the learning and teaching of the arts and sciences, with the help of the materials given by the above-menfioned Puruṣa.

इदानीं जगदुत्पत्तौ कालस्यावयवाख्या सामग्र्युच्यते ॥

---

* हविस्—√हु दानादनयोरादाने चेत्येके + इसि ॥ उ० २ । १०८ ॥

Now are described the divisions of time which are necessary elements in the production of the world.

वसन्तो*ऽस्यासीदाज्यं†=अस्य यज्ञस्य पुरुषादुत्पन्नस्य वा ब्रह्माण्डमयस्य वसन्त आज्यं घृतवदस्ति ॥

Vasanta (spring) is like the ghee in this yajña or in this universe produced by the Puruṣa.

ग्रीष्म‡ इध्मः§=ग्रीष्मर्तुरिध्म इन्धनान्यग्निर्वास्ति ॥

Grīṣma (the summer season) is like the fuel or fire.

शरद्धविः$=शरदृतुः पुरोडाशादिवद्धविर्हवनीयमस्ति ॥

Śarad (the winter) is like the purodāśa (sacrificial bread) or other oblations thrown into the fire.

NOTE. The Hindi commentary on this verse in the Ṛgvedādi-bhāṣya-bhūmikā is a supplement to the Sanskrit portion given above; hence, for a clear understanding of the text it is given below with an English translation:—

यत्पुरुषेण०—देव अर्थात् जो विद्वान लोग होते हैं उनको भी ईश्वर ने अपने अपने कर्मों के अनुसार उत्पन्न किया है और वे ईश्वर के दिये पदार्थों का ग्रहण करके पूर्वोक्त यज्ञ का विस्तार पूर्वक अनुष्ठान करते हैं और जो ब्रह्माण्ड का रचन, पालन और प्रलय करना रूप यज्ञ है उसी को जगत् बनाने की सामग्री बताते हैं।

The learned also are produced by God according to the residua of the actions of their past lives. Receiving the things produced by God they fully cooperate in the performance of the sacrifice mentioned above (vv. 6-9 and explain the divine sacrifice in the shape of creation, sustenance and dissolution of the cosmos itself to be the material for the creation of the universe.

---

* वसन्तः—√वस वासे निवासे आच्छादने च+झच् ॥ उ० ३ । १२८ ॥

† आज्यम्—आङ्+√अञ्जु मिश्रणे गतौ च+क्यप् ॥ अजेश्चोपसंख्यानं संज्ञायामिति वार्तिकेण ॥

‡ ग्रीष्म—√ग्रस अदने+मक् ॥ उ० १ । १४५ । १४६ ॥

§ इध्म—√ञिइन्धी दीप्तौ+मक् ॥ उ० १ । १४५ ॥

$ शरद्—√शॄ हिंसायाम्+अदि ॥ उ० १ । १३० ॥

वसन्तो०=पुरुष ने उत्पन्न किया जो यह ब्रह्माण्ड रूप यज्ञ है इसमें वसन्त ऋतु अर्थात् चैत्र और वैशाख घृत के समान है ॥

In this cosmic sacrifice that has been performed by Puruṣa (God), the spring season, comprising the two months of caitra and Vaiśakha, is the ghee.

ग्रीष्म इध्मः०=ग्रीष्म ऋतु जो ज्येष्ठ और आषाढ़ इन्धन है ॥

The summer season covering the two months of Jyeṣṭha and Āṣaḍha is the fuel.

श्रावण और भाद्रपद वर्षा ऋतु । आश्विन और कार्तिक शरद् ऋतु । मार्गशीर्ष और पौष हिम ऋतु और माघ तथा फाल्गुन शिशिर ऋतु कहाती है। यह इस यज्ञ में आहुति है ॥

The period covering the months of Śravaṇa and Bhadrapada is called the rainy season, that comprising Aśvina and Kartika the winter, that covering the two months Margaśirṣa and Pauṣa the frosty season and finally comes the autumn during the two months of Magha and Phalguna. All these are oblations in the cosmic sacrifice.

सो यहां रूपकालङ्कार से सब ब्रह्माण्ड का व्याख्यान जानना चाहिए ॥

It should be noted that in this manner the whole cosmos has been described in this verse (as a sacrifice) by means of a metaphor.

अन्वयः—देवाः पुरुषेण हविषा यद्यज्ञमतन्वतास्य वसन्त आज्यमासीद् ग्रीष्म इध्म शरच्च हविरासीत् ॥

Translation:—Of the sacrifice which the learned performed, do and will perform in the form of righteous works from the Agnihōtra to the Aśvamedha and the learning and teaching of the sciences and arts, the Spring is the ghee (essential like ghee to keep up the sacrificial fire ablaze and to diffuse atoms of health-giving material in the atmosphere), Summer the fuel (necessary like fuel to feed the fire) and the Winter and other seasons the oblations (useful like the sacrificial cake, incense and other fragrant and nourishing things to render the atmosphere of the locality pure and healthy).

NOTE. Another interpretation of this verse; slightly different, but beautiful and worth study is given by Maharṣi Dayānanda in his commentary on the Yajurveda. It is subjoined with a full English translation:—

पदार्थः=**Word-meaning:**—यत्=यदा=when. पुरुषेण=पूर्णेन परमात्मना=with God the perfect Being as the master of the Cosmic Sacrifice. हविषा=होतुमादातुमर्हेण=fit to be invoked, accepted at all times. देवाः=विद्वांसः=the enlightened. यज्ञम्=मानसं ज्ञानयज्ञम्=the spiritual sacrifice of contemplating on the cosmos itself as a sacrifice in which they are co-operating priests along with God the master thereof. अतन्वत=अन्वते विस्तृणन्ति=perform, extend. वसन्तः=पूर्वाह्णः=morning, forenoon. अस्य=यज्ञस्य= of this spiritual sacrifice. आसीत्=अस्ति=is. आज्यम्=घृतम्= ghee, molten butter; material to start the sacrifice with. ग्रीष्मः=मध्याह्नः=midday, afternoon. इध्मः=प्रदीपकः= fuel; material to feed or keep up the fire with. शरत्= अर्द्धरात्रः=midnight, evening and all the night till morning time. हविः=होतव्यंद्रव्यम्=oblations; material to burn in the sacrificial fire to diffuse fragrance and particles of healthy and disinfecting matter in the atmosphere.

अन्वयः—हे मनुष्या यद्धविषा पुरुषेण सह देवा यज्ञमतन्वत तदाऽस्य वसन्त आज्यं ग्रीष्म इध्मः शरद्धविरासीदिति यूयमपि विजानीत ॥

Translation:—Oh men! You should understand that when the enlightened perform the sacrifice of contemplating on (and teaching about) the cosmos itself as a huge sacrifice with God as the master thereof, the morning time serves as material for starting the fire of devotion in their souls, the midday becomes the fuel to keep it ablaze and the evening (and night) do duty, (so to say), for oblations to be thrown in to diffuse particles of matter endowed with purifying and health-giving influence over all creatures around.

भावार्थः—यदा बाह्यसामग्र्यभावे विद्वांसो सृष्टिकर्तुरीश्वरस्योपासनाख्यं मानसं ज्ञानयज्ञं विस्तारयेयुस्तदा पूर्वाह्णादिकाल एव साधनरूपेण कल्पनीयः ॥

Purport:—When, in the absence of external means, the enlightened engage themselves in the intellectual sacrifice offered mentally in the form of the adoration of God the Creator of the universe, the morning and other divisions of time themselves should be considered to be the matter for the performance thereof.

(९९) सप्तास्यासन्परिधयस्त्रिः सप्त समिधः कृताः
देवा यद्यज्ञं तन्वाना अबध्नन्पुरुषं पशुम् ॥१५॥

पदपाठः—सप्त अस्य आसन् परिऽधयः त्रिः सप्त समऽइधः कृताः
देवाः यत् यज्ञम् तन्वानाः अबध्नन् पुरुषम् पशुम् ॥

भाष्यम्=**Explanation**: – सप्तास्यासन्परिधयः=अस्य ब्रह्माण्डस्य सप्त* परिधयः† सन्ति । परिधिर्हि गोलस्योपरिभागस्य यावता सूत्रेण परिवेष्टनं भवति स परिधिर्ज्ञेयः । अस्य ब्रह्माण्डस्य ब्रह्माण्डान्तर्गतलोकानां वा सप्त सप्त परिधयो भवन्ति । समुद्र एकस्तदुपरि त्रसरेणुसहितो वायुर्द्वितीयः । मेघमण्डलं तत्रस्थो वायुस्तृतीयः । वृष्टिजलं चतुर्थस्तदुपरि-वायुः पञ्चमः अत्यन्तसूक्ष्मो धनञ्जयः षष्ठः । सूत्रात्मा सर्वत्र व्याप्तः सप्तमश्च । एवमेकैकस्योपरि सप्त सप्तावरणानि स्थितानि सन्ति तस्मात्ते परिधयो विज्ञेयाः ॥

The universe has seven circumferences. The line which passes round the outer surface of a sphere is called its circumference. There are seven concentric circles round the universe or the spheres comprised therein, namely, (1) the ocean, (2) the atmosphere together with the small particles (the motes), (3) the region of the clouds and the air thereof; (4) the rain-water, (5) the air above it, (6) the air of extreme rarity called Dhanañjaya and (7) the ubiquitous electricity, (Sūtratmā—literally, (the thread-soul). There are thus seven covers or circumferences one within the other.

---

* सप्तन् √षप समवाये + तुट् + कनिन् ॥ उ० १ । १५६ ॥ १५७ ॥

† परिधिः—परि + √डुधाञ् धारणपोषणयोः + कि ॥ पा० ३ । ३ । ९२ ॥

त्रिः* सप्त समिधः† कृताः—एकविंशतिः पदार्थाः सामग्र्यस्य चास्ति । प्रकृतिमहद्बुद्ध्याद्यन्तःकरणं जीवश्चैषैका सामग्री परमसूक्ष्मत्वात् । दशेन्द्रियाणि श्रोत्रं, त्वक् चक्षु जिह्वा नासिका वाक्पादौ हस्तौ पायुरुपस्थं-चेति । शब्दस्पर्शरूपरसगन्धाः पञ्चतन्मात्राः पृथिव्यापस्तेजोवायुराकाश-मिति पञ्चभूतानि च मिलित्वा दश भवन्ति । एवं सर्वां मिलित्वैकविंशतिर्भ-वन्त्यस्य ब्रह्माण्डरचनस्य समिधः कारणानि विज्ञेयानि । एतेषामवयव रूपाणि तु तत्त्वानि बहूनि सन्तीति बोध्यम् ॥

The constituent elements of the universe are twenty-one in number. (1) The subtle elements comprising Prakṛti (primordial matter), Mahat i. e., the internal organs—the intellect, &c., and jīvas (souls); (2-11) the ten organs of sensation and action, viz., the ears, the epidermis, the eyes, the tongue, the nose, the organ of speech, the feet, the hands, the organ of excretion and the generative organ, (12-16) the five Tanmātras (the potential perceptibilia, viz., sound, touch, sight, taste, and smell) and (17-21) the five Bhūtas (the elements) viz., earth, water, fire, air, and ether (ākāśa). These twenty-one are to be considered the chief ingredients in the construction of the world, although there are many more sub-ingredients derived from them.

यज्ञं तन्वाना‡=तदिदं येन पुरुषेण रचितं तं यज्ञपुरुषं पशुं सर्वद्रष्टारं सर्वैः पूजनीयं देवा विद्वांसोऽबध्नन्=ध्यानेन बध्नन्ति तं विहायेश्वरत्वेन कस्यापि ध्यानं नैव बध्नन्ति नैव कुर्वन्तीत्यर्थः ॥

The learned fasten with their contemplation the Puruṣa Who is All-seeing, the adorable Deity and the Maker of this universe. They do not concentrate their mind upon any other object than God.

अन्वयः—अस्य ब्रह्माण्डस्य सप्त परिधयः आसंस्त्रिः सप्त समिधश्च कृताः सन्ति । तदिदं येन रचितं तं पुरुषं पशुं यज्ञं तन्वाना देवा अबध्नन् ॥

Translation:—Of the altar of this Cosmic Sacrifice in the shape of the universe there are seven circumferences (viz., the ocean, the atmosphere with the motes, the region of the clouds along with the air thereof, the rain-water, the air above it, the Dhanañ-

* त्रिः—√तॄ प्लवनसंतरणयोः+ड्रि+डुच् ॥ उ० ५ । ६६ ॥ पा० ५।४।१८॥

† समिधः—सम्+√ञिइन्धी दीप्तौ+क्विप् ॥ पा० ३ । २ । १७८ ॥

‡ तन्वानाः—√तनु विस्तारे+शानच् ॥ पा० ३ । २ । १२४ ॥

jaya vāyu and the Sūtrātmā vāyu) and the sacrificial sticks to be burnt in it (in the shape of the ingredients of which it is made) are twenty-one (i. e., the primordial matter &c., the ten sense and motor organs, the five tanmātras, and the five mahābhūtas). The enlightened who perform the spiritual sacrifice of meditating on God the Creator of this universe, the All-seeing, bind Him, so to say, by contemplation.

भावार्थः—हे मनुष्या यूयमिममनेकविधकल्पितपरिध्यादिसामग्रीयुक्तं मानसं यज्ञं कृत्वा पूर्णमीश्वरं विज्ञाय सर्वाणि प्रयोजनानि साध्नुत ॥

Purport:—Oh men ! accomplish all your legitimate objects having arrived at a true knowledge of God by offering through contemplation the mental sacrifice described in this verse and constituted of the various circumferences and other parts.

(१००) यज्ञेन यज्ञमयजन्त देवास्तानि धर्माणि प्रथमान्यासन् । ते ह नाकं महिमानः सचन्त यत्र पूर्वे साध्याः सन्ति देवाः ॥१६॥

पदपाठः—यज्ञेन यज्ञम् अयजन्त देवाः तानि धर्माणि प्रथमानि आसन् ते ह नाकम् महिमानः सचन्त यत्र पूर्वे साध्याः सन्ति देवाः ॥

भाष्यम्=Explanation:—यज्ञेन०=ये देवा विद्वांसो यज्ञं यजनीयं पूजनीयं परमेश्वरं यज्ञेन तत्स्तुतिप्रार्थनोपासनरीत्या पूजनेन समेत्यायजन्त यजन्ते यक्ष्यन्ति च ॥

The enlightened have paid, do and will always pay homage to God the Worshipful, with praise, prayer and worship.

तानि धर्माणि०=तान्येव धर्माणि प्रथमानि† सर्वकर्मभ्य आदौ सर्वैर्मनुष्यैः कर्तव्यान्यासन् । न च तैः पूर्वं कृतैर्विना केनापि किंचित्कर्म कर्तव्यमिति ॥

All men ought to begin all actions with these and no one ought to do anything which is not preceded by them.

---

* धर्माणि—√धृञ् धारणे+मन् ॥ उ० १ । १४० ॥

† प्रथमानि—√प्रथ प्रख्याने+अमच् ॥ उ० १ । ६८ ॥

ते ह नाकम्०‡=त ईश्वरोपासका हेति प्रसिद्धं नाकं सर्वदुःखरहितं परमेश्वरं मोक्षं च महिमानः§ पूज्याः सन्तः सचन्त समवेता भवन्ति ॥

Verily do the worshippers of God, exalted in glory, attain to Him and emancipation in which there is no pain or suffering.

कीदृशं तत्। यत्र पूर्वे साध्याः०=साध्याः साधनवन्तः कृतसाधनाश्च देवाः विद्वांसः पूर्वे जातीता यत्र मोक्षाख्ये परमे पदे सुखिनः सन्ति। न तस्माद्ब्रह्मणः शतवर्षसंख्यातात्कालात्कदाचित्पुनरावर्तन्त इति किन्तु तमेव समसेवन्त ॥

The enlightened who qualified themselves in the past and those who are qualifying themselves now and those who will qualify themselves in the future, obtained and will obtain this highest state of bliss to be enjoyed for a hundred years of Brahma during which period there is no return to the cycle of births and deaths.

अत्राहुर्निरुक्तकारा यास्काचार्याः। यज्ञेन यज्ञमयजन्त देवा अग्निनाग्निमयजन्त देवा अग्निः पशुरासीत्तमालभन्त तेनायजन्तेति च ब्राह्मणम्। तानि धर्माणि प्रथमान्यासन्। ते ह नाकं महिमानः समसेवन्त यत्र पूर्वे साध्याः सन्ति देवाः साधना। द्युस्थानो देवगण इति नैरुक्ताः ॥ निरुक्त अ० १२। खं० ४१ ॥ अग्निना जीवेनान्तःकरणेन वाग्निं परमेश्वरमयजन्त। अग्निः पशुरासीत्तमेव देवा आलभन्त। सर्वोपकारकमग्निहोत्राद्यश्वमेधान्तं भौतिकाग्निनापि यज्ञं देवा समसेवन्तेति वा। साध्याः साधनवन्तो यत्र पूर्वे पूर्वं भूता मोक्षाख्यानन्दे पदे सन्ति। तमभिप्रेत्यात एव द्युस्थानो देवगण इति निरुक्तकारा वदन्ति। द्युस्थानः प्रकाशमयः परमेश्वरः स्थानं स्थित्यर्थं यस्य सः। यद्वा सूर्यप्राण¶ स्थानाः विज्ञानकिरणास्तत्रैव देवगणो देवसमूहो वर्तत इति ॥

On this verse Yaskacarya, the author of the Nirukta, observes: "The learned worshipped God with the soul and internal organs or they performed the universally beneficial yajñas (sacrifices) from the agnihotra up to the aśvamedha, with the help of the terrestrial fire. Those who adopted the prescribed means and qualified themselves in former times are enjoying the bliss of emancipation—the

‡ नाकम्—see p. 102. § महिमानः—√मह पूजायाम्+इमनिच् ॥ उ० ४। १४८=glorious, venerable. √मह+अति+इमनिच् ॥ उ० २। ८४ ॥ पा ५। १। १२२=glory. ¶ Breath inhailed through the right nostril is called 'Sūrya' while that inhailed through the left is termed 'Candra'. The phrase means "yogis who are adepts in the regulation of breathing."

highest state. The followers of the etymological school call this band of the learned (devas) the dwellers of the regions of light, i. e., God, who is self-effulgent or because the devas live in the rays of knowledge by perfect regulation of breath*.

अन्वयः—हे मनुष्या ये देवा यज्ञेन यज्ञमयजन्त तानि धर्माणि प्रथमान्यासंस्ते महिमानः सन्तो यत्र पूर्वे साध्या देवाः सन्ति तन्नाकं ह सचन्त तद्यूयमप्याप्नुत ॥

Translation:—Oh men! the enlightened have paid (do and will always pay) homage to God the worshipful with praise, prayer and worship, for, these are the most important duties which one should attend to before everything else. Those who thus worship God, exalted in glory attain to Him and emancipation in which there is no suffering, which highest state of bliss the learned who qualified themselves in the past obtained (and those who do so now and will do so in the future will obtain). You also should endeavour to attain it.

भावार्थः—मनुष्यैर्योगाभ्यासादिना सदा परमेश्वर उपासनीयः । अनेनानादिकालीनधर्मेण मुक्तिसुखं प्राप्य पूर्वविद्वद्वदानन्दितव्यम् ॥

Purport:—Men should always undergo yogic discipline or such other spiritual exercise and worship God. By the discharge of this duty prescribed from time immemorial one should obtain the bliss of emancipation and rejoice as the enlightened before them did.

(१०१) अद्भ्यः सम्भृतः पृथिव्यै रसाच्च विश्वकर्मणः समवर्तताग्रे । तस्य त्वष्टा विदधद्रूपमेति तन्मर्त्यस्य देवत्वमाजानमग्रे ॥१७॥

पदपाठः—अत्ऽभ्यः सम्ऽभृतः पृथिव्यै रसात् च विश्वऽकर्मणः सम् अवर्तत अग्रे तस्य त्वष्टा विऽदधत् रूपम् एति तत् मर्त्यस्य देवऽत्वम् आऽजानम् अग्रे ॥

* See p. 140.

भाष्यम्=**Explanation**:—अद्भ्यः संभृतः०—तेन पुरुषेण पृथिव्यै—पृथिव्युत्पत्त्यर्थमद्भ्यो रसः संभृतः । संगृह्य रसात्¶=तेन रसेन पृथिवी रचिता । एवमग्निरसेनाग्नेः सकाशादाप उत्पादिताः । अग्निश्च वायोः सकाशाद्वायुराकाशादुत्पादित आकाशः प्रकृतेः प्रकृतिः स्वसामर्थ्याच्च ॥

The Supreme Being, in order to form the earth made the attenuated matter (āpaḥ) solid and thus made the earth. Similarly He produced the attenuated matter from the igneous matter, the igneous from the gaseous and the gaseous from ether (ākāśa) and the etheric from the primordial (prakṛti) which He caused to evolve from His 'Sāmarthya'.

विश्वकर्मा*=विश्वं सर्वं कर्म क्रियमाणमस्य स विश्वकर्मा । तस्य परमेश्वरस्य सामर्थ्यमध्ये कारणाख्येऽग्रे† सृष्टेः प्राग्जगत्समवर्तत=वर्तमानमासीत् । तदानीं सर्वमिदं जगत्कारणभूतमेव नेदृशमिति ॥

The universe before the creation existed (potentially) in its cause called the Sāmarthya of God Who is called Viśvakarman—the Universal Architect because He is the Doer (par excellence) of all action. At that time the whole of this universe was in the causal state and not such (as it appears to us now).

तस्य सामर्थ्यस्यांशान्गृहीत्वा त्वष्टा‡=रचनकर्तेदं सकलं जगद्विदधत्=रचितवान् । पुनश्चेदं विश्वं रूपम्§=रूपवत्त्वमेति । तदेव मर्त्यस्य§=मरणधर्मकस्य विश्वस्य मनुष्यस्यापि च रूपवत्त्वं भवति ॥

The Tvaṣṭā—the Fashioner—made the universe with parts of that Sāmarthya. Then the whole universe assumed a perceptible form (rūpavat-tvam). Then also mortal man assumed a visible form (i. e., was created).

¶ रसात्—√रस आस्वादे+अच् ॥ पा० ३ । १ । १३४ ॥

* विश्वकर्मा—विश्वेषु कर्म यस्य—विश्व+√डुकृञ्+मनिन् ॥ उ० ४ । १४५ ॥ पा० २ । २ । २४ ॥

† अग्रे—√अगि गतौ+रन् ॥ उ० २ । २७ ॥ २८ ॥

‡ त्वष्टा—√त्वक्षू तनूकरणे+तृन् ॥ उ० २ । ९४ ॥ ९५ ॥ त्वष्टा तूर्णमश्नुत इति (√त्वर्+√अशूङ्+तृन्) नैरुक्ताः । त्विषेर्वा स्याद्दीप्तिकर्मणः (√त्विष्+तृन्) । त्वक्षतेर्वा स्यात्करोतिकर्मणः (√त्वक्ष्+तृन्) । इति निरुक्ते ८ । १३ ॥

§ रूपम्—√रु शब्दे+प ॥ उ० ३ । २३ ॥ २८ ॥

आजानमग्रे—वेदाज्ञापनसमये परमात्माज्ञप्तवान्वेदरूपामाज्ञां वत्तवान्मनुष्याय धर्मयुक्तेनैव सकामेन कर्मणा कर्मदेवत्वयुक्तं शरीरं धृत्वा विषयेन्द्रियसंयोगजन्यमिष्टं सुखं भवतु तथा निष्कामेन विज्ञानपरमं मोक्षाख्यं चेति ॥

At the time of revealing the Vedas, God promulgated this commandment for man through the Vedas themselves: "Thou shalt find the desired happiness arising from the contact of the objects with the senses by performing with thy action-body righteous works with attachment and thou shalt obtain the highest knowledge called emancipation by performing works without attachment".

अन्वयः—अग्रे तेन पुरुषेण पृथिव्या अद्भ्यो रसः सम्भृतस्तस्माद्रसाच्च पृथिवी रचिता । सर्वमिदं जगदग्रे विश्वकर्मणः सकाशात्स्वकारणरूपे सामर्थ्ये समवर्तत । तस्यैव त्वष्टेदं जगद्विद्धद्रूपमेति । तदेव मर्त्यस्य रूपमेति यं देवत्वमाजानं परमेश्वरः सृष्टवान् ॥

Translution:—In the beginning, for the making of the earth the attenuated matter was made solid by the Supreme Being and therefrom the earth fashioned; for the whole of this cosmos was, in the beginning, in its ultimate causal form, viz., the material Omnipotence of God which was with Him (under His control). The Almighty Fashioner fashioned of this the universe endowed with various forms. That itself under the hand of the Almighty Architect assumed the form of mortal man whom He made endowed with such potencies as would raise him to the highest position of the enlightened among men (if he followed His Vedic Law).

भावार्थः—हे मनुष्या योऽखिलकार्यकर्ता परमात्मा कारणात्कार्याणि निर्मिमीते सकलस्य जगतः शरीराणां रूपाणि विदधाति तज्ज्ञानं तदाज्ञापालनमेव देवत्वमस्तीति जानीत ॥

Purport:—Oh men ! know ye that wisdom consists in knowing and obeying the commandments of that Almighty God Who has the power to do everything, Who is the Promulgator of the law of causation and gives their shape to the world and all embodied beings.

मर्त्यस्य—√मृङ् प्राणत्यागे + तन् + यत् ॥ उ० ३ । ८६ ॥ पा० ५ । १ । ५ ॥

(१०२) वेदाहमेतं पुरुषं महान्तमादित्यवर्णं तमसः परस्तात् । तमेव विदित्वाऽतिमृत्युमेति नान्यः पन्था विद्यतेऽयनाय ॥१८॥

पदपाठः—वेद अहम् एतम् पुरुषम् महान्तम् आदित्यऽवर्णम् तमसः परस्तात् तम् एव विदित्वा अति मृत्युम् एति न अन्यः पन्थाः विद्यते अयनाय ॥

भाष्यम् = **Explanation**:—किं विदित्वा त्वं ज्ञानी भवसीति पृच्छ्यते । तदुत्तरमाह । यतः पूर्वोक्तलक्षणविशिष्टं सर्वेभ्यो महान्तं* । वृद्धतममादित्यवर्णं† स्वप्रकाशविज्ञानस्वरूपं तमसो‡ऽज्ञानाऽविद्यान्धकारात्परस्तात्पृथग्वर्तमानं परमेश्वरं पुरुषमहं वेद जानाम्यतोऽहं ज्ञान्यस्मीति निश्चयः ॥

This verse is an answer to the question 'By knowing what canst thou become wise ?' The answer is:—'I am certainly wise because I know the Puruṣa', the Supreme Lord Whose attributes have been described above, Who is the greatest of all, the Oldest, Self-effulgent, above and beyond the darkness of ignorance and nescience.'

नैव तमविदित्वा कश्चिज्ज्ञानी भवितुमर्हतीति । कुतः । तमेव विदित्वेत्यादि । मनुष्यस्तमेव पुरुषं परमात्मानं विदित्वाऽतिमृत्युं मृत्युमतिक्रान्तं

---

* महान्तम्—√मह पूजायाम्+अति ॥ उ० २ । ८४ ॥ तम् ॥

† आदित्यवर्णम्—स्वप्रकाशदानेन आदित्यं वृणोति प्रकाशयति अथवा स्वप्रकाशेन आदित्यं वारयति दूरीकरोति यद्वा स्वभक्तहृदयप्रकाशने आदित्यम् सूर्यमपि अतिशेते इति आदित्य +√वृञ्+न ॥ उ० ३ । ६ । १० ॥

‡ तमसः—तमस्तनोतेरिति श्री यास्काः ॥ २ । १६ ॥ √तनु विस्तारे+असुन् ॥ उ० ४ । १८६ ॥ खदार्थकात्तनिर् धातोरौणादिक असुन्प्रत्यय इति **क्षेमकरणदासकृत अथर्ववेदभाष्ये** अ० १ । २१ । २ ॥ तम् 4. P. 1. To choke, be suffocated.—2. To be exhausted or fatigued.—3 To be distressed (in body or mind), be uneasy or pained, pine, waste away.—4. To stop, become immovable.—5. To wish, desire इति प्रो० **आप्टेकृत संस्कृताङ्ग्लकोशे** । कांक्षायां √तमुधातोरौणादिकेनासुन् प्रत्ययेन **माधवीयधातुवृत्तौ** साधितः ॥

मृत्योः पृथग्भूतं मोक्षाख्यमानन्दमेति प्राप्नोति नैवातोऽन्यथेति ॥

No one can become wise without knowing Him because, by knowing the 'Puruṣa' the Supreme Lord alone, can a man cross death and attain to that state of the highest bliss (emancipation) which is beyond death. There is no other means of reaching that state.

एवकारात्तमीश्वरं विहाय नैव कस्यचिदन्यस्य लेशमात्राप्युपासना केनचित्कदाचित्कार्येति गम्यते । कथमिदं विज्ञायतेऽन्यस्योपासना नैव कार्येति ॥

The use of the word 'only' (eva) in the text shows that no one should ever offer the slightest worship to any one except God (as the Deity). That this in fact is the meaning is also apparent from the following words.

नान्यः पन्था* विद्यतेऽयनायेति† वचनात् । अयनाय व्यावहारिकपारमार्थिकसुखायाऽन्यो द्वितीयः पन्था मार्गो न विद्यते । किन्तु तस्यैवोपासनमेव सुखस्य मार्गोऽतो भिन्नस्येश्वरगणनोपासनाभ्यां मनुष्यस्य दुःखमेव भवतीति निश्चयः । अतः कारणादेव एव पुरुषः सर्वैरुपासनीय इति सिद्धान्तः ॥

'There is no other way for reaching the goal.' There is no other way of obtaining happiness either in the affairs of this world or those concerning the other world. The only road to happiness is the worship of God alone. There can be no doubt that by believing and worshipping another as God man comes to grief. The settled conclusion, therefore, is that the 'Puruṣa' alone is the (legitimate) object of worship for all men.

अन्वयः—अहमेतं महान्तमादित्यवर्णं तमसः परस्ताद्वर्तमानं पुरुषं वेद । तमेव विदित्वा मनुष्योऽतिमृत्युमेति । अयनायान्यः पन्था न विद्यते ॥

Translation:—I know this Supreme Being, the Greatest of all, the Self-effulgent Sun that dispels the darkness of ignorance that mars man's mind and is Himself ever beyond it. Man can reach his goal,

---

* पन्थाः—√पत गतौ+थ+इनि ॥ उ० ४ । ६ । १२ ॥ √पथे गतावित्यस्माद्धातोः पचाद्यचि (पा० ३ । १ । १३४ ॥) कृते पथः पथौ पथाः । इत्यदन्तोऽपि दृश्यत इति श्री महर्षि दयानन्दाः स्वकृतोणादिवृत्तौ ॥

† अयनाय—गमनाय—√अय गतौ+ल्युट् ॥ पा० ३ । ३ । ११५ ॥

emancipation, only by knowing and worshipping Him alone and there is no other way of achieving this.

भावार्थः—यदि मनुष्या ऐहिकपारमार्थिकसुखे इच्छेयुस्तर्हि सर्वेभ्यो बृहत्तमं स्वप्रकाशानन्दस्वरूपमज्ञानलेशाद्दूरे वर्तमानं परमात्मानं ज्ञात्वैव मरणाद्यगाधदुःखसागरात्पृथग्भवितुं शक्नुवन्त्ययमेव सुखप्रदो मार्गोऽस्ति। अस्मादन्यः कश्चिदपि मनुष्याणां मुक्तिमार्गो न भवति ॥

Purport:—If men wish to attain happiness in this world and the next, then (let it be known that) they can escape the unfathomable ocean of suffering and death only by knowing the Supreme Being Who is the Greatest of all, Whose essence is light and bliss and in Whom there can not be an iota of ignorance. This is the only way which can confer happiness on mankind. There is no other means by which man can secure emancipation.

(१०३) प्रजापतिश्चरति गर्भे अन्तरजायमानो बहुधा विजायते। तस्य योनिं परिपश्यन्ति धीरास्तस्मिन्ह तस्थुर्भुवनानि विश्वा ॥१९॥

पदपाठः—प्रजाऽपतिः चरति गर्भे अन्तः अजायमानः बहुधा वि जायते तस्य योनिम् परि पश्यन्ति धीराः तस्मिन् ह तस्थुः भुवनानि विश्वा ॥

भाष्यम्=**Explanation**:—प्रजापतिरिति*—स एव प्रजापतिः सर्वस्य स्वामी जीवस्यान्यस्य च जडस्य जगतोऽन्तर्गर्भे† मध्येऽन्तर्यामिरूपेणाजायमानो‡ऽनुत्पन्नोऽजः सन्नित्यं चरति। तत्सामर्थ्यादेवेदं सकलं जगद्बहुधा§ बहुप्रकारं विजायते विशिष्टतयोत्पद्यते ॥

* प्रजापतिः—प्रजानां पाता वा पालयिता वेति श्री यास्कमहर्षयः ॥ नि० १०।४२ ॥ पा० २।२।८ ॥ प्रजा—प्रकर्षेण जाता इति ॥ प्र+√जनी प्रादुर्भावे+ड ॥ पा० ३।२।६६ ॥ पतिः √पा पालने+डति ॥ उ० ४।५७ ॥

† गर्भे—मध्ये—√गॄ शब्दे+भन् ॥ उ० ३।१५२ ॥

‡ अजायमानः—नञ्+√जनी प्रादुर्भावे+मुक्+शानच् ॥ पा० ७।२।८२ ॥ ३।२।१२४ ॥ २।२।६ ॥ ६।३।७३ ॥

§ बहुधा—बहु+धा ॥ पा० १।२।३१ ॥ ५।३।४२ ॥

The Lord of creatures, the Ruler of all the animate and inanimate world, resides within it as its Indwelling Ruler. He is unborn and increate. By His might alone the whole world is decked out with variegated objects.

तस्य योनिं§—तस्य परब्रह्मणो योनिं सत्यधर्मानुष्ठानं वेदविज्ञानमेव प्राप्तिकारणं धीरा|| ध्यानवन्तः परिपश्यन्ति परितः सर्वतः प्रेक्षन्ते ॥

Those who can concentrate their mind upon Him obtain a perfect vision of His nature, i. e., they know that the way to realise Him is the performance of righteous acts and the acquisition of Vedic knowledge.

तस्मिन्ह तस्थुरित्यादि--यस्मिन्भुवनानि* विश्वानि† सर्वाणि सर्वे लोकास्तस्थुः स्थितिं चक्रिरे । हेति निश्चयार्थे । तस्मिन्नेव परमे पुरुषे धीरा ज्ञानिनो मनुष्या मोक्षानन्दं प्राप्य तस्थुः स्थिरा भवन्तीत्यर्थः ॥

In Him all the worlds find their support. 'Ha' is used here in the sense of certainty. Verily in Him—the Supreme Lord—do the constant and the wise rest satisfied and secure, by obtaining the bliss of emancipation.

अन्वयः—स एव प्रजापतिरजायमानो जीवस्यान्यस्य च जडस्य जगतोऽन्तर्गर्भे सन्नित्यं चरति । तत्सामर्थ्यविशेषैः सकलं जगद्बहुधा विजायते । तस्य योनिं धीराः परिपश्यन्ति । तस्मिन्ह विश्वा भुवनानि तस्थुः ॥

Translation:—That very Lord of creatures Who is Unborn, being Immanent everywhere in the animate as well as inanimate universe, ever moves in it (by His Providence). It is from His 'Material Omnipotence' (Samarthya) that the whole cosmos of motley forms

---

§ योनिम्—प्राप्तिकारणम्—√यु मिश्रणामिश्रणयोः+नि ॥ उ० ४ । ४८ ॥ ५१ ॥

|| धीराः—ध्यानवन्तः—√डुधाञ् धारणपोषणयोः+क्रन् ॥ उ० २ । २४ ॥ पा० ६ । ४ । ६६ ॥ अथवा √ध्यै चिन्तने+क्विप्+र ॥ पा० ३ । २ । १७८ ॥ पा० ध्यायतेः सम्प्रसारणं च ॥ पा० ५ । २ । ६४ ॥ अथवा धियमीरयतीति—धी+√ईर प्रेरणे+अण् ॥ पा० ३ । २ । १ ॥ २ । २ । १९ ॥ अथवा धियम्राति—धी+√रा दाने+क ॥ पा० ३ । २ । ३ ॥ २ । २ । १९ ॥

* भुवनानि—लोकाः—भवन्ति भूतान्यस्मिन्निति—√भू सत्तायाम्+क्युन् ॥ उ० २ । ८० ॥

† विश्वा—√विश प्रवेशने+क्वन् ॥ उ० १ । १५१ ॥ पा० ६ । १ । ७० ॥

comes into being. Those who are given to meditation see Him in His True Nature. In Him do all the worlds find their stay.

भावार्थः—योऽयं सर्वरक्षक ईश्वरः स्वयमनुत्पन्नः सन्स्वसामर्थ्याज्जगदुत्पाद्य तत्रान्तःप्रविश्य सर्वत्र विचरति यमनेकप्रकारेण प्रसिद्धं विद्वांस एव जानन्ति तं जगदधिकरणं सर्वव्यापकं परमात्मानं विज्ञाय मनुष्यैरानन्दितव्यम् ॥

Purport:—Men should rejoice by knowing that Supreme Being, the All-pervading Refuge of the whole world, the Saviour and Ruler of all, and Who, Himself Unborn, creates the universe out of His 'Omnipotence' (Sāmarthya) and entering into it (by His Divine Immanence) moves all through it and Whom, well-known as He is in several ways, only the enlightened know.

(१०४) यो देवेभ्य॑ आतपति यो देवानां पुरोहितः।
पूर्वो यो देवेभ्यो जातो नमो रुचाय ब्राह्मये ॥२०॥

पदपाठः—यः देवेभ्यः आऽतपति यः देवानाम् पुरःऽहितः पूर्वः यः देवेभ्यः जातः नमः रुचाय ब्राह्मये ॥

भाष्यम्=**Explanation**:—यो देवेभ्य* इति—यः पूर्णः पुरुषो देवेभ्यो विद्वद्भ्यस्तत्प्रकाशार्थमातपति आसमन्तात्तदन्तःकरणे प्रकाशयति नान्येभ्यश्च । यश्च देवानां विदुषां पुरोहितः† सर्वैः सुखैः सह मोक्षे विदुषो दधाति ॥

The All-pervading, the Perfect 'Puruṣa' sheds His lustre into the inner sense of the learned, but not into that of any one else, in order to illumine them. He is the Chief Priest and the Benefactor of the enlightened because He bestows on them the bliss of emancipation which contains all happiness.

पूर्वो‡ यो देवेभ्य जात इति—देवेभ्यो विद्वद्भ्यो यः पूर्वः पूर्वमेव सनातनत्वेन वर्तमानः सञ्जातः प्रसिद्धोऽस्ति ॥

---

* देवेभ्यः—see p. 5.

† पुरोहितः—see p. 5.

‡ पूर्वः—see p. 11.

He has been in existence from before the birth of the enlightened because He is Eternal.

नमो रुचायेति*—तस्मै रुचाय रुचिकराय ब्रह्मणे नमोऽस्तु । यश्च देवेभ्यो विद्वद्भ्यो ब्रह्मोपदेशं प्राप्य ब्रह्मरुचिर्ब्राह्मि•ब्रह्मणोऽपत्यमिव वर्तमानोऽस्ति । तस्मा अपि ब्रह्मनिष्ठकाय नमोऽस्तु ॥

Our salutations are due to the Lovable Brahma—the Supreme Being and also to His servants who, having acquired His knowledge from the learned, love Him with the love of a child for its parents

अन्वयः—यः पूर्णः पुरुषो देवेभ्य आतपति यो देवानां पुरोहितोऽस्ति यो देवेभ्य पूर्वो वर्तमानः सञ्जातस्तस्मै रुचाय ब्रह्मणे नमः । तदपत्यमिव वर्तमानाय तस्य भक्ताय ब्राह्मयेऽपि नमोऽस्तु ॥

Translation:—That Perfect Being sheds lustre into the hearts of the enlightened whom He leads to the bliss of emancipation and Who is known to have existed before them. May our obeisance be to that Supreme Being ! Salute also to that devotee of His who is like His son (owing to his religious life and submission to His commandments).

भावार्थः—हे मनुष्या यो जगदीश्वरः सर्वेषां विदुषां मनांसि स्वप्रकाशेन सूर्यवत्प्रकाशयति यः स्वभक्तान्पुत्रवत्पालयति च तस्यैवोपासना युष्माभिर्विधातव्या नान्यस्य तस्य सेवकाश्चादरणीया इति जानीत ॥

Purport:—Oh men ! know ye that you should adore none but that Lord of the universe, Who by His lustre like the sun illumines the mind of all the learned and who protects His devotees like His children, and that His servants should be respected by you.

(१०५) रुचं ब्राह्मं जनयन्तो देवा अग्रे तदब्रुवन् ।
यस्त्वैवं ब्राह्मणो विद्यात्तस्य देवा असन्वशे ॥२१॥

पदपाठः—रुचम् ब्राह्मम् जनयन्तः देवाः अग्रे तत् अब्रुवन् यः त्वा एवम् ब्राह्मणः विद्यात् तस्य देवाः असन् वशे ॥

---

* रुचाय—अभिप्रीताय—√रुच दीप्तावभिप्रीत्योः + क ॥ पा० ३ । १ । १३५ ॥

• ब्राह्मये—परमात्मनः पुत्रवद्वर्तमानाय सत्पुरुषाय । ब्रह्मन्+इञ् टिलोपः ॥ पा० ४ । १ । ९२ ॥

भाष्यम्=**Explanation**:—रुचं ब्राह्म*मिति—रुचं प्रीतिकरं ब्राह्मं ब्रह्मणोऽपत्यमिव ब्रह्मणः सकाशाज्जातं ज्ञानं जनयन्तो† उत्पादयन्तो देवा विद्वांसोऽन्येषामग्रे तज्ज्ञानं तज्ज्ञानसाधनं वाऽब्रुवन्ब्रुवन्तूपदिशन्तु च ॥

May the learned, who acquire this most lovable divine knowledge which is born of God and hence is called His child, teach it and the means of acquiring it, to others.

यस्त्वैवमिति—यस्त्वैवममुना प्रकारेण तद्ब्रह्म ब्राह्मणो‡ विद्यात्तु पश्चात्तस्यैव ब्रह्मविदो ब्राह्मणस्य देवा इन्द्रियाणि वशे§ऽसन्भवन्ति नान्यस्येति ॥

He, who acquires the knowledge of Brahma in this way, is called a Brahmaṇa. The senses come under the control of the Brahmaṇa who knows Brahma but never under the control of one who does not know Him.

अन्वयः—रुचं ब्राह्मं जनयन्तो देवा अन्येषामग्रे तद्ब्रुवन्। यो ब्राह्मणस्त्वैवं तद्ब्रह्म विद्यात्तस्य देवा वशे असन् ॥

Translation:—The enlightened, who acquire this lovable divine knowledge born of God, should teach it to others. He who acquires the knowledge of God thus, is called a Brahmaṇa and the senses of such a one come under his control.

भावार्थः—इदमेवाद्यं विद्वत्कृत्यमस्ति यद्वेदेश्वरधर्मादिषु रुचिसत्योपदेशाध्ययनाध्यापनधार्मिकत्वजितेन्द्रियत्वशरीरात्मबलवर्धनमेवं कृते सति सर्वे दिव्या गुणा भोगाश्च प्राप्तुं शक्याः ॥

Purport:—This is the first duty of the learned that they should inculcate in the minds of others a love for the Vedas, God and rectitude of life, propagation of truth, learning, teaching, uprightness, control of the senses and development of corporeal and spiritual vigour. This done, all superhuman virtues and bliss can be enjoyed.

---

* ब्राह्मम्—ब्रह्मसम्बन्धिनम्—ब्रह्मन्+अण् ॥ पा० ४ । २ । २४ ॥

† जनयन्तः—√जनी प्रादुर्भावे+णिच्+शतृ ॥ पा० ३ । १ । २६ ॥ २ । १२४ ॥

‡ ब्राह्मणः—ब्रह्म वेदं परमेश्वरं वा जानातीति ब्रह्मन्+अण् ॥ पा० ४ । २ । ५९ ॥

§ वशे—प्रभुत्वे—√वश कान्तौ+अप् ॥ वा० वशिरण्योरुपसंख्यानम् ॥

(१०६) श्रीश्च ते लक्ष्मीश्च पत्न्यावहोरात्रे पार्श्वे नक्षत्राणि रूपमश्विनौ व्यात्तम् । इष्णन्निषाणामुं म इषाण सर्वलोकं म इषाण ॥२२॥

पदपाठः—श्रीः च ते लक्ष्मीः च पत्न्यौ अहोरात्रे पार्श्वे नक्षत्राणि रूपम् अश्विनौ वि॰आत्तम् इष्णन् इषाण अमुम् मे इषाण सर्वऽलोकम् मे इषाण ॥

भाष्यम्=Explanation:—श्रीः (√श्रिञ् सेवायाम्+क्विप् U. II, 57)=सकला शोभा=all the glory or splendour. च=and. ते=तव=Thine. लक्ष्मीः (√लक्ष आलोचने+ई U. III, 160)=सर्वमैश्वर्यम्=all power. पत्न्यौ (√पा रक्षणे+डति+नुक्+ङीप् U. IV, 57; P. IV, 1, 32 and 1, 5)=स्त्रीवद्वर्तमाने=being like the wife, i, e., protecting and sustaining the universe. अहोरात्रे (अहश्च रात्रिश्चेति P. II, 2, 29 and V, 4, 87)=day and night. पार्श्वे (√स्पृश संस्पर्शने+श्वण् U. V, 27)=like the two sides. नक्षत्राणि (√णक्ष गतौ+अत्रन् U. III, 105; न विद्यते क्षत्रम् स्वतेजो येषाम् तानीति नञ्+क्षत्र, Vartika नञोऽस्त्यर्थानां वाच्यो वा चोत्तरपदलोपः and P. VI, 3, 75 also Nir. III, 20*)=the constellations, stars. रूपम् (√रु शब्दे+प U. III, 27)=like the form or countenance. अश्विनौ=सूर्याचन्द्रमसौ=the sun and the moon. व्यात्तम्=विकासितं मुखमिव। अत्र वि, आङ् पूर्वाद्डुदाञ् धातोः क्तः (P. III, 2, 102 and VII, 4, 47)=opened wide like the mouth. इष्णन् (√ईष आभीक्ष्ण्ये+शतृ P. III, 2, 124)=इच्छन्=wishing. इषाण=(imperative 2nd pers. sing.)=कामय=desire thou. अमुम्=इतः परं परोक्षं सुखम्=the unseen bliss hereafter. मे=मह्यम्=for me. इषाण=प्रापय=lead to, grant to attain. सर्वलोकम् (सर्व+√लोकृ दर्शने+घञ् P. III, 3, 19)=सर्वेषां दर्शनम्=sight, view, attainment,

अन्वयः—हे जगदीश्वर यस्य ते श्रीश्च लक्ष्मीश्च पत्न्यावहोरात्रे पार्श्वे यस्य ते सृष्टावश्विनौ व्यात्तं मुखमिव नक्षत्राणि रूपं सन्ति स त्वं मेऽमुमिष्णन्निषाण मे सर्वलोकमिषाण ॥

* नक्षत्राणि नक्षतेर्गतिकर्मणः । नेमानि क्षत्राणीति च ब्राह्मणम् ॥ नि॰ ३ । २० ॥

Translation:—Oh Almighty God, Lord of the world ! the whole splendour and all the power (and pelf) of the entire universe (visible and invisible) are completely submissive to Thy Divine Majesty like an obedient wife unto her husband. The day and night are like the front and back of Thy infinite body in the shape of the universe. The sun at daytime and the moon at night (during the bright half of the month) are like the open (unveiled) mouth (face) of that body of Thine. When there is no moon at night (during the dark half of the month) the constellations display the wonderful beauty of Thy body. Oh Lord Who commandest such power and glory, may it be Thy will to bless me with final beatitude (hereafter) and all true happiness (here).

भावार्थः—हे राजादयो मनुष्या यथेश्वरस्य न्यायादयो गुणा व्याप्तिः कृपा पुरुषार्थः सत्यं रचनं सत्या नियमाश्च सन्ति तथैव युष्माकमपि सन्तु यतो युष्माकमुत्तरोत्तरं सुखं वर्द्धेतेति ॥

Purport:—Oh ye who rule over and lead others and ye who are ruled and led ! May you all be blest with good and great virtues like unto God Almighty Whose attributes, as justice &c., are perfect, Who is all-pervading, gracious, ever active, Whose disposal (of the cosmos) is truthful (=everlasting) and Whose dispensations (=laws) are perfect.

This is the commentary on the Puruṣa-sūkta by the Maharṣi Dayānanda Sarasvatī. How reasonable it is, can be seen from the following extract from the Muṇḍakopaniṣad. As for its scholarly handling of Vedic matter the innumerable quotations given in it are enough to convince any fair-minded person:—

तदेतत्सत्यं यथा सुदीप्तात्पावकाद्विस्फुलिङ्गाः सहस्रशः प्रभवन्ते सरूपाः । तथाक्षरा*त्पुरूपाः† सोम्य भावाः प्रजायन्ते तत्रैवापियन्ति ॥१॥

दिव्यो ह्यमूर्तः पुरुषः स बाह्याभ्यन्तरो ह्यजः । अप्राणो ह्यमनाः शुभ्रो ह्यक्षरात्परतः परः ॥२॥

एतस्माज्जायते प्राणो मनः सर्वेन्द्रियाणि च । खं वायुर्ज्योतिरापः पृथिवी विश्वस्य धारिणी ॥३॥

---

* अक्षरात्=प्रकृतेः=from the Primordial Matter.

† पुरुषाः=शरीरिणः=embodied beings and not souls.

अग्निर्मूर्धा चक्षुषी चन्द्रसूर्यौ दिशः श्रोत्रे वाग्विवृताश्च वेदाः । वायुः प्राणो हृदयं विश्वमस्य पद्भ्यां पृथिवी ह्येष सर्वभूतान्तरात्मा ॥४॥

तस्मादग्निः समिधो यस्य सूर्यः सोमात्पर्जन्य ओषधयः पृथिव्याम् । पुमान्रेतः सिञ्चति योषितायां बह्वीः प्रजाः पुरुषात्सम्प्रसूताः ॥५॥

तस्मादृचः साम यजूंषि दीक्षा यज्ञाश्च सर्वे क्रतवो दक्षिणाश्च । संवत्सरं च यजमानश्च लोकाः सोमो यत्र पवते यत्र सूर्यः ॥६॥

तस्माच्च देवा बहुधा सम्प्रसूताः साध्या मनुष्याः पशवो वयांसि । प्राणापानौ व्रीहियवौ तपश्च श्रद्धा सत्यं ब्रह्मचर्यं विधिश्च ॥७॥

सप्त प्राणाः प्रभवन्ति तस्मात्सप्तार्चिषः समिधः सप्त होमाः । सप्त इमे लोका येषु चरन्ति प्राणा गुहाशया निहिताः सप्त सप्त ॥८॥

अतः समुद्रा गिरयश्च सर्वेऽस्मात्स्यन्दन्ते सिन्धवः सर्वरूपाः । अतश्च सर्वा ओषधयो रसश्च येनैष भूतैस्तिष्ठते ह्यन्तरात्मा ॥९॥

पुरुष एवेदं विश्वं कर्म तपो ब्रह्म परामृतम् । एतद्यो वेद निहितं गुहायां सोऽविद्याग्रन्थिं विकिरतीह सोम ॥१०॥

मुण्डकोपनिषदि २ । १ ॥

Chapter IX.

The External Form and Content of the Vedas.

Sāmavēda II, 21, 7.

(१०७) ओ३म् ॥ नमः सखिभ्यः पूर्वसद्भ्यो नमः साकंनिषेभ्यः । युञ्जे वाचꣳ शतपदीम् ॥१॥

पदपाठः—नमः । सऽखिभ्यः । पूर्वऽसद्भ्यः । नमः । साकम्ऽनिषेभ्यः । युञ्जे । वाचम् । शतऽपदीम् ॥

अन्वयः—पूर्वसद्भ्यः सखिभ्यः नमः, साकंनिषेभ्यः सखिभ्यः नमः । अहम् शतपदीम् वाचम् युञ्जे ॥

Word-meaning &c:—सखिभ्यः=to friends पूर्वसद्भ्यः (पूर्वम् पूर्वस्मिन् दिशायां वा सीदतीति पूर्व+√षद्लृ+क्विप् P. III, 2, 61) =that have been already seated; those who are sitting towards the east or in the front. साकंनिषेभ्यः (साकं+नि+√षद्लृ+ड P. III, 4, 96)=that are sitting in company with. युञ्जे=I use. वाचम्=speech; the Vedic speech. शतपदीम् (शतं पादाः यस्याः सा शत+√पद+क्विप्+ङीप् P. IV, 1, 8,=of hundred feet; rich in vocabulary and metres.

Translation:—(The person who has just arrived at the assembly says:—) Salute to those friends that have already been sitting at the assembly and salute also to those that are sitting with me. (With your permission) I sing the (splendid) Vedic poetry that is rich in vocabulary and metres.

Comment:—This is the opening of a Vedic Assembly held according to the principles laid down in the famous Samjñana sūkta, Ṛgvēda X, 71. This stanza describes the external form of the Vedas. The Vedic style is essentially poetical, rich in vocabulory and metres, and full of figures of speech.

(१०८) युञ्जे वाचँ शतपदीं गाये सहस्रवर्तनि ।
गायत्रं त्रैष्टुभं जगत् ॥२॥

पदपाठः—युञ्जे । वाचम् । शतऽपदीम् । गाये । सहस्रऽवर्तनि ।
गायऽत्रम् । त्रैऽस्तुभम् । जगत् ॥

अन्वयः—अहम् शतपदीम् वाचम् युञ्जे, सहस्रवर्तनि गायत्रम्, त्रैष्टुभम्, जगत् च गाये ॥

Word-meaning &c :—गाये=I sing. सहस्रवर्तनि (सहस्रेषु वर्तनिषु सहस्र+√वृतु+अनि U. II, 106)=in a thousand ways. गायत्रम् (√गै+युक्+अत्रन् U. III, 105 and P. VII, 3, 33; गायत्रं गायतेः स्तुतिकर्मणः । निरुक्ते १ । ८ ॥ or √गै+शतृ+√त्रै पालने+क P. III, 2, 3)=the metre called gayatrī; God the Protector of His devotee. त्रैष्टुभम् (त्रि+√ष्टुभ निरोधे+क्विप्+अण् P. III, 2, 177 and V, 4, 38)=the triṣṭubh metre. जगत् (√गम्लृ+अति U. II, 84)=the jagatī metre.

Translation:—I use charming Vedic poetry rich in phraseology singing it in a thousand ways, as it is adorned in innumerable metres like the gayatrī, the triṣṭubh, the jagatī &c.

Comment:—The expression 'śatapadīm' is explained in this verse. The external form of Vedic poetry is clearly described here by the words 'sahasravartani', 'gayatram', 'traiṣṭubhaṃ' and 'jagat'. The Vedic psalms or hymns—whatever they may be called—can be sung in various ways. At the head of most of the chapters in this book the metre as well as the key has been mentioned. The names of the three metres in the stanza include by implication all the other metres as well.

"The gāyatrī usually consists of twenty-four syllables, variously arranged, but generally as a triplet of three Padas (=feet or quarters) of eight syllables each, or in one line of sixteen syllables and a second line of eight. There are eleven varieties of this metre, and the number of syllables in the stanza varies accordingly from nineteen to thirtythree syllables. The jagatī consists of fortyeight syllables arranged in four Pādas of twelve syllables each, two Pādas forming a line or hemistich. The Triṣṭubh consists of four Pādas of eleven syllables each."*

(१०९) गायत्रं त्रैष्टुभं जगद्विश्वा रूपाणि संभृता ।
देवा ओकाꣳसि चक्रिरे ॥३॥

पदपाठः—गायत्रम् । त्रैऽस्तुभम् । जगत् । विश्वा । रूपाणि ।
सम्ऽभृता । देवाः । ओकांसि चक्रिरे ॥

अन्वयः विश्वा रूपाणि संभृता गायत्रं त्रैष्टुभं जगत् देवाः ओकांसि चक्रिरे ॥

Word-meaning &c.:—विश्वा=all. रूपाणि=forms. संभृता =assuming; putting on. देवाः=all beneficial objects. ओकांसि=(√अव+कक् U. III, 41 or कु U. IV, 216)=abodes. चक्रिरे=have made. देवा ओकांसि चक्रिरे=in which all beneficial objects and laws are clearly and infallibly described.

Translation:—This poetry of the Holy Vedas dressed in its innumerable forms of the gāyatrī, triṣṭubh, jagatī and other metres, contains a clear and faultless account of all objects and laws beneficial to humanity.

* Griffith in his Translation of the Ṛgvēda.

Comment:—In this stanza the inner content or subject matter of the Vedas is mentioned. They are the refuge or abode (ओकस्), so to say, of all beneficent things. At the time of the dissolution of the world, the norm or standard of the being and essential features of all created things subsists only in the Vedas—Divine Knowledge—the Knowledge of God. It is in the Mind of the Supreme Being that the form, nature and differentia of each created object has its true specimen, and when the period of the great dissolution (महाप्रलय) is over, this Divine Knowledge serves as a guide for material creation. R. V. I, 164, 39 states the same fact but with greater force as follows: "All Vedic statements (ऋचः) have their denotation in the Most High (परमे), Imperishable (अक्षरे), Omnipresent God (व्योमन्), in Whom (यस्मिन्) all beneficent beings and objects (विश्वे देवाः) have their refuge (अधि निषेदुः). What profit (किम्) can that man derive (करिष्यति) from the Vedas (ऋचा) who (यः) does not realise (न वेद) the Supreme Being (तत्) [but blindly studies the Sacred Text] ? [But on the other hand] all these beneficent agents (ते इमे) fully resort (समासते) only (इत्) to them who (ये) realise (विदुः) that Supreme Being (तत्) [in their Vedic studies]."*

Manu also says that "it is from the Vedic Law itself that the Supreme Being in the beginning, severally fashioned different institutions assigning different names and walks in life to different beings."†

---

* ऋचो अक्षरे परमे व्योमन्यस्मिन्देवा अधि विश्वे निषेदुः । यस्तन्न वेद किमृचा करिष्यति य इत्तद्विदुस्त इमे समासते ॥ ऋ० १ । १६४ । ३९ ॥

† सर्वेषां तु स नामानि कर्माणि च पृथक् पृथक् । वेदशब्देभ्य एवादौ पृथक्संस्थाश्च निर्ममे ॥ म० १ । २१ ॥

Similarly in the Vedanta Sūtra I, 3, 28 we have the following aphorism शब्द इति चेन्नातः प्रभवात्प्रत्यक्षानुमानाभ्याम् on which Śaṃkarācarya remarks:—अतः प्रभवात् ।

अत एव हि वैदिकाच्छब्दाद्देवादिकं जगत्प्रभवति। ननु 'जन्माद्यस्य यतः' (१।१।२) इत्यत्र ब्रह्मप्रभवत्वं जगतोऽवधारितं कथमिह शब्दप्रभवत्वमुच्यते। अपि च यदि नाम वैदिकाच्छब्दादस्य प्रभवोऽभ्युपगतः कथमेतावता विरोधः शब्दे परिहृतो यावता वसवो रुद्रा आदित्या विश्वेदेवा मरुत इत्येतेऽर्थाः अनित्या एवोत्पत्तिमत्त्वात्। तदनित्यत्वे च तद्वाचिनां वैदिकानां वस्वादिशब्दानामनित्यत्वं केन निवार्यते। प्रसिद्धं हि लोके देवदत्तस्य पुत्र उत्पन्ने यज्ञदत्त इति तस्य नाम क्रियत इति। तस्माद्विरोध एव शब्द इति चेत्। न। गवादिशब्दार्थसम्बन्धनित्यत्वदर्शनात्। नहि गवादिव्यक्तीनामुत्पत्तिमत्त्वे तदाकृतीनामप्युत्पत्तिमत्त्वं स्यात्। द्रव्यगुणकर्मणां हि व्यक्तय एवोत्पद्यन्ते नाकृतयः। आकृतिभिश्च शब्दानां सम्बन्धो न व्यक्तिभिः।

× × × × ×

स्थिते वाचकात्मना नित्ये शब्दे नित्यार्थसम्बन्धिनि शब्दव्यवहारयोग्यार्थव्यक्तिनिष्पत्तिरतः प्रभव इत्युच्यते ॥ ब्रह्मसूत्रशांकरभाष्य Nirṇaya Sagara edition p. 122, 123.

Chapter X.

Glorification of God and Prayer for Prosperity.

Sāmaveda II, 397-406.

Seer:—Hiraṇyastūpa.

Subject:—Glorification of and supplication for prosperity to, God the Most Holy, Generator of all.

Metre:—Stanzas 1, 3, 4 and 10 gāyatrī; 2, 5, 8 and 9 nicṛd-gāyatrī, 6 and 7 virāḍ-gāyatrī.

(११०) ओ३म् ॥ सना च सोम जेषि च पवमान
महि श्रवः । अथा नो वस्यसस्कृधि ॥१॥

पदपाठः—सन । च । सोम । जेषि । च । पवमान । महि ।
श्रवः । अथ । नः । वस्यसः । कृधि ॥

अन्वयः—हे सोम पवमान त्वं शत्रून्सर्वदा जेषि तवैव महि श्रवश्च । अथ च नो धनं सन नो वस्यसः कृधीति प्रार्थयामहे ॥

Word-meaning &c.:—सन=give (wealth &c.). सोम Oh Most Loving Lord ! जेषि=Thou dost always overcome Thy antagonists or the wicked. पवमान=Most Holy; sanctifying others; Holy and Sanctifying Thy devotees. महि=great. श्रवः=glory. अथ=hence; therefore. वस्यसः(√वस्+तृच्+ईयसुन् P. V, 3, 59 and VI, 4, 154)=dwelling most happily; happy; most or very happy.

Translation:—Oh Most Loving and Gentle God ! Thou dost always put down the wicked, and Thine is all Greatness and Glory. Bestow on us, we beseech Thee, wealth, great peace and happiness in life.

Purport:—God, to Whom alone real greatness and glory belongs and Who is always victorious over wickedness, has all at His Omnipotent disposal. He confers on the devotee prosperity and liberation according to the latter's deserts. Hence every man or woman should endeavour to grow better and better spiritually day by day, in the sight of God.

(१११) सना ज्योतिः सना स्वाऽ३ऽर्विश्वा च सोम सौभगा । अथा नो वस्यसस्कृधि ॥२॥

पदपाठः—सन । ज्योतिः । सन । स्वः । विश्वा । च । सोम । अथ । नः । वस्यसः । कृधि ॥

अन्वयः—हे सोम नो ज्योतिः स्वो विश्वा च सौभगा सन । अथ नो वस्यसः कृधि ॥

Word-meaning &c.:—**ज्योतिः**=light (to see and grasp matters spiritual and other difficult affairs where ordinary worldly intelligence is of no use). **स्वर्**= heaven i. e., heavenly happiness (the highest happiness in mundane life is meant here); Divine Lustre or Splendour. **सना ज्योतिः सना स्वः**=give us light to see Thy Divine Splendour. **सौभगा (सुभग+अञ्** P. V, 1, 129; =**सौभगानि** VII, 1, 39)=things that bring prosperity.

Translation:—Oh Most Bountiful Lord ! give us light that we may see Thy splendour (in every thing), bestow on us all that is required to make us prosper in the world and make our life peaceful and happy.

Purport:—God is ever Pure, Wise and Happy. It is only by resorting to Him that we shall become enlightened and secure true happiness.

(११२) सना दक्षमुत क्रतुमप सोम मृधो जहि ।
अथा नो वस्यसस्कृधि ॥३॥

पदपाठः—सन । दक्षम् । उत । क्रतुम् । अप । सोम । मृधः । जहि । अथ । नः । वस्यसः । कृधि ॥

अन्वयः—हे सोम ! नो दक्षमुत क्रतुं धेहि, मृधोऽप जहि अथ नो वस्यसः कृधि ॥

Word-meaning &c.:—दक्षम् (√दक्ष वृद्धौ + अच्; Nig. II, 9)=cleverness, intelligence, dexterity, strength. क्रतुम् (√डुकृञ् करणे + कतु U. I, 76 Nig. II, 1)=power or strength to work; perseverance in our duties. मृधः (√मृध हिंसायाम् + क्विप्; Nir. VII, 2)=enemies (like lust anger and other passions). जहि=destroy.

Translation:—Oh Most Generous God ! confer on us the intelligence and strength to do our duty in life, crush all our foes in the shape of lust, anger and other passions and bestow on us great peace and happiness.

Purport:—Our worst enemies are our passions which have first to be disposed of if we have to succeed in life. To expel them is possible only through the grace of God Who gives to His devotees all the strength required to combat them. What is most essential in the fight for us is our pursuance of our duty with right understanding and perseverance.

(११३) पवीतारः पुनीतन सोममिन्द्राय पातवे ।
अथा नो वस्यसस्कृधि ॥४॥

पदपाठः—पवीतारः । पुनीत । न । सोमम् । इन्द्राय । पातवे । अथ । नः । वस्यसः । कृधि ॥

अन्वयः—हे पवीतारो यूयमिन्द्राय पातवे नो जीवनम्पुनीत न । अथ नो वस्यसः कृधि ॥

Word-meaning &c.:—पवितारः (√पू+तृच्)=the wise who cleanse the hearts of others by good advice. पुनीत =purify, cleanse. न = expletive of certainty. सोमम्= gentle; brimming with gentleness and love for all, इन्द्राय=for Almighty God. पातवे (√पा पाने+तवेन् P. III, 4, 9)=that it may be acceptable to.

Translation:—Oh wise men ! who by your guidance cleanse the hearts of men, please do purify our lives and render them loving towards all so that we may be acceptible to the Lord Almighty. Make us worthy of the highest happiness.

Purport:—At the time of initiation or the solemn observance of any rite, the man, learned in the Vedas and of a virtuous life, should, at the very outset advise the principal person concerned and also all that are assembled, about the Loving, Peaceful and Gentle Nature of God, then about worldly prosperity and liberation, thus enabling them to see their way in life so as to become most acceptable to God.

(११४) त्वं सूर्ये न आ भज तव क्रत्वा तवोतिभिः । अथा नो वस्यसस्कृधि ॥५॥

पदपाठः—त्वम् । सूर्ये । नः । आ । भज । तव । क्रत्वा । तव । ऊतिऽभिः । अथ । नः । वस्यसः । कृधि ॥

अन्वयः—हे सोम ! त्वं तव क्रत्वा तवोतिभिर्नः सूर्यं आभज । अथ नो वस्यसः कृधि ॥

Word-meaning &c.:—सूर्ये*=in the sun; when men are engaged in work; when the sun rises; at day; आ भज resort or come to us; make us approach Thee. क्रत्वा= by religious or philanthropic work. (√अव रक्षण &c.+ क्तिन् P. III, 3, 97 & VI, 4, 20)=acts of protection from various dangers.

Translation:—Oh Most Generous God, protect us from all dangers and give us the right impulse when we go about our duties on sunrise thus leading us to highest happiness in life.

Purport:—In his daily duties man should seek, in his remembrance of God, protection from various dangers and Divine impulse to be always in the right. This attitude is a great source of happiness.

२ ३ २ ३ २ ३ १ २ ३ १ २
(११५) तव क्रत्वा तवोतिभिर्ज्योक्पश्येम सूर्यम् ।
१ २ ३ १ २
अथा नो वस्यसस्कृधि ॥६॥

पदपाठः—तव । क्रत्वा । तव । ऊतिभिः । ज्योक् । पश्येम ।
सूर्यम् । अथ । नः । वस्यसः । कृधि ॥

अन्वयः—हे परमात्मंस्तव क्रत्वा, तवोतिभिर्वयं ज्योक् सूर्यं पश्येम । अथ नो वस्यसः कृधि ॥

Word-meaning &c.:—ज्योक्=long.

Translation:—Oh Most Loving God, may we, by Thy impulse, and through Thy acts of protection from all sides, see many days of active life, so bless Thou us with peace and happiness.

---

*The word सूर्य according to P. III, 1, 114, is derived either from √सृ or √सू by adding the suffix क्यप् which after √सू will take the augment रुट्, (√सृ+क्यप् or सू+रुट्+क्यप्), the latter meaning that which prevails upon man to work. All begin to work when the sun rises. Hence सूर्ये in the present stanza means also when we go about our duties on sunrise. (Vide Mahabhāṣya, III, 1, 6 on P. III, 1, 114).

Purport:—Man can attain long life only by active, peaceful and innocent life. This should be the ideal for all who wish to live long. Any other way of living is a bane to humanity.

(११६) अभ्यर्ष स्वायुध सोम द्विबर्हसंँ रयिम्।
अथा नो वस्यसस्कृधि ॥७॥

पदपाठः—अभि। अर्ष। सुऽआयुध। सोम। द्विऽबर्हसम्।
रयिम्। अथ। नः। वस्यसः। कृधि॥

अन्वयः—हे स्वायुध सोम! द्विबर्हसं रयिमस्मभ्यमभ्यर्ष। अथ नो वस्यसः कृधि॥

Word-meaning &c.:—अभ्यर्ष=confer on (us). स्वायुध (सु+आ+√युध्+अच्)=Who helps to fight well (enemies like lust, anger &c.). सोम (√सु+मन् U. I, 140)=Creator. द्विबर्हसम् (द्वयोः स्थानयोः परिवृढः द्वि+√बृह+असि U. IV, 227; Nir. VI, 17)=exalted in two places—the earth and the heaven; in both lives, before death and after. वस्यसः= most joyful and rejoicing.

Translation:—Oh Lord God, Creator of the universe! Thou Who helpest us to fight well all enemies, lead us to that happiness which is exalted both here and hereafter and so bless us with the greatest joy.

Purport:—Man's aim should be the highest happiness whatever may the odds be in the way of attaining it. The means to fight and overcome all difficulties is by peacefully attending to our duty feeling the presence of God wherever we may be.

(११७) अभ्यऽ३ऽर्षानपच्युतो वाजिन्त्समत्सु सासहिः। अथा नो वस्यसस्कृधि ॥८॥

पदपाठः—अभि । अर्ष । अनु । अपच्युत । वाजिन् । स । मत्सु । ससहिः । नः । वस्यसः । कृधि ॥

अन्वयः—हे सोम त्वमनपच्युतः ससहिरस्त्यथ नो रयिमभ्यर्ष नः समत्सु वस्यसः कृधि ॥

Word-meaning &c. :—अनपच्युतः=unconquerable. अभ्यर्ष (अभि+ √ऋषी गतौ)=succour us. समत्सु (सम्+ √अद भक्षणे or सम्+ √मदी हर्षे+क्विप् P. III, 2, 178 ; Nig. II, 17). *=in battles ससहिः (√षह मर्षणे+कि P. III, 2, 171, Vartika सासहिवावहिचाचलिपापतीनां निपातनम् Vide Mahabhaṣya) =Who overcomes His foes. वस्यसः=victorious. वाजिन्= most powerful.

Translation:—Oh Most Powerful God, Thou art unquerable and ever vanquishest the antagonist; give us wealth and make us victorious on our foes in our battles.

Purport:—God supports the just and helps them subdue their foes, but He is ever opposed to the wicked whom He subdues.

(११८) त्वां यज्ञैरवीवृधन्पवमान विधर्मणि । अथा नो वस्यसस्कृधि ॥९॥

पदपाठः—त्वाम् । यज्ञैः । अवीवृधन् । पवमान । विऽधर्मणि । अथ । नः । वस्यसः । कृधि ॥

अन्वयः—हे पवमान सोमोपासकास्त्वां यज्ञैरवीवृधन् । स त्वम् नो विधर्मणि रक्ष । अथ नो वस्यसः कृधि ॥

Word-meaning &c.:—यज्ञैः=by such religious duties as worship &c. अवीवृधन्=establish, glorify. पवमान (√पूङ् पवने+शानच् P. III, 2, 18 and VII, 2, 82)=Who sanctifies

---

* समदः समदो वाऽत्तेः । सम्मदो वा मदतेः ॥ नि० ६ । १७ ॥ This word is used only in the plural.

or purifies. विधर्मणि (वगतः धर्मः यस्मात् P. II, 2, 24 and V. 4, 124)=sinful things. मन्द्यसः=full of joy. उपासकाः (उप+√आस उपवेशने+ण्वुल् P. III, 1, 133)=the devotees. रक्ष=protect (us).

Translation:—Oh Most Holy God the Sanctifier of all ! Thy devotees glorify Thee by acts of piety. Do Thou protect us amidst sinful things, so that we may always rejoice.

Purport:—The devotee must take care that he does not forget his lofty spiritual aim in the midst of impure and sinful surroundings. It is better to shift oneself from such either bodily or mentally as necessary and keep the goal always in sight. Therefore company to be consorted with, books to be read and work to be done should always be scrutinised and seen whether they agree with one's goal or not, and anything contrary should always be decisively rejected. This is the way to grow in spiritual life and requires an assiduous practice of the presence of God.

(११९) रयिं नश्चित्रमश्विनमिन्दो विश्वायुमा भर। अथा नो वस्यसस्कृधि ॥१०॥

पदपाठः—रयिम् । नः । चित्रम् । अश्विनम् । इन्दो । विश्व ऽ आयुम् । आ । भर । अथ । नः । वस्यसः । कृधि ॥

अन्वयः—हे इन्दो ! चित्रमश्विनं, विश्वायुं रयिमाभर । अथ नो वस्यसः कृधि ॥

Word-meaning &c.:—चित्रम् (√चित् चयने+क्त U. IV, 164)=various types of. अश्विनम्=vast, enormous. विश्वायुम् (विश्वम् आयुः यस्य यद्वा विश्वम् आयुः येन साधनेन जीव्यते तत्)=lasting for or enabling one to enjoy the full span of life. इन्दो =Most Opulent God ! आ भर=fully bestow on us.

Translation:—Oh Most Opulent God! bestow on us, we beseech Thee, wealth of various types, vast and lasting a lifetime, and thus help us enjoy true happiness in life.

Purport:—Money, lands and cattle are worldly possessions which enable a man to be called rich. Good offspring also is a blessing. Good education, moral and spiritual advancement are other and higher types of wealth. On one side the endeavour of man and on the other the bestowal of them by God according to man's deserts, are the factors essential for its acquisition. Hence it is the duty of every man or woman to try to acquire them by all just and righteous means.

Prayers and Exhortations.

ॐ ॥ आ ब्रह्मन्ब्राह्मणो ब्रह्मवर्चसी जायतामा राष्ट्रे राजन्यः शूर इषव्योऽतिव्याधी महारथो जायताम् ॥ दोग्ध्री धेनुर्वोढाऽनड्वानाशुः सप्तिः पुरन्धिर्योषा जिष्णू रथेष्ठाः सभेयो युवाऽस्य यजमानस्य वीरो जायताम् ॥ निकामे निकामे नः पर्जन्यो वर्षतु । फलवत्यो न ओषधयः पच्यन्ताम् ॥ योगक्षेमो नः कल्पताम् ॥ यजुर्वेदे २२, २२ ॥

"Oh Great God ! let there be born in our kingdom men devoted to learning and teaching full of spiritual splendour; let there be born warriors skilled in military enterprise, heroic in spirit, masters of the science of military weapons and mighty fighters who can totally vanquish the enemy; let there be born cows giving abundant milk, oxen, carriers of heavy loads, and horses of high speed; women skilled in various industries, and may the son of Thy devotee shine in the assembly of the great while he attains his youth, may he be a heroic, all-conquering and a good wielder of the war chariot. May the clouds rain on every required occasion may the fruit-bearing trees bear for us ripe fruit in abundance and may the power of acquiring and preserving property ever remain with us."

न पापासो मनामहे नारायासो न जह्लवः । यदिन्न्विन्द्रं वृषणं सचा सुते सखायं कृणवामहै ॥ ऋ० ८ । ६१ । ११ ॥

"We do not approach Almighty God, the Dispenser of all good, being ourselves steeped in sin, void of charity and doing no righteous works; (but we have to our credit a life of purity, charity and pious works), wherefore only it is that we now make the Lord God Almighty our Friend by all joining together in good deeds."

प्रियं मा कृणु देवेषु प्रियं राजसु मा कृणु । प्रियं सर्वस्य पश्यत उत शूद्र उतार्ये ॥ अथर्व० १६; ६२ ॥

"Oh Lord God Almighty, grant me such qualities of head and heart as would endear me to the enlightened and learned among us, to the ruling class and to all men that have eyes to see whether agriculturist and trader or artizan and labourer"

रुचं नो धेहि ब्राह्मणेषु रुचꣳ राजसु नस्कृधि । रुचं विश्येषु शूद्रेषु मयि धेहि रुचा रुचम् ॥ य० १८, ४८ ॥

"Oh Lord of the universe! impart, we beseech Thee. out of Thy refulgence, lustre to those of us that are devoted to learning and contemplation of Thee; bestow on our rulers amiability of disposition, on our commercial and agricultural, artizan and labouring classes light; and enlighten me also with a ray of Thy splendour".

यत्र ब्रह्मविदो यान्ति दीक्षया तपसा सह । ब्रह्मा मा तत्र नयतु ब्रह्मा ब्रह्म दधातु मे । ब्रह्मणे स्वाहा ॥ अ० १९ । ४३ । ८ ॥

"May the Supreme Lord bestow on me the knowledge of His Eternal Vedas and lead me into that bliss into which the knowers of God and His Law enter by a regulated and mortified life. Glory be to God Almighty".

एतो न्विन्द्रं स्तवाम शुद्धं शुद्धेन साम्ना । शुद्धैरुक्थैर्वावृध्वांसं शुद्ध आशीर्वान्ममत्तु ॥ ऋ० ८ । ९५ । ७॥

Come (brethren), let us, now, with the singing of the Samaveda and the chant of the Ṛgveda both correct in pronunciation and accent, propitiate the Lord God the Bestower of all good, Whose Glory is always on the increase, and Who is capable of imparting bliss to us. May He make us happy !"

अरं त इन्द्र श्रवसे गमेम शूर त्वावतः । अरं शक्र परेमणि ॥ सा० २ २०९ ॥

"Oh Strong and Omnipresent God ! Vouchsafe, we beseech Thee, the grace to approach Thee always and everywhere in Thy Glory—Thee, Who hast no equal—and under all circumstances to take refuge in Thee."

विश्वतोदावन्विश्वतो न आ भर । यं त्वा शविष्ठमीमहे ॥ सा० १ । ४३७ ॥

Oh Lord God! Who conferest benefits on Thy devotees from all round, support us from all directions we beseech Thee Who art the Most Powerful."

अग्ने विवस्वदा भरास्मभ्यमूतये महे । देवो ह्यसि नो दृशे ॥ सा० १ । १० ॥

"Oh Most Refulgent God! Vouchsafe, we beseech Thee, that we may accomplish such religious and philanthropic works as would confer on us perfect safety (in life), for Thou art Illuminator with Whose light we are able to percieve with our senses (and realise the truth)."

द्यौः शान्तिरन्तरिक्षँ शान्तिः पृथिवी शान्तिरापः
शान्तिरोषधयः शान्तिः । वनस्पतयः शान्तिर्विश्वे देवाः
शान्तिर्ब्रह्म शान्तिः सर्वँ शान्तिः शान्तिरेव शान्तिः
सा मा शान्तिरेधि ॥ य० ३६ । १७ ॥

"Oh Lord! May there be peace in the celestial regions, may there be peace in the intermediate regions, may there be peace on earth; may the waters be appeasing, may herbs be wholesome and may trees and plants bring peace to all; may all beneficent beings bring peace to us, may the Vedic Law propagate peace all through the world May all things be a source of peace to us and let peace itself bestow peace on all and may that peace come to me also".

॥ ॐ ॥ शान्तिः । शान्तिः । शान्तिः ॥ ॐ ॥

"May there be peace to all from external material objects, may there be peace from our own selves, may there be peace from Divine Wrath"

APPENDIX I.

Index to the first lines of Vedic verses and other matter.

In this index short quotations from the Brāhmaṇas and Upaniṣads as well as partial quotations from other sources are not included. The bold print in this appendix refers to the principal Vedic verses, the middling, to those Vedic stanzas that have either been translated or simply quoted. The small type indicates statements from other sources such as the Upaniṣads, Mahabharata &c. Figures within brackets are the serial numbers of verses in the book and those outside refer to pages.

अ

आ

इ

उ

ऋ

ए

ऐ

ओ

क

ग

च

ज

त

द

ध

न

प

ब

भ

म

य

र

व

श

स

ह

END OF VOLUME I.